OECD HISTORICAL SERIES
COLLECTION HISTORIQUE DE L'OCDE

The European Reconstruction 1948-1961

La reconstruction européenne

Bibliography
on the Marshall Plan and the
Organisation for European
Economic Co-operation (OEEC)

Bibliographie
sur le Plan Marshall
et l'Organisation européenne
de coopération économique (OECE)

ORGANISATION FOR ECONOMIC CO-OPERATION AND DEVELOPMENT
ORGANISATION DE COOPÉRATION ET DE DÉVELOPPEMENT ÉCONOMIQUES

ORGANISATION FOR ECONOMIC CO-OPERATION AND DEVELOPMENT

ORGANISATION DE COOPÉRATION ET DE DÉVELOPPEMENT ÉCONOMIQUES

Pursuant to Article 1 of the Convention signed in Paris on 14th December 1960, and which came into force on 30th September 1961, the Organisation for Economic Co-operation and Development (OECD) shall promote policies designed:

- to achieve the highest sustainable economic growth and employment and a rising standard of living in Member countries, while maintaining financial stability, and thus to contribute to the development of the world economy;
- to contribute to sound economic expansion in Member as well as non-member countries in the process of economic development; and
- to contribute to the expansion of world trade on a multilateral, non-discriminatory basis in accordance with international obligations.

The original Member countries of the OECD are Austria, Belgium, Canada, Denmark, France, Germany, Greece, Iceland, Ireland, Italy, Luxembourg, the Netherlands, Norway, Portugal, Spain, Sweden, Switzerland, Turkey, the United Kingdom and the United States. The following countries became Members subsequently through accession at the dates indicated hereafter: Japan (28th April 1964), Finland (28th January 1969), Australia (7th June 1971), New Zealand (29th May 1973), Mexico (18th May 1994) and the Czech Republic (21st December 1995). The Commission of the European Communities takes part in the work of the OECD (Article 13 of the OECD Convention).

En vertu de l'article 1er de la Convention signée le 14 décembre 1960, à Paris, et entrée en vigueur le 30 septembre 1961, l'Organisation de Coopération et de Développement Économiques (OCDE) a pour objectif de promouvoir des politiques visant :

- à réaliser la plus forte expansion de l'économie et de l'emploi et une progression du niveau de vie dans les pays Membres, tout en maintenant la stabilité financière, et à contribuer ainsi au développement de l'économie mondiale ;
- à contribuer à une saine expansion économique dans les pays Membres, ainsi que les pays non membres, en voie de développement économique ;
- à contribuer à l'expansion du commerce mondial sur une base multilatérale et non discriminatoire conformément aux obligations internationales.

Les pays Membres originaires de l'OCDE sont : l'Allemagne, l'Autriche, la Belgique, le Canada, le Danemark, l'Espagne, les États-Unis, la France, la Grèce, l'Irlande, l'Islande, l'Italie, le Luxembourg, la Norvège, les Pays-Bas, le Portugal, le Royaume-Uni, la Suède, la Suisse et la Turquie. Les pays suivants sont ultérieurement devenus Membres par adhésion aux dates indiquées ci-après : le Japon (28 avril 1964), la Finlande (28 janvier 1969), l'Australie (7 juin 1971), la Nouvelle-Zélande (29 mai 1973), le Mexique (18 mai 1994) et la République tchèque (21 décembre 1995). La Commission des Communautés européennes participe aux travaux de l'OCDE (article 13 de la Convention de l'OCDE).

''Never in my experience before and after the Marshall Plan, have I known an international team moved by such an intensive desire to accomplish a joint endeavour, the success of which represented at that time a matter of life and death for Europe and for each member country, and to see that it succeeded in conditions such that each participant might derive equal benefits.''

Secretary general of the OEEC
Robert Marjolin
1948-1955

«Jamais dans mon expérience, avant et après le Plan Marshall, je n'ai connu une équipe internationale animée d'un désir aussi intense de faire réussir une entreprise commune, dont le succès apparaissait alors comme une question de vie ou de mort pour l'Europe et pour chaque pays Membre, et de faire qu'elle réussît dans les conditions telles que chacun en tirât profit également.»

Secrétaire général de l'OECE
Robert Marjolin
1948-1955

FOREWORD

In the fall of 1992, the Organisation for Economic Co-operation and Development (OECD) opened for research the archives of its predecessor, the Organisation for European Economic Co-operation (OEEC). In conjunction with the opening of the historical archives, the OECD commissioned a series of historical research papers for publication in a volume entitled *Explorations in OEEC History,* which is being published in the same series as this bibliography.

While much historical literature has been written on post World War II Europe, little has been written on the OEEC or on the other international organisation which played a part in post-war recovery. As the *Explorations* was being compiled, relevant literature was uncovered but not always cited. In order to support and encourage the further development of historical research in post-war economic development, this bibliography was compiled by OECD staff, with the co-operation of the historians who prepared *Explorations* volume, so that a convenient, up-to-date reference tool on post-war economic recovery can help elucidate the role of the OEEC and other international organisations in a broader context.

The archival programme at the Organisation continues to grow and to systematically make available to historical records of the OEEC, and of the OECD. Archives are opened after a thirty year period. With the recent collapse of the Soviet Union, the role of international organisations in developing the economic underpinnings of Western Europe's economic stability and growth is a very current topic.

This work is published on the responsibility of the Secretary-General of the OECD.

AVANT-PROPOS

A l'automne de 1992, l'Organisation de Coopération et de Développement Economiques (OCDE) a ouvert aux chercheurs les archives de son prédécesseur, l'Organisation Européenne de Coopération Economique (OECE). En même temps qu'elle rendait accessible ces archives historiques, l'OCDE a commandé une série d'études historiques à publier dans un volume intitulé *Explorations dans l'histoire de l'OECE,* qui paraît dans la même série que cette bibliographie.

Si beaucoup d'ouvrages et d'études ont été consacrés à l'histoire de l'Europe après la Seconde guerre mondiale, on a peu écrit sur l'OECE ou sur les autres organisations internationales qui ont joué un rôle dans le relèvement de l'après-guerre. Au moment de la préparation des *Explorations,* les études correspondantes ont été mises au jour mais pas toujours citées. Afin d'aider et d'encourager le développement des recherches historiques, la bibliographie en a été établie par le personnel de l'OCDE avec la coopération des historiens qui ont contribué au volume *Explorations,* de façon qu'un outil de référence commode et à jour sur le redressement économique d'après-guerre puisse servir pour éclairer le rôle de l'OECE et des autres organisations internationales dans un contexte plus large.

Le programme concernant les archives de l'Organisation continue de se développer; il rend accessibles d'une façon systématique les archives historiques de l'OECE et de l'OCDE qui sont en effet ouvertes au bout de 30 ans. Avec le récent effondrement de l'Union soviétique, le rôle des organisations internationales dans l'instauration des bases de la stabilité et de la croissance économique de l'Europe occidentale est tout à fait d'actualité.

Ce travail est publié sous la responsabilité du Secrétaire général de l'OCDE.

TABLE OF CONTENTS

TABLE DES MATIÈRES

INTRODUCTION

The contribution of the Organisation for European Economic Co-operation (OEEC) to Western Europe's efforts towards unity between 1948 and 1961 is still largely unrecognised by historians, researchers and the general public. The OEEC archives, which had been kept secret until 1992, are at last available for consultation; they, together with certain basic reference works on the OEEC, should shed new light on the post-war era of European reconstruction as well as on the events of today.

The OEEC represented the first institutional stage in the organisation of post-war Europe. In 1948 it was appointed to distribute Marshall Plan aid and implement an economic recovery programme for the western European countries. It furthered the development of its Member countries in the domains of industry, agriculture, energy and technology, and contributed to the process of trade liberalisation and currency convertibility in Europe. In 1961, when its work had been completed, it was replaced by the Organisation for Economic Co-operation and Development (OECD) which extended membership to the United States and Canada and continued some of the activities of the OEEC. The two North American countries were joined later by Japan (1964), Finland (1969), Australia (1971), New Zealand (1973) and Mexico (1994).

The monographs, expert reports and periodicals published by the OEEC testify to the work accomplished by the Organisation and by its ancillary bodies (European Productivity Agency, European Nuclear Energy Agency and the Office for Scientific and Technical Personnel). This bibliography lists these publications in a layout based on the Secretariat organigrams and the Historical Archives Plan – the latter will be made available to researchers when they consult the archives (see below). A brief description of author committees and programmes is given.

The OEEC, and the Marshall Plan in particular, have been extensively written about by authors outside the Organisation. This bibliography lists a selection of their books and press articles published since 1970 – the OECD having brought out in 1967, on the occasion of the 20th Anniversary of the Marshall Plan, a first bibliography (produced by Mrs. Tarr, OECD 1967) and a number of basic reference works.

The bibliographical data here are preceded by the text of the Convention for European Economic Co-operation signed in Paris on 16 April 1948, the instrument establishing the OEEC, and by a chronology of the main events that marked the Organisation's work.

This bibliography should facilitate consultation of the historical archives of the OEEC, of which a first segment has been deposited with the European University Institute, Villa il Poggiolo, Piazza Edison 11, Florence (Italy) to be made available to the public. Further segments will be added as arrangements are made to house them.

The first deposit, made in November 1992, comprises the minutes of the Council and the Executive Committee, together with the records of Member country accession, the European Payments Union and the negotiations on the establishment of a European free trade area.

It is hoped that the publication of this bibliography, in conjunction with the opening of the OEEC archives, will prompt new studies, not only retrospective but also forward-looking. The idea has been put forward that a new type of Marshall Plan might be launched to aid the Central and Eastern European Countries (CEECs) and the New Independent States of the ex-Soviet Union (NIS), and that inspiration might be drawn from the forms of cooperation practised in the OEEC. The history of that Organisation abounds in lessons on the ways and means of undertaking programmes of structural adjustment, multilateralisation of trade and payments, and elimination of economic imbalances, as well as the necessary stages in the process of opening up national economies, the institutional structures that encourage ongoing dialogue, the exchange of information and mutual supervision, and the socio-cultural conditions propitious to productivity growth. In this last context, the experience of the European Productivity Agency, although not without relevance, cannot simply be reproduced in order to solve the problem of productivity now confronting the economies engaged in the process of reform. That experience can, however, supply useful references with which to investigate the institutional and organisational aspects of the approach that should be adopted in launching an enterprise of multilateral assistance.

This bibliography was compiled under the direction of the Documentation Resources Management Division of the Directorate for General Administration and Personnel, with the assistance of historians, OECD officials, consultants, former staff of the OEEC, and specialised libraries.

INTRODUCTION

La contribution de l'Organisation Européenne de Coopération Économique (OECE) aux efforts d'unité de l'Europe occidentale entre 1948 et 1961 demeure méconnue du public en général et même, quelquefois, des historiens et chercheurs. L'ouverture au public, en 1992, des archives historiques de l'OECE, jusqu'à ce jour restées largement confidentielles, associée à la lecture de certains ouvrages de base sur l'OECE, devraient apporter un éclairage nouveau sur cette époque, importante pour la reconstruction de l'Europe et les évènements d'aujourd'hui.

L'OECE a constitué la première étape institutionnelle de l'organisation de l'Europe occidentale d'après-guerre. En 1948, elle a été chargée de répartir l'aide du Plan Marshall et de mettre en œuvre un programme de relèvement économique entre pays d'Europe occidentale. Elle a contribué au développement industriel, agricole, énergétique et technologique de ses pays Membres et au processus de libéralisation des échanges et de convertibilité des monnaies européennes. Son œuvre achevée, elle fut remplacée en 1961 par l'Organisation de Coopération et de Développement Économiques (OCDE) auquelle s'est joint les États-Unis et le Canada afin de poursuivre l'action entreprise, dans une optique plus large. Ils furent suivis du Japon (1964), de la Finlande (1969), de l'Australie (1971), de la Nouvelle-Zélande (1973) et du Mexique (1994).

Les ouvrages, rapports d'experts et revues périodiques publiés par l'OECE témoignent des efforts poursuivis par cet organisme et ses organes auxiliaires (Agence européenne de productivité, Agence européenne pour l'énergie nucléaire et Bureau du personnel scientifique et technique). Cette bibliographie en dresse l'inventaire et tente de l'organiser autour d'un plan qui s'inspire de l'organigramme du Secrétariat et du Plan d'archives historiques – ce dernier sera mis à la disposition des chercheurs lors de la consultation de ces archives (voir infra). Une brève description est donnée des comités et programmes auteurs.

L'OECE et particulièrement le Plan Marshall ont fait l'objet de nombreux écrits par des auteurs extérieurs à l'Organisation. La présente bibliographie recense donc une sélection des ouvrages et articles de revues publiés depuis 1970 – l'OCDE ayant réalisé en 1967, à l'occasion du XXème Anniversaire du Plan Marshall, une première bibliographie (rédigée par Mme Tarr, OCDE 1967) et quelques ouvrages de base et de référence.

Les données bibliographiques présentées dans le présent ouvrage, sont précédées du texte de la Convention de coopération économique européenne signée à Paris le 16 avril 1948, acte constitutif de l'OECE, et complétées par des repères chronologiques dans lesquels sont énumérés les principaux événements ayant marqué les travaux de l'Organisation.

La consultation de cet ouvrage devrait faciliter l'analyse des archives historiques de l'OECE dont la première partie a été déposée auprès de l'Institut Universitaire Européen (IUE), Villa il Poggiolo, Piazza Edison 11, à Florence (Italie), pour être ouvertes au public. Progressivement, ces archives seront complétées par d'autres dépôts au fur et à mesure de leur organisation physique.

Ce premier dépôt, effectué en novembre 1992, comprenait les procès-verbaux du Conseil et du Comité Exécutif, ainsi que les archives sur l'adhésion des pays Membres, sur l'Union Européenne de Paiements et sur les négociations sur la constitution d'une zone européenne de libre-échange.

Il est à souhaiter que la publication de cet ouvrage, associée à l'ouverture des archives historiques de l'OECE, donnera lieu à la préparation de nouvelles études non seulement à caractère rétrospectif mais également prospectif. L'idée est avancée de lancer un nouveau «Plan Marshall» pour venir en aide aux pays d'Europe centrale et orientale (PECO) et aux nouveaux États indépendants (NEI) ou de s'inspirer des formes de coopération pratiquées au sein de l'OECE. L'histoire de cette organisation est riche d'enseignements sur les mécanismes nécessaires pour entreprendre des programmes d'ajustement structurel, de multilatéralisation des échanges et des paiements et d'élimination des déséquilibres économiques, sur les étapes nécessaires à l'ouverture des économies nationales, les structures institutionnelles qui favorisent le dialogue continu, l'échange d'informations et la surveillance mutuelle, les conditions socio-culturelles propres à favoriser le développement de la productivité. Dans ce dernier cas, bien qu'elle ne soit pas sans rapport, l'expérience de l'Agence européenne de productivité ne peut être simplement reproduite pour résoudre les problèmes de productivité tel qu'ils se posent dans les économies engagées dans le processus de réforme. Cette

expérience peut, toutefois, fournir des références utiles pour explorer dans ses aspects institutionnels ou organisationnels l'approche qu'il conviendrait d'adopter pour lancer une initiative d'assistance multilatérale.

Cet ouvrage bibliographique a été réalisé sous la direction de la Division de la Gestion des Ressources Documentaires de la Direction de l'Administration Générale et du Personnel, avec la collaboration d'historiens, d'agents de l'OCDE, de consultants, d'anciens agents de l'OECE et de Bibliothèques spécialisées.

I. CONVENTION FOR EUROPEAN ECONOMIC CO-OPERATION

The text of the Convention for European Economic Co-operation is reproduced after the Final Act of the Second Session of the Committee of European Economic Co-operation. They are followed by the Supplementary Protocol No. I on the Legal Capacity, Privileges and Immunities of the Organisation and by the Supplementary Protocol No. II on the Financial Regulations of the Organisation. This section also lists the States who have ratified or acceded to Convention and Supplementary Protocols, which came into force on the 28th July 1948.

*

* *

FINAL ACT OF THE SECOND SESSION OF THE COMMITTEE OF EUROPEAN ECONOMIC CO-OPERATION

With a view to determining the manner of the European economic co-operation contemplated in the General Report adopted on the 22nd September, 1947, by the Committee of European Economic Cooperation, and, in particular, in order to set up the Organisation contemplated by paragraph 113 of the said Report, the Governments of Austria, Belgium, Denmark, France, Greece, Ireland, Iceland, Italy, Luxemburg, Norway, the Netherlands, Portugal, the United Kingdom, Sweden, Switzerland and Turkey, having invited the Commanders-in-Chief of the French, United Kingdom and United States Zones of Occupation of Germany to participate in the work.

Initiated in Paris on the 15th March, 1948, through their representatives, the preparations necessary for this purpose.

These preparations terminated on the 16th April, 1948, and have resulted in the framing of the following instruments:

1. Convention for European Economic Cooperation;
2. Supplementary Protocol No. I on the Legal Capacity, Privileges and Immunities of the Organisation for European Economic Co-operation;
3. Supplementary Protocol No. II on the Financial Regulations of the Organisation.

The following Resolutions were also adopted:

1. Resolution on the Functions of the Organisation;
2. Resolution on Relations between the Organisation and the United States Special Representative in Europe;
3. Resolution on the Rules of Procedure of the Organisation;
4. Resolution on the Financing of the Initial Budget of the Organisation;
5. Resolution on the Interim Financing of the Organisation;
6. Resolution on the Staff Regulations of the Organisation;
7. Resolution on the Location of the First Meeting of the Council of the Organisation.

All the above mentioned Governments and Authorities will have the right to participate at once in the initial work of the Organisation on the provisional putting into operation of the Convention as provided for in Article 24*b*.

The Signatories of the present Final Act who become signatories of the Convention will be deemed to be original Members of the Organisation as from the date of the deposit of their instruments of ratification.

In faith whereof the Representatives of the above mentioned Governments and Authorities have signed the present Final Act.

Done in Paris this sixteenth day of April, Nineteen Hundred and Forty Eight, in the English and French languages, both texts being equally authentic, in a single copy which shall remain deposited in the Archives of the Government of the French Republic, by which certified copies will be communicated to all the other Signatories.

CONVENTION FOR EUROPEAN ECONOMIC CO-OPERATION

The Governments of Austria, Belgium, Denmark, France, Greece, Ireland, Iceland, Italy, Luxemburg, Norway, the Netherlands, Portugal, the United Kingdom, Sweden, Switzerland and Turkey, and the Commanders-in-Chief of the French, United Kingdom and United States Zones of Occupation of Germany:

CONSIDERING that a strong and prosperous European economy is essential for the attainment of the purpose of the United Nations, the preservation of individual liberty and the increase of general well-being, and that it will contribute to the maintenance of peace;

RECOGNISING that their economic systems are inter-related and that the prosperity of each of them depends on the prosperity of all;

BELIEVING that only by close and lasting co-operation between the Contracting Parties can the prosperity of Europe be restored and maintained, and the ravages of war made good;

RESOLVED to implement the principles and to achieve the aims set forth in the General Report of the Committee of European Economic Co-operation, particularly the speedy establishment of sound economic conditions enabling the Contracting Parties as soon as possible to achieve and maintain a satisfactory level of economic activity without extraordinary outside assistance, and to make their full contribution to world economic stability;

DETERMINED to combine their economic strength to these ends, to join together to make the fullest collective use of their individual capacities and potentialities, to increase their production, develop and modernise their industrial and agricultural equipment, expand their commerce, reduce progressively barriers to trade among themselves, promote full employment and restore or maintain the stability of their economies and general confidence in their national currencies;

TAKING NOTE of the generous resolve of the American people expressed in the action taken to furnish the assistance without which the aims set forth above cannot be fully achieved;

RESOLVED to create the conditions and establish the institutions necessary for the success of European economic co-operation and for the effective use of American aid, and to conclude a Convention to this end;

HAVE ACCORDINGLY APPOINTED the undersigned Plenipotentiaries who, having presented their full powers, found in good and due form, have agreed on the following provisions:

Article 1

The Contracting Parties agree to work in close co-operation in their economic relations with one another.

As their immediate task, they will undertake the elaboration and execution of a joint recovery programme. The object of this programme will be to achieve as soon as possible and maintain a satisfactory level of economic activity without extraordinary outside assistance, and to this end the programme will take special account of the need of the Contracting Parties to develop their exports to non-participating countries to the maximum extent possible.

Accordingly the Contracting Parties pledge themselves to carry out, by their efforts of self-help and in a spirit of mutual aid, the following General Obligations, and hereby set up an Organisation for European Economic Co-operation, hereinafter referred to as the Organisation.

PART I – General Obligations

Article 2

The Contracting Parties will, both individually and collectively, promote with vigour the development of production, through efficient use of the resources at their command, whether in their metropolitan or overseas territories, and by the progressive modernisation of equipment and techniques, in such manner as may best assist the accomplishment of the joint recovery programme.

Article 3

The Contracting Parties will, within the framework of the Organisation and as often and to such extent as may be necessary, draw up general programmes for the production and exchange of commoditics and services. In so doing they will take into consideration their several estimates or programmes and general world economic conditions.

Each Contracting Party will use its best endeavours to secure the fulfilment of such general programmes.

Article 4

The Contracting Parties will develop, in mutual co-operation, the maximum possible interchange of goods and services. To this end they will continue the efforts already initiated to achieve as soon as possible a multilateral system of payments among themselves, and will co-operate in relaxing restrictions on trade and payments between one another, with the object of abolishing as soon as possible those restrictions which at present hamper such trade and payments.

In the application of this Article, the Contracting Parties will take due account of the necessity that they should, collectively and individually, correct or avoid excessive disequilibrium in their financial and economic relations, both amongst themselves and with non-participating countries.

Article 5

The Contracting Parties agree to strengthen their economic links by all methods which they may determine will further the objectives of the present Convention. They will continue the study of Customs Unions or analogous arrangements such as free trade areas, the formation of which might constitute one of the methods of achieving these objectives. Those Contracting Parties which have already agreed in principle to the creation of Customs Unions will further the establishment of such Unions as rapidly as conditions permit.

Article 6

The Contracting Parties will co-operate with one another and with other like-minded countries in reducing tariff and other barriers to the expansion of trade, with a view to achieving a sound and balanced multilateral trading system such as will accord with the principles of the Havana Charter.

Article 7

Each Contracting Party will, having due regard to the need for a high and stable level of trade and employment and for avoiding or countering the dangers of inflation, take such steps as lie within its power to achieve or maintain the stability of its currency and of its internal financial position, sound rates of exchange and, generally, confidence in its monetary system.

Article 8

The Contracting Parties will make the fullest and most effective use of their available manpower.

They will endeavour to provide full employment for their own people and they may have recourse to manpower available in the territory of any other Contracting Party. In the latter case they will, in mutual agreement, take the necessary measures to facilitate the movement of workers and to ensure their establishment in conditions satisfactory from the economic and social point of view.

Generally, the Contracting Parties will co-operate in the progressive reduction of obstacles to the free movement of persons.

Article 9

The Contracting Parties will furnish the Organisation with all the information it may request of them in order to facilitate the accomplishment of its tasks.

PART II – The Organisation

Article 10

MEMBERSHIP

The Members of the Organisation shall be the Parties to the present Convention.

Article 11

AIM

The aim of the Organisation shall be the achievement of a sound European economy through the economic co-operation of its Members. An immediate task of the Organisation will be to ensure the success of the European recovery programme, in accordance with the undertakings contained in Part I of the present Convention.

Article 12

FUNCTIONS

Within the limits of such powers as are or may be agreed for the Organisation, its functions shall be:

a) to prepare and implement, within the sphere of the collective action of the Members concerned, the measures necessary to achieve the aim laid down in Article 11 and to facilitate, promote and co-ordinate the individual action of the Members;

b) to facilitate and review the implementation of the present Convention; to take such action as may be found appropriate in order to ensure its execution; and to this end, to provide for systems of observation and review adequate to ensure the efficient use both of external aid and of indigenous resources;

c) to provide the United States Government with such assistance and information as may be agreed in relation to the execution of the European recovery programme and to address recommendations to that Government;

d) at the request of the interested parties, to assist in the negotiation of such international agreements as may be necessary for the better execution of the European recovery programme.

The Organisation may also assume such other functions as may be agreed.

Article 13

POWERS

In order to achieve its aim as set out in Article 2 the Organisation may:

a) take decisions for implementation by Members;

b) enter into agreements with its Members, non-member countries, the United States Government and International Organisations;

c) make recommendations to the United States Government, to other Governments and to International Organisations.

Article 14

DECISIONS

Unless the Organisation otherwise agrees for special cases, decisions shall be taken by mutual agreement of all the Members. The abstention of any Members declaring themselves not to be interested in the subject under discussion shall not invalidate decisions, which shall be binding for the other Members.

Article 15

THE COUNCIL

a) A Council composed of all the Members shall be the body from which all decisions derive;

b) The Council shall designate annually from among the Members a Chairman and two Vice-Chairmen;

c) The Council shall be assisted by an Executive Committee and a Secretary-General. The Council may set up such technical committees or other bodies, as may be required for the performance of the functions of the Organisation. All such organs shall be responsible to the Council.

Article 16

THE EXECUTIVE COMMITTEE

a) The Executive Committee shall consist of seven Members to be designated annually by the Council. It shall carry on its work in accordance with the general and specific instructions of the Council and shall report on it to the Council;
b) The Council shall designate annually from among the Members of the Executive Committe a Chairman and a Vice-Chairman. It may also designate annually a Rapporteur-General and specify his functions;
c) Any Member of the Organisation not represented on the Executive Committee may take part in all the discussions and decisions of that Committee on any item specially affecting the interests of that Member.

The Members of the Organisation shall be informed of the proceedings of the Executive Committee by the circulation in good time of agenda and summary records.

Article 17

THE SECRETARY-GENERAL

a) The Secretary-General shall be assisted by a first and a second Deputy Secretary-General;
b) The Secretary-General and the Deputy Secretaries-General shall be appointed by the Council. The Secretary-General shall be under the instructions of the Council;
c) The Secretary-General shall attend or be represented at the meetings of the Council, the Executive Committee and, as required, at meetings of the technical committees and the other bodies, with the right to participate in discussion. He will prepare the meetings of the Council and of the Executive Committee and will ensure the execution of their decisions in accordance with the general and specific instructions of the Council and the Executive Committee.

Additional provisions as to the functions of the Secretary-General are set out in the Annex to the present Convention.

Article 18

SECRETARIAT

a) The Secretary-General shall appoint such staff as the Organisation may require. Senior staff appointments and the staff regulations shall be subject to approval by the Council;
b) Having regard to the international character of the Organisation, the Secretary-General and the staff shall neither seek nor receive instructions from any of the Members or from any Government or authority external to the Organisation.

Article 19

TECHNICAL COMMITTEES AND OTHER BODIES

Technical committees and other bodies set up under Article 15*c* shall be under the instructions of the Council. They shall be composed of the Members most concerned and will so organise their work that other interested Members may take part as may be necessary.

Article 20

RELATIONSHIP WITH OTHER INTERNATIONAL ORGANISATIONS

a) The Organisation shall establish such formal or informal relationships with the United Nations, its principal organs and subsidiary bodies and with the Specialised Agencies, as may best facilitate collaboration in the achievement of their respective aims;
b) The Organisation may also maintain relationships with other international bodies.

Article 21

HEADQUARTERS

The Headquarters of the Organisation shall be determined by the Council at its first session. The Council, the several committees or the other bodies may meet elsewhere than at the Headquarters of the Organisation should they so decide.

Article 22

LEGAL CAPACITY, PRIVILEGES AND IMMUNITIES

a) The Organisation shall enjoy in the territory of each of its Members such legal capacity as may be necessary for the exercise of its functions and the fulfilment of its purposes, as defined in Supplementary Protocol No. I, to the present Convention;

b) The Organisation, its officials, and representatives of the Members of the Organisation shall be entitled to the privileges and immunities set out in the above mentioned Supplementary Protocol.

Article 23

FINANCIAL REGULATIONS

a) The Secretary-General shall present to the Council for approval an annual budget and accounts drawn up in accordance with the Financial Regulations set out in Supplementary Protocol No. II, to the present Convention;

b) The financial year of the Organisation shall begin on the 1st July;

c) The expenses of the Organisation shall be borne by Members and shall be apportioned in accordance with the provisions of the above mentioned Supplementary Protocol.

PART III – Final Clauses

Article 24

RATIFICATION AND COMING INTO FORCE

a) The present Convention shall be ratified. Instruments of ratification shall be deposited with the Government of the French Republic. The Convention shall come into force upon the deposit of instruments of ratification by not less than six of the Signatories. For each Signatory ratifying thereafter, the Convention shall come into force upon the deposit of its instrument of ratification;

b) Nevertheless, pending the coming into force of the Convention in the manner provided by the Preceding paragraph, the Signatories agree, in order to avoid delay in its execution, to put it into operation on signature on a provisional basis and in accordance with their several constitutional requirements.

Article 25

ACCESSION

At any time after not less than ten instruments of ratification of the Present Convention have been deposited, any non-signatory European country may accede to it by notification addressed to the Government of the French Republic, and with the assent of the Council of the Organisation. Accessions shall take effect on the date of such assent.

Article 26

NON-FULFILMENT OF OBLIGATIONS

If any Member of the Organisation ceases to fulfil its obligations under the present Convention, it shall be invited to conform to the provisions of the Convention. If the said Member should not so conform within the period indicated

in the invitation, the other Members may decide, by mutual agreement, to continue their co-operation within the Organisation without that Member.

Article 27
WITHDRAWAL

Any of the Contracting Parties may terminate the application of the present Convention to itself by giving twelve months' notice to that effect to the Government of the French Republic.

Article 28
COMMUNICATION OF RATIFICATIONS, ACCESSIONS AND WITHDRAWALS

Upon the receipt of any instrument of ratification or accession, or of any notice of withdrawal, the Government of the French Republic shall give notice thereof to all the Contracting Parties and to the Secretary-General of the Organisation.

ANNEX

Additional Provisions concerning the Functions of the Secretary-General

Provisions concerning the functions of the Secretary-General additional to those specified in Article 17 are set out below:

1. He may submit proposals to the Council and to the Executive Committee.
2. He shall provide, in agreement with the Chairmen of the technical committees, for these committees to be convened as required and for the necessary secretarial arrangements. He shall transmit to them, as necessary, the instructions of the Council and of the Executive Committee.
3. He shall follow the work of the other bodies referred to in Article 15*c* and transmit to them, as necessary the instructions of the Council and of the Executive Committee.
4. He shall, having regard to the provisions of Article 20 and in accordance with the instructions of the Council and the Executive Committee, make the necessary arrangements for liaison with other International Organisations.
5. He shall exercise all such other functions necessary for the efficient administration of the Organisation as may be entrusted to him by the Council or by the Executive Committee.

In faith whereof the undersigned Plenipotentiaries, being duly authorised to that effect, have signed the present Convention and have affixed thereto their Seals.

Done in Paris this sixteenth day of April, Nineteen Hundred and Forty Eight, in the English and French languages, both texts being equally authentic, in a single copy which shall remain deposited in the Archives of the Government of the French Republic, by which certified copies will be communicated to all the other Signatories.

SUPPLEMENTARY PROTOCOL No. I
TO THE CONVENTION FOR EUROPEAN ECONOMIC CO-OPERATION
ON THE LEGAL CAPACITY, PRIVILEGES AND IMMUNITIES OF THE ORGANISATION

The Government and Authorities signatories to the Convention for European Economic Cooperation:

CONSIDERING that according to the provisions of Article 22 of the Convention, the Organisation for European Economic Co-operation shall enjoy in the territory of each of its Members such legal capacity as may be necessary for the exercise of its functions and the fulfilment of its purposes and that the Organisation, its officials, and representatives of the Members of the Organisation shall be entitled to the privileges and immunities set out in a Supplementary Protocol;

HAVE AGREED on the following provisions:

PART I – Personality, Capacity

Article 1

The Organisation shall possess juridical personality. It shall have the capacity to conclude contracts, to acquire and dispose of movable and immovable property and to institute legal proceedings.

PART II – Property, Funds and Assets

Article 2

The Organisation, its property and assets wherever located and by whomsoever held, shall enjoy immunity from every form of legal process except insofar as in any particular case it has expressly waived its immunity. It is, however, understood that no waiver of immunity shall extend to any measure of execution.

Article 3

The premises of the Organisation shall be inviolable. The property and assets of the Organisation, wherever located and by whomsoever held, shall be immune from search, requisition, confiscation, expropriation and any other form of interference, whether by executive, administrative, judicial or legislative action.

Article 4

The archives of the Organisation, and in general all documents belonging to it or held by it, shall be inviolable wherever located.

Article 5

Without being restricted by financial controls, regulations or moratoria of any kind:

a) the Organisation may hold currency of any kind and operate accounts in any currency;
b) the Organisation may freely transfer its funds from one country to another or within any country and convert any currency held by it into any other currency.

Article 6

The Organisation, its assets, income and other property shall be:

a) exempt from all direct taxes; it is understood, however, that the Organisation will not claim exemption from rates and taxes which are in fact no more than charges for public utility services;
b) exempt from customs duties and prohibitions and restrictions on imports and exports in respect of articles imported or exported by the Organisation for its official use. It is understood however that articles imported

under such exemption will not be sold in the country into which they were imported except under conditions agreed with the Government of that country;

c) exempt from customs duties and prohibitions and restrictions on imports and exports in respect of its publications.

Article 7

While the Organisation will not, as a general rule, claim exemption from excise duties and from taxes on the sale of movable and immovable property which forms part of the price to be paid, nevertheless when the Organisation is making important purchases for official use of property on which such duties and taxes have been charged or are chargeable, Members will, whenever possible, make appropriate administrative arrangements for the remission or return of the amount of duty or tax.

PART III – Facilities in Respect of Communications

Article 8

The Organisation shall enjoy in the territory of each Member, for its official communications, treatment not less favourable than that accorded by the Government of that Member to any other Government including its diplomatic mission in the matter of priorities, rates and taxes on mails, cables, telegrams, radiograms, telephotos, telephone and other communications and press rates for information to the press and radio. No censorship shall be applied to the official correspondence and other official communications of the Organisation.

PART IV – The Representatives of Members

Article 9

Representatives of Members to the principal and subsidiary organs of the Organisation shall, while exercising their functions and during their journey to and from the place of meeting, enjoy the privileges, immunities and facilities normally enjoyed by diplomatic envoys of comparable rank.

Article 10

Privileges, immunities and facilities are accorded to the representatives of Members not for the personal benefit of the individuals concerned, but in order to safeguard the independent exercise of their functions in connexion with the Organisation. Consequently, a Member has not only the right but the duty to waive the immunity of its representative in any case where, in the opinion of the Member, the immunity would impede the course of justice, and it can be waived without prejudice to the purpose for which the immunity is accorded.

Article 11

The provisions of Article 9 are not applicable as between a representative and the authorities of the State of which he is a national or of which he is or has been the representative.

Article 12

In this Part IV the expression ''representatives'' shall be deemed to include all delegates, alternates, advisers, technical experts and secretaries of delegations.

PART V – Officials

Article 13

The Secretary-General will specify the categories of officials to which the provisions of this Part V shall apply. He shall submit a list of these categories to the Council. Thereafter this list shall be communicated to all Members. The names of the officials included in these categories shall from time to time be made known to Members.

Article 14

Officials of the Organisation shall:

a) be immune from legal process in respect of things done by them in their official capacity; they shall continue to be so immune after completion of their functions as officials of the Organisation;
b) enjoy the same exemption from taxation in respect of the salaries and emoluments paid to them as is enjoyed by officials of the principal International Organisations and on the same conditions;
c) be immune, together with their spouses and dependent relatives, from immigration restrictions and alien registration;
d) be accorded the same privileges in respect of exchange facilities as are accorded to the officials of comparable rank forming a part of diplomatic missions;
e) be given, together with their spouses and dependent relatives, the same repatriation facilities in time of international crisis as members of diplomatic missions;
f) have the right to import free of duty their furniture and effects at the time of first taking up their post in the country in question.

Article 15

In addition to the privileges, immunities, exemptions and facilities specified in Article 14, the Secretary-General shall be accorded in respect of himself, his spouse and children under the age of 21, the privileges, immunities, exemptions and facilities accorded to heads of diplomatic missions in conformity with international law.

The Deputy Secretaries-General shall enjoy the privileges, immunities, exemptions and facilities accorded to diplomatic representatives of comparable rank.

Article 16

Privileges, immunities and facilities are granted to officials in the interests of the Organisation and not for the personal benefit of the individuals concerned. The Secretary-General shall have the right and the duty to waive the immunity of any official in any case where, in his opinion, the immunity would impede the course of justice and can be waived without prejudice to the interests of the Organisation. In the case of the Secretary-General and the Deputy Secretaries-General the Council shall have the right to waive immunity.

Article 17

The Organisation shall co-operate at all times with the appropriate authorities of Members to facilitate the proper administration of justice, secure the observance of police regulations and prevent the occurrence of any abuse in connexion with the privileges, immunities, exemptions and facilities mentioned in this Part V.

PART VI – Experts on Missions for the Organisation

Article 18

Experts (other than officials coming within the scope of Part V) performing missions for the Organisation shall be accorded such privileges, immunities and facilities as are necessary for the independent exercise of their functions during the period of their missions, including the time spent on journeys in connexion with their missions. In particular they shall be accorded:

a) immunity from personal arrest or detention and from seizure of their baggage;
b) in respect of things done by them in the course of the performance of their mission, immunity from legal process of every kind;
c) inviolability for all papers and documents.

Article 19

Privileges, immunities and facilities are granted to experts in the interests of the Organisation and not for the personal benefit of the individuals concerned. The Secretary-General shall have the right and the duty to waive the immunity of any expert in any case where, in his opinion, the immunity would impede the course of justice and it can be waived without prejudice to the interests of the Organisation.

PART VII – Supplementary Agreements

Article 20

The Organisation may conclude with any Member or Members supplementary agreements adjusting the provisions of the present Protocol so far as that Member or those Members are concerned.

In faith whereof the undersigned Plenipotentiaries, being duly authorised to that effect, have signed the present Protocol.

Done in Paris this sixteenth day of April, Nineteen Hundred and Forty Eight, in the English and French languages, both texts being equally authentic, in a single copy which shall remain deposited in the Archives of the Government of the French Republic, by which certified copies will be communicated to all the other Signatories.

SUPPLEMENTARY PROTOCOL No. II
TO THE CONVENTION FOR EUROPEAN ECONOMIC CO-OPERATION
ON THE FINANCIAL REGULATIONS OF THE ORGANISATION

The Governments and Authorities signatories to the Convention for European Economic Cooperation:

CONSIDERING that Article 23 of the Convention provides that a Supplementary Protocol on Financial Regulations of the Organisation for European Economic Co-operation shall be drawn up;

HAVE AGREED on the following provisions:

Article 1

BUDGET

The Secretary-General shall not later than May 1st in each year submit to the Council for consideration and approval detailed estimates of expenditure for the following financial year.

Estimates of expenditure shall be divided under general headings. Transfers within the budget shall not be permitted except by authority of the Executive Committee. The exact form of estimates shall be determined by the Secretary-General.

Travelling and subsistence expenses of representatives of Members shall normally be borne by the Members concerned. The Council may authorise the reimbursement in special cases of expenditure incurred by representatives of Members in connexion with special tasks laid upon them by the Organisation.

Article 2

SUPPLEMENTARY BUDGET

The Council may require the Secretary-General to present a supplementary budget if circumstances make it necessary. The Secretary-General shall submit to the Council an estimate of the cost of all resolutions submitted to the Council. No resolution involving additional expenditure shall be deemed to be approved by the Council until it has approved an estimate of the additional expenditure involved.

Article 3

BUDGET COMMITTEE

A Budget Committee composed of representatives of Members of the Organisation shall be set up by the Council. The Secretary-General shall submit the budget to this Committee for preliminary examination before submitting it to the Council.

Article 4

BASIS OF CONTRIBUTIONS

Approved budget expenditure shall be met by contributions from the Members of the Organisation in accordance with a scale approved by the Council.

The Secretary-General shall notify the amount of their contributions to Members and invite them to remit their contribution at a date to be fixed by him.

Article 5

CURRENCY OF CONTRIBUTIONS

The budget of the Organisation shall be expressed in the currency of the country in which the Headquarters of the Organisation are established. The contributions of members shall be made in that currency.

The Council may, however, require Members to pay a fraction of their contributions in any currency which may be needed for the work of the Organisation.

Article 6

WORKING CAPITAL FUND

Until the contributions have been assessed and paid, the Council shall call upon Members from time to time as may be necessary to make advances of working capital in the same currency or currencies as the contributions. These advances shall be reimbursed during the same financial year by appropriate deductions from contributions. The amount of such advances shall be assessed on the basis of the criterion used in calculating the contributions themselves.

Article 7

ACCOUNTS AND AUDITING

The Secretary-General shall cause an accurate account to be kept of all receipts and disbursements.

The Council shall appoint auditors who will serve for three years in the first instance and may be re-appointed. The function of the auditors shall be to examine the accounts of the Organisation particularly in order to certify that expenditure has conformed to the provisions made in the budget.

The Secretary-General shall furnish the auditors with such facilities as they may require to carry out their duties.

Article 8

FINANCIAL REGULATIONS

The Secretary-General shall submit to the Council for approval as soon as possible after the establishment of the Organisation detailed financial regulations drawn up in accordance with the principles set out herein and designed to ensure sound financial administration and economy of expenditure.

Article 9

PROVISIONAL BUDGET

Exceptionally, the Secretary-General shall, not later than two months after the coming into force of the Convention, present to the Council a first budget which will cover the period from the coming into force of the Convention up to June 30th, 1949, together with proposals regarding the amount of the advances of working capital required.

In faith whereof the undersigned Plenipotentiaries, being duly authorised to that effect, have signed the present Protocol.

Done in Paris this sixteenth day of April, Nineteen Hundred and Forty Eight, in the English and French languages, both texts being equally authentic, in a single copy which shall remain deposited in the Archives of the Government of the French Republic, by which certified copies will be communicated to all the other Signatories.

RATIFICATION, COMING INTO FORCE, ACCESSIONS

Ratification

In accordance with its Article 24, the Convention for European Economic Co-operation was ratified by the Signatories on the dates indicated below:

UNITED KINGDOM	10th June, 1948
UNITED KINGDOM AND UNITED STATES ZONES OF OCCUPATION OF GERMANY	15th June, 1948
IRELAND	16th July, 1948
FRANCE	28th July, 1948
AUSTRIA	28th July, 1948
ICELAND	28th July, 1948
SWEDEN	28th July, 1948
FRENCH ZONE OF OCCUPATION OF GERMANY	29th July, 1948
DENMARK	29th July, 1948
ITALY	24th August, 1948
NORWAY	24th August, 1948
THE NETHERLANDS	25th August, 1948
BELGIUM	4th September, 1948
TURKEY	27th October, 1948
SWITZERLAND	26th November, 1948
PORTUGAL	4th April, 1949
LUXEMBURG	14th April, 1949
GREECE	20th October, 1949

Accessions

In accordance with Article 25 of the Convention for European Economic Co-operation, the British-United States Zone of the Free Territory of Trieste acceded to that Convention with the assent of the Council of the Organisation, given at its meeting on 14th October, 1948 and Spain acceded to that Convention with the assent of the Council of the Organisation, given at its meeting on 20th July 1959.

Change in the representation of a Contracting Party

As from 25th October, 1949, the Government of the Federal Republic of Germany has succeeded the Commanders in Chief of the French, United Kingdom and United States Zones of Occupation of Germany in the representation of Western Germany in the Organisation. The Council of the Organisation took note of this change on 31st October, 1949.

I. CONVENTION DE COOPÉRATION ÉCONOMIQUE EUROPÉENNE

Le texte de la Convention de Coopération Économique Européenne (Paris, 16 avril 1948) est précédé de l'Acte Final de la Seconde Session du Comité de Coopération Économique Européenne et est suivi du Protocole Additionnel nº I sur la Capacité Juridique, les Privilèges et les Immunités de l'Organisation ainsi que du Protocole Additionnel nº II sur le Régime Financier de l'Organisation. Enfin, il est fait état des pays ayant ratifié ou adhéré à la Convention et aux Protocoles Additionnels, qui sont entrés en vigueur le 28 juillet 1948.

*

* *

ACTE FINAL DE LA SECONDE SESSION DU COMITÉ DE COOPÉRATION ÉCONOMIQUE EUROPÉENNE

En vue de déterminer les formes de la coopération économique européenne projetée dans le Rapport général adopté le 22 septembre 1947 par le Comité de Coopération Économique Européenne, et notamment afin d'instituer l'Organisation envisagée au paragraphe 113 dudit Rapport, les Gouvernements de l'Autriche, de la Belgique, du Danemark, de la France, de la Grèce, de l'Irlande, de l'Islande, de l'Italie, du Luxembourg, de la Norvège, des Pays-Bas, du Portugal, du Royaume-Uni, de la Suède, de la Suisse et de la Turquie, qui ont invité les Commandants-en-chef des Zones d'occupation en Allemagne de la France, du Royaume-Uni et des États-Unis d'Amérique à participer à ces travaux ;

Ont entrepris le 15 mars 1948, à Paris, par l'entremise de leurs représentants, les travaux nécessaires à cet effet.

Ces travaux ont pris fin le 16 avril 1948 et ont abouti à l'élaboration des instruments suivants :

1. Convention de Coopération Économique Européenne ;
2. Protocole Additionnel nº I sur la capacité juridique, les privilèges et les immunités de l'Organisation Européenne de Coopération Économique ;
3. Protocole Additionnel nº II sur le régime financier de l'Organisation.

Les Résolutions suivantes ont été également adoptées :

1. Résolution sur les tâches de l'Organisation ;
2. Résolution sur les relations entre l'Organisation et le représentant spécial des États-Unis en Europe ;
3. Résolution sur le règlement intérieur de l'Organisation ;
4. Résolution sur le financement du budget initial de l'Organisation ;
5. Résolution sur le financement intérimaire de l'Organisation ;
6. Résolution sur le statut du personnel de l'Organisation ;
7. Résolution sur le lieu de la première réunion du Conseil de l'Organisation.

Tous les Gouvernements et Autorités mentionnés ci-dessus auront le droit de participer immédiatement aux travaux initiaux de l'Organisation, dès la mise en application provisoire de la Convention prévue à l'Article 24*b*.

Les Signataires du présent Acte Final qui auront signé la Convention seront réputés Membres originaires de l'Organisation dès le dépôt de leur instrument de ratification.

En foi de quoi les Représentants des Gouvernements et Autorités susmentionnés ont signé le présent Acte.

Fait à Paris, le seize avril mil neuf cent quarante-huit, en français et en anglais, les deux textes faisant également foi, en un seul exemplaire qui restera déposé aux Archives du Gouvernement de la République Française, qui en communiquera copie certifiée conforme à tous les autres signataires.

CONVENTION DE COOPÉRATION ÉCONOMIQUE EUROPÉENNE

Les Gouvernements de l'Autriche, de la Belgique, du Danemark, de la France, de la Grèce, de l'Irlande, de l'Islande, de l'Italie, du Luxembourg, de la Norvège, des Pays-Bas, du Portugal, du Royaume Uni, de la Suède, de la Suisse, de la Turquie et les Commandants-en-chef des Zones d'occupation en Allemagne de la France, du Royaume-Uni et des États-Unis d'Amérique :

CONSIDÉRANT qu'une économie européenne forte et prospère est essentielle pour atteindre les buts des Nations Unies, sauvegarder les libertés individuelles, accroître le bien-être général et qu'elle contribuera au maintien de la paix ;

RECONNAISSANT que leurs économies sont interdépendantes et que la prospérité de chacune d'elles dépend de la prospérité de toutes ;

ESTIMANT que seule une coopération étroite et durable des Parties Contractantes permet de restaurer et de maintenir la prospérité de l'Europe et de relever les ruines de la guerre ;

RÉSOLUS à mettre en œuvre les principes du rapport général du Comité de Coopération Économique Européenne et à atteindre les objectifs qu'il définit, notamment à établir rapidement des conditions économiques saines qui permettront aux Parties Contractantes de parvenir aussitôt que possible et de se maintenir à un niveau d'activité satisfaisant sans aide extérieure d'un caractère exceptionnel, ainsi que d'apporter leur pleine contribution à la stabilité économique du monde ;

DÉTERMINÉS à conjuguer à ces fins leurs forces économiques, à s'entendre sur l'utilisation la plus complète de leurs capacités et de leurs possibilités particulières, à augmenter leur production, développer et moderniser leur équipement industriel et agricole, accroître leurs échanges, réduire progressivement les entraves à leur commerce mutuel, favoriser le plein emploi de la main-d'œuvre, restaurer ou maintenir la stabilité de leurs économies ainsi que la confiance dans leurs devises nationales ;

PRENANT ACTE de la volonté généreuse du Peuple américain exprimée par les mesures prises pour apporter l'aide sans laquelle les objectifs assignés ne pourraient pleinement être atteints ;

DÉCIDÉS à créer les conditions et à établir les institutions nécessaires au succès de la coopération économique européenne et à l'usage efficace de l'aide américaine et à conclure une Convention à cette fin ;

ONT DÉSIGNÉ les Plénipotentiaires soussignés, lesquels, après présentation de leurs pleins pouvoirs, trouvés en bonne et due forme, sont convenus des dispositions suivantes :

Article 1

Les Parties Contractantes conviennent de pratiquer une étroite coopération dans leurs relations économiques mutuelles.

Elles s'assignent comme tâche immédiate l'établissement et l'exécution d'un programme commun de relèvement. Ce programme aura pour objet de permettre aux Parties Contractantes de parvenir aussitôt que possible et de se maintenir à un niveau d'activité économique satisfaisant sans aide extérieure de caractère exceptionnel. A cet effet, le programme devra notamment tenir compte de leur besoin de développer dans toute la mesure du possible leurs exportations vers les pays non participants.

A ces fins, les Parties Contractantes s'engagent à remplir, par leurs efforts individuels et dans un esprit d'entraide, les obligations générales ci-après et instituent une Organisation Européenne de Coopération Économique, dénommée ci-dessous l'Organisation.

TITRE I – Obligations générales

Article 2

Les Parties Contractantes s'engagent à promouvoir avec énergie tant individuellement que collectivement le développement de la production, par l'utilisation des ressources dont elles disposent dans la Métropole comme dans

les territoires d'Outre-Mer et par la modernisation progressive de leur équipement et de leurs techniques, dans les conditions les mieux appropriées à la réalisation du programme commun de relèvement.

Article 3

Les Parties Contractantes établiront dans le cadre de l'Organisation, aussi souvent et pour autant que nécessaire, des programmes généraux de production et d'échanges de biens et de services, en prenant en considération les prévisions ou programmes de chacune d'elles et les conditions générales de l'économie mondiale.

Chaque Partie Contractante fera tous ses efforts pour assurer la réalisation de ces programmes généraux.

Article 4

Les Parties Contractantes développeront dans la plus large mesure possible et de façon concertée leurs échanges réciproques de biens et de services. Elles poursuivront à cet effet les efforts entrepris pour parvenir aussitôt que possible entre elles à un régime de paiements multilatéraux et coopéreront pour atténuer les restrictions à leurs échanges et à leurs paiements réciproques, en vue d'abolir dès que possible celles qui les entravent actuellement.

Dans l'application du présent article, les Parties Contractantes tiendront dûment compte de la nécessité, pour l'ensemble et pour chacune d'entre elles, de réduire ou d'éviter des déséquilibres excessifs dans leurs relations économiques et financières, tant entre elles que vis-à-vis des pays non participants.

Article 5

Les Parties Contractantes s'engagent à resserrer leurs liens économiques par tous les moyens qu'elles estimeront propres à réaliser les objectifs de la présente Convention. Elles poursuivront leurs études en cours sur les Unions douanières ou les régimes analogues tels que les zones de libre-échange, dont l'institution pourrait constituer un des moyens d'atteindre ces objectifs. Celles des Parties Contractantes qui ont déjà admis entre elles le principe d'une Union douanière en assureront l'établissement aussi rapidement que possible.

Article 6

Les Parties Contractantes coopéreront entre elles avec les autres pays animés des mêmes intentions pour réduire les tarifs et autres obstacles à l'expansion des échanges, en vue de réaliser un régime multilatéral d'échanges viable et équilibré, conformément aux principes de la Charte de La Havane.

Article 7

Chaque Partie Contractante, en tenant compte de la nécessité de maintenir ou d'atteindre un niveau élevé et stable dans le volume des échanges et de l'emploi et de prévenir ou combattre les dangers de l'inflation, prendra telles dispositions en son pouvoir afin d'instaurer ou de maintenir la stabilité de sa monnaie et l'équilibre de ses finances, ainsi qu'un taux de change approprié et, d'une manière générale, la confiance dans son système monétaire.

Article 8

Les Parties Contractantes utiliseront de la façon la plus complète et la plus rationnelle la main-d'œuvre disponible.

Elles s'efforceront de réaliser le plein emploi de leur main-d'œuvre nationale et pourront avoir recours à la main-d'œuvre disponible dans le territoire de toute autre Partie Contractante. Pour ce dernier cas, elles prendront d'un commun accord les mesures nécessaires pour faciliter le mouvement et assurer l'établissement des travailleurs dans des conditions satisfaisantes au point de vue économique et social.

D'une manière générale, les Parties Contractantes coopéreront en vue de réduire progressivement les obstacles au libre mouvement des personnes.

Article 9

Les Parties Contractantes fourniront à l'Organisation toutes les informations que celle-ci pourrait leur demander en vue de faciliter l'accomplissement de ses tâches.

TITRE II – Organisation

Article 10

MEMBRES

Sont Membres de l'Organisation les Parties à la présente Convention.

Article 11

OBJECTIF

L'objectif de l'Organisation est la réalisation d'une économie européenne saine par la voie de la coopération économique de ses Membres. L'une des tâches immédiates de l'Organisation est d'assurer le succès du programme de relèvement européen, conformément aux engagements figurant au Titre I de la présente Convention.

Article 12

FONCTIONS

L'Organisation est chargée de remplir les fonctions suivantes dans les limites des pouvoirs qui lui sont ou pourraient lui être reconnus :

a) élaborer et mettre en œuvre, dans le domaine de l'action collective des Parties intéressées, les mesures nécessaires pour assurer la réalisation de l'objectif visé à l'Article 11 ; faciliter, susciter et coordonner l'action individuelle des Membres ;

b) faciliter et surveiller l'exécution de la présente Convention ; prendre les mesures propres à assurer cette exécution : à cette fin, pourvoir à l'établissement de mécanismes de surveillance et de contrôle susceptibles d'assurer la meilleure utilisation, tant de l'aide extérieure que des ressources nationales ;

c) fournir au Gouvernement des États-Unis l'aide et les informations à convenir, relatives à l'exécution du programme de relèvement européen, et lui adresser des recommandations ;

d) sur la demande des Parties intéressées, prêter son concours à la négociation des conventions internationales qui pourraient être nécessaires à la meilleure exécution du programme de relèvement européen.

L'Organisation pourra également assumer toute autre fonction dont il sera convenu.

Article 13

POUVOIRS

En vue d'atteindre son objectif tel qu'il est défini à l'Article 2, l'Organisation peut :

a) prendre des décisions que les Membres exécuteront ;

b) conclure des accords avec ses Membres ou des pays non membres, avec le Gouvernement des États-Unis et avec les organisations internationales ;

c) faire des recommandations au Gouvernement des États-Unis, à d'autres gouvernements et aux organisations internationales.

Article 14

DÉCISIONS

A moins que l'Organisation n'en décide autrement pour des cas spéciaux, les décisions sont prises par accord mutuel de tous les Membres. Dès lors qu'un Membre déclare ne pas être intéressé à une question, son abstention ne fait pas obstacle aux décisions, qui sont obligatoires pour les autres Membres.

Article 15

CONSEIL

a) Un Conseil composé de tous les Membres est l'organe duquel émanent toutes les décisions ;

b) Le Conseil désigne chaque année parmi ses Membres un Président et deux Vice-Présidents ;

c) Le Conseil est assisté d'un Comité Exécutif et d'un Secrétaire Général. Il peut créer tout Comité Technique ou autre organisme nécessaire à l'exercice des fonctions de l'Organisation. Tous ces organes sont responsables devant le Conseil.

Article 16

COMITÉ EXÉCUTIF

a) Le Comité Exécutif se compose de sept Membres désignés chaque année par le Conseil. Il poursuit ses travaux conformément aux instructions et directives du Conseil, et il lui en rend compte ;
b) Le Conseil désigne chaque année parmi les Membres du Comité Exécutif, un Président et un Vice-Président. Il peut également désigner chaque année un Rapporteur général dont il précisera les fonctions ;
c) Tout Membre de l'Organisation qui n'est pas représenté au Comité Exécutif peut prendre part à toutes les discussions et décisions de ce Comité qui affectent en particulier les intérêts dudit Membre.

Les Membres de l'Organisation seront tenus informés des délibérations du Comité Exécutif par la communication en temps utile des ordres du jour et des comptes rendus sommaires.

Article 17

SECRÉTAIRE GÉNÉRAL

a) Le Secrétaire Général est assisté d'un premier et d'un second Secrétaire Général Adjoint ;
b) Le Secrétaire Général et les Secrétaires Généraux Adjoints sont nommés par le Conseil. Le Secrétaire Général est placé sous l'autorité du Conseil ;
c) Le Secrétaire Général assiste avec voix consultative aux séances du Conseil, du Comité Exécutif, et, s'il y a lieu, aux séances des Comités techniques et des autres organismes. Il peut s'y faire représenter. Il prépare les délibérations du Conseil et du Comité Exécutif et assure l'exécution de leurs décisions conformément à leurs instructions et directives.

Les fonctions du Secrétaire Général font l'objet de dispositions complémentaires figurant en Annexe à la présente Convention.

Article 18

SECRÉTARIAT

a) Le Secrétaire Général nomme le personnel utile au fonctionnement de l'Organisation. La nomination du personnel de direction se fait sur avis conforme du Conseil. Le statut du personnel est soumis à l'approbation du Conseil ;
b) Étant donné le caractère international de l'Organisation, le Secrétaire Général et le personnel ne solliciteront ni recevront de directives d'aucun des Membres de l'Organisation, ni d'aucun gouvernement ou autorité extérieurs à l'Organisation.

Article 19

COMITÉS TECHNIQUES ET AUTRES ORGANISMES

Les Comités techniques et les autres organismes prévus à l'Article 15*c*, sont placés sous l'autorité du Conseil. Ils sont composés des Membres les plus intéressés et organisent leur travail de telle sorte que les autres Membres intéressés puissent y participer s'il est nécessaire.

Article 20

RELATIONS AVEC LES AUTRES ORGANISATIONS INTERNATIONALES

a) L'Organisation établit avec les Nations Unies, leurs organes principaux, leurs organes subsidiaires et avec les institutions spécialisées toutes relations propres à assurer une collaboration conforme à leurs fins respectives ;
b) L'Organisation peut également entretenir des relations avec d'autres organismes internationaux.

Article 21

SIÈGE

Le siège de l'Organisation sera fixé par le Conseil à sa première session.

Le Conseil, les différents Comités ou les autres organismes peuvent se réunir en un lieu autre que le siège de l'Organisation s'ils en décident ainsi.

Article 22

CAPACITÉ JURIDIQUE, PRIVILÈGES ET IMMUNITÉS

a) L'Organisation jouit, sur le territoire de chacun de ses Membres, de la capacité juridique qui lui est nécessaire pour exercer ses fonctions et pour atteindre ses buts, dans les conditions prévues par le Protocole Additionnel n° I à la présente Convention;

b) L'Organisation, ses fonctionnaires ainsi que les représentants de ses Membres bénéficient des privilèges et immunités définis dans le Protocole Additionnel précité.

Article 23

RÉGIME FINANCIER

a) Le Secrétaire Général soumet à l'approbation du Conseil un budget annuel et des comptes, établis conformément aux règles financières fixées par le Protocole Additionnel n° II à la présente Convention;

b) L'année financière de l'Organisation commence le 1er juillet;

c) Les dépenses de l'Organisation sont supportées par les Membres et réparties conformément aux dispositions du Protocole Additionnel précité.

TITRE III – Dispositions finales

Article 24

RATIFICATION ET ENTRÉE EN VIGUEUR

a) La présente Convention sera ratifiée. Les instruments de ratification seront déposés auprès du Gouvernement de la République Française. La Convention entrera en vigueur dès que six au moins des signataires auront déposé leurs instruments de ratification; Pour tout signataire qui la ratifiera ultérieurement, la Convention entrera en vigueur dès le dépôt de l'instrument de ratification;

b) Toutefois, en attendant l'entrée en vigueur de la Convention dans les conditions prévues au paragraphe précédent, les signataires conviennent, afin d'éviter tout délai dans son exécution, de la mettre en application dès sa signature, à titre provisoire, et conformément à leurs règles constitutionnelles respectives.

Article 25

ADHÉSION

Dès le dépôt de dix instruments de ratification au moins, tout pays d'Europe non signataire pourra adhérer à la Convention par notification adressée au Gouvernement de la République Française, et avec l'accord du Conseil de l'Organisation. L'adhésion prendra effet à la date de cet accord.

Article 26

INEXÉCUTION DES OBLIGATIONS

Si l'un des Membres de l'Organisation cesse de remplir les obligations qui découlent de la présente Convention, il sera invité à se conformer aux dispositions de la Convention. Si ledit Membre ne se conformait pas à cette invitation

dans le délai qui lui serait imparti, les autres Membres pourraient, par accord mutuel, décider de poursuivre sans lui leur coopération au sein de l'Organisation.

Article 27
RETRAIT

Toute Partie Contractante pourra mettre fin, en ce qui la concerne, à l'application de la présente Convention, en donnant un préavis d'un an à cet effet au Gouvernement de la République Française.

Article 28
COMMUNICATION DES RATIFICATIONS, ADHÉSIONS ET RETRAITS

Dès la réception des instruments de ratification, d'adhésion ou de préavis de retrait, le Gouvernement de la République Française en donnera communication à toutes les Parties Contractantes et au Secrétaire Général de l'Organisation.

ANNEXE

Dispositions complémentaires relatives aux fonctions du Secrétaire Général

Les fonctions du Secrétaire Général définies à l'Article 17 font l'objet des dispositions complémentaires ci-dessous :

1. Il peut soumettre des propositions au Conseil et au Comité Exécutif.
2. En accord avec les Présidents des Comités techniques, il prend toutes dispositions pour réunir ces Comités chaque fois que cela est nécessaire et pour en assurer le Secrétariat. Il leur communique, en tant que de besoin, les instructions du Conseil et du Comité Exécutif.
3. Il suit les travaux des autres organismes mentionnés à l'Article 15*c* et leur transmet, en tant que de besoin, les instructions du Conseil et du Comité Exécutif.
4. Il prend eu égard aux dispositions de l'Article 20 et en accord avec les instructions du Conseil et du Comité Exécutif les mesures nécessaires pour assurer la liaison avec les autres organisations internationales.
5. Il assume toutes les autres fonctions utiles à la bonne marche de l'Organisation, qui lui sont confiées par le Conseil ou par le Comité Exécutif.

En foi de quoi les Plénipotentiaires soussignés, dûment autorisés à cet effet, ont signé la présente Convention et y ont apposé leurs sceaux.

Fait à Paris, le 16 avril 1948, en français et en anglais, les deux textes faisant également foi, en un seul exemplaire qui restera déposé aux Archives du Gouvernement de la République Française, qui en communiquera copie certifiée conforme à tous les autres signataires.

PROTOCOLE ADDITIONNEL nº I
A LA CONVENTION DE COOPÉRATION ÉCONOMIQUE EUROPÉENNE
SUR LA CAPACITÉ JURIDIQUE, LES PRIVILÈGES ET LES IMMUNITÉS DE L'ORGANISATION

Les Gouvernements et Autorités signataires de la Convention de Coopération Économique Européenne;

CONSIDÉRANT qu'aux termes de l'Article 22 de la Convention, l'Organisation Européenne de Coopération Économique jouit sur le territoire de chacun de ses Membres de la capacité juridique qui lui est nécessaire pour exercer ses fonctions et pour atteindre ses buts et que l'Organisation, ses fonctionnaires ainsi que les représentants de ses Membres bénéficient des privilèges et immunités définis dans un Protocole Additionnel;

SONT convenus de ce qui suit :

TITRE I – Personnalité, capacité

Article 1

L'Organisation possède la personnalité juridique. Elle a la capacité de contracter, d'acquérir et aliéner des biens immobiliers et mobiliers et d'ester en justice.

TITRE II – Biens, fonds et avoirs

Article 2

L'Organisation, ses biens et avoirs, quels que soient leur siège et leur détenteur, jouissent de l'immunité de juridiction, sauf dans la mesure où l'Organisation y a expressément renoncé dans un cas particulier. Il est toutefois entendu que la renonciation ne peut s'étendre à des mesures d'exécution.

Article 3

Les locaux de l'Organisation sont inviolables. Ses biens et avoirs, où qu'ils se trouvent et quel que soit leur détenteur, sont exempts de perquisition, réquisition, confiscation, expropriation ou de toute autre forme de contrainte exécutive, administrative, judiciaire ou législative.

Article 4

Les archives de l'Organisation et, d'une manière générale, tous les documents lui appartenant ou détenus par elle, sont inviolables où qu'ils se trouvent.

Article 5

Sans être astreinte à aucun contrôle, réglementation ou moratoire financiers, l'Organisation peut :

a) détenir des devises quelconques et avoir des comptes en n'importe quelle monnaie;

b) transférer librement ses fonds, d'un pays dans un autre ou à l'intérieur d'un pays quelconque et convertir toutes devises détenues par elle en toute autre monnaie.

Article 6

L'Organisation, ses avoirs, revenus et autres biens sont :

a) exonérés de tout impôt direct. Toutefois, l'Organisation ne demandera pas l'exonération d'impôts qui ne constituent que la simple rémunération de services d'utilité publique;

b) exonérés de tous droits de douane et prohibitions et restrictions d'importation ou d'exportation pour son usage officiel. Il est entendu, toutefois, que les articles ainsi importés en franchise ne seront pas vendus sur le territoire du pays dans lequel ils auront été introduits, à moins que ce ne soit à des conditions agréées par le Gouvernement de ce pays;

c) exonérés de tout droit de douane et de toutes prohibitions et restrictions d'importation et d'exportation à l'égard de ses publications.

Article 7

Bien que l'Organisation ne revendique pas, en principe, l'exonération des droits d'accise et des taxes à la vente entrant dans le prix des biens mobiliers ou immobiliers, cependant, quand elle effectue pour son usage officiel des achats importants dont le prix comprend des droits et taxes de cette nature, les Membres prendront, chaque fois qu'il leur sera possible, les dispositions administratives appropriées en vue de la remise ou du remboursement du montant de ces droits et taxes.

TITRE III – Facilités de communications

Article 8

L'Organisation bénéficiera sur le territoire de chaque Membre, pour ses communications officielles, d'un traitement au moins aussi favorable que le traitement accordé par lui à tout autre gouvernement, y compris sa mission diplomatique, en ce qui concerne les priorités, tarifs et taxes sur le courrier, les câblogrammes, télégrammes, radiotélégrammes, téléphotos, communications téléphoniques et autres communications, ainsi que sur les tarifs de presse pour les informations à la presse et à la radio. La correspondance officielle et les autres communications officielles de l'Organisation ne pourront être censurées.

TITRE IV – Représentants des Membres

Article 9

Les représentants des Membres auprès des organes principaux et subsidiaires de l'Organisation jouissent, durant l'exercice de leurs fonctions et au cours des voyages à destination ou en provenance du lieu de la réunion, des privilèges, immunités et facilités dont jouissent les agents diplomatiques de rang comparable.

Article 10

Ces privilèges, immunités et facilités sont accordés aux représentants des Membres, non à leur avantage personnel, mais dans le but d'assurer en toute indépendance l'exercice de leurs fonctions en rapport avec l'Organisation. Par conséquent, un Membre a non seulement le droit, mais le devoir de lever l'immunité de son représentant dans tous les cas où, à son avis, l'immunité empêcherait que justice soit faite et où elle peut être levée sans nuire au but pour lequel l'immunité est accordée.

Article 11

Les dispositions de l'Article 9 ne sont pas applicables dans le cas d'un représentant vis-à-vis des autorités de l'État dont il est ressortissant ou dont il est ou a été le représentant.

Article 12

Au sens du présent titre, le terme « représentants » est considéré comme comprenant tous les délégués, suppléants, conseillers, experts techniques et secrétaires de délégation.

TITRE V – Fonctionnaires

Article 13

Le Secrétaire Général déterminera les catégories de fonctionnaires auxquels s'appliquent les dispositions du présent titre. Il en soumettra la liste au Conseil et en donnera ensuite communication à tous les Membres. Les noms des fonctionnaires compris dans ces catégories seront communiqués périodiquement aux Membres.

Article 14

Les fonctionnaires de l'Organisation :

a) jouiront de l'immunité de juridiction pour les actes accomplis par eux en leur qualité officielle ; ils continueront à bénéficier de cette immunité après la cessation de leurs fonctions ;

b) jouiront, en ce qui concerne les traitements et émoluments versés par l'Organisation, des mêmes exonérations d'impôts que celles dont bénéficient les fonctionnaires des principales Organisations internationales et dans les mêmes conditions ;

c) ne seront pas soumis, non plus que leurs conjoints et les membres de leur famille vivant à leur charge, aux dispositions limitant l'immigration et aux formalités d'enregistrement des étrangers ;

d) jouiront, en ce qui concerne les facilités de change, des mêmes privilèges que les fonctionnaires d'un rang comparable appartenant aux missions diplomatiques auprès du Gouvernement ;

e) jouiront, ainsi que leurs conjoints et les membres de leur famille vivant à leur charge, des mêmes facilités de rapatriement que les membres des missions diplomatiques en période de crise internationale ;

f) jouiront du droit d'importer en franchise leur mobilier et leurs effets à l'occasion de leur première prise de fonction dans le pays intéressé.

Article 15

Outre les privilèges, immunités, exemptions et facilités prévus à l'Article 14, le Secrétaire Général, tant en ce qui le concerne qu'en ce qui concerne son conjoint et ses enfants mineurs, jouira des privilèges, immunités, exemptions et facilités accordés, conformément au droit international, aux chefs de missions diplomatiques.

Les Secrétaires Généraux Adjoints jouiront des privilèges, immunités, exemptions et facilités accordés aux représentants diplomatiques de rang comparable.

Article 16

Les privilèges, immunités et facilités sont accordés aux fonctionnaires dans l'intérêt de l'Organisation et non à leur avantage personnel. Le Secrétaire Général pourra et devra lever l'immunité accordée à un fonctionnaire dans tous les cas où, à son avis, cette immunité empêcherait que justice soit faite et pourra être levée sans porter préjudice aux intérêts de l'Organisation. A l'égard du Secrétaire Général et des Secrétaires Généraux Adjoints le Conseil a qualité pour prononcer la levée des immunités.

Article 17

L'Organisation collaborera, en tous temps, avec les autorités compétentes des Membres en vue de faciliter la bonne administration de la justice, d'assurer l'observation des règlements de police et d'éviter tout abus auquel pourraient donner lieu les privilèges, immunités, exemptions et facilités énumérés dans le présent titre.

TITRE VI – Experts en mission pour l'Organisation

Article 18

Les experts (autres que les fonctionnaires visés au Titre V), lorsqu'ils accomplissent des missions pour l'Organisation, jouissent, pendant la durée de cette mission, y compris le temps du voyage, des privilèges, immunités et facilités nécessaires pour exercer leurs fonctions en toute indépendance, notamment de :

a) l'immunité d'arrestation personnelle ou de détention et de saisie de leurs bagages ;

b) l'immunité de juridiction en ce qui concerne les actes accomplis par eux au cours de leurs missions ;

c) l'inviolabilité de tous papiers et documents.

Article 19

Les privilèges, immunités et facilités sont accordés aux experts dans l'intérét de l'Organisation, et non à leur avantage personnel. Le Secrétaire Général pourra et devra lever l'immunité accordée à un expert, dans tous les cas où, à son avis, cette immunité empêcherait que justice soit faite et où elle pourrait être levée sans porter préjudice aux intérêts de l'Organisation.

TITRE VII – Accords complémentaires

Article 20

L'Organisation pourra conclure avec un ou plusieurs Membres des accords complémentaires, aménageant en ce qui concerne ce Membre ou ces Membres les dispositions du présent Protocole.

En foi de quoi les Plénipotentiaires soussignés, dûment autorisés à cet effet, ont signé le présent Protocole.

Fait à Paris, le 16 avril 1948, en français et en anglais, les deux textes faisant également foi, en un seul exemplaire qui restera déposé aux Archives du Gouvernement de la République Française, qui en communiquera copie certifiée conforme à tous les autres signataires.

PROTOCOLE ADDITIONNEL nº II
A LA CONVENTION DE COOPÉRATION ÉCONOMIQUE EUROPÉENNE
SUR LE RÉGIME FINANCIER DE L'ORGANISATION

Les Gouvernements et les Autorités signataires de la Convention de Coopération Économique Européenne :

CONSIDÉRANT que l'Article 23 de la Convention prévoit l'établissement d'un Protocole additionnel sur le régime financier de l'Organisation Européenne de Coopération Économique;

SONT convenus de ce qui suit :

Article 1

BUDGET

Le Secrétaire Général soumet au Conseil, pour examen et approbation, au plus tard le 1er mai de chaque année, des prévisions détaillées de dépenses pour l'exercice budgétaire suivant.

Les prévisions de dépenses sont groupées par chapitres. Les virements de chapitre à chapitre sont interdits, sauf autorisation du Comité Exécutif. La forme précise du projet du budget est déterminée dans son détail par le Secrétaire Général.

Les frais de voyage et les indemnités de séjour des représentants des Membres incombent normalement aux Membres. Le Conseil peut autoriser, dans certains cas, le remboursement des frais qu'aura entraînés, pour certains représentants, l'accomplissement de missions spéciales dont ils auront été chargés par l'Organisation.

Article 2

BUDGET ADDITIONNEL

Si les circonstances l'exigent, le Conseil peut demander au Secrétaire Général de présenter un budget additionnel. Le Secrétaire Général soumet au Conseil une évaluation des dépenses qu'implique l'exécution de chacune des résolutions présentées au Conseil. Une résolution dont l'exécution entraîne des dépenses supplémentaires n'est considérée comme approuvée par le Conseil que lorsque celui-ci a également approuvé les prévisions de dépenses supplémentaires correspondantes.

Article 3

COMMISSION DU BUDGET

Une Commission du budget composée de représentants de Membres de l'Organisation sera créée par le Conseil. Avant de présenter le budget au Conseil, le Secrétaire Général le soumet à cette Commission en vue d'un examen préalable.

Article 4

BASE DE CALCUL DES CONTRIBUTIONS

Les dépenses budgétaires approuvées sont couvertes par les contributions des Membres de l'Organisation, conformément à un barème arrêté par le Conseil.

Le Secrétaire Général informe les Membres du montant de leurs contributions et les invite à verser ces contributions à une date qu'il détermine.

Article 5

MONNAIE ADOPTÉE POUR LE PAIEMENT DES CONTRIBUTIONS

Le budget de l'Organisation est établi dans la monnaie du pays où l'Organisation a son siège; les contributions des Membres sont payables en cette monnaie.

Le Conseil peut toutefois inviter les Membres à payer une partie de leurs contributions en toute monnaie dont l'Organisation aura besoin pour accomplir ses tâches.

Article 6

FONDS DE ROULEMENT

Jusqu'à la fixation et au versement des contributions, le Conseil invitera les Membres à faire, chaque fois que cela sera nécessaire, des avances de fonds de roulement dans la monnaie ou les monnaies prévues pour le paiement des contributions. Ces avances seront remboursées, au cours du même exercice budgétaire, par imputation sur les contributions de sommes correspondantes. Le montant des avances sera fixé d'après le critère employé par le calcul des contributions elles-mêmes.

Article 7

COMPTES ET VÉRIFICATIONS

Le Secrétaire Général fait établir un compte exact de toutes les recettes et dépenses de l'Organisation.

Le Conseil désigne des Commissaires aux Comptes, dont le premier mandat est de trois ans et peut être renouvelé. Ces commissaires sont chargés d'examiner les comptes de l'Organisation, notamment en vue de certifier que les dépenses ont été conformes aux prévisions budgétaires.

Le Secrétaire Général fournit aux Commissaires aux Comptes toutes les facilités dont ils peuvent avoir besoin dans l'accomplissement de leur tâche.

Article 8

RÈGLEMENT FINANCIER

Le Secrétaire Général soumet au Conseil, pour approbation, dans un délai aussi bref que possible après la création de l'Organisation, un règlement financier détaillé établi conformément aux principes énoncés au présent Protocole et conçu de manière à assurer à l'Organisation une gestion financière saine et économique.

Article 9

BUDGET INITIAL

A titre exceptionnel, le Secrétaire général soumettra au Conseil, deux mois au plus tard après l'entrée en vigueur de la Convention, un budget initial couvrant la période allant de la date d'entrée en vigueur jusqu'au 30 juin 1949, ainsi que des propositions relatives au montant des avances de fonds de roulement.

En foi de quoi les Plénipotentiaires soussignés, dûment autorisés à cet effet, ont signé le présent Protocole.

Fait à Paris, le 16 avril I948, en français et en anglais, les deux textes faisant également foi, en un seul exemplaire qui restera déposé aux Archives du Gouvernement de la République Française, qui en communiquera copie certifiée conforme à tous les autres signataires.

RATIFICATIONS ET ADHÉSIONS

Ratifications

La Convention de Coopération Économique Européenne a été ratifiée par les signataires conformément à l'Article 24 de la Convention, aux dates indiquées ci-dessous :

ROYAUME-UNI	le 10 juin 1948
ZONE D'OCCUPATION EN ALLEMAGNE DU ROYAUME-UNI ET DES ÉTATS-UNIS D'AMÉRIQUE	le 15 juin 1948
IRLANDE	le 16 juillet 1948
FRANCE	le 28 juillet 1948
AUTRICHE	le 28 juillet 1948
ISLANDE	le 28 juillet 1948
SUÈDE	le 28 juillet 1948
ZONE D'OCCUPATION EN ALLEMAGNE DE LA FRANCE	le 29 juillet 1948
DANEMARK	le 29 juillet 1948
ITALIE	le 24 août 1948
NORVÈGE	le 24 août 1948
PAYS-BAS	le 25 août 1948
BELGIQUE	le 4 septembre 1948
TURQUIE	le 27 octobre 1948
SUISSE	le 26 novembre 1948
PORTUGAL	le 4 avril 1949
LUXEMBOURG	le 14 avril 1949
GRÈCE	le 20 octobre 1949

Adhésions

Conformément à l'Article 25 de la Convention de Coopération Économique Européenne, la Zone anglo-américaine du Territoire Libre de Trieste a adhéré à la Convention avec l'accord du Conseil de l'Organisation, donné à sa séance du 14 octobre 1948 et l'Espagne a adhéré à la Convention avec l'Accord du Conseil de l'Organisation, donné à sa séance du 20 juillet 1959.

Changement dans la représentation d'une Partie Contractante

A compter du 25 octobre 1949, le Gouvernement de la République Fédérale d'Allemagne a succédé aux Commandants-en-chef des Zones d'occupation en Allemagne de la France, du Royaume-Uni et des États-Unis d'Amérique pour la représentation de l'Allemagne Occidentale au sein de l'Organisation. Le Conseil de l'Organisation a pris acte de ce changement le 31 octobre 1949.

II. OEEC PUBLICATIONS/PUBLICATIONS DE L'OECE

This section lists the monographs and periodicals published by the OEEC (1948 to 1961) and by its former Committee. They are presented in chronological and alphabetical order of the English-language title and grouped under author divisions or committees.

Most publications are available at OECD Secretariat on microfiche or paper form.

1. Origin of the OEEC

The OEEC originated in the Conference on European Economic Co-operation held in Paris from 12 July 1947 in response to General Marshall's proposal of American aid for the reconstruction of Europe. The speech delivered by the US Secretary of State at Harvard University on 5 June 1947 stated not simply that the United States was prepared to help Europe, but also that it was for the Europeans to work out a programme for the reconstruction of their economies in mutual agreement. This announcement of the "Marshall Plan" prompted the sixteen countries of Western Europe to meet, at the invitation of France and the United Kingdom. They produced a report on the **European Recovery Programme** which was sent to the US Government.

This report, drawn up by the **Committee of European Economic Co-operation,** was adopted on 22 September 1947. It defined the essential problems of European economic recovery, and on its strength, the US Congress a few months later approved the release of $5.055 million for the first year of the programme. This preliminary report was followed by two others setting out the distribution of American aid for the first two annual programmes.

The need to set up a permanent co-ordinating body able to give a strong impetus to the efforts of European countries was becoming more and more pressing. On 15 January 1948 the French and British governments proposed the creation of the permanent economic organisation proposed in the Report of the Paris Conference. On 16 April 1948, the Foreign Ministers of the sixteen participating European countries and the Commanders in Chief of the Western Zones of Occupation in Germany signed the Convention for European Economic Co-operation, bringing the OEEC into being.

Cette section dresse la liste des monographies et des revues périodiques publiées par l'OECE (1948 à 1961) et par le Comité l'ayant précédée. Elle est présentée selon l'ordre chronologique et alphabétique du titre de la version anglaise et regroupée sous les divisions ou comités-auteurs.

La plupart des publications sont disponibles au Secrétariat de l'OCDE sur format papier ou microfiche.

1. Origine de l'OECE

L'origine de l'OECE remonte à la Conférence de Coopération Économique Européenne, ouverte à Paris le 12 juillet 1947, en réponse à la proposition du Général Marshall d'aide américaine pour la reconstruction de l'Europe. Le discours du Secrétaire d'État Américain, le 5 juin 1947, à l'Université de Harvard énonçait non seulement que les États-Unis étaient disposés à aider l'Europe, mais également qu'il revenait aux européens d'élaborer un programme de reconstruction de leurs économies d'un commun accord. Cette annonce du Plan Marshall a incité seize pays d'Europe occidentale à se réunir, à l'initiative de la France et du Royaume-Uni. Ils élaborèrent un rapport sur le **Programme de relèvement européen** qui fut transmis au Gouvernement des États-Unis.

Ce rapport, préparé par le **Comité de Coopération Économique Européenne,** fut adopté le 22 septembre 1947. Il définissait les problèmes essentiels à résoudre pour relever l'économie européenne et donna lieu, quelques mois plus tard, au vote par le Congrès américain de 5.055 millions de dollars pour la première année du programme. Ce rapport préliminaire fut suivi de deux autres qui exposèrent la répartition de l'aide américaine pour les deux premiers programmes annuels.

Le besoin de constituer un organisme permanent de coordination, susceptible de donner une impulsion vigoureuse aux efforts des pays Membres, devenait de plus en plus urgent. Le 15 janvier 1948, les gouvernements français et britannique proposèrent la création de l'organisation économique permanente envisagée dans le Rapport de la Conférence de Paris. Le 16 avril 1948, les Ministres des Affaires Étrangères de seize pays européens et les Commandants en chef des zones occidentales d'occupation en Allemagne signèrent la Convention de Coopération Économique Européenne, acte de naissance de l'OECE.

Publications:

Committee of European Economic Co-operation (1947), Report, 2 vols., HMSO, London.

Committee of European Economic Co-operation/Comité de Coopération Économique Européenne (1948), *Report of the Secretary General on the Development of the European Economic Co-Operation: 15th March/Rapport du Secrétaire Général sur le développement de la coopération économique européenne : 15 mars,* Paris.

Committee of European Economic Co-operation (1948), *Resolutions Transmitted to the Council of the OEEC, 16th April,* Paris.

Committee of European Economic Co-operation (1948), *Convention for European Economic Co-operation,* Paris.

2. Council, Executive Committee and External Relations

Governance of the Organisation was assigned to the Council assisted by an Executive Committee and a Secretary General. The **Council** comprised representatives of the Member countries: Austria, Belgium, Denmark, France, Greece, Iceland, Ireland, Italy, Luxembourg, Netherlands, Norway, Portugal Sweden, Switzerland, Turkey and the United Kingdom since 1948, Germany since 1949 (succeeding to the Commanders in Chief of the occupied Zones), and finally Spain in 1959. It met periodically, either at ministerial level (once a year) or at the level of permanent delegations (on average two to three times a month).

The Council was responsible for the administration and general policy of the Organisation. It set up technical committees and other bodies necessary for the performance of its tasks. The preparatory work of the various bodies of the Organisation and the Secretariat was submitted to it for approval. It took decisions binding on Member governments regarding their economic policies.

The Council set up, on a temporary basis and in some cases with restricted membership, specific Working Parties to execute technical issues:

- *No. 1 Rules of Procedure*
- *No. 2 Systems of Observation and Review (ad hoc)*
- *No. 3 Co-operation in matters of Scientific and Technical Information*
- *No. 4 The Telephone Communications Network in the Mediterranean Basin (ad hoc)*
- *No. 5 Selective Expansion*
- *No. 6 Internal Financial Stability*
- *No. 7 Financing of Investments*
- *No. 8 Organisation of Inland Transport in Western Europe*
- *No. 9 Italian Economic Development Plan*
- *No. 10 Methods of Co-operation in the Peaceful Use of Nuclear Power*

Publications :

Comité de Coopération Économique Européenne (1947), Rapport, 2 vols., Imprimerie Nationale, Paris.

Committee of European Economic Co-operation/Comité de Coopération Économique Européenne (1948), *Report of the Secretary General on the Development of the European Economic Co-Operation: 15th March/Rapport du Secrétaire Général sur le développement de la coopération économique européenne : 15 mars,* Paris.

Comité de Coopération Économique Européenne (1948), *Résolutions transmises au Conseil de l'OECE, 16 avril,* Paris.

Comité de Coopération Économique Européenne (1948), *Convention de Coopération Économique Européenne,* Paris.

2. Conseil, Comité Exécutif et Relations Extérieures

La direction de l'Organisation était confiée à un Conseil, assisté d'un Comité Exécutif et d'un Secrétaire Général. Le **Conseil** était composé des représentants des pays Membres: Autriche, Belgique, Danemark, France, Grèce, Irlande, Islande, Italie, Luxembourg, Norvège, Pays-Bas, Portugal, Royaume-Uni, Suède, Suisse et Turquie dès 1948, de l'Allemagne depuis 1949 (succédant aux Commandants en chef des zones d'occupation) et enfin de l'Espagne en 1959. Le Conseil se réunissait périodiquement soit au niveau ministériel une fois par an, soit au niveau des Délégations permanentes (en moyenne deux ou trois fois par mois).

Le Conseil était responsable de l'administration et de la politique générale de l'Organisation. Il a créé des Comités techniques et d'autres organismes nécessaires à l'exercice de ses fonctions. Les travaux préparatoires des organes divers de l'Organisation ou du Secrétariat lui étaient soumis. Il prenait les décisions engageant les gouvernements des pays Membres dans leur politique économique.

Le Conseil a créé, à titre temporaire et parfois de composition restreinte, des groupes de travail pour l'exécution de questions techniques précises :

- *n° 1 Juridique : règles de procédure*
- *n° 2 Ad hoc pour l'établissement des mécanismes de surveillance et de contrôle*
- *n° 3 Coopération en matière d'information scientifique et technique*
- *n° 4 Ad hoc, réseau des communications téléphoniques du Bassin méditerranéen*
- *n° 5 Expansion économique*
- *n° 6 Stabilité financière intérieure*
- *n° 7 Financement des investissements*
- *n° 8 Organisation des transports intérieurs en Europe occidentale*
- *n° 9 Plan italien de développement économique*
- *n° 10 Coopération dans l'utilisation pacifique de l'énergie nucléaire*

– *No. 11 Enquiry into the Spanish Economic Situation*
– *No. 12 Ministerial Directives relating to the study of Effects of the Disposal of Agricultural Surpluses*
– *No. 13 Public Relations Policy of the OEEC*
– *No. 14 Energy*
– *No. 15 Economic Co-operation with the Yugoslav Government*
– *No. 16 General Review of the Operations of the Organisation*
– *No. 17 The Relationship between the Proposed European Customs Union and Member Countries not taking part therein*
– *No. 18 Association of Spain with the Organisation*
– *No. 19 Current Economic Situation in Member Countries*
– *No. 20 Joint Publicity Campaign in the United States for the Development of American Tourism in Europe*
– *No. 21 Conditions under which a European Free Trade Area could be brought into being*
– *No. 22 Agriculture*
– *No. 23 Countries with Special Economic Difficulties which would not allow them to accept the General Obligations of a European Free Trade Area*
– *No. 24 Participation of the Organisation in the Brussels Universal and International Exhibition in 1958*
– *No. 25 Shortages of Highly Qualified Scientists and Engineers*
– *No. 26 Future of the European Productivity Agency*

Other working parties assured ongoing relations with the Council of Europe, the European Conference of Ministers of Transport (ECMT), the other international organisations concerned with European economic co-operation, and non-governmental organisations.

The **Executive Committee** comprised representatives of seven Member countries appointed each year by the Council, which also appointed the chairman and vice-chairman. The Council could also appoint a ''rapporteur general'' to the Executive Committee who, if he did not represent a country with membership of the committee, could participate in the committee's discussions and decisions. The Executive Committee met at least once a week at the ambassadorial level and could meet at ministerial level if required. It examined all questions to be submitted to the Council for decision concerning the general policy of the Organisation or the progress of its work. It co-ordinated this work in accordance with the instructions and directives of the Council and reported to the latter. It set up the Technical Assistance Group and Working Groups to deal with the following questions:

– *No. 1 Long Term Programme*
– *No. 2 Internal Financial Stability of Member Countries*

– *n° 11 Participation de l'Espagne aux travaux de l'Organisation*
– *n° 12 Directives ministérielles pour les effets de l'écoulement des excédents agricoles*
– *n° 13 Politique d'information de l'OECE*
– *n° 14 Énergie*
– *n° 15 Coopération économique avec le Gouvernement Yougoslave*
– *n° 16 Examen général des activités de l'Organisation*
– *n° 17 Rapports entre l'Union douanière européenne envisagée et les Pays Membres n'y participant pas (Marché Commun)*
– *n° 18 Modalités de l'association de l'Espagne avec l'Organisation*
– *n° 19 Situation économique actuelle des Pays Membres*
– *n° 20 Campagne de publicité collective aux États-Unis pour le développement du tourisme américain en Europe*
– *n° 21 Conditions de l'établissement d'une Zone européenne de libre-échange*
– *n° 22 Agriculture*
– *n° 23 Pays présentant des difficultés économiques qui les empêcheraient d'accepter les obligations d'une Zone européenne de libre-échange*
– *n° 24 Participation de l'Organisation à l'Exposition internationale et universelle de Bruxelles en 1958*
– *n° 25 Pénuries du personnel scientifique et technique hautement qualifié*
– *n° 26 Activités futures de l'Agence Européenne de Productivité*

D'autres groupes de travail ont assuré le suivi des relations avec le Conseil de l'Europe, la Conférence Européenne des Ministres des Transports (CEMT), les autres organisations intéressées à la coopération économique européenne et avec les organisations non gouvernementales.

Le **Comité Exécutif** se composait des représentants de sept pays Membres désignés chaque année par le Conseil; celui-ci désignait un Président et un Vice-Président. Le Conseil pouvait aussi désigner un Rapporteur général du Comité Exécutif qui, s'il ne représentait pas un pays Membre du Comité Exécutif, pouvait participer aux discussions et décisions de ce Comité. Au niveau des Ambassadeurs, le Comité Exécutif se réunissait au moins hebdomadairement et pouvait se réunir au niveau des ministres. Il étudiait toutes les questions relatives à la politique générale de l'Organisation ou à l'avancement des travaux à soumettre pour décision au Conseil. Il coordonnait les travaux conformément aux instructions et directives du Conseil et lui en rendait compte. Il a créé le Groupe d'assistance technique et les groupes de travail pour les questions suivantes :

– *n° 1 Programme à long terme*
– *n° 2 Stabilité financière intérieure des pays Membres*

– *No. 3 Harmonization of Member Countries' Policies. To prepare 2nd Interim Report*
– *No. 4 Study of American Work Statistics and Productivity Procedure*
– *No. 5 Preparation of 3rd Report*
– *No. 6 European Integration (Stikker-Pella-Petsch Plans)*

– *n° 3 Harmonisation des politiques des pays Membres : préparation du 2ᵉ rapport*
– *n° 4 Productivité*
– *n° 5 Préparation du 3ᵉ rapport*
– *n° 6 Intégration (Plans Stikker-Pella-Petsch)*

Annual report of the OEEC

The OEEC published twelve annual reports drawn up by the Economic Committee and approved by the Council. Each report had a title that reflected the major concerns of the Organisation at the time of publication.

The first, entitled *Interim Report on the European Recovery Programme* (1948), comprised three volumes of which Volume 1 identified the economic problems of Western Europe with a view to the development of a joint recovery programme, while Volume 2 described the recovery programmes of each individual Member country.

The next three reports *European Recovery Programme,* (1950); *Economic Progress and Problems of Western Europe,* (1951); *Europe – The Way Ahead : Towards Economic Expansion and Dollar Balance,* (1952) dealt with progress in European recovery, ongoing national and co-operative programmes and methods for ensuring that complete recovery would be achieved. Only the fourth report, like the first, contained individual country chapters.

The fifth report *Progress and Problems of the European Economy,* (1954) presents a very brief review of the Organisation's activities and an equally brief summary of the European situation in general, followed by a set of detailed studies on economic conditions in the Member and Associated countries.

The sixth and seventh reports *From Recovery Towards Economic Strength,* 2 vol., (1955); *Economic Expansion and its Problems,* (1956) went back to the initial formula: progress in European recovery (with a review as from 1948 in the sixth report), statement of new tasks, country chapters.

The eighth report *Europe Today and in 1960,* 2 vol., (1957) has a new pattern. It contains no country chapters, referring the reader instead to the series of brochures entitled *Economic Conditions* (see above § 13 a). After reviewing developments in the European situation since 1953, it assesses the economic prospects for the period 1956-1960. Finally, it presents for the first time an account of the Organisation's activities to date.

Rapports annuels de l'OECE

L'OECE a publié douze rapports annuels préparés par le Comité économique et approuvés par le Conseil. Chacun d'entre eux porte un titre qui définit les préoccupations majeures de l'Organisation à l'époque de sa parution.

Le premier, intitulé *Rapport intérimaire sur le programme de relèvement européen* (1948), tente, dans un premier volume, de préciser les problèmes économiques de l'Europe occidentale en vue de l'élaboration d'un programme commun de relèvement et décrit, dans un second volume, les programmes de relèvement de chacun des pays Membres.

Les trois suivants *Programme de relèvement européen,* (1950); *L'Évolution de la situation économique et ses perspectives en Europe occidentale,* (1951); *Perspectives de l'économie européenne – expérience économique – balance dollar,* (1952) traitent des progrès réalisés dans le relèvement de l'Europe, des programmes nationaux et coopératifs en cours ainsi que des méthodes propres à assurer un redressement complet de la situation. Seul le quatrième comporte, comme le premier, des chapitres par pays.

Le cinquième rapport *Progrès et problèmes de l'économie européenne,* (1954), après un très bref rappel des activités de l'Organisation et un non moins bref résumé de la situation européenne en général, présente une série d'études détaillées sur les conditions économiques dans les pays Membres et Associés.

Avec le sixième et le septième rapport, *De la reconstruction à l'expansion,* 2 vol., (1955) ; *L'expansion économique et ses problèmes,* (1956), on revient à la formule initiale : évolution du relèvement européen (avec, dans le sixième rapport, une rétrospective à partir de 1948), énoncé des tâches nouvelles, chapitres par pays.

Le huitième rapport *L'Europe d'aujourd'hui et en 1960,* 2 vol., (1957) répond au contraire à une conception nouvelle. Il ne contient pas de chapitres par pays, mais se contente de renvoyer à la série de brochures *Situation et problèmes de l'économie.* Il tente, après un rappel de l'évolution de la situation européenne depuis 1953, d'évaluer les perspectives économiques pour la période 1956-1960; enfin, pour la première fois, il donne un compte-rendu des activités de l'Organisation.

The ninth report *A Decade of Co-operation: Achievements and Perspectives,* (1958) differs from all the others. Produced to coincide with the tenth anniversary of the OEEC, it is in a sense a publicity document that outlines the activities of the various branches of the Organisation and attempts to assess their results.

The tenth and eleventh reports *Policies for Sound Economic Growth,* (1959); *Europe and the World Economy,* (1960) are capsule reviews of economic developments in Europe over the previous twelve months; they contain no country chapters.

The twelfth and last report, untitled (1961), is essentially a progress report, drawn up with a view to the transfer of tasks from the OEEC to the OECD. Analysis of the economic situation occupies only a very small place.

Publications:

OEEC (1947), *Report to the Economic Co-operation Administration on the First Annual Programme.*

____. (1948-1959), *Acts of the Organisation,* vol. 1-19. (*Recapitulative Index,* 16 April 1948 – 29 September 1961).

____. (1948-1961), *Annual Report,* No. 1-12.

____. (1949-1950), *Report to the Economic Co-operation Administration on the 1949-1950 Programme,* 2 vol.

____. (1950), *General Memorandum on the 1950-51 and 1951-52 Programmes,* 16 Country Chapters.

____. (1960), *A Remodelled Economic Organisation.*

____. (1960), *Convention on the OECD.*

____. (1960), *Organisation for Economic Co-operation and Development: Convention, Report of the Preparatory Committee.*

OECD (1961), *Acts of the OEEC Remaining in Force After Its Reconstitution, OECD/C(61)41.*

3. Secretariat General

The **Secretariat General** carried out all the duties necessary for the efficient administration of the Organisation, assigned to it by the Council or the Executive Committee. It was headed by a Secretary-General – who attended, in a consultative capacity, the meetings of the Council and the Executive Committee and, as required, those of the technical committees and other bodies – and two deputy secretaries-general appointed by the Council. This team prepared the meetings of the Council and the Executive Committee, submitted proposals to them, saw that their decisions were carried out, maintained relations with the other international organisations, furnished the press with information concerning the Organisation's work and issued press communiqués.

Le neuvième rapport *Dix ans de coopération : Réalisations et perspectives,* (1958) diffère de tous les autres. Établi à l'occasion du Dixième Anniversaire de l'OECE, c'est un document en quelque sorte publicitaire, qui résume les activités des différentes branches de l'Organisation et tente d'évaluer leurs résultats.

Les dixième et onzième rapports *Les éléments d'une expansion saine,* (1959) ; *L'Europe et l'économie mondiale,* (1960) sont des résumés assez sommaires de l'évolution économique de l'Europe au cours de l'exercice précédent ; ils ne comportent pas de chapitres par pays.

Enfin le douxième et dernier rapport, non titré, (1961) est essentiellement un compte-rendu d'activité, établi dans la perspective du transfert des tâches de l'OECE à l'OCDE. L'analyse de la situation économique n'y tient qu'une place minime.

Publications :

OECE (1947), *Rapport à l'Administration de coopération économique sur le premier programme annuel.*

____. (1948-1959), *Actes de l'Organisation,* vol. 1-19. (*Index récapitulatif,* 16 Avril 1948 – 29 Septembre 1961).

____. (1948-1961), *Rapport annuel,* n° 1-12.

____. (1949-1950), *Rapport à l'Administration de coopération économique sur le programme 1949-1950,* 2 vol.

____. (1950), *Mémorandum général sur les programmes 1950-51 et 1951-52,* 16 fascicules.

____. (1960), *Une organisation économique rénovée.*

____. (1960), *Convention relative à l'OCDE.*

____. (1960), *Organisation de coopération et de développement économique, Convention, Rapport du comité préparatoire.*

OCDE (1961), *Actes de l'OECE maintenus en application après sa reconstitution, OECD/C(61)41.*

3. Secrétariat Général

Le **Secrétariat général** assumait les fonctions nécessaires à la bonne marche de l'Organisation, assignées par le Conseil ou par le Comité exécutif. Il était dirigé par un Secrétaire général qui assistait avec voix consultative aux séances du Conseil, du Comité exécutif et, s'il y avait lieu, aux séances des comités techniques et des autres organismes, et par deux secrétaires généraux adjoints nommés par le Conseil. Cette équipe préparait les délibérations du Conseil et du Comité exécutif, leur soumettait des propositions, assurait l'exécution des décisions prises ainsi que la liaison avec les autres organisations internationales, la diffusion des informations relatives aux travaux de l'Organisation destinées à la presse, et l'élaboration des communiqués de presse.

As head of the Secretariat, the Secretary-General was empowered to appoint staff, regulate their conditions of employment and enforce discipline; these administrative duties extended to the Organisation's finances and property. Mr. Robert Marjolin was Secretary-General from 1948 to 1955 and was succeeded by Mr. René Sergent (1955-1961).

The Secretariat, staffed by international civil servants, was divided into directorates which were normally named in a manner appropriate to the committees and working groups they had to serve and to the other tasks they had to perform. The main directorates dealt with the following areas:

– administration and conferences
– trade and payments
– economics and statistics
– technical services
– food and agriculture
– productivity
– scientific and technical personnel
– nuclear energy

Publications:

OEEC (1949), *Report on the Progress of Western European Recovery.*

___. (1949-1961), *History and Structure.* 1st-9th ed.

___. (1951-1956), *European Economic Co-operation : Report prepared for the Council of Europe,* No. 1-7.

___. (1954), *Comments on the Strasbourg Plan.*

___. (1955), *European Payments Union: Convertibility of Currencies 1951-1954,* OEEC Bibliographies No. 1.

___. (1956), *American Aid to Europe 1947-1956: Selected Bibliography.*

___. (1956), *International Trade. Theory of International Trade. International Trade Policy. Trade Liberalisation 1950-1955, OEEC Bibliographies* No. 2.

___. (1957), *Automation: Technology and Fields of Application. Economic and Social Impact. Policy – Achievements 1955-1956, OEEC Bibliographies* No. 3.

___. (1958), *Catalogue of Publications OEEC: 1948-1958.*

OECD (1967), *European Recovery Program, Special Annotated Bibliography* No. 14.

4. Trade and payments

It was in the field of liberalisation of intra-European trade and payments that the Organisation performed most durably and obtained the most tangible results. In the aftermath of the war, Europe, anxious to increase its

Chef du Secrétariat, le Secrétaire Général détenait le pouvoir de nomination, de règlementation des conditions de travail des fonctionnaires et de la discipline; ces fonctions administratives s'étendaient également aux finances et à la gestion des biens de l'Organisation. M. Robert Marjolin a été Secrétaire général de 1948 à 1955 et a été suivi de M. René Sergent (1955-1961).

Le Secrétariat, composé d'agents internationaux, était divisé en directions dont la dénomination variait, en principe, selon l'évolution des comités et groupes de travail qu'elles avaient à servir et en fonction d'autres tâches qu'elles avaient à accomplir. Les principales directions ont traité des questions suivantes :

– affaires générales et conférences
– échanges et paiements
– affaires économiques et statistiques
– services techniques
– alimentation et agriculture
– productivité
– personnel scientifique et technique
– énergie nucléaire

Publications :

OECE (1949), *Rapport sur l'amélioration de la situation économique en Europe occidentale.*

___. (1949-1961), *Historique et structure,* 1re-9e éd.

___. (1951-1956), *La coopération économique européenne: Rapport préparé au Conseil de l'Europe par l'OECE,* n° 1-7.

___. (1954), *Commentaires sur le Plan de Strasbourg.*

___. (1955), *Union Européenne de Paiements : Convertibilité des monnaies 1951-1954, Bibliographies de l'OECE* n° 1.

___. (1956), *Aide américaine à l'Europe 1947-1956 : Bibliographie sélectionnée.*

___. (1956), *Commerce international. Théorie de l'échange international. Politique commerciale internationale. Libération des échanges 1950-1955, Bibliographie de l'OECE* n° 2.

___. (1957), *Automation: Technique et domaine d'application. Effets sociaux et économiques. Politique – réalisations 1955-1956, Bibliographie de l'OECE* n° 3.

___. (1958), *Catalogue des publications OECE : 1948-1958.*

OCDE (1967), *Programme de relèvement européen, Bibliographie spécialisée analytique* n° 14.

4. Échanges et paiements

C'est en matière de libéralisation des échanges et des paiements intra-européens que le rôle de l'Organisation a été le plus durable et qu'elle a obtenu les résultats les plus tangibles. Au lendemain de la guerre, l'Europe,

exports, needed to remove trade restrictions. The OEEC's action therefore focused on the removal of quantitative import restrictions and impediments to the free movement of goods, capital, services and labour (see also Section 6.6).

4.1 Trade

As regards the liberalisation of intra-European trade, the OEEC concerned itself with drawing up, improving and applying the Code of Liberalisation designed to bring about the dismantlement of quantitative restrictions on trade in goods and services and of such other impediments as state trading, export aids, import restrictions, and administrative and technical obstacles to trade. Between 1957 and 1960, the OEEC devoted a part of its work to the negotiation of a Free Trade Area and relations between the European Economic Community and the other Member countries of the OEEC (**Intergovernmental Committee on the establishment of a European Free Trade Area**).

As regards trade relations between Europe and the rest of the world, the OEEC addressed such matters as liberalisation of trade with the dollar area and non-member countries, problems of trade with state-trading countries, relations with low-wage countries, and the reduction of customs tariffs being taken over by the GATT.

The **Joint Trade and Intra-European Payments Committee,** set up in 1948, comprised representatives of Member country governments. It examined and transmitted to the Council, together with any comments from Member countries, the reports drawn up by the three independent bodies, namely the Steering Board for Trade, the Managing Board of the European Monetary Agreement and the Committee for Invisible Transactions. It reviewed periodically the trade liberalisation measures taken by Member countries *vis-à-vis* the United States and Canada, and studied the multilateralisation of trade and payments with non-member countries.

It set up the following Working Parties:

- *No. 1 Liberalisation of Invisible Transactions*
- *No. 2 Simplification of Financial Studies*
- *No. 3 Examination of the 2nd Report of the Economic Committee*
- *No. 4 Special Facilities for Re-exports*
- *No. 5 Exceeding of Quotas*
- *No. 6 Dollar Imports*
- *No. 7 Bilateral Trade*
- *Joint with Maritime Transport Committee*
- *Joint with Inland Transport Committee*
- *Supervisory Sub-Committee*
- *Insurance Sub-Committee (see below)*

désireuse d'augmenter ses exportations, devait se débarasser des restrictions aux échanges. L'action de l'OECE a donc porté sur la suppression des restrictions quantitatives aux importations et sur l'abolition des entraves à la libre circulation des biens, des capitaux, des services et de la main d'œuvre (voir également section 6.6).

4.1 Échanges

En matière de libéralisation des échanges intra-européens, l'OECE s'est occupée de l'élaboration, du perfectionnement et de l'application du Code de la libération. Ce Code visait à l'élimination des restrictions quantitatives aux échanges de biens et de services, et à la suppression des autres entraves au commerce: commerce d'état, aides à l'exportation, restrictions aux importations, obstacles administratifs et techniques aux échanges. Entre 1957 et 1960, l'OECE a consacré une partie de ses travaux à la négociation d'une Zone de libre échange et aux relations entre la Communauté économique européenne et les autres pays Membres de l'OECE (**Comité intergouvernemental sur l'établissement d'une Zone européenne de libre échange**).

Quant aux relations commerciales entre l'Europe et le monde extérieur, l'OECE a abordé les questions de libéralisation des échanges vis-à-vis de la zone dollar et des pays tiers, les problèmes de commerce avec les pays à Commerce d'état, les relations avec les pays à bas salaires et l'abaissement des droits de douane relevant de la responsabilité du GATT.

Le **Comité mixte des échanges et des paiements,** créé en 1948, se composait de représentants gouvernementaux des pays Membres. Il a examiné et transmis au Conseil, avec les commentaires éventuels des pays Membres, les rapports établis par les trois organes indépendants : Comité de direction des échanges, Comité directeur de l'Accord monétaire européen et Comité des transactions invisibles. Il a été chargé d'encourager la libéralisation des échanges à l'égard de la zone dollar (États-Unis et Canada) et d'examiner périodiquement les mesures prises par les pays Membres. Il a également étudié la multilatéralisation des échanges et des paiements avec des pays non-membres.

Ce même Comité a créé les groupes de travail consacrés aux problèmes suivants :

- *n° 1 libéralisation des transactions invisibles*
- *n° 2 simplification des études financières*
- *n° 3 examen du 2ᵉ rapport du Comité économique*
- *n° 4 facilités spéciales aux réexportations*
- *n° 5 dépassement des quotas*
- *n° 6 importations dollar*
- *n° 7 échanges libéraux*
- *Mixte avec le Comité des transports maritimes*
- *Mixte avec le Comité des transports intérieurs*
- *Sous-comité de surveillance*
- *Sous-comité des assurances (voir ci-dessous)*

The **Trade Committee** was set up on 15 July 1948 and comprised representatives of all the Member countries. It examined Member countries' notifications of measures taken in observance of the Code of Liberalisation. It succeeded the Intra-European Trade Committee which had come into being when the Intra-European Trade and Payments Committee was split.

It set up the following Working Parties:

- *No. 1 Principles of Trade Policy*
- *No. 2 Liberalisation of Trade*
- *No. 3 Tariffs*
- *No. 4 Exports to non-participating countries*
- *Joint with the Food and Agriculture Committee on Tobacco*

The **Steering Board for Trade,** set up by decision of the Council on 18 April 1952 and responsible for trade policy matters, comprised seven experts chosen on a personal basis by the Council. Its terms of reference were fixed by Article 36 of the Code of Liberalisation. It set up Joint Working Party No. 1 with the Steering Committee for Nuclear Energy.

Publications:

OEEC (1950), *Liberalisation of Invisible Transactions between Member Countries.*

___. (1950), *Nomenclature of Products.*

___. (1951-1956), *Code de la Libération/Code of Liberalisation,* 1-4 ed.

___. (1960), *Code of Liberation,* new ed.

___. (1954), *Foreign Trade Zones in the USA, Technical Assistance Mission* No. 28.

___. (1955), *Liberalisation of Europe's Dollar Trade,* 1st report.

___. (1957), *Liberalisation of Europe's Dollar trade,* 2nd report.

___. (1957), *Report on the Possibility of Creating a Free Trade Area in Europe.*

OUIN, Marc (1958), *OEEC and the Common Market: Why Europe Needs an Economic Union of Seventeen Countries.*

OEEC (1958), *Terms Used in International Trade and Payments and National Accounts: Glossary and Definitions.*

___. (1959), *European Free Trade Association Convention.*

4.2 Payments

From 1948 onwards, the OEEC tried to render the system of bilateral payments agreements between Member countries more flexible and to ease the quantitative

Créé le 15 juillet 1948, le **Comité des échanges** se composait de représentants de tous les pays Membres. Il a examiné les notifications adressées à l'Organisation par les pays Membres sur les mesures prises en exécution du Code de la Libéralisation. Il a succédé au Comité des échanges intra-européens lui-même résultant d'une scission du Comité des échanges et des paiements intra-européens. Il était assisté d'un Comité des suppléants.

Il a constitué les Groupes de travail destinés à étudier les problèmes suivants:

- *n° 1 principes de politique commerciale*
- *n° 2 libéralisation des échanges*
- *n° 3 tarifs douaniers*
- *n° 4 exportations vers les pays non-participants*
- *Mixte sur le tabac avec le Comité de l'alimentation et de l'agriculture*

Le **Comité de direction des échanges,** institué par Décision du Conseil du 18 avril 1952, et compétent en matière de politique commerciale, se composait de sept experts choisis à titre personnel par le Conseil. Son mandat était fixé par l'article 36 du Code de la Libération. Il a créé le Groupe de travail mixte n° 1 avec le Comité spécial de l'énergie nucléaire.

Publications :

OECE (1950), *Libération des transactions invisibles entre les pays Membres.*

___. (1950), *Nomenclature des produits.*

___. (1951-1956), *Code de la Libération/Code of Liberalisation,* 1-4 éd.

___. (1960), *Code de la libération,* nouvelle éd.

___. (1954), *Zones franches aux USA, Mission d'assistance technique* n° 28.

___. (1955), *Libération des échanges de l'Europe avec la zone Dollar,* 1er rapport.

___. (1957), *Libération des échanges de l'Europe avec la zone Dollar,* 2e rapport.

___. (1957), *Rapport sur la possibilité d'instituer une Zone de libre-échange en Europe.*

OUIN, Marc (1958), *OECE et le marché commun, Les raisons d'être d'une union économique des 17.*

OECE (1958), *Terminologie des échanges et paiements internationaux et de la comptabilité nationale : Glossaire et Définitions.*

___. (1959), *Association européenne de libre échange, Convention.*

4.2 Paiements

A partir de 1948, l'OECE s'est efforcée d'assouplir le réseau d'accords bilatéraux de paiements entre pays Membres et d'atténuer les restrictions quantitatives sur

restrictions on imports which were the corollary of that system. In October 1948, the Member countries signed the first Agreement governing payments and compensations between European countries, and, in September 1949, a second agreement which was replaced in 1950 by the Agreement establishing a European Payments Union, and ultimately to be succeeded by the European Monetary Agreement in 1958.

Various committees were set up. The **Intra-European Payments Committee,** came into being on 4 June 1948 when the Intra-European Trade and Payments Committee was divided. It worked to develop – through multilateralisation of payments (*i.e.* the easing of restrictions on transferability of payments in international settlements) – trade in goods and services and capital investment between Member countries and their currency areas. It examined Member countries' notifications of measures taken to liberalise invisible transactions. To assist it, it set up a *Working Party on Payments Agreements (1948-1949) and the following Working Parties:*

- *No. 1 Determination of Quotas*
- *No. 2 Units of Account*
- *No. 3 Consolidation of Existing Resources*
- *No. 6 Drafting of Payments Agreements (EPU)*
- *No. 7 Drafting of EPU Directives*

The **Managing Board of the European Payments Union,** set up on 12 September 1950 under the Agreement on the Establishment of a European Payments Union, was instructed to supervise the operations of the Union, which were communicated for accounting purposes to the Bank for International Settlements acting as Agent for the Organisation.

The **Managing Board of the European Monetary Agreement,** a restricted body of seven members appointed each year by the Council in the capacity of independent experts, was set up under Article 19 of the European Monetary Agrement (EMA), concluded on 5 August 1955, and entered into operation on 27 September 1958. Its meetings were also attended by one representative from the US government, the Managing Director of the IMF and the Bank for International Settlements acting as Agent of the OEEC, and by the Chairman of the Intra-European Payments Committee.

The Board supervised the implementation of the EMA and acted as technical adviser to the Council in the matter of Member countries' balances of payments and international financial problems connected with the operation of the EMA. Twice yearly it reviewed each country's economic and financial situation. Between sessions the Board's tasks were performed by acting members.

les importations, corollaires de ce système. En octobre 1948, les pays Membres ont signé un premier accord, puis en 1949, un second Accord de paiements et de compensations entre pays Européens, remplacé en 1950 par l'Accord sur l'établissement d'une Union Européenne de Paiements, auquel a succédé en 1958 l'Accord Monétaire Européen.

Divers comités ont été institués. Le **Comité des Paiements Intra-européens,** créé le 4 juin 1948, résultait de la division du Comité des Échanges et des Paiements Intra-européens. Il a étudié les problèmes relatifs au développement par la multilatéralisation des paiements (c'est-à-dire l'atténuation des restrictions sur la libre transférabilité des paiements dans les règlements internationaux) et par tout autre moyen, des échanges de biens et de services et des investissements de capitaux entre les pays Membres et leurs zones monétaires. Il a examiné les mesures de libéralisation des transactions invisibles, notifiées par les pays Membres à l'OECE. Pour l'assister, il a créé un *Groupe de travail sur les Accords de paiements* (1948-1949), ainsi que les groupes de travail suivants:

- *n° 1 détermination des quotas*
- *n° 2 unités de compte*
- *n° 3 consolidation des ressources existantes*
- *n° 6 rédaction des accords de paiements (UEP)*
- *n° 7 rédaction des directives de l'UEP*

Le **Comité de Direction de l'Union Européenne des Paiements,** créé le 12 septembre 1950 dans le cadre de l'Accord sur l'établissement d'une Union Européenne des Paiements, a été chargé de surveiller l'exécution des opérations de l'Union compatibilisées par un Agent (la Banque des Règlements Internationaux).

Le **Comité directeur de l'Accord monétaire européen,** organe restreint de sept membres désignés chaque année par le Conseil en qualité d'experts indépendants, a été créé en vertu de l'article 19 de l'Accord Monétaire Européen (AME) conclu le 5 août 1955 et entré en vigueur le 27 septembre 1958. Assistaient également à ses réunions un représentant du gouvernement américain, du Directeur général du FMI, de la Banque des règlements internationaux en qualité d'agent de l'OECE, et le Président du Comité des paiements intra-européens.

Ce comité a veillé à l'exécution de l'AME et a joué un rôle de conseiller technique, avisant le Conseil sur la balance des paiements des pays Membres et les problèmes financiers internationaux liés au fonctionnement de l'AME. Il a examiné bi-annuellement la situation économique et financière de chaque pays. Des Suppléants remplissaient les tâches du Comité entre les sessions.

The **Committee for Invisible Transactions,** a body with restricted membership set up in June 1955 under Article 39 of the Code of Liberalisation, comprised seven independent experts. The Chairman of the Intra-European Payments Committee, a representative of the US government and a representative of the Managing Director of the IMF, attended the meetings as observers. Acting members met every month to prepare the meetings of the Committee, which advised the Council on the liberalisation of current invisible transactions and transfers (*e.g.*application by Member countries of Part II of the Code of Liberalisation) and capital movements (*e.g.* drafting of a Code of Liberalisation of Capital Movements, and of the Draft Convention on Protection of Investments and Private Ownership Rights of Residents or Nationals of other Member Countries).

The Committee set up two Working Parties to study:

– *Liberalisation of Invisible Transactions and Capital Movements within a European Free Trade Area*
– *Joint with the ECMT: Liberalisation of Road Transport*

The **Insurance Sub-Committee of the Joint Trade and Intra-European Payments Committee,** set up by the Council on 18 November 1955, was a plenary body in which each Member country was represented. Its work, sometimes done in collaboration with other committees, focused on the liberalisation of insurance transactions and transfers, conditions of establishment and operations of foreign insurers in Member countries, nuclear risk insurance and motor vehicle insurance. It set up the following Working Parties:

– *ad hoc: Minimum Solvency Standard*
– *ad hoc: Reinsurance*
– *Nuclear Risks*
– *Insurance Supervision*

Publications:

OEEC (1950), *Directives for the Application of the Agreement for the Establishment of a European Payments Union.*

___. (1951-1959), *European Payments Union: Annual Reports.*

___. (1951), *OEEC Bankers' Mission to the USA, Technical Assistance Mission* No. 31.

___. (1958), *Agreement for the Establishment of an EPU.*

___. (1960), *Code of Liberalisation of Capital Movements.*

___. (1960), *European Monetary Agreement: 5th August 1955.*

OEEC/OECD (1960-1972), *European Monetary Agreement: Annual Report.*

Le **Comité des transactions invisibles,** organe restreint créé en juin 1955 en vertu de l'article 39 du Code de la Libération, était composé de sept experts indépendants. Le président du Comité des paiements intra-européens, un représentant du gouvernement des États-Unis et du Directeur général du FMI assistaient aux réunions à titre d'observateur. Des Suppléants siégaient tous les mois pour préparer les réunions du Comité qui avisait le Conseil sur la libéralisation des transactions invisibles courantes et des transferts (*ex* : application par les pays Membres du Titre II du Code de la libération) et des mouvements de capitaux (*ex* : élaboration d'un Code de la libération des mouvements de capitaux et de projets de convention sur la protection assurée aux investissements et aux droits de propriété privée des résidents ou ressortissants des autres pays Membres).

Le comité a créé deux Groupes de travail pour étudier :

– *la libération des transactions invisibles et des mouvements de capitaux dans le cadre d'une Zone européenne de libre-échange*
– *mixte avec la CEMT, la libéralisation des transports routiers*

Le **Sous-comité des assurances du Comité mixte des échanges et des paiements,** créé par le Conseil le 18 novembre 1955, était un organe plénier dans lequel chaque pays Membre était représenté. Ses travaux, parfois réalisés en collaboration avec d'autres Comités, ont porté sur la libéralisation des transactions et des transferts en matière d'assurances et les conditions d'établissement et d'opérations des assureurs étrangers des pays Membres, d'assurance des risques nucléaires et d'assurances automobiles. Il a constitué les Groupes de travail suivants :

– *ad hoc, standard minimum de solvabilité*
– *ad hoc, réassurance*
– *risques nucléaires*
– *contrôles des assurances*

Publications :

OECD (1950), *Directives pour l'exécution de l'accord sur l'établissement d'une Union européenne de paiements.*

___. (1951-1959), *Union européenne de paiements : Rapports Annuels.*

___. (1951), *Mission bancaire de l'OECE aux USA, Mission d'assistance technique* n° 31.

___. (1958), *Accord sur l'établissement d'une UEP.*

___. (1960), *Code de libération des mouvements de capitaux.*

___. (1960), *Accord monétaire européen : 5 août 1955.*

OECE/OCDE (1960-1972), *Accord monétaire européen : rapport annuel.*

OEEC (1961), *Liberalization of Current Invisibles and Capital Movements.*

4.3 Fiscal Affairs

The **Fiscal Committee,** a plenary body, was set up by the Council on 16 March 1956 to study double taxation and other technical tax-related questions. It drew up common rules for Member countries to apply in their bilateral double taxation agreements regarding income and capital.

These rules were drafted in the following Working Parties:

- *No. 1 Permanent Establishment*
- *No. 2 Fiscal Domicile*
- *No. 3 Enumeration and Definition of Income and Capital Taxes, including Taxes on Inheritances and Estates, which should be covered by Double Taxation Conventions*
- *No. 4 Tax Discrimination for reasons of Nationality or other similar reasons*
- *No. 5 Taxation of Income and Capital of Shipping, Inland Waterways Transport and Air Transport Enterprises and their Crews*
- *No. 6 Taxation of Inland Waterway Transport Enterprises and of Enterprises not solely engaged in Maritime or Air Transport activities*
- *No. 7 Definition of Profits and their Distribution among the Head Office of an Enterprise, its Permanent Establishments and its Subsidiaries*
- *No. 8 Direct Taxation of Royalties*
- *No. 9 Taxation of Income from Immovable Property*
- *No. 10 Taxation of Profits and Remunerations of Dependent and Independent Professional Activities*
- *No. 11 Taxation of Interest*
- *No. 12 Taxation of Dividends*
- *No. 13 Taxation of Capital*
- *No. 14 Definitions, Mutual Agreement and General Provisions*
- *No. 15 Avoidance of Double Taxation*
- *No. 16 Tax Regulations for Nuclear Risk Insurance*
- *No. 17 Taxes on Inheritances and Estates*

Publications:

OEEC (1958-1961), *Elimination of Double Taxation.*

5. Economics and Statistics

As an organisation concerned with economic development, the OEEC, from the outset, set about collecting the statistical data available in the various countries which were essential to its work. It had to draw up

OECE (1961), *Libération des transactions invisibles courantes et des mouvements de capitaux.*

4.3 Fiscalité

Le **Comité fiscal,** comité plénier, a été créé par le Conseil le 16 mars 1956 pour étudier la double imposition et les questions fiscales techniques similaires. Il a établi des règles communes destinées à servir de modèle aux dispositions de conventions bilatérales de double imposition sur le revenu et la fortune conclues entre pays Membres.

L'élaboration de ces règles a été préparée dans les groupes de travail suivants :

- *n° 1 établissement stable*
- *n° 2 domicile fiscal*
- *n° 3 énumération et définition des impôts sur le revenu et la fortune y compris sur les successions qui devraient être couverts par les conventions de double imposition*
- *n° 4 discrimination de taxation pour motifs de nationalité ou autres motifs similaires*
- *n° 5 imposition sur le revenu et la fortune des entreprises de navigation maritime, fluviale et aérienne et des équipages*
- *n° 6 imposition des entreprises de navigation fluviale et des entreprises n'exerçant pas exclusivement une activité maritime ou aérienne*
- *n° 7 définition et répartition des bénéfices entre le siège principal d'une entreprise, ses établissements permanents et ses filiales*
- *n° 8 imposition directe des redevances*
- *n° 9 imposition du revenu des biens immobiliers*
- *n° 10 imposition des bénéfices ou des rémunérations des professions dépendantes et indépendantes*
- *n° 11 imposition des intérêts*
- *n° 12 imposition des dividendes*
- *n° 13 imposition du capital*
- *n° 14 définitions, procédure amiable et clauses générales*
- *n° 15 comment éviter la double imposition*
- *n° 16 réglementations fiscales de l'assurance des risques nucléaires*
- *n° 17 impôts sur les successions*

Publications :

OECE (1958-1961), *Élimination des doubles impositions.*

5. Affaires économiques et statistiques

En tant qu'organisme à vocation économique, l'OECE a dû dès sa création rassembler les données statistiques disponibles dans les divers pays et indispensables à ses travaux. Il lui a fallu élaborer certaines séries, favoriser

certain statistical series, develop ways of improving the quantity and quality of national statistics, and above all devise concepts and methods of classification that would improve data comparability across countries. These statistical data served to chart economic progress in Western Europe and each of its constituent countries and, in some cases, the United States and Canada.

l'amélioration (en quantité comme en qualité) des statistiques nationales, et surtout élaborer les concepts et modes de classification propres à améliorer la comparabilité des données entre pays. Ces données statistiques ont ainsi permis de suivre l'évolution économique de l'Europe occidentale et de chacun des pays qui la composent, et, dans certains cas, des États-Unis et du Canada.

5.1 Economics, country studies, statistics and national accounts

The **Economic Committee,** established by Resolution of the Council on 9 June 1950, succeeded the Programmes Committee (see Section 6). It prepared the annual report and the special reports of the OEEC and examined the annual reports of the Technical Committees. It conducted periodic reviews of the economic and financial situation in Member countries. It compared the economic, financial, social, tariff and investment policies of those countries, with a view to achieving the degree of harmony necessary for the development of closer economic and monetary understandings between them.

It set up the following Working Parties:

- *No. 1 Preparation of the Questionnaire for the Annual Report*
- *No. 2 Preparation of the Annual Report*
- *No. 3 Preparation of an Expert Report on Financial Stability*
- *No. 4 Request for a Special Credit presented by Turkey*
- *No. 5 Programme of French Imports of Staple Products*
- *No. 6 American Private Investment Abroad*
- *No. 7 Stabilisation of Markets for Raw Materials and Primary Commodities*
- *No. 8 Disequilibrium in the EPU Leading to the Extreme Creditor Position of Germany*
- *No. 9 Renewal of the EPU*
- *No. 10 Structure of Trade*
- *No. 11 Relaxation of Restrictions on Dollar Imports*
- *No. 12 Vertical Committees' Reports on the Economic Situation*
- *No. 13 Economic Situation in Member Countries*
- *No. 14 Examination of the Annual Report*
- *Joint with the Trade Committee and with the Food and Agriculture Committee*

The **Group of Economic Experts,** composed of independent government experts, met from September 1953 about four times a year to exchange confidential views on the economic policy stance of Member and Associated countries.

5.1 Affaires économiques, études nationales, statistiques et comptes nationaux

Le **Comité économique,** créé par Résolution du Conseil le 9 juin 1950, a succédé au Comité des programmes (voir section 6). Il préparait le rapport annuel et les rapports spéciaux de l'OECE et examinait les rapports annuels des Comités techniques. Il effectuait des examens périodiques de la situation économique et financière des pays Membres. Les politiques financière, économique, sociale, tarifaire et d'investissement faisaient l'objet d'examen, par la confrontation, afin de leur apporter le degré d'harmonie nécessaire à la réalisation d'ententes économiques et monétaires plus étroites entre pays Membres.

Il a créé les Groupes de travail pour étudier les questions suivantes :

- *n° 1 préparation du questionnaire pour le rapport annuel*
- *n° 2 préparation du rapport annuel*
- *n° 3 préparation d'un rapport d'experts en matière de stabilité financière*
- *n° 4 demande d'un crédit spécial présentée par la Turquie*
- *n° 5 programme d'importations de la France des incompressibles*
- *n° 6 investissements privés américains à l'étranger*
- *n° 7 stabilisation des marchés de matières premières et produits de base*
- *n° 8 déséquilibre au sein de l'UEP conduisant à la position de créditeur extrême de l'Allemagne*
- *n° 9 reconduction de l'UEP*
- *n° 10 structure des échanges*
- *n° 11 assouplissement des restrictions aux importations dollar*
- *n° 12 rapports de conjoncture des comités verticaux*
- *n° 13 situation économique des Pays membres*
- *n° 14 préparation du rapport annuel*
- *Mixte avec le Comité des échanges, le Comité de l'alimentation et de l'agriculture*

Le **Groupe d'experts économiques,** composé d'experts gouvernementaux indépendants, s'est réuni depuis septembre 1953 environ quatre fois par an pour échanger des vues confidentielles sur l'orientation des politiques économiques des pays Membres et associés.

The **Economic Policy Committee,** set up by a Resolution of the Council of 29 April 1959, replaced a Council working party instructed to co-ordinate general economic policies. Composed of high-ranking government officials, it kept the economic and financial situation of Member countries under review for the purpose of co-ordinating the policies needed to maintain a high level of employment, economic expansion, financial stability and the general conditions required for the pursuit of liberal policies in the field of international trade.

It set up the following Working Parties:

- *No. 1 Preparation of the Code of Good Conduct*
- *No. 2 Measures to encourage Economic Growth*
- *No. 3 Measures to ensure better Equilibrium of International Payments*

Publications:

OEEC (1949), *Internal Financial Stability in Member Countries.*

___. (1950), *Internal Financial Stability in member countries.*

___. (1950), *A Simplified System of National Accounts.*

___. (1950), *Report on International Investment.*

___. (1950-1951), *General Statistical Bulletin.*

___. (1952), *A Standardised System of National Account.*

___. (1959), *A Standardised System of National Account,* rev. ed.

OECE/OEEC (1950-1958), *Commerce extérieur par zones géographiques/Foreign trade by areas.*

OEEC (1951), *Financial Stability and the Fight Against Inflation.*

___. (1951), *Industrial Censuses in Western Europe.*

___. (1951), *Intra-european Investments.*

___. (1951-1953), *National Accounts Studies,* (7 Nos, 6 countries.)

OECE/OEEC (1957), *Commerce extérieur par produits et par origines et destinations : 1951-1956/Foreign Trade by Commodity and by Origin and Destination: 1951-1956,* 2 vols.

OEEC (1952), *Definitions and Methods, Statistical bulletins.*

___. (1953-1955), *Definitions and Methods, Statistical bulletins,* 2nd. ed., 4 vol.

___. (1958-1960), *Definition and Methodes, Statistical bulletins,* 3rd ed., 2 vol.

___. (1952), *Internal Financial Situation in Member and Associated Countries.*

___. (1952-1961), *General Statistics of OEEC.*

Le **Comité de politique économique,** institué par une Résolution du Conseil du 29 avril 1959, remplaçait un Groupe de travail du Conseil chargé de coordonner les politiques économiques générales. Composé de fonctionnaires de rang élevé, il observait la situation économique et financière des pays Membres afin d'assurer la coordination des politiques nécessaires au maintien d'un niveau élevé de l'emploi, de l'expansion économique, de la stabilité financière et des conditions générales qui leur permettaient de pratiquer une politique libérale dans le domaine des échanges internationaux.

Il a créé les Groupes de travail suivants :

- *n° 1 préparation du Code de bonne conduite*
- *n° 2 mesures favorisant la croissance économique*
- *n° 3 mesures assurant un meilleur équilibre des paiements internationaux*

Publications :

OECD (1949), *Rapport sur la stabilité financière intérieure.*

___. (1950), *Rapport sur la stabilité financière intérieure.*

___. (1950), *Système simplifié de comptabilité nationale.*

___. (1950), *Rapport sur les investissements internationaux.*

___. (1950-1951), *Bulletin général de statistique.*

___. (1952), *Système normalisé de comptabilité nationale.*

___. (1959), *Système normalisé de comptabilité nationale,* éd. rév.

OECE/OEEC (1950-1958), *Commerce extérieur par zones géographiques/Foreign trade by areas.*

OECE (1951), *La stabilité financière et la lutte contre l'inflation.*

___. (1951), *Les recensements industriels en Europe occidentale.*

___. (1951), *Les investissements intra-européens.*

___. (1951-1953), *Études sur la comptabilité nationale,* (3 n°, 3 pays.)

OECE/OEEC (1957), *Commerce extérieur par produits et par origines et destinations : 1951-1956/Foreign Trade by Commodity and by Origin and Destination: 1951-1956,* 2 vols.

OECE (1952), *Définitions et méthodes, Bulletins statistiques.*

___. (1953-1955), *Définitions et méthodes, Bulletins statistiques,* 2e éd., 4 vol.

___. (1957-1959), *Définitions et méthodes, Bulletins statistiques,* 3e éd., 2 vol.

___. (1952), *La situation financière intérieure dans les pays membres et associés.*

___. (1952-1961), *Statistiques générales de l'OECE.*

___. (1952-1958), *Foreign trade of selected commodities.*

OECE/OEEC (1953), *Statistiques de base de la production industrielle : 1913-1952/Basic Statistics of Industrial Production: 1913-1952.*

OEEC (1953-1957), *Economic Conditions.*

OEEC/OECD (1958), *Economic Surveys.*

OECE/OEEC (1954), *Statistiques de base de l'alimentation et de l'agriculture/Basic Statistics of Food and Agriculture, Bulletins statistiques/Statistical bulletins.*

OEEC (1954), *Industrial Censuses in the USA.*

European Productivity Agency (1954), *Labour Force Statistics: Sample Survey Method,* OEEC, Paris.

OEEC (1954), *Private United States Investment in Europe and the Overseas Territories.*

OEEC. Economic Committee (1954), *Report on the Pattern of Western European Trade Between 1948 and 1953, Paris.*

OEEC. Council. Working Party No. 5 (1954), *Report on Selective Expansion,* Paris.

GILBERT, M., and KRAVIS, I.B. (1954), *International Comparison of National Products and the Purchasing Power of Currencies: A Study of the United States, the United Kingdom, France, Germany and Italy.*

OEEC (1954), *Outline of development of income and employment in Italy in the ten-year period 1955-64.*

___. (1954), *The Measurement of Agricultural Production and Food Consumption.*

Institut Suisse de Recherche pour les Arts et Métiers et OECE (1956), *Rapport sur les bases statistiques des petites et moyennes entreprises dans le commerce et les problèmes des enquêtes d'économies de l'entreprise.* (available only in French)

OEEC (1957), *Foreign Trade Statistics, 1951-1956: The ''SIX'': Belgium, Luxembourg, the Netherlands, Germany (Fed.Rep.), France, Italy,* 2 vol.

___. (1957), *The Network of Intra European Trade: trade by Product in 1956.*

European Productivity Agency (1957), *The Supply of Capital Funds for Industrial Development in Europe: resources, structure, methods, Technical Assistance Mission* No. 292, suppl. No. 2 and No. 3, OEEC, Paris.

Agence Européenne de Productivité (1957), *Le financement du développement industriel en Europe : ressources, structure, méthodes,* Mission d'assistance technique n° 292, suppl. n° 1, OECE, Paris. (available only in French)

___. (1952-1958), *Commerce extérieur de certains produits.*

OECE/OEEC (1953), *Statistiques de base de la production industrielle : 1913-1952/Basic Statistics of Industrial Production: 1913-1952.*

OECE (1953-1957), *Situation et problèmes économiques.*

OECE/OCDE (1958), *Études économiques.*

OECE/OEEC (1954), *Statistiques de base de l'alimentation et de l'agriculture/Basic Statistics of Food and Agriculture, Bulletins statistiques/Statistical bulletins.*

OECE (1954), *Les recensements industriels aux États-Unis.*

Agence Européenne de Productivité (1954), *Statistiques de main-d'œuvre : Méthodes d'enquête par sondage,* OECE, Paris.

OECE (1954), *Investissements privés américains en Europe et dans les territoires d'outre-mer.*

OECE. Comité économique (1954), *Rapport sur la structure des échanges de l'Europe occidentale entre 1948 et 1953,* Paris.

OECE. Conseil. Groupe de travail n° 5 (1954), *Rapport sur l'expansion sélective,* Paris.

GILBERT, M., and KRAVIS, I.B. (1954). *Étude comparative des produits nationaux et du pouvoir d'achat des monnaies, États-Unis, Royaume-Uni, France, Allemagne, Italie.*

OECE (1954), *Études sur le développement du revenu national et de l'emploi en Italie au cours de la période 1955-64.*

___. (1954), *Mesure de la production agricole et de la consommation alimentaire.*

Institut Suisse de Recherche pour les Arts et Métiers et OECE (1956), *Rapport sur les bases statistiques des petites et moyennes entreprises dans le commerce et les problèmes des enquêtes d'économies de l'entreprise.*

OECE (1957), *Statistiques du commerce extérieur, 1951-1956 : Les « SIX » : Belgique, Luxembourg, Pays-Bas, Allemagne (Rép. Féd.), France, Italie,* 2 vol.

___. (1957), *Structure du commerce intra-européen : les échanges de produits en 1956.*

European productivity Agency (1957), *The Supply of Capital Funds for Industrial Development in Europe: resources, structure, methods, Technical Assistance Mission* No. 292, suppl. No. 2 and No. 3, OEEC, Paris. (disponible seulement en anglais)

Agence Européenne de Productivité et OECE (1957), *Le financement du développement industriel en Europe : ressources, structure, méthodes,* Mission d'assistance technique n° 292, suppl. n° 1, OECE, Paris.

OEEC (1957), *Statistical Summary of Agricultural Production and Food Consumption in OEEC Countries.*

___. (1958), *Comparative national Products and Price Levels, Study of Western Europe and the United States.*

___. (1958), *Structure of European Economy in 1953, Tentative Input-Output Table for the OEEC Member Countries.*

OEEC/OECD (1958), *Economic Surveys.*

PAIG, D. and BOMBACH, G. (1958), *Comparison of National Output and Productivity of the United Kingdom and the United States.*

OEEC(1958), *Statistics of Sources and Uses of Finance, 1948-1958.*

___. (1959), *Work of the Conference on Financial Assistance to Turkey and on Turkish Debts.*

OEEC/OECD (1960), *Main Economic Indicators.*

OEEC (1960), *Industrial statistics: 1900-1959/Statistiques industrielles : 1900-1959, Statistical bulletins/Bulletins statistiques.*

___. (1961), *Flow of Financial Resources to Countries in Course of Economic Development: 1956-1959.*

OECD (1962), *Flow of Financial Resources to Countries in Course of Economic Development: 1960.*

___. (1963), *Flow of Financial Resources to Countries in Course of Economic Development: 1961.*

BAADE, Fritz (1961), *Exports and Invisible Receipts in Turkey.*

STONE, Richard (1961), *Input-Output and National Accounts,* re-ed.

OECD (1969), *Standardized System of National Accounts: 1958.*

OECE (1957), *Résumé statistique de la production agricole et de la consommation alimentaire dans les pays de l'OECE.*

___. (1958), *Comparative national Products and Price Levels, Study of Western Europe and the United States.* (disponible seulement en anglais)

___. (1958), *Structure de l'économie européenne en 1953, Essai d'établissement d'un tableau des relations inter-industrielles des pays membres de l'OECE.*

OECE/OCDE (1958), *Études économiques.*

PAIG, D. and BOMBACH, G. (1958), *Comparison of National Output and Productivity of the United Kingdom and the United States.* (disponible seulement en anglais)

OEEC(1958), *Statistics of Sources and Uses of Finance, 1948-1958.* (disponible seulement en anglais)

___. (1959), *Travaux de la conférence sur l'aide financière à la Turquie et sur les dettes turques.*

OECE/OCDE (1960), *Principaux indicateurs économiques.*

OECE (1955), *Statistiques industrielles : 1900-1955/Industrial Statistics: 1900-1955, Bulletins statistiques/Statistical bulletins.*

___. (1961), *Moyens financiers mis à la disposition des pays en voie de développement: 1956-1959.*

OCDE (1962), *Moyens financiers mis à la disposition des pays en voie de développement : 1960.*

___. (1963), *Moyens financiers mis à la disposition des pays en voie de développement : 1961.*

BAADE, Fritz (1961), *Exportation et recettes invisibles en Turquie.*

STONE, Richard (1961), *Input-Output and National Accounts,* re-ed. (disponible seulement en anglais)

OECE (1958), *Système normalisé de comptabilité nationale.*

5.2 Overseas Territories

The **Overseas Territories Committee,** set up by Decision of the Council on 28 March 1949, comprised representatives of Member countries with overseas territories (Belgium, Spain from July 1959, France, Italy from 1950, and the Netherlands, Portugal and United Kingdom). It concerned itself with the part which those territories who would exercice a role in European economic recovery and expansion. On 21 May 1949 it reported to the Council on their situation and technical assistance requirements; subsequently it carried out studies on their needs with regard to local investment, production and market outlets.

It set up *Joint Working Parties with the Textiles Committee, the Food and Agriculture Committee and the Manpower Committee,* as well as the following groups:

5.2 Territoires d'Outre-Mer

Le **Comité des territoires d'Outre-Mer,** créé par Décision du Conseil du 28 mars 1949, se composait des pays Membres ayant des responsabilités outre-mer (Belgique et Espagne depuis juillet 1959, France et Italie depuis 1950, et Pays-Bas, Portugal et Royaume-Uni). Il s'est intéressé au rôle que pouvaient jouer ces territoires dans le relèvement et l'expansion de l'économie européenne. Il fit rapport au Conseil le 21 mai 1949 de la situation et des besoins des territoires en matière d'assistance technique et, par la suite, prépara des études relatives aux investissements à y effectuer, et sur la production et les débouchés offerts aux produits de ces territoires.

Il a créé des *Groupes de travail mixte avec le Comité des textiles, le Comité de l'alimentation et de l'agriculture et le Comité de la main d'œuvre* et les groupes suivants:

– *No. 2 Preparation of the Committee's Programmes*
– *No. 4 Preparation of the Programme of Work*
– *No. 6 Draft Report on Investment in Africa South of the Sahara*
– *No. 7 Organisation of Production*
– *No. 8 Energy*

plus the following *Expert Groups:*

– *Increased use of Tropical Timber*
– *Pasture Land and Irrigation for the Agricultural Economy in Africa South of the Sahara*

Publications:

OEEC (1951), *African Tropical Timber.*

___. (1951), *African Tropical Timber: Nomenclature Description.*

___. (1951), *Investments in Overseas Territories in Africa, South of the Sahara.*

___. (1953), *Energy in Overseas Territories in Africa South of the Sahara and in Surinam.*

___. (1953), *Techniques de culture des arachides en Afrique occidentale.* (available only in French)

___. (1955), *Cotton: The Main Products of the Overseas Territories.*

___. (1956), *Cacao : Les productions principales des territoires d'outre-mer.*

___. (1957), *Développement économique des pays et territoires d'outre-mer associés aux pays membres de l'OECE.* (available only in French)

___. (1957), *Oilseeds, The Main Products of the Overseas Territories.*

___. (1957), *Statistics of Exports from the Overseas Territories.*

___. (1958), *Economic Development of Overseas Countries and Territories Associated with OEEC Member Countries.*

___. (1960), *Systems of National Accounts in Africa.*

1960-1961, *Taxation Systems Applicable to Investments in the Overseas Countries Associated with Member Countries of OEEC as at 31st December 1959,* 2 vol.

OEEC (1961), *Problem of Rising Prices,* by W. Fellner (*et al.*).

___. (1961), *Systèmes de comptabilité nationale en Afrique.* (available only in French)

6. Technical Services

Co-operation within the OEEC extended to numerous sectors of economic activity (agriculture, energy, industry, transport) which were handled by various technical committees also known as "Vertical Committees".

– *n° 2 établissement des programmes des comités*
– *n° 4 établissement du programme de travail*
– *n° 6 projet de rapport sur les investissements en Afrique au sud du Sahara*
– *n° 7 organisation de la production*
– *n° 8 énergie*

ainsi que des *groupe d'experts :*

– *pour l'intensification de l'utilisation des bois tropicaux, et*
– *sur les pâturages et l'irrigation pour l'économie agricole en Afrique au sud du Sahara*

Publications :

OECE (1951), *Bois tropicaux africains.*

___. (1951), *Bois tropicaux africains: Nomenclature caractéristiques.*

___. (1951), *Les investissements dans les territoires d'Outre-Mer en Afrique, au sud du Sahara.*

___. (1953), *Énergie dans les territoires d'outre-mer, en Afrique au sud du Sahara et au Surinam.*

___. (1953), *Techniques de culture des arachides en Afrique occidentale.*

___. (1955), *Le coton : Les productions principales des territoires d'outre-mer.*

___. (1956), *Cocoa: The Main Products of the Overseas Territories.*

___. (1957), *Développement économique des pays et territoires d'outre-mer associés aux pays membres de l'OECE.*

___. (1957), *Oléagineux, les productions principales des territoires d'outre-mer.*

___. (1957), *Statistiques des produits exportés par les territoires d'outre-mer.*

___. (1960), *Développement économique des pays et territoires d'outre-mer associés aux pays membres de l'OECE.*

___. (1960), *Systems of National Accounts in Africa.* (disponible seulement en anglais)

1960-1961, *Régime fiscal des investissements dans les pays d'outre-mer associés aux pays membres de l'OECE au 31 décembre 1959,* 2 vol.

OECE (1961), *Problème des hausses de prix,* par W. Fellner (*et al.*).

___. (1961), *Systèmes de comptabilité nationale en Afrique.*

6. Services techniques

La coopération au sein de l'OECE s'est exercée dans de nombreux secteurs de l'activité économique (agriculture, énergie, industrie, transports) par l'action de comités techniques, également dénommés «Comités verticaux».

At the outset the chief task of these committees was to assess Member countries' needs in individual sectors, so as to ensure optimum utilisation of resources when Marshall Plan aid was distributed. Soon, however, their attention was directed to longer-term issues, such as productivity growth, and the introduction of national programmes to promote sectors with a potential contribution to make towards improving the balance of payments in particular.

A Programmes Committee, which on 11 May 1948 replaced the Committee of Methods, drew up programmes relating to production, industrial machinery and investment. On 9 June 1950 it became the Economic Committee (see Section 5).

6.1 Food and Agriculture

The **Food and Agriculture Committee,** set up on 11 May 1948, sought to ensure that Member countries slanted their agricultural production in such a way as to reduce their imports from the dollar area as far as possible, with subsequent steps to encourage growth of farm output as a whole and the removal of European trade barriers. On the technical level it worked to promote agricultural productivity growth, better utilisation of labour and capital, and modernisation of rural management methods. In 1955 its work was taken over by the Ministerial Committee for Agriculture and Food (see Section 7).

In 1949 the Council set up a Food Consumption Levels Working Party and the following Sub-Committees:

- *Agricultural Production Plans and Programmes*
- *Agricultural Machinery*
- *Fertilisers, Insecticides and Fungicides*
- *Fisheries*

The activities of some of these bodies were carried on by the *Working Parties* set up by the Food and Agriculture Committee:

- *No. 1 Livestock Products*
- *No. 2 Fruit and Vegetables*
- *No. 3 Industrial Crops*
- *No. 4 Statistics*
- *No. 5 Consumption Levels*
- *No. 6 Agricultural Machinery*
- *No. 7 Pasture Land*
- *No. 8 Animal Health*
- *No. 9 Information and Advices*
- *No. 10 Ad Hoc: Rural Economics*
- *No. 11 Ad Hoc: Dairy Products*
- *No. 12 Ad Hoc: Eggs and Pigmeat*
- *No. 13 Ad Hoc: Fruit and Vegetables*
- *Joint Working Parties with the Machinery Committee, the Trade Committee and the Chemical Products Committee*

Au départ, ces comités devaient surtout contribuer à évaluer les besoins des pays Membres dans leurs secteurs particuliers de façon à assurer la meilleure utilisation possible des ressources lors de la répartition de l'aide du Plan Marshall. Rapidement leur attention porta sur des problèmes à plus long terme, tel le développement de la productivité, et sur la mise en oeuvre de programmes nationaux destinés à relever des secteurs susceptibles, notamment, de contribuer à l'amélioration de la balance des paiements.

Un Comité des programmes, qui remplaça le 11 mai 1948 le Comité des méthodes, élabora des programmes de production, d'équipement et d'investissement. Le 9 juin 1950, il devint le Comité économique (voir section 5).

6.1 Alimentation et agriculture

Le **Comité de l'alimentation et de l'agriculture,** créé le 11 mai 1948, s'est efforcé d'obtenir que les pays Membres orientent leur production agricole de façon à réduire le plus possible les besoins d'importation en provenance de la zone dollar pour ensuite favoriser l'accroissement de la production agricole globale et l'abaissement des barrières commerciales entre les pays Membres. Sur le plan technique, il a encouragé l'accroissement de la productivité agricole, une meilleure utilisation de la main d'œuvre et des capitaux, et la modernisation des principes de gestion rurale. Ses travaux ont été repris en 1955 par le Comité ministériel de l'agriculture et de l'alimentation (voir section 7).

En 1949, le Conseil a créé un Groupe de travail des niveaux de consommation alimentaire et les Sous-comités suivants :

- *Programmes et plans de production agricole*
- *Machinisme agricole*
- *Engrais et produits insecticides et fongibles*
- *Pêches*

L'activité de certains d'entre eux a été poursuivie par les *Groupes de travail* constitués par le Comité de l'alimentation et de l'agriculture :

- *n°1 produits de l'élevage*
- *n°2 fruits et légumes*
- *n°3 cultures industrielles*
- *n°4 statistiques*
- *n°5 niveaux de consommation*
- *n°6 machinisme agricole*
- *n°7 pâturages*
- *n°8 hygiène animale*
- *n°9 information et vulgarisation*
- *n°10 ad hoc, économie rurale*
- *n°11 ad hoc, produits laitiers*
- *n°12 ad hoc, oeufs et la viande porcine*
- *n°13 ad hoc, fruits et légumes*
- *Groupes de travail mixte avec le Comité de l'équipement, le Comité des échanges et le Comité des produits chimiques*

Publications:

OEEC (1950), *Agricultural Advisory Services in European Countries.*

___. (1950), *Hybrid Maize in European Countries.*

___. (1951), *Agricultral Extension Services in the USA.*

___. (1951), *Fertilisers, Trade Regulations in OEEC Countries.*

___. (1951), *Seed Production Testing and Distribution in European Countries.*

___. (1951), *The Mechanisation of Small Farms in European Countries.*

___. (1952), *Fertilisers, Methods of Analysis used in OEEC Countries.*

___. (1952), *Fish Marketing in OEEC Countries.*

___. (1952), *Hybrid Maize: Progress in OECE Countries*

___. (1952), *Situation of the Agricultural Engineering Industry in Member Countries in 1950.*

___. (1954-1957), *Market for Apples and Pears in OEEC Countries, 3 issues.*

___. (1954), *Stone Fruit: Prospects for the 1954 Season.*

___. (1954), *Exploitation des herbages, y compris la création de paturages temporaires et la conservation de l'herbe.* (available only in French)

6.2 Energy

The serious damage done by the war to the energy-producing industries affected the overall development of the European economy. Although post-war reconstruction addressed some of the deficiencies, European energy output was outstripped by demand and energy imports rose continuously. In addition, the successive shocks caused by the Korean War and the Suez crisis revealed the precariousness of the energy balance and prompted the OEEC to look for ways of resolving the general problem of energy supply and the difficulties being encountered in the different energy sectors. Its technical committees covered all the sectors: coal, oil, electricity and, later, nuclear energy and gas.

6.2.1 Coal

Set up on 11 May 1948, the **Coal Committee** dealt with every type of solid mineral fuel. Its first tasks were to assess Europe's needs and the economic and technical implications for its coal industry, much weakened by the war. Subsequently, it drew up annual reports on the coal

Publications :

___. (1950), *Les services consultatifs agricoles dans les pays européens.*

___. (1950), *Le maïs hybride dans les pays européens.*

___. (1951), *Les services consultatifs agricoles aux États-Unis.*

___. (1951), *Engrais, Réglementation du commerce dans les pays de l'OECE.*

___. (1951), *Production, contrôle et distribution des semences dans les pays européens.*

___. (1951), *La mécanisation des petites exploitations agricoles dans les pays européens.*

___. (1952), *Méthode d'analyse en usage dans les pays de l'OECE.*

___. (1952), *Marché du poisson dans les pays de l'OECE.*

___. (1952), *Le maïs hybride : développement de la production dans les pays de l'OECE.*

___. (1952), *Situation de l'industrie des machines agricoles et des tracteurs dans les pays membres en 1950.*

___. (1954-1957), *Marché des pommes et des poires dans les pays de l'OECE, 3 issues.*

___. (1954), *Fruits à noyaux : Perspectives pour la campagne 1954.*

___. (1954), *Exploitation des herbages, y compris la création de paturages temporaires et la conservation de l'herbe.*

6.2 Énergie

Le potentiel de production d'énergie, gravement touché par la guerre, affectait le développement général de l'économie. Bien que la phase de reconstruction ait permis de combler certaines insuffisances, la production européenne d'énergie a augmenté moins vite que les besoins, de sorte que les importations n'ont cessé de s'accroître. De plus, les chocs successifs créés par la guerre de Corée et la crise de Suez ont révélé la précarité du bilan énergétique et incité l'OECE à trouver des solutions au problème général de l'approvisionnement et aux difficultés rencontrées dans les divers secteurs de l'énergie. L'activité de ces comités s'est exercée dans toutes les branches : charbon, pétrole, électricité, et, plus tard, énergie nucléaire et gaz.

6.2.1 Charbon

Créé le 11 mai 1948, le **Comité du charbon** avait compétence à traiter des combustibles minéraux solides de toute sorte. Ses premières tâches ont porté sur l'évaluation des besoins européns et sur les conséquences économiques et techniques pour l'industrie charbonnière,

market and medium-term trends in coal demand by sector, and co-operated with the Energy Committee and the Energy Advisory Commission in their work. It set up a joint working party with the Oil Committee and the following *Working Parties:*

- *No. 1 Technical Assistance (Turkish Investment Programme)*
- *No. 2 Study of long-term programmes and more especially that of the Bizone*
- *No. 3 Rapid growth of production in Producing Countries*

Set up by Resolution of the Council on 26 February 1951, the **Supply and Distribution Sub-Committee** examined the short-term outlook for the coal market, and in cases of severe shortage – as occurred during the Korean War – apportioned coal supplies fairly among the Member countries. Its other tasks were to make forecasts for imports of American coal, analyse the freight shipping situation, and in the event of shipment difficulties, to co-ordinate imports by means of a special group of trade experts working in association with the Maritime Transport Committee.

Publications:

OEEC (1952), *Coal and European Economic Expansion.*

___. (1952), *Coal production: Short-Term Programmes of Western Europe.*

___. (1953), *Coal Production and Supplies for Western Europe in 1952 and 1953.*

___. (1953), *Coal Gasification: Underground Gasification : Gasification of Mined Coal, Technical Assistance Mission* No. 99.

___. (1954-1961), *The Coal Industry in Europe.*

___. (1955), *New Coking Processes.*

___. (1956), *Drainage and Use of Methane from Coal-Fields (Fire Damp).*

___. (1958), *Drainage and Use of Methane from Coal-Fields Fire Damp: Developments since 1956.*

6.2.2 Oil and Gas

Set up on 11 May 1948, the **Oil Committee** dealt with questions relating to crude oil and petroleum products, natural gas, refinery gas and substitute fuels. The first task entrusted to it was to distribute the funds earmarked for the creation of a European refining industry. Subsequently it co-ordinated the development of refineries in Europe and compiled half-yearly statistics on supplies and uses of crude oil and petroleum products. It submitted recommendations and reports to the Council on the need to increase European oil storage capacity and oil

sortie très affaiblie de la guerre. Depuis lors, il a préparé les rapports annuels sur le marché charbonnier avec les tendances sur l'évolution à moyen terme de la demande de charbon par secteur, et coopéré avec le Comité de l'énergie et la Commission consultative de l'énergie dans leurs travaux. Il a créé un groupe de travail mixte avec le Comité du pétrole et des *groupes de travail :*

- *n° 1 assistance technique (Programme d'investissement en Turquie)*
- *n° 2 étude des programmes à long terme et plus spécialement de la Bizone*
- *n° 3 croissance rapide de production dans les pays producteurs*

Créé par Résolution du Conseil du 26 février 1951, le **Sous-comité de l'approvisionnement et de la distribution** a examiné les perspectives du marché charbonnier à court terme et, en cas de pénurie sérieuse – comme pendant la guerre de Corée – a réparti équitablement les disponibilités charbonnières à l'exportation entre tous les pays Membres. Il avait également pour tâche la prévision des importations de charbon américain, l'analyse de la situation des affrètements et en cas de difficultés de transports maritimes, la coordination des importations par un Groupe spécial d'experts commerciaux, en liaison avec le Comité des transports maritimes.

Publications :

OECE (1952), *Charbon et expansion économique européenne.*

___. (1952), *Production du charbon, Perspectives immédiates de l'Europe occidentale.*

___. (1953), *Production du charbon: approvisionnement de l'Europe occidentale en 1952 et 1953.*

___. (1953), *Gazéification des charbons. Gazéification souterraine. Gazéification des charbons extraits, Mission d'assistance technique* n° 99.

___. (1954-1961), *L'industrie du charbon en Europe.*

___. (1955), *Les procédés nouveaux de coxéfaction.*

___. (1956), *Drainage et utilisation du méthane des charbonnages (Grisou).*

___. (1958), *Captage et utilisation du méthane des charbonnages (grisou) : évolution depuis 1956.*

6.2.2 Pétrole et gaz

Créé le 11 mai 1948, le **Comité du pétrole** a traité des questions de pétrole brut et de produits pétroliers, de production de gaz naturel, de gaz de raffinerie et de carburants de remplacement. La première tâche qui lui ait été confiée fut la répartition des fonds affectés à la création d'une industrie européenne du raffinage. Par la suite, il assura la coordination du développement de l'industrie du raffinage et le rassemblement des données statistiques semestrielles sur les approvisionnements et les affectations du pétrole brut et des produits pétroliers.

stocks. In 1956-1957, following the suspension of Middle East oil shipments to Europe, it allocated the available supply among the countries of Western Europe in co-operation with the oil industry. It studied projects for intra-European crude oil pipelines (at the request of the European Conference of Ministers of Transport – ECMT) and the technical and economic implications of exploitation of North Saharan natural gas resources. It set up the following *Working Parties:*

- *Steering*
- *Technical Questions*
- *Ad Hoc: Statistics*
- *Mining Experts*
- *Geological Experts*
- *General*
- *Study of Programmes*
- *Standing*
- *Storage Capacity and Oil Stocks*
- *Special: Exploitation of North Saharan Natural Gas Resources*
- *Ad Hoc: Allocations*

To assist the Committee, the Council set up on 30 November 1956 the OEEC Petroleum Emergency Group.

Established by Decision of the Council on 27 January 1957, the **Gas Committee** dealt with questions relating to production, transportation, distribution and utilisation of gas, with the exception of natural and refinery gas production. Its main tasks were to prepare reports on the influence of taxes on gas costs and prices, safety in the use of gas, the technical and economic problems posed by the use of natural gas as extracted or processed, the problems of interchangeability of gas products and their production, and the development of gas use for domestic heating purposes. In the course of its existence the Committee was assisted by the following *Working Parties:*

- *No. 1 Ad Hoc: Programme and Methods*
- *No. 2 Ad Hoc: Statistics*
- *No. 3 Gasification*
- *No. 4 Investment*
- *No. 5 Annual Report*

- *Working Party*
- *Group of Experts*

Publications:

OEEC (1949-1953), *Co-ordination of Oil Refinery Expansion in the OEEC Countries: report,* No. 1-3.

___. (1953), *Production of Drilling and Refining Oil Equipment in the USA,* Technical Assistance Mission No. 57.

Il a soumis au Conseil des recommandations et rapports sur la nécessité d'augmenter la capacité européenne de stockage et les stocks de pétrole. En 1956-1957, à la suite de l'interruption des livraisons pétrolières du Moyen-Orient en Europe, il devait répartir, en coopération avec l'industrie, le pétrole disponible entre les pays de l'Europe occidentale. Il étudia les projets de pipelines de pétrole brut intra-européen (à la demande de la Conférence européenne des Ministres des transports (CEMT)), et les implications techniques et économiques de l'exploitation des ressources en gaz naturel du Nord Sahara. Il a créé les *groupes suivants :*

- *Direction*
- *questions techniques*
- *ad hoc, sur les statistiques*
- *experts miniers*
- *géologues*
- *toutes questions*
- *étude des programmes*
- *permanent*
- *capacité de stockage et constitution des stocks*
- *spécial, exploitation des ressources en gaz naturel du Nord Sahara*
- *ad hoc pour les allocations*

Pour l'assister, le Conseil a créé, le 30 novembre 1956, un Groupe industriel spécial de l'OECE pour le pétrole.

Créé par Décision du Conseil du 27 janvier 1957, le **Comité du gaz** a étudié les questions de production, transport, distribution et utilisation du gaz, à l'exception de la production du gaz naturel ou de rafinerie. Il eut pour tâches principales de préparer des rapports sur l'influence des taxes sur le coût et le prix du gaz, la sécurité dans l'emploi du gaz, les problèmes technico-économiques posés par l'utilisation du gaz naturel en l'état ou réformé, les problèmes de l'interchangeabilité des gaz de la deuxième famille, et sur leur production, le développement de l'emploi du gaz pour le chauffage des locaux. Au cours de son existence, il a été assisté de *groupes de travail :*

- *n° 1 ad hoc, programmes et méthode*
- *n° 2 ad hoc, statistiques*
- *n° 3 gazéification*
- *n° 4 investissements*
- *n° 5 rapport annuel*

- *Groupe de travail*
- *Groupe d'experts*

Publications :

OECE (1949-1953), *Coordination du développement du raffinage du pétrole dans les pays de l'OECE : rapport,* n° 1-3.

___. (1953), *Équipement pétrolier aux USA, Fabrication de matériel de forage et de raffinage, Mission d'assistance technique* n° 57.

——. (1955-1961), *Oil Equipment in Europe,* 2 vol.

——. (1956), *Oil: The Outlook for Europe 1955: a Study.*

——. (1957), *Search for an Exploitation of Crude Oil and Natural Gas in the OEEC Area.*

——. (1958), *Europe's Need for Oil: Implications and Lessons of the Suez Crisis.*

——. (1960), *Gas in Europe: Production, Availabilities, Consumption.*

——. (1960), *Pétrole en Turquie.* (available only in French)

——. (1961), *Oil: Recent Developments in OEEC Area: 1960.*

6.2.3 Electricity

Established on 11 May 1948, the **Electricity Committee** endeavoured to resolve the problems connected with production, distribution and rational utilisation of electric power. The electric power equipments were the subject of surveys and annual reports. The Committee also analysed electricity demand, exchanges between countries by means of interconnected networks, the hydroelectric resources still available in Europe and the overseas territories, long-distance power transmission and combined production of heat and power, financing of investment and related problems such as electricity prices and administrative regulations concerning power supply, and the development of exchanges of electric power between adjacent countries. Its activities led to the establishment of the Union for the Co-ordination of the Production and Transport of Electricity on 19 December 1950.

It set up the following *Working Parties:*

- *No. 1 Presentation of International and Complementary Programmes and Analytical Documentation concerning Power Stations*
- *No. 2 Financing of Emergency Programmes*
- *No. 3 Long-term development of the Electricity Economy*
- *Group of Experts on Electricity Rates*
- *Liaison Group with the Energy Committee*

Publications:

OEEC (1950-1961), *Electric Power Equipment,* survey No. 1-14.

——. (1950), *Interconnected Power Systems in the USA and Western Europe : Report of the Tecaid Mission, Technical Assistance Mission* No. 1.

——. (1950), *Note on the Technical Development of Thermal Power Stations.*

——. (1951), *The Position of Electricity Industry in OEEC Countries,* 1st Survey.

——. (1955-1961), *L'équipement pétrolier en Europe,* 2 vol.

——. (1956), *Pétrole : Perspectives européennes 1955 : étude.*

——. (1957), *La Recherche et l'exploitation du pétrole brut et du gaz naturel dans la zone OECE.*

——. (1958), *Besoins de l'Europe en pétrole : incidences et enseignements de la crise de Suez.*

——. (1960), *Gaz en Europe : production, disponibilités, consommation.*

——. (1960), *Pétrole en Turquie.*

——. (1961), *Pétrole : Nouvelle évolution dans la zone OECE : 1960.*

6.2.3 Électricité

Créé le 11 mai 1948, le **Comité de l'électricité** s'est efforcé de résoudre les problèmes que posent la production, la distribution et l'utilisation rationnelle de l'électricité. L'équipement électrique a donné lieu à des enquêtes et des rapports annuels. Le Comité s'est également préoccupé d'analyser la demande d'énergie électrique, les échanges entre pays par réseaux interconnectés, les ressources hydroélectriques encore disponibles en Europe et dans les territoires d'outre-mer, le transport de l'énergie électrique à longue distance, la production combinée de chaleur et d'électricité, le financement des investissements ainsi que les problèmes connexes, tel que le prix de l'électricité, les règlementations administratives liées à sa fourniture, et le développement des échanges d'électricité entre pays limitrophes. Ses activités ont abouti à la création le 19 décembre 1950 de l'Union pour la coordination de la production et du transport de l'électricité.

Il a créé les *groupes de travail :*

- *nº 1 présentation des programmes internationaux et complémentaires et documentation analytique concernant les centrales*
- *nº 2 financement de programmes d'urgence*
- *nº 3 développement à long terme de l'économie d'électricité*
- *Groupe d'experts de la tarification*
- *Groupe de liaison avec le Comité de l'énergie*

Publications :

OECE (1950-1961), *Équipement électrique,* enquête nº 1-14.

——. (1950), *Structure des interconnexions aux États-Unis et en Europe Occidentale : rapport de la mission Tecaid, Mission d'assistance technique* nº 1.

——. (1950), *Note sur l'évolution technique des centrales thermiques.*

——. (1951), *Situation de l'industrie de l'électricité dans les pays de l'OECE,* 1re enquête.

___. (1952-1954), *Position of the Electricity Industry in OEEC Countries,* 1st-4th enquiry. (Replaced by, *Electricity Supply Industry in Europe* from 1954.)

___. (1953-1954), *Fuel Consumption of Thermal Power Stations,* 1st-3rd enquiry.

___. (1953), *Gasification of Coal, Underground Gasification, Gasification of Mined Coal.*

___. (1954-1962), *Electricity Supply Industry in Europe,* 5th-12th survey.

___. (1954), *Price of Electricity and Its Relation to Investment in the Electricity Supply Industry.*

___. (1957), *Electricity Rates.*

___. (1957), *Production, Transmission and Distribution of Electricity in Europe.*

___. (1958), *Theory of Marginal Cost and Electricity Rates.*

___. (1958), *Trend of the Selling Price of Electricity and its Relation to the Financing of New Plant.*

___. (1952-1954), *Situation de l'industrie électrique dans les pays de l'OECE,* 1e-4e enquête. (Remplacé par, *Industrie de l'électricité en Europe,* de 1954.)

___. (1953-1954), *Consommation de combustibles des centrales thermiques,* 1re-3e enquête.

___. (1953), *La gazéification des charbons, Gazéification souterraine, gazéification des charbons extraits.*

___. (1954-1962), *Industrie de l'électricité en Europe,* 5e-12e enquête.

___. (1954), *Prix de l'électricité et leur influence sur le financement des investissements dans l'industrie électrique.*

___. (1957), *Tarification de l'électricité.*

___. (1957), *Production, transport et distribution de l'électricité en Europe.*

___. (1958), *Théorie du coût marginal et de la tarification de l'électricité.*

___. (1958), *Évolution du prix de vente de l'électricité et les problèmes financiers d'expansion de l'industrie électrique.*

6.2.4 Energy

Acting on the suggestions contained in a report submitted to the Organisation in May 1955 by Mr. Louis Armand, Chairman of the Board of Management of the French National Railways, the Council set up a **Commission for Energy** on 10 June 1955. The Commission considered Europe's growing energy requirements and the best means of meeting them and submitted its report in May 1956. To implement the report's recommendations and to carry on the work that had been begun, the Council of the OEEC set up by Decision of 4 June 1957 an **Energy Committee** and an **Energy Advisory Commission.** (On nuclear energy, see Section 10.)

The **Energy Committee** comprised representatives of the Member countries, the chairmen of the OEEC committees dealing with energy questions and the chairman of the Economic Committee, an observer from the High Authority of the ECSC and one from the ECE. Its terms of reference were to study and compare the methods used by Member countries to resolve general energy problems that lay outside the competence of the Vertical Committees, to co-ordinate energy policies, to study the problems posed by energy surpluses and to introduce improved energy statistics (quantities and prices). Its *Working Party No. 1* studied the rational utilisation of fuels and the possibility of establishing a co-ordinated European energy policy.

The **Energy Advisory Commission** comprised nine independent experts. It studied general energy problems

6.2.4 Énergie

Suite aux suggestions contenues dans le rapport de M. Louis Armand, Président du conseil d'administration de la Société nationale des chemins de fer français, établi en mai 1955, le Conseil a créé le 10 juin 1955 une **Commission de l'énergie.** Celle-ci a étudié les besoins croissants en énergie de l'Europe, les meilleurs moyens d'y faire face et présenté son rapport en mai 1956. Pour mettre en œuvre les recommandations contenues dans ce rapport et continuer la tâche entreprise, le Conseil de l'OECE a institué par Décision du 4 juin 1957, un **Comité de l'énergie** et une **Commission consultative de l'énergie.** (Sur l'énergie nucléaire, voir section 10).

Le **Comité de l'énergie** était constitué des représentants des pays Membres, des présidents des comités de l'OECE s'occupant de questions énergétiques, du président du Comité économique et d'un observateur de la Haute Autorité de la CECA et de la CEE/ONU. Il avait pour tâche d'étudier la confrontation des méthodes appliquées par les pays Membres pour résoudre les problèmes généraux énergétiques qui dépassaient la compétence des Comités verticaux, la coordination des politiques énergétiques, l'étude des problèmes du surplus énergétique et l'amélioration des statistiques de l'énergie (quantités, prix). Son *Groupe de travail n° 1* étudiait l'utilisation rationnelle de combustibles et la possibilité d'élaboration d'une politique énergétique européenne coordonnée.

La **Commission consultative de l'énergie** était composée de neufs experts indépendants. Elle a étudié les

and energy investment projects and their financing, and established forecasts of energy consumption and production levels. It worked in close association with the Energy Committee and the vertical committees for coal, oil, electricity and gas, as well as with the Economic Committee. It had two *Working Parties:*

- *Deputies of Members of the Commission to prepare its work*
- *Investment and its Financing*

Publications:

ARMAND, Louis (1955), *Some Aspects of the European Energy Problem: report.*

OEEC (1956), *Europe's Growing Needs of Energy.*

___. (1960), *Towards a New Energy Pattern in Europe.*

6.3 Industry

The "Vertical Committees" were the setting for continuous co-operation on problems facing specific industries. These committees, most of which were carried over to the OECD, covered (with the energy bodies) the following sectors: machinery, iron and steel, non-ferrous metals, chemical products, timber, textiles, pulp and paper, hides and skins, and miscellaneous products.

The vertical committees had been set up to resolve the problems connected with European recovery and to interest business and industry circles in productivity issues. Prior to the creation of the European Productivity Agency (EPA) in 1953, there had been several missions of experts to the United States and in Europe, and subsequently the committees co-operated with the EPA. They reacted to the critical shortages that occurred by establishing, for example, an international system of raw materials distribution. They were called upon to give their opinion on trade liberalisation questions of concern to the industries they covered, and from 1954 their principal activities were to study the situation and outlook for those industries and investigate ways of resolving specific short-term difficulties.

6.3.1 Machinery

Set up on 5 June 1948, the **Machinery Committee** dealt with all the mechanical and electrical engineering industries (including transport equipment, precision engineering and watchmaking) and studied the opportunities for European co-operation in this sector from the economic, statistical, commercial and productivity-related standpoints. It drew up periodical reports on the situation in the sector and annual reports on output of and demand

problèmes énergétiques généraux, les questions d'investissement et de financement en énergie et projeté les niveaux de consommation et de production d'énergie. Elle a travaillé en liaison étroite avec le Comité de l'énergie et les comités verticaux compétents pour le charbon, le pétrole, l'électricité et le gaz ainsi qu'avec le Comité économique. Elle a disposé de *2 groupes de travail :*

- *Adjoints des membres de la Commission pour en préparer les travaux*
- *investissements et leur financement*

Publications :

ARMAND, Louis (1955), *Quelques aspects du problème européen de l'énergie : rapport.*

OECE (1956), *L'Europe face à ses besoins croissants en énergie.*

___. (1960), *Énergie en Europe : nouvelles perspectives.*

6.3 Industrie

La coopération n'a cessé de s'exercer dans les « Comités verticaux » à l'égard de problèmes que rencontrent certaines industries. Ces Comités, dont la plupart ont été reconduits au sein de l'OCDE, couvraient (avec les comités de l'énergie) les secteurs suivants de l'économie: équipement, sidérurgie, métaux non-ferreux, produits chimiques, bois, textiles, pâtes et papiers, produits divers, cuirs et peaux.

Ces comités avaient été créés pour résoudre des problèmes propres à la période de relèvement et pour intéresser les milieux d'affaires et industriels aux questions de productivité. Avant la création de l'Agence européenne de productivité (AEP), en 1953, plusieurs missions d'experts avaient visité les États-Unis et l'Europe. Les Comités ont coopéré avec l'AEP depuis sa création. Ils ont réagi aux périodes de crise en mettant sur pied, par exemple, un système international de répartition des matières premières, et ont donné leur avis sur les questions de la libération des échanges intéressant leur industrie. A partir de 1954, leur principale activité a consisté à étudier la situation et les perspectives de leur industrie, ou à effectuer des enquêtes spécifiques sur les solutions à apporter à de graves problèmes de conjoncture.

6.3.1 Équipement

Créé le 5 juin 1948, le **Comité de l'équipement** était compétent à traiter de l'ensemble des industries mécaniques et électriques (y compris le matériel de transport, la mécanique de précision et l'horlogerie) dont il étudiait la coopération européenne sous ses aspects économiques, statistiques, commerciaux et de productivité. Il prépara un rapport périodique sur la situation dans le secteur et un rapport annuel sur la production et la demande de

for power station equipment. In the area of trade liberalisation it examined the technical and administrative regulations impeding trade, the arrangements applicable to government buying of engineering products, the state of liberalisation and customs duties and import charges, and competition from non-member countries on third markets. It set up the following *Working Parties:*

- *No. 1 General (Steering Group)*
- *No. 2 Mining Equipment*
- *No. 3 Electrical Equipment*
- *No. 4 Machine Tools*
- *No. 5 Textile Machinery*
- *No. 6 Civil Engineering*
- *No. 7 Technical Assistance*
- *No. 8 Motor Vehicles*
- *No. 9 Statistical Experts*

Publications:

OEEC (1949-1952), *Machinery and Equipment,* 1st-5th ed.

___. (1949), *Machine Tools.*

___. (1950), *Manufacture in Europe of Spare Parts for Civil Engineering and Tracklaying Tractors of American Origine.*

World Metallurgical Congress (1951, Detroit) (1954), *Papers, Technical Assistance Mission* No. 80, 9 booklets, OEEC, Paris.

World Metallurgical Congress (1951, Detroit) (1954), *Steel Making and Refining, Technical Assistance Mission* No. 80, OEEC, Paris.

World Metallurgical Congress (1951, Detroit) (1954), *Non-ferrous Refining, Rolling and Fabrication, Technical Assistance Mission* No. 80, OEEC, Paris.

World Metallurgical Congress (1951, Detroit) (1954), *Ferrous Fabrication in Lighter Industry, Technical Assistance Mission* No. 80, OEEC, Paris.

World Metallurgical Congress (1951, Detroit) (1954), *Heat Treatment, 2 parts, Technical Assistance Mission* No. 80, OEEC, Paris.

World Metallurgical Congress (1951, Detroit) (1954), *Welding and Joining, Technical Assistance Mission* No. 80, OEEC, Paris.

World Metallurgical Congress (1951, Detroit) (1954), *Testing and Inspection, Technical Assistance Mission* No. 80, OEEC, Paris.

World Metallurgical Congress (1951, Detroit) (1954), *Metallurgical Education, Technical Assistance Mission* No. 80, OEEC, Paris.

World Metallurgical Congress (1951, Detroit) (1954), *Research and laboratories, Technical Assistance Mission* No. 80, OEEC, Paris.

matériel lourd pour centrales électriques. En matière de libéralisation des échanges, il a examiné les réglementations techniques et administratives formant obstacle aux échanges, les régimes applicables aux achats gouvernementaux de biens d'équipement, l'état de libéralisation et les droits de douane et taxes à l'importation et la concurrence des pays non-membres sur les marchés tiers. Il a créé les *groupes de travail* traitant les questions suivantes:

- *n° 1 général (Groupe de direction)*
- *n° 2 matériel des mines*
- *n° 3 matériel électrique*
- *n° 4 machines-outils*
- *n° 5 machines textiles*
- *n° 6 génie civil*
- *n° 7 assistance technique*
- *n° 8 automobiles*
- *n° 9 experts statisticiens*

Publications :

OECE (1949-1952), *Biens d'équipement,* 1re-5e éd.

___. (1949), *Machines-outils.*

___. (1950), *Fabrication en Europe de pièces de rechange pour matériel de génie civil et tracteurs à chenille d'origine américaine.*

Congrès mondial de la métallurgie (1951, Detroit) (1954), *Comptes rendus, Mission d'assistance technique n° 80, 9 brochures, OECE, Paris.*

Congrès mondial de la métallurgie (1951, Detroit) (1954), *Fabrication et affinage de l'acier, Mission d'assistance technique* n° 80, OECE, Paris.

Congrès mondial de la métallurgie (1951, Detroit) (1954), *Affinage, laminage et transformation des métaux non ferreux, Mission d'assistance technique* n° 80, OECE, Paris.

Congrès mondial de la métallurgie (1951, Detroit) (1954), *Transformation des produits ferreux dans l'industrie légère, Mission d'assistance technique* n° 80, OECE, Paris.

Congrès mondial de la métallurgie (1951, Detroit) (1954), *Traitement thermique, 2 parties, Mission d'assistance technique* n° 80, OECE, Paris.

Congrès mondial de la métallurgie (1951, Detroit) (1954), *Soudure et assemblage, Mission d'assistance technique* n° 80, OECE, Paris.

Congrès mondial de la métallurgie (1951, Detroit) (1954), *Essais et contrôle, Mission d'assistance technique* n° 80, OECE, Paris.

Congrès mondial de la métallurgie (1951, Detroit) (1954), *Enseignement de la métallurgie, Mission d'assistance technique* n° 80, OECE, Paris.

Congrès mondial de la métallurgie (1951, Detroit) (1954), *Recherche et laboratoires, Mission d'assistance technique* n° 80, OECE, Paris.

OEEC (1952), *Swedish Shale Oil: Production Methods in Sweden, Teachnical Assistance Mission* No. 93.

——. (1953), *European Foundries and Productivity: Some Recent Experiments and Achievements, Technical Assistance Mission* No. 122.

——. (1953), *Galvanizing Techniques in the USA, Technical Assistance Mission* No. 78.

——. (1953), *Some Aspects of the Motor Vehicle Industry in the USA, Technical Assistance Mission* No. 92.

——. (1955-1960), *Engineering Industries in Europe.*

——. (1955), *Buyer's Guide to European Machinery.*

——. (1955), *Welding Techniques and Uses in the USA, Technical Assistance Mission* No. 143.

——. (1956), *Cooking and Heating Appliances in the USA: Production and Distribution, EPA Project* No. 246.

——. (1957), *List of European Trade Associations in the Engineering Industries: EQ(57)12.*

——. (1958), *Low Grade Ores: a Survey of American Research Methods, EPA Project* No. 228.

European Productivity Agency (1959), *Metal Testing in the United States: a Survey of Destructive and Non-Destructive Methods, EPA Project* No. 388, OEEC, Paris.

OECE. Machinery Committee (1960), *The Demand for Engineering Products in Less Industrialized Countries.*

OEEC (1961), *Government Buying of Engineering Products: Responsible Departments, Products Bought, Procedure.*

OCDE/OECD (1962), *Liste des associations internationales intéressant les industries mécaniques et électriques :* 1961/*List of International Associations Connected with the Engineering:* 1961.

6.3.2 Iron and Steel

The **Iron and Steel Committee** was set up on 11 May 1948. It dealt with questions pertaining to iron and steel products, manganese ore, iron ore and ferrous scrap and ferro-alloys, and worked to promote rational reconstruction and development of the industry. It drew up annual reports on general trends in the industry, conducted annual surveys on raw materials and production capacity for iron and steel with periodic reviews of investment projects, and studied related technical questions. It set up a *Steering Group* (comprising the Committee's chairman, the vice-chairmen and the working party chairmen) and the following *Working Parties:*

OECE (1952), Huile de schiste en Suéde : Méthodes suédoises de production, Mission d'assistance technique nº 93.

——. (1953), *Fonderie européenne et productivité : expériences et réalisations récentes, Mission d'assistance technique* nº 122.

——. (1953), *La galvanisation aux États-Unis, Mission d'assistance technique* nº 78.

——. (1953), *Aspects de l'industrie automobile aux USA, Mission d'assistance technique* nº 92.

——. (1955-1960), *Industries mécaniques et électriques en Europe.*

——. (1955), *Guide de l'acheteur de biens d'équipement en Europe.*

——. (1955), *Technique et emploi de la soudure aux États-Unis, Mission d'assistance technique* nº 143.

——. (1956), *Cuisine et chauffage domestiques aux États-Unis : fabrication et distribution, Projet AEP* nº 246.

——. (1957), *Liste des associations professionnelles européennes dans les industries mécaniques et électriques : EQ(57)12.*

——. (1958), *Minerais pauvres : exposé des méthodes de recherche américaines, Projet AEP* nº 228.

Agence Européenne de Productivité (1960), *Essai des métaux aux États-Unis : procédés destructifs et non destructifs, Projet AEP* nº 388, OECE, Paris.

OECE. Comité de l'équipement (1960), *Demande de produits mécaniques et électriques dans les pays moins industrialisés : études sur l'Amérique latine et sur l'Inde.*

OECE (1961), *Achats gouvernementaux de produits des industries mécaniques et électriques : services responsables, produits achetés, procédure en vigueur.*

OCDE/OECD (1962), *Liste des associations internationales intéressant les industries mécaniques et électriques :* 1961/*List of International Associations Connected with the Engineering:* 1961.

6.3.2 Sidérurgie

Créé le 11 mai 1948, le **Comité de la sidérurgie** a traité des questions relatives aux produits sidérurgiques, minerai de manganèse, minerai de fer, ferrailles et ferro-alliages, et a promu la reconstruction et le développement rationnels de cette industrie. Il a réalisé des rapports annuels sur les tendances générales de l'industrie, des enquêtes annuelles sur les matières premières et la capacité de production de fonte et d'acier. Il a examiné périodiquement des projets d'investissements, et étudié des questions techniques. Il a constitué un *Groupe de direction,* composé du président, des vice-présidents et des présidents des groupes de travail, et les *groupes de travail* suivants:

– *No. 1 Annual Report*
– *No. 2 Raw Materials*
– *No. 3 Technical Questions*
– *No. 4 Investment Projects, Sector Studies*
– *No. 5 Replies to Questionnaire and*
– *Group of Experts-Statisticians*

Publications:

OEEC (1953), *Manganese in the Iron and Steel Industry: Use Recovery-Supplies.*

___. (1953), *Technical Improvements in the Use of Steel.*

___. (1955-1961), *Iron and Steel Industry in Europe.*

___. (1958), *Market Sampling Study on Iron and Steel Products: Results of a Pilot Study Carried out in Switzerland, EPA Project* No. 328.

6.3.3 Non-Ferrous Metals

The **Non-Ferrous Metals Committee** was set up on 22 May 1948 to deal with matters concerning non-ferrous ores, metals and semi-finished products. It had to distribute Marshall aid for European imports of raw materials (ores and metals), then harmonize restrictions on metal use during the period of shortage in 1950-1. Subsequently it concerned itself with liberalisation of trade in non-ferrous metals, and later with ways of preventing excessive fluctuations in lead and zinc prices. It reviewed twice yearly the situation in the mining, metal and metal fabrication industries, and published an annual report and a monthly report in the press on mining and metal production of lead and zinc. The Committee studied metal consumption by end-uses and the structure of the scrap market (obstacles to trade). It set up the following *Working Parties:*

– *No. 1 Steering Group*
– *No. 2 Lead and Zinc, ad hoc*
– *No. 3 Availabilities*
– *No. 4 Light Metals*
– *No. 5 Productivity*
– *No. 6 Co-ordination of Restrictions on Consumption*
– *Statistics*
– *Liberalisation of Trade in Scrap*

Publications:

OEEC (1952), *Secondary Aluminium Industry in the USA, Technical Assistance Mission* No.° 19.

___. (1953), *Non-Ferrous Ore Dressing in the USA : Report, Technical Assistance Mission* No. 54.

___. (1954), *Non-Ferrous Heavy Metal Fabrication in the USA, Technical Assistance Mission* No. 79.

– *n*° *1 rapport annuel*
– *n*° *2 matières premières*
– *n*° *3 questions techniques*
– *n*° *4 investissements et études par secteur*
– *n*° *5 réponses au questionnaire, et*
– *Groupe d'experts statisticiens*

Publications :

OECE (1953), *Manganèse dans la sidérurgie : utilisation, récupération, approvisionnement.*

___. (1953), *Améliorations techniques dans l'utilisation du fer.*

___. (1955-1961), *Industrie sidérurgique en Europe.*

___. (1958), *Étude par sondage du marché des produits sidérurgiques : résultats d'une étude pilote effectuée en Suisse, Projet AEP* n° 328.

6.3.3 Métaux non-ferreux

Les travaux du **Comité des métaux non-ferreux,** créé le 22 mai 1948, ont porté sur les minerais et les métaux et semi-produits non-ferreux. Il a réparti l'aide du plan Marshall pour l'importation européenne de matières premières (minerais et métaux) et harmonisé les interdictions d'emploi de métaux pendant la période de pénurie 1950-1951. Il s'est ensuite préoccupé de la libéralisation des échanges des métaux non-ferreux et, plus tard, de la façon d'éviter les fluctuations excessives des prix du plomb et du zinc. Il suivait bi-annuellement la situation des industries minières et des métaux de première transformation, et publiait un rapport annuel et mensuel dans la presse sur la production minière et métallurgique du plomb et du zinc. Le comité a étudié la consommation des métaux d'après leur utilisation finale et la structure du marché des déchets (obstacles aux échanges). Il a créé les *groupes de travail* suivants:

– *n*° *1 « Groupe de direction »*
– *n*° *2 ad hoc, plomb et zinc*
– *n*° *3 disponibilité*
– *n*° *4 métaux non-ferreux légers*
– *n*° *5 productivité*
– *n*° *6 coordination des restrictions à la consommation statistiques*
– *étude de la Libération des déchets*

Publications :

OECE (1952), *Industrie de l'aluminium deuxième fusion aux États-Unis, Mission d'assistance technique* n° 19.

___. (1953), *Préparation des minerais non ferreux aux États-Unis : rapport, Mission d'assistance technique* n° 54.

___. (1954), *Transformation des métaux non-ferreux lourds aux USA, Mission d'assistance technique* n° 79.

———. (1954-1955), *Technical Assistance Mission* No. 85, 2 vol.

———. (1954), *Copper Smelting and Refining in the USA, Technical Assistance Mission* No. 85, vol. 1.

———. (1955), *Zinc and Lead Smelting and Refining in the USA, Technical Assistance Mission* No. 85, vol. 2.

———. (1955), *Mining and Dressing of Low-Grade Ores in Europe, Technical Assistance Mission* No. 127

———. (1955-1956), *Non-Ferrous Metal Industry in Europe.* (Replaced by, Statistics of Non Ferrous Metals from 1957-1959.)

DUMAS, A. (1957), *Present Situation and Prospects of the Light Metal Industry.*

OEEC (1957-1959), *Statistics of Non Ferrous Metals.* (Replaced by, Non Ferrous metals from 1960-1984.)

———. (1958), *Situation of the Lead and Zinc Mining Industry in Europe.*

OEEC/OECD (1960-1984), *Non Ferrous Metals.*

OEEC (1961), *European Non-Ferrous Scrap Metal Market.*

———. (1954-1955), *Mission d'assistance technique* nº 85, 2 vol.

———. (1954), *Fusion et affinage du cuivre aux États-Unis, Mission d'assistance technique* nº 85, vol. 1.

———. (1955), *Fusion et affinage du plomb et du zinc aux États-Unis, Mission d'assistance technique* nº 85, vol. 2.

———. (1955), *Extraction et préparation des minerais pauvres en Europe, Mission d'assistance technique* nº 127.

———. (1955-1956), *Industrie des métaux non-ferreux en Europe.* (Remplacé par, Statistiques des métaux non-ferreux de 1957-1959.)

DUMAS, A. (1957), *Situation actuelle et perspectives de l'industrie des métaux légers.*

OECE (1957-1959), *Statistiques des métaux non-ferreux.* (Remplacé par, Métaux non-ferreux de 1960-1984.)

———. (1958), *Situation de l'industrie minière du plomb et du zinc en Europe.*

OECE/OCDE (1960-1984), *Métaux non ferreux.*

OECE (1961), *Marché Européen des déchets de métaux non ferreux.*

6.3.4 Chemical Products

Set up on 22 May 1948, the **Chemical Products Committee** studied the problems posed by the production and marketing of fertilisers, sulphur, dyestuffs, pharmaceuticals, plastic materials, industrial chemical products, synthetic rubber, oil derivatives, glass and glassware. After reviewing the situation of the European chemical industry in 1948-1949, the Committee concerned itself more particularly with sulphur, tanning materials and, in 1950-1951, exportable surpluses. It produced detailed annual situation reports on the chemical industry, statistical reports on fertilisers (in association with the appropriate agricultural body), and studies on the technical and administrative obstacles to trade in pharmaceuticals. It set up the following *Working Parties:*

- *No. 1 "Steering Committee"*
- *No. 2 Tanning Materials*
- *No. 3 Paints and Varnishes*
- *No. 4 Nitrogenous Fertilisers*
- *No. 5 Phosphatic Fertilisers*
- *No. 6 Potassic Fertilisers*
- *No. 7 Petroleum Chemicals*
- *No. 8 Dyestuffs*
- *No. 9 Soaps and Detergents*
- *No. 10 Statistics*
- *No. 11 Plastic Materials*
- *Recovery of Sulphur in the Textile Industry*
- *Joint with the Food and Agriculture Committee*

6.3.4 Produits chimiques

Créé le 22 mai 1948, le **Comité des produits chimiques** examinait les problèmes posés par la production et la commercialisation des engrais, du soufre, des colorants, des produits pharmaceutiques, des matières plastiques, des produits chimiques industriels, du caoutchouc, des produits dérivés de la chimie du pétrole, du verre et de la verrerie. Après avoir étudié en 1948-1949, la situation de l'industrie chimique européenne, le Comité s'est préoccupé notamment du soufre, des matières tannantes et, en 1950-1951, des surplus exportables. Il a préparé un rapport annuel détaillé de conjoncture sur ce secteur, des rapports statistiques sur les engrais (en liaison avec l'instance agricole correspondante), et des études sur les obstacles techniques et administratifs aux échanges de produits pharmaceutiques. Il a créé les *groupes de travail* suivants:

- *nº 1 « Groupe de direction »*
- *nº 2 matières tannantes*
- *nº 3 peintures et vernis*
- *nº 4 engrais azotés*
- *nº 5 engrais phosphatés*
- *nº 6 engrais potassiques*
- *nº 7 industrie pétrochimique*
- *nº 8 matières colorantes*
- *nº 9 savons et détergents*
- *nº 10 statistiques*
- *nº 11 matières plastiques*
- *récupération du soufre dans l'industrie textile*
- *mixte avec le Comité de l'alimentation et de l'agriculture*

Publications:

OEEC (1950), *Vegetable Tanning Extracts.*

___. (1950-1951), *Chemicals Products Exportable Surpluses,* No. 1, 3, 4.

___. (1952), *Sulphur: Could the Position be Improved in Europe?*

___. (1953), *Sulphuric Acid and the Manufacture of Phosphatic Fertilisers.*

___. (1954), *Corrosion, Problems and Prevention in the Chemical and Petro-Chemical Industries in the USA, Technical Assistance Mission* No. 130.

___. (1954-1961), *Chemical Industry in Europe: Trends in Economic Sectors.* (Published by OECD under the title, Chemical Industry from 1962-1980.)

___. (1957), *Industrial Uses of Nitrogen in the United States, Technical Assistance Mission* No. 371.

___. (1961), *Technical and Administrative Regulations on Pharmaceutical Products on OEEC Countries.*

6.3.5 Timber

The **Timber Committee,** which was set up on 22 May 1948, dealt with all questions pertaining to timber, cork and their finished products. It periodically analysed developments in the timber market and short-term trends. It published an annual report on products of first-stage wood processing and detailed statistics on tropical timber production and trade. It dealt with such questions as supplies of rail ties, increased use of hardwoods in the pulp industry, development of forestry production, trade restrictions, trade with the Eastern countries, plant health regulations in international trade in forest products and handling operations in the timber industries. It set up the *Working Party on Statistics* and the following *Working Groups:*

- *No. 1 Steering Group*
- *Urgent Economic Problems*
- *No. 2 Group of Experts to study the Use of certain Tropical Plants in Mines (Increased Use of Tropical Timber)*
- *No. 3 Group to study Economies in Timber Use*
- *Joint with the Overseas Territories Committee*

Publications:

OEEC (1950), *Possibilities of Increasing the Use of Tropical Timber.*

___. (1951), *American Forest Operations and Tropical Timber Production, Technical Assistance Mission* No. 18A (1951).

Publications :

OECE (1950), *Extraits tannants végétaux.*

___. (1950-1951), *Surplus exportables en produits chimiques,* n° 1, 3, 4.

___. (1952), *Soufre : pourrait-on améliorer la situation européenne?*

___. (1953), *Acide sulphurique et la fabrication des engrais phosphatés.*

___. (1954), *Lutte contre la corrosion dans les industries chimique et pétro-chimique aux USA, Mission d'assistance technique* n° 130.

___. (1954-1961), *Industrie chimique en Europe : la situation dans les secteurs économiques.* (Publié par l'OCDE sous le titre, Industrie chimique de 1962-1980.)

___. (1957), *Applications industrielles de l'azote aux États-Unis, Mission d'assistance technique* n° 371.

___. (1961), *Réglementations techniques et administratives relatives aux produits pharmaceutiques dans les pays membres de l'OECE.*

6.3.5 Bois

Créé le 22 mai 1948, le **Comité du bois** traitait des questions relatives au bois, au liège, et à leurs produits finis. Il effectuait périodiquement l'analyse de l'évolution récente du marché et de ses tendances à court terme. Il publiait annuellement un rapport sur les produits de première transformation du bois, et des statistiques détaillées de la production et des échanges de bois tropicaux. Il a abordé les questions d'approvisionnements en traverses de chemin de fer, d'expansion de l'utilisation des bois feuillus dans l'industrie des pâtes, du développement de la production forestière, des restrictions aux échanges, du commerce avec les pays de l'Est, des règlementations phytosanitaires dans les échanges internationaux de produits forestiers et de manutention dans les industries du bois. Il a créé le *Groupe de travail « statistiques »*, et les *groupes de travail* suivants:

- *n° 1 Groupe de direction: problèmes économiques urgents*
- *n° 2 Groupe d'experts pour l'étude de l'utilisation dans les mines de certains végétaux tropicaux (intensification de l'utilisation des bois tropicaux)*
- *n° 3 Groupe pour l'étude des économies dans l'emploi du bois*
- *mixte avec le Comité des Territoires d'Outre-Mer*

Publications :

OECE (1950), *Possibilités d'accroître l'utilisation des bois tropicaux.*

___. (1951), *Techniques forestières américaines et production des bois tropicaux, Mission d'assistance technique* n° 18A (1951).

——. (1951), *The Americain Poplar: its Importance for Europe, Technical Assistance Mission* No. 13.

——. (1952), *American Sylviculture and Tropical Forest Problems, Technical Assistance Mission* No. 18A (1952).

——. (1952), *Diseases of the Chestnuts and Poplar in Europe, Technical Assistance Mission* No. 29.

——. (1952), *Statistiques des produits forestiers dans les pays membres de l'OECE /Statistics of Forest Products in OEEC countries.*

——. (1952), *Timber: American Forest Operations and Increase of European Productivity, Technical Assistance Mission* No. 18 pt. 1.

——. (1952), *Ecology of American Forest Species: Erosion and Reafforestation, Technical Assistance Mission* No. 18 pt. 2.

——. (1953), *Nomenclature of Timber Associations and Technical Publications.*

——. (1953), *The Timber Industries in the USA, Technical Assistance Mission* No. 59A-B, 4 vol.

——. (1953), *Timber and the Furniture Industry, The Timber Industries in the USA:* vol. 1., *Technical Assistance Mission* No. 59A.

——. (1953), *Timber and the Building Industry, The Timber Industries in the USA:* vol. 2., *Technical Assistance Mission* No. 59A.

——. (1953), *Woodware, The Timber Industries in the USA:* vol. 3, *Technical Assistance Mission* No. 59B.

——. (1953), *The treatment and Preservation of Timber, The Timber Industries in the USA:* vol. 4, *Technical Assistance Mission* No. 59B.

——. (1953), *Tropical Timber: Production and Consumption Prospects.*

——. (1954), *Productivité dans l'industrie de la forêt et du bois, Mission d'assistance technique* n° 132. (available only in French and German.)

——. (1954-1956), *Timber Industry in Europe, Trends in economic sectors.* (Replaced by, Timber Statistics from 1957.)

——. (1957), *Wood Research in Europe, Technical Assistance Mission* No. 242.

OEEC/OECD (1957-1965), *Timber Statistics.*

OEEC/OECD (1957-1969), *Statistics on Tropical Timber.*

OEEC (1958), *Laminated Timber.*

——. (1959), *Plant Health Regulations Governing International Trade in Forest Products.*

——. (1951), *Les peupliers américains : leurs importance pour l'Europe, Mission d'assistance technique* n° 13.

——. (1952), *Sylviculture américaine et problèmes forestiers tropicaux, Mission d'assistance technique* n° 18A (1952).

——. (1952), *Les maladies du chataîgnier et du peuplier en Europe, Mission d'assistance technique* n° 29.

——. (1952), *Statistiques des produits forestiers dans les pays membres de l'OECE/Statistics of Forest Products in OEEC countries.*

——. (1952), *Le bois : méthodes de production américaines et accroissement de la productivité européenne, Mission d'assistance technique* n° 18 pt. 1.

——. (1952), *Ecologie des essences forestières américaines : érosion et reboisement, Mission d'assistance technique* n° 18 pt. 2.

——. (1953), *Nomenclature des associations et publications techniques du bois.*

——. (1953), *Les industries du bois aux USA, Mission d'assistance technique* n° 59A-B, 4 vol.

——. (1953), *Bois dans l'ameublement, Les industries du bois aux USA :* Vol. 1., *Mission d'assistance technique* n° 59A.

——. (1953), *Bois dans la construction, Les industries du bois aux USA :* vol. 2., *Mission d'assistance technique* n° 59A.

——. (1953), *Boissellerie, Les industries du bois aux USA :* vol. 3, *Mission d'assistance technique* n° 59B.

——. (1953), *Traitement et préservation du bois, Les industries du bois aux USA :* vol. 4, *Mission d'assistance technique* n° 59B.

——. (1953), *Bois tropicaux : perspectives de production et de consommation.*

——. (1954), *Productivité dans l'industrie de la forêt et du bois, Mission d'assistance technique* n° 132. (édition française et allemande.)

——. (1954-1956), *Industrie du bois en Europe, Situation dans les secteurs économiques.* (Remplacé par Statistiques du bois de 1957.)

——. (1957), *Recherche sur le bois en Europe, Mission d'assistance technique* n° 242.

OECE/OCDE (1957-1965), *Statistiques du bois.*

OECE/OCDE (1957-1969), *Statistiques des bois tropicaux.*

OECE (1956), *Bois lamellés.*

——. (1959), *Réglementations phytosanitaires appliquées dans les échanges internationaux de produits forestiers.*

6.3.6 Textiles

Set up on 22 May 1948, the **Textiles Committee** dealt with questions relating to animal and vegetable textile fibres, artificial and synthetic fibres and yarn, semi-manufactured articles and manufactured textile products. It monitored developments in the European textile industry and published an annual report, as well as detailed statistics on textile production, consumption and trade. It concerned itself with the distribution of Marshall Plan aid, raw material supplies, structural problems, imports from Asian countries, statistics on distribution of textile products, trends in consumption of textile fibres (International Advisory Committee for Cotton and FAO) and ways of promoting productivity in the textile industry (in co-operation with the EPA). It set up the following *Working Parties:*

- No. 1 *Flax and Hemp*
- No. 2 *Hard Fibres*
- No. 3 *Wool*
- No. 4 *Artificial Fibres*
- No. 5 *Cotton*
- No. 6 *Productivity*
- No. 7 *Statistics*
- No. 11 *Liberalisation of Trade in Flax*
- No. 12 *Liberalisation of Trade in Printed Fabrics*
- No. 13 *Liberalisation of Trade in Synthetic Fibres*
- No. 14 *Liberalisation of Trade in Jute*
- No. 15 *Preparation of the Situation Report*

Publications:

OEEC (1952), *Situation of the Textile Machinery Industry in Member Countries in 1950.*
___. (1953-1955), *European Textile Industry, Trends in Economic Sectors, 1953.* (Replaced by, Textile Industry in Europe from 1955-1960.)

OEEC/OECE (1955-1960), *Textile Industry in Europe/ Industrie textile en Europe.* (Published by OECD (1962-1982) under ''Textile Industry in OECD Countries/Industrie textile dans les Pays de l'OCDE''.)

TORNQVIST, G. (1957), *Distribution Problems in Textiles.*

OEEC (1957), *Future of the European Cotton Industry.*

Problèmes de distribution et de marketing des articles textiles (1958, Turin) (1958), *Compte rendu sommaire,* OEEC, Paris. (available only in French)

MOUGIN, G. (1960), *Working Conditions in the European Textile Industry.*

6.3.6 Textiles

Créé le 22 mai 1948, le **Comité des textiles** s'est occupé de fibres textiles animales et végétales, de fibres et fils artificiels et synthétiques, d'articles semi-manufacturés et de produits textiles manufacturés. Il a suivi l'évolution de l'industrie textile européenne et a publié un rapport annuel ainsi que des statistiques détaillées sur la production, la consommation et les échanges de produits textiles. Il a examiné la répartition de l'aide du Plan Marshall, l'approvisionnement en matières premières, les problèmes de structure, les importations en provenance des pays asiatiques, les statistiques de distribution des produits textiles, l'évolution de la consommation de fibres textiles (Comité consultatif international du coton et FAO) et les moyens de promouvoir la productivité dans l'industrie textile (en coopération avec l'AEP). Il a constitué les *groupes de travail* sur les questions suivantes :

- n° 1 *lin et chanvre*
- n° 2 *fibres dures*
- n° 3 *laine*
- n° 4 *fibres artificielles et synthétiques*
- n° 5 *coton*
- n° 6 *productivité*
- n° 7 *statistiques*
- n° 11 *libération des échanges-lin*
- n° 12 *libération des échanges-tissus imprimés*
- n° 13 *libération des échanges-fibres synthétiques*
- n° 14 *libération des échanges-jute*
- n° 15 *préparation du Rapport de conjoncture*

Publications :

OECE (1952), *Situation de l'industrie des machines textiles dans les pays membres en 1950.*
___. (1953-1955), *Industrie textile européenne, Situation dans les secteurs économiques, 1953.* (Remplacé par, Industrie textile en Europe de 1955-1960.)

OEEC/OECE (1955-1960), *Textile Industry in Europe/ Industrie textile en Europe.* (Publié par l'OCDE (1962-1982 sous « Textile Industry in OECD Countries/ Industrie textile dans les Pays de l'OCDE ».)

TORNQVIST, G. (1957), *Problèmes de la distribution des textiles.*

OECE (1957), *Avenir de l'industrie cotonnière européenne.*

Problèmes de distribution et de marketing des articles textiles (1958, Turin) (1958), *Compte rendu sommaire,* OECE, Paris.

MOUGIN, G. (1960), *Conditions de travail dans l'industrie textile européenne.*

6.3.7 Pulp and Paper

The **Pulp and Paper Committee,** set up on 22 May 1948, dealt with: miscellaneous pulp, including textile pulp and other fibres used in the manufacture of paper and paper-board; paper, paper-board, and paper or paper-board articles, excluding printed matter and other graphic art products. Its half-yearly and yearly statistics on developments in the European pulp and paper market gave the official figures for production, consumption and trade in Member countries and in Finland; the latter country was represented at meetings as an observer, as were the secretariats of the FAO and the ECE. Its studies focused on: problems connected with raw material supplies (wood and pulp); inter-enterprise productivity measurement; trends in production capacity and utilisation; production of fibreboard. In association with the EPA it promoted the dispatch of task forces to the United States to study fruit and vegetable packaging. It set up the following *Working Parties:*

- *No. 1 To study the Negative List of Wallboards*
- *No. 2 To draft a Report on the Structure and Trend of Wallboard Production in Europe*

Publications:

OEEC (1951), *Pulp and Paper Industry in the USA.*

___. (1954), *Pulp and Paper Industry in Europe : Development and Prospects.*

___. (1955-1956), *Six-Monthly Statistics for Pulp and Paper.*

___. (1955-1959), *Pulp and Paper Statistics.*

___. (1957), *Pulp and Paper Industry in Europe : Its Trend from 1950 to 1955: Its Future Prospects.*

OEEC/OECD (1959-1985), *Pulp and Paper.*

6.3.8 Miscellaneous Products (Cement)

The **Miscellaneous Products Committee** was dissolved on 20 May 1952 but its Working Party on Cement remained active. The latter produced a yearly report on developments in the cement industry, forecasts for its short-term development and the investments needed, and forecasts for Member countries' exports and extra-European exports.

Publications:

OEEC/OECD (1954-1973), *Cement Industry in Europe.*

6.3.9 Hides and Skins

Set up by Resolution of the Council on 13 May 1955, the **Hides and Skins Committee** dealt with questions

6.3.7 Pâtes et papiers

Créé le 22 mai 1948, le **Comité des pâtes et papiers** traitait des pâtes diverses, y compris les pâtes textiles et autres matières fibreuses servant à la fabrication des papiers, cartons et articles en papier ou carton, sauf les produits des arts graphiques. Ses statistiques semestrielles et annuelles sur l'évolution du marché européen des pâtes et papiers ont fourni les chiffres officiels de production, de consommation et des échanges des pays Membres et de la Finlande ; ce dernier pays assistant aux réunions à titre d'observateur, comme l'ont fait les secrétariats de la FAO et de la CEE/ONU. Ses études portèrent sur : les problèmes d'approvisionnements en matières premières (bois et pâtes) ; la mesure inter-entreprise de la productivité ; l'évolution et l'utilisation des capacités de production; les panneaux de fibres. En liaison avec l'AEP, il a favorisé l'envoi de missions aux États-Unis pour étudier l'emballage des fruits et légumes. Il a créé les *groupes de travail* suivants :

- *n° 1 pour examiner la liste négative des panneaux de revêtement*
- *n° 2 pour établir un rapport sur la structure et l'évolution des panneaux de revêtements en Europe*

Publications :

OECE (1952), *Industrie des pâtes et papiers aux USA.*

___. (1954), *Industrie des pâtes et papiers en Europe : Évolution et perspectives.*

___. (1955-1956), *Statistiques semestrielles des pâtes et papiers.*

___. (1955-1959), *Statistiques des pâtes et papiers.*

___. (1957), *Industries des pâtes et papiers en Europe, son évolution de 1950 à 1955, ses perspectives d'avenir.*

OECE/OCDE (1959-1985), *Pâtes et papiers.*

6.3.8 Produits divers (ciment)

Le **Comité des matériaux et produits divers** a été supprimé le 20 mai 1952. Son Groupe de travail sur le ciment est toutefois demeuré actif. Celui-ci préparait un rapport annuel sur l'évolution de l'industrie, les prévisions sur son développement à court terme et les investissements nécessaires, ainsi que sur les exportations des pays Membres, et hors d'Europe.

Publications :

OECE/OCDE (1954-1973), *Industrie du ciment en Europe.*

6.3.9 Cuirs et peaux

Créé par Résolution du Conseil du 13 mai 1955, le **Comité des cuirs et peaux** traitait des questions de

relating to hides and skins, leather, footwear and other leather articles and furs. In addition to publishing yearly statistical reports, it produced two reports (1955 and 1959) on supply and demand trends and the structure of the European tanning and footwear industries. It studied distribution in the footwear sector, trade problems such as export restrictions, manpower problems in the tanning and footwear industries and the improvement of skin quality. It promoted meetings of principals of specialised schools in the Member countries and contacts between tanners and footwear manufacturers and distributors.

It set up the following *Working Parties:*
- *No. 1 Productivity*
- *No. 2 Preparation of the Annual Report*
- *No. 3 Improvement of Skins*

It assigned the preparation of specific segments of the annual review to the following *Working Groups:*

- *Raw Materials*
- *Tanning*
- *Footwear*

Publications:

OEEC/OECD (1955-1959), *Hides and Skins Industry in Europe.*

OEEC (1958), *Distribution in the Footwear Trade in Europe.*

___. (1960), *Vocational Training in the Footwear Industry.*

6.4 Transport

6.4.1 Inland Transport

The **Inland Transport Committee,** set up on 11 May 1948, studied the problems of rebuilding transport systems destroyed or damaged by the war. From the outset it concerned itself with distributing Marshall Plan aid and establishing schedules for dollar-billed imports of transport equipment. Subsequently it carried out technical and economic studies. To ensure better co-ordination of the different transport modes it seemed preferable to replace this committee, composed of government experts, by a Committee of Ministers [(see Section 11: European Conference of Ministers of Transport (ECMT)].

It set up the following *Working Parties:*

- *No. 1 Rail Tariffs*
- *No. 2 Motor Vehicle Industry*
- *No. 3 Electrification of Railways*
- *No. 5 Sleeping Cars*

cuirs et peaux bruts et tannés, de pelleterie, de chaussures et autres produits manufacturés en cuir et de fourrures. Outre la publication de rapports statistiques annuels, il a préparé deux rapports (1955 et 1959) sur l'évolution de l'offre et de la demande et sur la structure des industries européénnes de la tannerie et de la chaussure. Il a étudié la distribution dans le secteur de la chaussure, les problèmes d'échange tels les restrictions à l'exportation, les problèmes de main d'œuvre dans les industries de la tannerie et de la chaussure, l'amélioration de la qualité des peaux. Il a favorisé les rencontres de directeurs d'écoles spécialisées des pays Membres et les contacts entre tanneurs, industriels de la chaussure et distributeurs.

Il a créé les *groupes de travail :*
- *n° 1 productivité*
- *n° 2 élaboration du rapport annuel*
- *n° 3 amélioration de la qualité des cuirs et peaux bruts*

Il a confié la préparation d'aspects de l'examen annuel à des *groupes de travail :*
- *matières premières*
- *tannerie*
- *chaussures*

Publications :

OECE/OCDE (1955-1959), *Industrie des cuirs et peaux en Europe.*

OECE (1958), *Distribution dans le secteur de la chaussure en Europe.*

___. (1960), *Formation professionnelle dans l'industrie de la chaussure.*

6.4 Transports

6.4.1 Transports intérieurs

Créé le 11 mai 1948, le **Comité des transports intérieurs** a étudié les problèmes de reconstruction des systèmes de transport détruits ou endommagés par la guerre. Il s'est attaché, dès l'origine, à distribuer l'aide du Plan Marshall et à mettre en œuvre des programmes d'importation de matériel de transport payable en dollars. Il a ultérieurement entrepris des études techniques et économiques. Pour assurer une meilleure coordination des différents moyens de transport, il a semblé préférable de remplacer ce Comité, composé d'experts gouvernementaux, par un Comité des ministres [voir section 11 : Conférence européenne des Ministres des transports (CEMT)].

Il a créé des *groupes de travail* pour les domaines suivants:

- *n° 1 tarifs ferroviaires*
- *n° 2 industrie automobile*
- *n° 3 électrification des chemins de fer*
- *n° 5 wagons-lits*

– *No. 6 Follow-up to the Report of Mission No. 17 (Cold Chain)*
– *No. 7 Integration of Rolling Stock and Productivity*

Publications:

OEEC (1952), *Cold Chain in the USA, Technical Assistance Mission* No. 17, 2 vol.

___. (1952), *Railroads in the USA, Technical Assistance Mission* No. 14.

European Inland Transport Conference (Paris, 1953) (1953), Report, OEEC, Paris.

OEEC (1953), Federal Regulation of Transport in the USA: How Transport Problems are Solved in a System of Federal States, Technical Assistance Mission No. 103.

___. (1953), *Material Handling Equipment and Methods in the USA, Technical Assistance Mission* No. 42.

___. (1954), *Repercussions in the Field of Transport of the Programme of Economic Expansion.*

Eurofima (Société Européenne pour le financement de matériel ferroviaire) (1955), *Actes constitutifs : Berne, 20 Octobre 1955,* OECE, Paris. (available in French, Italian and German)

6.4.2 Shipping

Set up on 11 May 1948, the **Maritime Transport Committee** was instructed, within the context of the Marshall Plan, to advise the Council on all shipping questions and, especially, to assess Europe's shipping requirements. The Committee undertook, *vis-à-vis* the US Administration, to ensure compliance with Section 111(*a*)2 of the Economic Co-operation Act which required that at least 50 per cent of the commodities procured in the United States with funds of the European Recovery Programme should be shipped in United States flag ships. In the discharge of its mandate the Committee met every month as from May 1948. Its meetings also covered the other problems connected with maritime transport.

The policy of the Member countries was based on the principle of circulation of shipping in free and fair competition. The Committee periodically examined all cases of discriminatory practices and endeavoured to eliminate them through concerted action. It produced an annual report on the general situation and developments in maritime transport, discussed such questions as flag discrimination and registration under flag of convenience and, in co-operation with the Coal and Oil Committees, kept the freight market under review. It set up a *Steering Group,* an *Ad Hoc Working Party on Coastal Shipping,* a joint working party with the Tourism Committee, and the following *Working Parties:*

– *n° 6 examen des suites à donner au Rapport de la Mission n° 17 (chaîne du froid)*
– *n° 7 intégration du matériel roulant et productivité*

Publications :

OECE (1952), *Chaîne du froid aux États-Unis, Mission d'assistance technique* n° 17, 2 vol.

___. (1952), *Chemins de fer aux USA, Mission d'assistance technique* n° 14.

Conférence sur les transports intérieurs européens (Paris, 1953) (1953), Rapport, OECE, Paris.

OECE (1953), Réglementation fédérale des transports aux USA : problèmes et solutions dans une fédération d'états, Mission d'assistance technique n° 103.

___. (1953), *Matériel et méthodes de manutention aux USA, Mission d'assistance technique* n° 42.

___. (1954), *Répercussions dans le domaine des transports du programme d'expansion économique.*

Eurofima (Société Européenne pour le financement de matériel ferroviaire) (1955), *Actes constitutifs : Berne, 20 Octobre 1955,* OECE, Paris. (édition trilingue français, italien, allemand)

6.4.2 Transports maritimes

Créé le 11 mai 1948, le **Comité des transports maritimes** a été chargé, dans le cadre du plan Marshall, d'aviser le Conseil sur toutes les questions relevant de ce secteur, et surtout d'en évaluer les besoins. Le Comité s'est engagé vis-à-vis de l'administration américaine à surveiller l'application de la Section 111(*a*)2 de la Loi de coopération économique qui prévoyait que 50 % au moins des marchandises fournies au moyen de fonds du Programme de relèvement européen devait être transporté par des navires battant pavillon des États-Unis. Pour s'acquitter de son mandat, le Comité a tenu, à partir de mai 1948, des réunions tous les mois. Celles-ci portaient également sur les autres problèmes liés aux transports maritimes.

La politique des pays Membres se fondait sur le principe de la circulation sous un régime de libre concurrence des navires effectuant des transports internationaux. Le Comité examinait périodiquement tous les cas de pratiques discriminatoires et s'efforçait de les éliminer par une action concertée. Il préparait un rapport annuel sur la situation générale et le développement des transports maritimes, discutait de questions telles les privilèges de pavillon et d'immatriculation sous pavillon de complaisance, et surveillait en coopération avec les Comités du charbon et du pétrole la situation du marché des frêts. Il a constitué un *Groupe de travail (Groupe de direction),* un *groupe de travail « ad hoc » sur la question du cabotage,* mixte avec le Comité de tourisme, et les *groupes de travail* suivants :

– *No. 1 Compliance with Section 111(a)2 of the Economic Co-operation Act*
– *No. 2 General*
– *No. 3 Productivity*

Publications:

OEEC/OECD (1954-), *Maritime Transport.*

___. (1959), *Story of the Maritime Transport Committee of the OEEC 1947-1959.*

___. (1961), *Pipelines and Tankers: Report on the Effect of the Use of Pipelines on the Transport of Oil by Tankers.*

6.5 Tourism

The **Tourism Committee,** a plenary body, was set up in March 1949 to study the possibilities of the ''expansion of tourism within the framework of the European Recovery Programme, particularly with a view to increasing the dollar resources of Member countries''. Having initially concerned itself with the ways and means of attracting American tourists to Europe (transport, abolition of visas, customs facilities, publicity), the Committee turned to intra-European tourism and proposed measures to facilitate its development: abolition of visas, duty-free facilities, increased foreign currency allowances for tourists.

To assist it in its work, it set up the following *Working Parties:*

– *No. 1 Dealing with Questions of Investment in the Hotel Industry*
– *No. 2 Dealing with Staggering of Holidays in liaison with Manpower and Social Tourism*
– *No. 3 To study certain Customs Facilities to encourage Tourism*
– *No. 4 To study Economic and Financial questions in the field of Tourism*
– *No. 5 Technical Assistance*
– *No. 6 To study the Committee's Programme*
– *Ad Hoc: To study Visas and Passports*
– *Customs Experts*
– *Tourist Statistics*
– *Social Tourism*
– *Ad Hoc: Transport Problems*
– *Ad Hoc: Standardization of National Registration Cards for Motor Vehicles*

Publications:

OEEC (1951), *Hotel Industry in the USA.*

___. (1951), *Tourism and European Recovery.*

___. (1955-1961), *Tourism in Europe.*

6.6 Manpower

Set up on 30 June 1948, the **Manpower Committee,** one of the ''Horizontal Committees'', was instructed to promote the fullest and most effective use of available manpower (Preamble and Article 8 of the Convention of

– *n° 1 mise en application de la Section 111(a)2 de la Loi de coopération économique*
– *n° 2 toutes questions*
– *n° 3 productivité*

Publications :

OECE/OCDE (1954-), *Transports Maritimes.*

___. (1959), *Story of the Maritime Transport Committee of the OEEC 1947-1959.*

___. (1961), *Oléoducs et pétroliers : rapport sur l'incidence de l'utilisation des oléoducs sur les transports maritimes pétroliers.*

6.5 Tourisme

Le **Comité du tourisme,** comité plénier, fut créé en mars 1949 pour étudier les possibilités «de développement du tourisme dans le cadre du programme de relèvement européen notamment en vue d'accroître les ressources en dollar des pays Membres». Après s'être intéressé aux problèmes relatifs aux touristes d'Amérique du Nord (transport, suppression des visas, facilités douanières, publicité), le Comité a discuté des questions de tourisme intra-européen. A cet effet, il a fait adopter des mesures destinées à faciliter son développement: suppression des visas, franchises douanières, relèvement des allocations touristiques de devises.

Pour l'aider dans ses travaux, il a constitué les *groupes de travail* pour les questions suivantes:

– *n° 1 étude des questions d'investissements dans l'industrie hôtelière*
– *n° 2 problèmes d'étalement des vacances en liaison avec la main d'œuvre et le tourisme social*
– *n° 3 étude de certaines mesures de tolérance douanière en faveur du tourisme*
– *n° 4 étude des questions économiques et financières dans le domaine du tourisme*
– *n° 5 assistance technique*
– *n° 6 étude du programme du Comité*
– *ad hoc, étude des visas et passeports*
– *experts douaniers*
– *statistiques touristiques*
– *tourisme social*
– *ad hoc, problèmes de transport*
– *ad hoc, uniformisation des cartes d'immatriculation nationales des véhicules automobiles*

Publications :

OECE (1951), *Industrie hôtelière aux États-Unis.*

___. (1951), *Tourisme et relèvement de l'Europe.*

___. (1955-1961), *Tourisme en Europe.*

6.6 Main-d'œuvre

Créé le 30 juin 1948, le **Comité de la main-d'œuvre,** comité horizontal, était chargé de promouvoir l'utilisation la plus complète et la plus rationnelle de la main-d'œuvre disponible (préambule et art. 8 Convention

the OEEC). It accordingly took steps to improve the functioning of employment and vocational training services in each of the Member countries and to remove the obstacles to the free movement of workers across national borders. In the latter connection, it supervised the application of the Council Decision of October 1953 relating to the employment of nationals of Member countries and drew up Recommendations designed to simplify and harmonize the administrative regulations pertaining to entry, employment and residence of workers and their families. Alerted by the Sub-Committee for Scientific Research to the critical shortage of highly qualified scientists and engineers, it carried out two surveys on the question.

Representatives of the labour ministries of Member countries attended its meetings and, with observer status, representatives of the International Labour Office, the Council of Europe, the ECSC, the EEC, the Inter-Governmental Committee for European Migration and the Office of the United Nations High Commissioner for Refugees. It reviewed the annual labour market situation in Member countries and carried out occasional studies. The Committee set up the following *Working Parties* and *Groups:*

- *No. 1 To draw up the Committee's Revised 49-50 Programme*
- *No. 2 Emigration Statistics*
- *No. 3 Work of the ILO concerning Migration*
- *No. 4 Manpower Statistics*
- *No. 5 Adult Vocational Training*
- *No. 6 Availabilities and Utilisation of Skilled Manpower; Organisation of Employment Services*
- *Administrative Practices*
- *Manpower Liberalisation*

Finally, the **Joint Consultative Group on Manpower Utilisation,** set up by the Council in 1953, comprised representatives of the employers' organisations and trade unions recognised by the OEEC (Trade Union Advisory Committee and Council of European Industrial Federations). It advised the Manpower Committee on the main points in its programme of activities.

Publications:

The Manpower Conference (1948, Rome) (1948), *Reports [by the] Committee of European Economic Co-Operation,* HMSO, London.

European Productivity Agency (1984), *Labour Force Statistics: Sample Survey Methods.*

OEEC (1955), *Shortages and Surpluses of Highly Qualified Scientists and Engineers in Western Europe.*

——. (1957), *Problem of Scientific and Technical Manpower in Western Europe, Canada and the United States.*

OECE). A cet effet, il a pris des mesures visant à améliorer le fonctionnement des services de l'emploi et la formation professionnelle dans chacun des pays Membres et à lever les obstacles qui entravaient la libre circulation de la main-d'œuvre d'un pays à l'autre. Dans ce dernier cas, il a contrôlé l'application de la décision qui, depuis octobre 1953, régissait l'emploi des ressortissants des pays Membres et a préparé des Recommandations visant à simplifier et à harmoniser les procédures administratives qui régissaient l'introduction, l'emploi et le séjour des travailleurs et de leurs familles. Alerté par le Sous-comité de la recherche scientifique du caractère urgent de la pénurie de personnel scientifique et technique hautement qualifié, il effectua deux enquêtes sur la question.

Les représentants des ministères du travail des pays Membres assistaient à ses réunions et, en tant qu'observateur, les représentants du Bureau international du travail, du Conseil de l'Europe, de la CECA, de la CEE, du Comité intergouvernemental pour les migrations européennes et du Haut commissariat pour les réfugiés. Il a étudié la situation annuelle du marché de travail dans les pays Membres et effectué des enquêtes occasionnelles. De ce Comité ont dépendu les *groupes de travail* suivants :

- *n° 1 pour établir le programme révisé 49-50 du Comité*
- *n° 2 statistiques d'émigration*
- *n° 3 travail de l'OIT relatif aux migrations*
- *n° 4 statistiques de main-d'œuvre*
- *n° 5 formation professionnelle des adultes*
- *n° 6 disponibilité et utilisation de la main-d'œuvre qualifiée; organisation des services de l'emploi*
- *pratiques administratives*
- *libération de la main-d'œuvre*

Enfin, le **Groupe consultatif mixte sur l'utilisation de la main-d'œuvre,** créé par le Conseil en 1953, comprenait des représentants des organisations patronales et syndicales accréditées auprès de l'OECE (Commission consultative syndicale et Conseil des fédérations industrielles d'Europe). Il avisait le Comité de la main-d'œuvre sur les principaux points de son programme d'activités.

Publications :

La conférence de la main-d'œuvre (1948, Rome) (1948), *Rapports [du] Comité de coopération économique européenne,* Imprimerie Nationale, Paris.

Agence Européenne de Productivité (1948), *Statistiques de Main-d'œuvre : méthodes d'enquête par sondage.*

OECE (1955), *Pénuries et excédents de personnel scientifique et technique hautement qualifié dans les pays de l'OECE.*

——. (1957), *Problèmes du personnel scientifique et technique en Europe occidentale, aux États-Unis et au Canada.*

6.7 Productivity and Applied Research

The general policy of economic recovery needed to be completed by a whole range of measures designed to stimulate productivity in most sectors. The Committee for Scientific and Technical Matters was established on 26 February 1951 together with a set of sub-committees that were later replaced by the Advisory Sub-Committee for Increasing Productivity through Standardization and subsequently, when the EPA was formed, by the Productivity and Applied Research Committee. Given in particular a climate of psychological resistance to technical change and the traditional fear of productivity growth as a cause of unemployment, the OEEC decided to entrust the task of promoting productivity to an operational body. In May 1953 the Council set up the European Productivity Agency (EPA) (see Section 8), which would interact more directly with industrial and agricultural circles, and with the public.

Publications:

OECE/OEEC (1950), *Terminologie de la productivité/ Terminology of Productivity.*

OEEC (1951), *Documentation Techniques in the United-States, Technical Assistance Mission* No. 40.

___. (1952), *Cost Accounting and Productivity : the Use and Practice and Cost Accounting in the USA: report, Technical Assistance Mission* No. 50.

___. (1952), *Fire Prevention and Control, Technical Assistance Mission* No. 67.

___. (1952), *Measurement of Productivity: Methods Used by the Bureau of Labour Statistics in the USA, Technical Assistance Mission* No. 7, 10, 11.

7. Food and Agriculture

The **Ministerial Committee for Agriculture and Food** replaced, by Decision of the Council of 14 January 1955, the Food and Agriculture Committee set up in 1948. By this decision the OEEC took on the activities of the European Conference on the Organisation of Agricultural Markets (''Green Pool''). The Ministerial Committee's essential function was to examine the farming and food situation in the Member countries, together with the agricultural implications of more general problems and of the possible solutions studied by the Organisation. It agreed on measures to be taken by the participating ministers within the limits of their competence, and when decisions binding on governments were required it submitted proposals to the Council. The Committee's major tasks included the confrontation of agricultural policies of the Member countries and the Associated countries (Spain 1955-1959 and Yugoslavia 1955-1961) and the development of productivity and application of modern techniques in agriculture. It set up the following *Working Parties:*

6.7 Productivité et recherche appliquée

Une politique générale de redressement économique se devait d'être utilement complétée par tout un ensemble de mesures destinées à stimuler la productivité dans la plupart des secteurs. Un Comité des questions scientifiques et techniques a été créé le 26 février 1951 ainsi qu'un ensemble de sous-comités qui furent remplacés par le Groupe consultatif pour l'augmentation de la productivité par la normalisation, puis, lors de la création de l'AEP, par le Comité de la Productivité et de la Recherche appliquée. Face notamment à une opposition d'ordre psychologique au changement technique et à la crainte traditionnelle que l'accroissement de la productivité ne conduise au chômage, l'OECE décida de confier la tâche de promouvoir la productivité à un organe opérationnel. Le Conseil créa en mai 1953 l'Agence européenne de productivité (AEP) (voir section 8) qui allait agir par des voies plus directes sur les milieux industriels, agricoles et sur le public.

Publications :

OECE/OEEC (1950), *Terminologie de la productivité/ Terminology of Productivity.*

OECE (1951), *Les techniques de documentation aux États-Unis, Mission d'assistance technique* n° 40.

___. (1952), *Comptabilité industrielle et productivité, le rôle de la comptabilité industrielle aux USA : rapport, Mission d'assistance technique* n° 50.

___. (1952), *Prévention et contrôle de l'incendie, Mission d'assistance technique* n° 67.

___. (1952), *Mesure de la productivité : méthodes pratiquées par le Bureau des statistiques du travail aux USA, Mission d'assistance technique* n° 7, 10, 11.

7. Alimentation et agriculture

Le **Comité ministériel de l'agriculture et de l'alimentation** a succédé, par Décision du Conseil du 14 janvier 1955, au Comité de l'agriculture et de l'alimentation créé en 1948. L'OECE acquérait alors les activités de la Conférence européenne de l'Organisation des marchés agricoles («Pool vert»). Le Comité ministériel avait pour fonction d'examiner la situation agricole et alimentaire des pays Membres et l'incidence des questions et des projets d'ordre général étudiés par l'Organisation pour règler ces problèmes. Il convint de mesures à prendre par les ministres participants, dans la limite de leurs compétences et lorsque les décisions engageant les gouvernements devaient être prises, il soumettait des propositions au Conseil. Une des tâches majeures du Comité fut la confrontation des politiques agricoles des pays Membres et Associés (Espagne 1955-1959 et Yougoslavie 1955-1961), le développement de la productivité et l'application des techniques modernes dans l'agriculture. Il a créé les *Groupes de travail :*

- *Joint: Fertilisers*
- *Ad Hoc: Confrontation of Agricultural Policies*
- *Ad Hoc: Productivity*
- *Agricultural Statistics*
- *Ad Hoc: Cereals*

Set up by the same Decision of the Council on 14 January 1955, the **Committee of Deputies for Agriculture and Food** implemented the directives of the Ministerial Committee. It set up the following *Ad Hoc Working Parties:*

- *No. 1 Confrontation of Agricultural Policies*
- *No. 2 Productivity*
- *No. 3 Agricultural Statistics*
- *No. 4 Fruit and Vegetables*
- *No. 5 Meat*
- *No. 6 Dairy Products*
- *No. 7 Cereals*
- *No. 8 Fish*
- *No. 9 Industrial Crops*
- *No. 10 Farm Management*
- *No. 11 Fertilisers*
- *No. 12 Farm Machinery*

Publications:

OEEC (1951-1960), *Fertilizers.* (Replaced by Fertilizers in Europe, from 1961.)

___. (1956-1961), *Agricultural Policies in Europe and North America,* report No. 1-5.

International Dairy Conference (1960, Paris) (1960), *Summary Report, EPA Project* No. 6/11-IIB.

OEEC (1960), *Fishery Policies in Western Europe and North America.*

___. (1960), *Market for Apples and Pears During the Last Few Years: Provisional Data on the 1960-61 Season.*

___. (1961-1962), *Fertilizers in Europe.* (Replaced by Fertilizers/Engrais from 1963.)

___. (1961), *Agriculture, 1961: Production and Consumption Figures.*

8. European Productivity Agency

The European Productivity Agency (EPA) was an international body working within the framework of the OEEC. Set up by the OEEC Council on 24 March 1953, the Agency acted, first, as a clearing house to provide to newly created national productivity centres and, where appropriate, international professional assocations with information and other services to help them in their work and, second, as a centre for study and discussion to guide European efforts towards greater productivity. To stimulate the productivity drive in Member countries it used a wide range of methods (missions, expert

- *mixte sur les engrais*
- *ad hoc sur la confrontation des politiques agricoles*
- *ad hoc sur la productivité*
- *sur les statistiques agricoles*
- *ad hoc sur les céréales*

Institué par la même Décision du Conseil du 14 janvier 1955, le **Comité des suppléants des ministres de l'agriculture et de l'alimentation** mettait en œuvre les directives du Comité ministériel. Il a créé des *groupes de travail ad hoc:*

- *n° 1 confrontation des politiques agricoles*
- *n° 2 productivité*
- *n° 3 statistiques agricoles*
- *n° 4 fruits et légumes*
- *n° 5 viande*
- *n° 6 produits laitiers*
- *n° 7 céréales*
- *n° 8 poisson*
- *n° 9 cultures industrielles*
- *n° 10 gestion-exploitation*
- *n° 11 engrais*
- *n° 12 machinisme agricole*

Publications :

OECE (1951-1960), *Les engrais.* (Remplacé par Les engrais en Europe à compter de 1961.)

___. (1956-1961), *Les politiques agricoles en Europe et en Amérique du Nord,* rapport n° 1-5.

Conférence internationale sur les questions laitières (1960, Paris) (1960), *Compte rendu, Projet AEP* n° 6/11-IIB.

OECE (1960), *Politiques de pêche en Europe et en Amérique du Nord.*

___. (1960), *Market for Apples and Pears During the Last Few Years: Provisional Data on the 1960-61 Season.* (disponible seulement en anglais)

___. (1961-1962), *Engrais en Europe.* (Remplacé par Fertilizers/Engrais à compter de 1963.)

___. (1961), *Agriculture, 1961 : chiffres de production et de consommation.*

8. Agence européenne de productivité

L'Agence européenne de productivité (AEP) fut un organisme international dont l'activité s'est insérée dans le cadre de l'OECE. Créée par le Conseil de l'OECE le 24 mars 1953, l'AEP a joué le rôle, en premier lieu, d'un centre d'échange conçu en vue de fournir aux organismes nationaux de productivité, nouvellement créés, et, le cas échéant, aux organismes professionnels internationaux des informations et des services leur permettant de mieux diriger leur propre mission et, en second lieu, d'un centre d'études et de discussions, conçu en vue d'orienter les efforts qui tendaient à promouvoir

consultancy services, international study courses, conferences, publications, etc.) reflected in specific projects.

These projects originated either in a Member country, or in the Agency's Directorate, or even in an OEEC committee which might be said to have "placed an order" with the Agency for action it considered useful. From 1957, project implementation had basically to be approved at two levels: a majority vote of the **Governing Body** and a declaration of participation or interest from a specified minimum number of countries.

8.1 Structure and Working Procedure

When the EPA was set up, the Council instructed the **Productivity and Applied Research Committee** to supervise the Agency, fix its rules and methods of work, approve projects of medium importance and keep under review the activities of the Agency's Director, whom it guided by means of directives. The following *Working Parties* were set up:

- *No. 1 Intergovernmental Document Exchanges and International Service for Technical Information*
- *No. 2 Intergovernmental Document Exchanges and Auxiliary Audio-Visual Services*

A number of Sub-Committees were formed, which in turn set up working parties:

The *Sub-Committee for Co-operation in Scientific Research* **(GR),** which later became the **Committee for Applied Research,** set up the following *Working Parties:*

- *No. 1 Long-Distance Transport of Gas*
- *No. 2 To study the Use of Wind Power*
- *No. 3 Gasification of Solid Fuels*
- *No. 4 To study the Manufacture of Phosphate Fertilisers without Sulphuric Acid*
- *No. 5 To study the Mixture of Man-Made Fibres with Wool*
- *No. 6 New Coking Processes*
- *No. 7 To study Cartographic Problems*
- *No. 8 Desalination of Brackish Water*
- *No. 9 Use of Low-Grade Ores*

The *Productivity Sub-Committee* **(PG)** set up a *Working Party on Systems of Remuneration likely to encourage Productivity* as well as the following *Working Parties:*

- *No. 1 To study Work Analysis and Measurement Methods*
- *No. 3 To study the influence of Tax Legislation on Productivity*
- *No. 4 Human Factors*
- *No. 5 To study Simplification of Manufactured Products*

en Europe un développement continu de la productivité. Pour stimuler l'effort de productivité des pays Membres, elle eut recours à de nombreuses méthodes (missions, envois d'experts, études internationales, conférences, publications, etc.) lesquelles s'inscrivaient dans des projets distincts.

Ces projets émanaient soit d'un pays Membre, soit de la Direction, soit même d'un comité de l'OECE, qui, en quelque sorte, passait commande à l'Agence d'une action qui lui paraissait utile. A partir de 1957, la mise en œuvre des projets était en principe soumise à une double approbation: un vote majoritaire du **Comité de direction,** et une déclaration de participation ou d'intérêt de la part d'un nombre minimum de pays.

8.1 Structure et fonctionnement

Lors de la création de l'AEP, le Conseil a chargé le **Comité de la productivité et de la recherche appliquée** de la contrôler, de déterminer les règles et les méthodes de travail, d'approuver les projets d'importance moyenne et de suivre l'activité du Directeur de l'AEP qu'il éclairait de ses directives. Il a créé les *groupes de travail* suivants :

- *n° 1 échanges de documents intergouvernementaux et service international de renseignements techniques*
- *n° 2 échanges de documents intergouvernementaux et services auxiliaires audio-visuels*

Plusieurs Sous-comités ont été constitués et ont créé des groupes de travail :

Le *Sous-comité de la coopération dans la recherche scientifique* **(GR),** devenu le **Comité de la recherche appliquée,** a créé les *groupes de travail* ci-après :

- *n° 1 transport du gaz à grande distance*
- *n° 2 étude de l'utilisation de l'énergie éolienne*
- *n° 3 gazéification des combustibles*
- *n° 4 étude des engrais phosphatés dont la production ne nécessite pas l'emploi d'acide sulfurique*
- *n° 5 étude du mélange de certaines fibres synthétiques avec la laine*
- *n° 6 nouveaux procédés de cokéfaction*
- *n° 7 étude des problèmes cartographiques*
- *n° 8 déssalement des eaux saumâtres*
- *n° 9 minerais pauvres*

Le *Sous-comité de la productivité* **(PG)** a créé des *groupes de travail sur les systèmes de rémunérations propres à stimuler la productivité :*

- *n° 1 étude des méthodes d'analyse et des mesures du travail*
- *n° 3 étude de l'influence de la législation fiscale sur la productivité*
- *n° 4 facteurs humains*
- *n° 5 étude de la simplification des produits manufacturés*

The *Sub-Committee for Business Administration and Organisation* **(BA)** set up the following *Working Parties:*

- *No. 1 To study Work Analysis and Measurement Methods*
- *No. 4 To study Human Factors of Productivity*

When the Council decided to continue the activities of the Agency on 27 February 1957 it altered its structure. A **Governing Body** consisting of a representative of each of the Member countries, the United States, and Canada replaced the PRA Committee as the deliberative body of the Agency. Its terms of reference were to deal with all matters relating to the Agency's aims, to examine general questions of principle in connection with productivity and to submit appropriate proposals to the Council, to which it transmitted an annual report and estimates of operating expenditure. It adopted the projects proposed under the Agency's programme.

An **Advisory Board,** set up at the same time as the PRA Committee, guided the Agency's work; its statutes were revised by the Council in 1957. The Board was composed of 14 members appointed by the Council from among the persons nominated by the professional associations maintaining relations with the OEEC. Its terms of reference were to advise the Governing Body and the Secretary-General on the Agency's work, its relations with public opinion and its long-term policy. It examined the annual programme and report and submitted comments to the Governing Body. It set up the *Working Party on Underdeveloped Areas.*

On technical matters the Agency could request an opinion from the committees and working parties of the OEEC, or from the two special committees set up for that purpose on 26 July 1957, the **Committee for Applied Research** and the **Productivity Committee.** The latter consisted of representatives of productivity centres and was required to give technical opinions to the Secretary-General, who transmitted them to the Governing Body, on all the operational phases of projects adopted under the Agency's annual programme. It dealt with activities that would develop relations between national productivity centres or other similar bodies and enable the Agency to act as an international centre for information exchanges and joint review of common problems.

The **Committee for Applied Research** consisted of representatives of the national applied research institutes and dealt with questions relating to co-operation and coordination in research in the field of applied science and technological development. Like the Productivity Committee, it was required to give the Secretary-General its technical opinions on all the operational phases of the projects adopted under the Agency's annual programme. In 1961 its functions were transferred to the Committee for Scientific Research.

Le *Sous-comité pour l'administration et l'organisation des entreprises* **(BA)** a créé les *groupes de travail :*

- *n° 1 étude des méthodes d'analyse et de mesure du travail*
- *n° 4 étude des facteurs humains de la productivité*

Lorsque le Conseil décida de continuer les activités de l'Agence, le 27 janvier 1957, il en modifia la structure. Le **Conseil de direction,** composé des représentants de tous les pays Membres, des États-unis et du Canada, remplaça le Comité PRA comme organe délibérant de l'Agence. Il était compétent pour traiter de toutes les questions se rapportant à l'objet de l'Agence, examiner des questions de principe d'ordre général en matière de productivité et présenter des propositions appropriées au Conseil à qui il transmettait le rapport annuel et les évaluations de dépenses de fonctionnement. Il adopta les projets proposés au titre du programme.

Un **Comité consultatif,** créé en même temps que le Conseil de direction orienta ses travaux et ses statuts furent révisés par le Conseil en 1957. Le Comité comprenait 14 membres nommés par le Conseil parmi les personnes désignées par les organismes professionnels entretenant des relations avec l'OECE. Il avait pour mandat d'aviser le Conseil de direction et le Sécretaire général des travaux de l'Agence, de ses relations avec l'opinion publique, et de sa politique à long terme. Il en examinait le programme et les rapports annuels et soumettait ses commentaires au Conseil de direction. Il a notamment créé le *Groupe de travail sur les régions sous-développées.*

Sur le plan technique, l'Agence pouvait demander l'avis des comités et groupes de travail de l'OECE, des groupes ad hoc d'experts nommés par le Directeur de l'Agence, ou des deux comités spéciaux créés le 26 juillet 1957 à cet effet : le **Comité de la recherche appliquée** et le **Comité de la productivité.** Composé des représentants des centres de productivité, ce dernier était appelé à donner au Secrétaire général qui les transmettait au Comité de direction, des avis techniques à chaque phase du déroulement d'un projet adopté au titre du programme annuel de l'Agence. Il traita des activités propres à développer les relations entre les centres nationaux de productivité ou autres organismes correspondants et à permettre à l'Agence de jouer le rôle d'un centre international pour les échanges de renseignements et l'examen collectif des problèmes communs.

Composé des représentants des instituts nationaux de recherche appliquée, le **Comité de la recherche appliquée** a traité des questions de coopération et de coordination dans la recherche en matière de sciences appliquées et de développement technique. Comme le Comité de la productivité, il a été appelé à donner au Secrétaire général des avis techniques au cours des phases du déroulement d'un projet adopté au titre du programme annuel de l'Agence. En 1961, ses fonctions ont été transférées au Comité de la recherche scientifique.

Publications:

European Productivity Agency, 1954-1961, *Information Bulletin of the European Productivity Agency,* No. 1-40. (Index No. 1-40)

OECE (1961), *Cinq ans d'assistance technique à l'OECE.* (available in French only)

8.2 Productivity

The principal aim of the **European Productivity Agency** was to raise living standards through productivity growth, in other words, to produce more by effectively using the human and material resources available in the Member countries. The economic part of the EPA programme focused on methods of productivity measurement and the influence of general economic factors on productivity growth.

The Agency's publications dealt with basic productivity concepts, productivity measurement and techniques of analysing productivity differentials between firms, industries and countries. The study of general factors of productivity gave rise to published reports on restrictive business practices, tax legislation, investment, capital resources and distribution.

Publications:

European Productivity Agency (1955-1961), *Productivity Measurement Review,* No. 1-26.

___. (1955-1956), *Productivity Measurement,* 2 vol.

___. (1957), *Productivity: Prices and Wages.*

___. (1957), *Supply of Capital Funds for Industrial Development in Europe: Resources – Structure – Methods, EPA Project* No. 292.

___. (1957), *The Influence of Sales Taxes on Productivity, EPA Project* No. 315.

___. (1958), *Consumer's Food-buying Habits, EPA Project* No. 169.

MUNTHE, Preben (1958), *Freedom of Entry into Industry and Trade, EPA Project* No. 259.

GAMMELGAARD, Soren (1958), *Resale Price Maintenance, EPA Project* No. 238.

NORBYE, O.D.K. (1959), *Restrictive Business Practices in the United States, Technical Assistance Mission* No. 414.

European Productivity Agency (1960), *Industrial Growth in the Jet Age.*

European Productivity Agency (1961), *Series of Lectures on Economic Growth at University of Madrid,* OEEC, Paris.

8.3 Business Management

At the time, certain Europeans explained the high productivity of American firms by the efforts made in

Publications :

Agence Européenne de Productivité, 1954-1961, *Bulletin d'information de l'Agence Européenne de Productivité,* n° 1-40. (Index n° 1-40)

OECE (1961), *Cinq ans d'assistance technique à l'OECE.*

8.2 Productivité

L'objectif principal de l'**Agence européenne de productivité** était d'élever le niveau de vie par l'accroissement de la productivité, c'est à dire produire plus en utilisant les ressources humaines et matérielles dont les pays Membres disposaient. La partie économique du programme de l'AEP a porté sur les méthodes propres à mesurer le niveau de productivité et sur l'influence de facteurs économiques généraux sur son développement.

Des publications traitent des concepts de base de la productivité, des méthodes pour la mesurer et des procédés d'analyse des différences de productivité entre entreprises, industries et pays. L'étude des facteurs généraux de productivité a donné lieu à la publication de rapports sur les pratiques commerciales restrictives, la législation fiscale, les investissements, les ressources en capitaux et la distribution.

Publications :

Agence Européenne de Productivité (1955-1961), *Revue de la mesure de la productivité,* n° 1-26.

___. (1955-1956), *Mesure de la productivité,* 2 vol.

___. (1957), *Productivité : prix et salaires.*

___. (1957), *Financement du développement industriel de l'Europe : Ressources – structures – méthodes, Projet AEP* n° 292.

___. (1957), *Régime fiscal du chiffre d'affaires et son incidence sur la productivité, Projet AEP* n° 315.

___. (1958), *Comportement de l'acheteur de produits alimentaires, Projet AEP* n° 169.

MUNTHE, Preben (1958), *Liberté d'accès à l'industrie et au commerce, Projet AEP* n° 259.

GAMMELGAARD, Soren (1958), *Système des prix imposés, Projet AEP* n° 238.

NORBYE, O.D.K. (1959), *Pratiques commerciales restrictives aux États-Unis, Mission d'assistance technique* n° 414.

Agence Européenne de Productivité (1960), *Expansion industrielle à l'époque de l'avion à réaction.*

Agence Européenne de Productivité (1961), *Cycle de conférences sur le développement économique, Université de Madrid,* OECE, Paris.

8.3 Conduite des entreprises

A l'époque, certains européens expliquaient le haut niveau de productivité des entreprises américaines

the United States to study the best methods of business management and organisation. Taking US business administration as a model, the EPA accordingly endeavoured to disseminate its principal techniques. The Agency's activities with regard to management of industrial and commercial firms focussed on three areas:

- development of business management science, evaluation of basic and advanced training programmes in Member countries, and comparison of returns from new and traditional methods of distribution;

- assistance to establishments teaching busines management (basic and advanced training). In this respect, the EPA was instructed in setting up the INSEAD business school in France;

- dissemination of modern management techniques, by making American and European consultants available to Member countries, by aiding the consultancy services which were developing in most countries, or by organising exchanges of information on new methods through conferences or written information.

Publications:

European Productivity Agency (1953), *Material Handling Equipment and Methods in the USA, Technical Assistance Mission* No. 42.

United States. Bureau of Labor Statistics (1954), *Cost Savings Through Standardisation, Simplification, Specialisation in the Building Industry, Technical Assistance Mission* No. 126, OEEC, Paris.

United States. Bureau of Labor Statistics (1954), *Cost Savings Through Standardisation, Simplification, Specialisation in the Clothing Industry, Technical Assistance Mission* No. 126, OEEC, Paris.

United States. Bureau of Labor Statistics (1954), *Cost Savings Through Standardisation, Simplification, Specialisation in Containers, Technical Assistance Mission* No. 126, OEEC, Paris.

European Productivity Agency (1954), *Paper and Board Packaging, Technical Assistance Mission* No. 64.

notamment par les efforts poursuivis aux États-Unis pour étudier les meilleures méthodes d'organisation et de conduite des affaires. Inspiré de ce modèle, l'AEP s'est donc efforcée d'en faire connaître les principales techniques. Ses activités en matière de gestion des entreprises industrielles et commerciales ont porté sur trois aspects :

- le développement de la science de la gestion des entreprises, l'évaluation des programmes de formation et de perfectionnement existant dans les pays Membres et la comparaison du rendement des méthodes nouvelles et traditionnelles de distribution ;

- une aide aux établissements d'enseignement et de perfectionnement en matière de gestion des entreprises (centres de formation et de perfectionnement des cadres). Notons que l'AEP a été à l'origine de la création de l'Institut européen d'administration des affaires (INSEAD) en France ;

- un programme de dissémination des techniques modernes de gestion et de distribution soit en mettant des consultants américains et européens à la disposition des pays Membres, soit en aidant les « services consultatifs » qui se développaient dans la plupart des pays, soit en organisant un échange d'expériences sur des méthodes nouvelles, par des conférences, ou sous forme écrite.

Publications :

Agence Européenne de Productivité (1953), *Matériel et méthode de manutention aux USA, Mission d'assistance technique* n° 42.

United States. Bureau of Labor Statistics (1954), *Cost Savings Through Standardisation, Simplification, Specialisation in the Building Industry, Technical Assistance Mission* n° 126, OEEC, Paris. (Disponible seulement en anglais.)

United States. Bureau of Labor Statistics (1954), *Cost Savings Through Standardisation, Simplification, Specialisation in the Clothing Industry, Technical Assistance Mission* n° 126, OEEC, Paris. (Disponible seulement en anglais.)

United States. Bureau of Labor Statistics (1954), *Cost Savings Through Standardisation, Simplification, Specialisation in Materials Handling Equipment, Technical Assistance Mission* n° 126, OEEC, Paris. (Disponible seulement en anglais.)

Agence Européenne de Productivité (1954), *Emballages en papier et carton, Mission d'assistance technique* n° 64.

JEFFERYS, J.B., HAUSBERGER, S. and LINDBLAD, G. (1954), *Productivity in the Distributive Trade in Europe: Wholesale and Retails Aspects.*

European Productivity Agency (1954), *Problems of Business Management: American opinions: European Opinions, Technical Assistance Mission* No. 129.

HARTMANN, Heinz (1955), *Education for Business Leadership: the Role of the German ''Hochschulen'', EPA Project* No. 346.

European productivity Agency (1955), *Specialized Training in the Field of Work Study, Technical Assistance Mission* No. 195.

___. (1956), *The Automotive Equipments and Parts Industry in the United States, Technical Assistance Mission* No. 131.

Turin Conference on Business Management Education (1956, Turin) (1956), *[Conference Papers], EPA Project* No. 378.

Turin Conference on Business Management Education (1956, Turin) (1956), *Breakdown of Courses in the Setting up of a Programme,* by G. C. CILLARIO, *Projet AEP* No. 378.

Turin Conference on Business Management Education (1956, Turin) (1956), *Institute of Business Administration of the University of Paris,* by R. GOETZ-GIRCY, *EPA project* No. 378.

Turin Conference on Business Management Education (1956, Turin) (1956), *Outline of a Postgraduate Programme of General Management Studies of the University of Manchester,* by T. E. CHESTER, *EPA Project* No. 378.

Turin Conference on Business Management Education (1956, Turin) (1956), *Programme for Basic Sciences as Preparatory Background for studies of Business Management,* by A. PLANT, *EPA Project* No. 378.

Turin Conference on Business Management Education (1956, Turin) (1956), *The Relationship between Management Training Programmes organised inside individual firms and Programmes organised by Universities Training Centres and other outside bodies,* by A. J. VLERICK, *EPA Project* No. 378.

Turin Conference on Business Management Education (1956, Turin) (1956), *What Subjects Should be Included in a Full Programme of Business Administration and Management Studies: Financial Management,* by P. TABATONI, *EPA Project* No. 378.

JEFFERYS, J.B., HAUSBERGER, S. and LINDBLAD, G. (1954), *Productivité dans la distribution en Europe : Commerce de gros et de détail.*

Agence Européenne de Productivité (1954), *Problèmes de gestion des entreprises : opinions américaines : opinions européennes, Mission d'assistance technique* n° 129.

HARTMANN, Heinz (1955), *Formation des dirigeants d'entreprises : le rôle des universités et grandes écoles techniques allemandes, Projet AEP* n° 346.

Agence Européenne de Productivité (1955), Formation des spécialistes de l'étude du travail, Mission d'assistance technique n° 195.

___. (1956), *L'industrie des pièces détachées et des équipements automobiles aux États-Unis, Mission d'assistance technique* n° 131.

Conférence de Turin sur la formation des dirigeants des entreprises (1956, Turin) (1956), *[Comptes rendus], Projet AEP* n° 378.

Conférence de Turin sur la formation des dirigeants des entreprises (1956, Turin) (1956), *Différentes possibilités de subdiviser l'ensemble des cours d'un programme en administration des entreprises,* par G. C. CILLARIO, *Projet AEP* n° 378.

Conférence de Turin sur la formation des dirigeants des entreprises (1956, Turin) (1956), *Centre d'administration des entreprises de l'Université de Paris,* par R. GOETZ-GIRCY, *Projet AEP* n° 378.

Conférence de Turin sur la formation des dirigeants des entreprises (1956, Turin) (1956), *Esquisse d'un programme post-universitaire en direction générale à l'Université de Manchester,* par T. E. CHESTER, *Projet AEP* n° 378.

Conférence de Turin sur la formation des dirigeants des entreprises (1956, Turin) (1956), *Quel serait le meilleur programme en matière de sciences comme préparation à des études d'administration des entreprises ?* par A. PLANT, *Projet AEP* n° 378.

Conférence de Turin sur la formation des dirigeants des entreprises (1956, Turin) (1956), *Quelle peut-être la relation entre les programmes de perfectionnement des cadres organisés dans les firmes et les programmes établis par des organismes extérieurs ?* par A. J. VLERICK, *Projet AEP* n° 378.

Conférence de Turin sur la formation des dirigeants des entreprises (1956, Turin) (1956), *Quelles matières convient-il d'inclure dans un programme complet d'études sur l'administration et la gestion des entreprises : direction financière,* par P. TABATONI, *Projet AEP* n° 378.

Turin Conference on Business Management Education (1956, Turin) (1956), *What Subjects Should be Included in a Full Programme of Business Administration and Management Studies: Financial Management,* by C. P. TERRIER, *EPA Project* No. 378.

Conférence de Turin sur la formation des dirigeants des entreprises (1956, Turin) (1956), *Quelles matières convient-il d'inclure dans un programme complet d'études sur l'administration et la gestion des entreprises : direction financière,* par C. P. TERRIER, *Projet AEP* nº 378.

Turin Conference on Business Management Education (1956, Turin) (1956), *What Subjects Should be Included in a Full Programme of Business Administration and Management Studies: General Management,* by Folke KRISTENSSON, *EPA Project* No. 378.

Conférence de Turin sur la formation des dirigeants des entreprises (1956, Turin) (1956), *Quelles matières convient-il d'inclure dans un programme complet d'études sur l'administration et la gestion des entreprises : direction générale et la direction commerciale,* par Folke KRISTENSSON, *Projet AEP* nº 378.

Turin Conference on Business Management Education (1956, Turin) (1956), *What Subjects Should be Included in a Full Programme of Business Administration and Management Studies: Personnel Management,* by B. Nancy SEEAR, *EPA Project* No. 378.

Conférence de Turin sur la formation des dirigeants des entreprises (1956, Turin) (1956), *Quelles matières convient-il d'inclure dans un programme complet d'études sur l'administration et la gestion des entreprises : direction du personnel,* par B. Nancy SEEAR, *Projet AEP* nº 378.

Turin Conference on Business Management Education (1956, Turin) (1956), *What Subjects should be Included in a Full Programme of Business Administration and Management Studies: Production Management,* by Vittorio ZIGNOLI, *EPA Project* No. 378.

Conférence de Turin sur la formation des dirigeants des entreprises (1956, Turin) (1956), *Quelles matières convient-il d'inclure dans un programme complet d'études sur l'administration et la gestion des entreprises : Direction de la production,* par Vittorio ZIGNOLI, *Projet AEP* nº 378.

Turin Conference on Business Management Education (1956, Turin) (1956), *What Subjects Should be Included in a Full Programme of Business Administration and Management Studies: Sales Management,* by Ulf af TROLLE, *EPA Project* No. 378.

Conférence de Turin sur la formation des dirigeants des entreprises (1956, Turin) (1956), *Quelles matières convient-il d'inclure dans un programme complet d'études sur l'administration et la gestion des entreprises : direction commerciale,* par Ulf af TROLLE, *Projet AEP* nº 378.

CHESTER, T. E. (1956), *Outline of a Postgraduate Programme of General Management Studies of the University of Manchester,* Turin Conference on Business Management Education (1956, Turin), *EPA Project* No. 378.

CHESTER, T. E. (1956), *Esquisse d'un programme post-universitaire en direction générale à l'Université de Manchester,* Conférence de Turin sur la formation des dirigeants des entreprises (1956, Turin), *Projet AEP* nº 378.

CILLARIO, G. C. (1956), *Breakdown of Courses in the Setting up of a Programme for Business management,* Turin Conference on Business Management Education (1956, Turin), *EPA Project* No. 378.

CILLARIO, G. C. (1956), *Différentes possibilités de subdiviser l'ensemble des cours d'un programme en administration des entreprises,* Conférence de Turin sur la formation des dirigeants des entreprises (1956, Turin), *Projet AEP* nº 378.

GOETZ-GIRCY, R. (1956), *Institute of Business Administration of the University of Paris,* Turin Conference on Business Management Education (1956, Turin), *EPA Project* No. 378.

GOETZ-GIRCY, R. (1956), *Centre des entreprises de l'Université de Paris,* Conférence de Turin sur la formation des dirigeants des entreprises (1956, Turin), *Projet AEP* nº 378.

KRISTENSSON, Folke (1956), *What Subjects Should be Included in a Full Programme of Business Administration and Management Studies : General Management,* Turin Conference on Business Management Education (1956, Turin), *EPA Project* No. 378.

KRISTENSSON, Folke (1956), *Quelles matières convient-il d'inclure dans un programme complet d'études sur l'administration et la gestion des entreprises : direction générale et direction commerciale,* Conférence de Turin sur la formation des dirigeants des entreprises (1956, Turin), *Projet AEP* nº 378.

PLANT, A. (1956), *Programme for Basic Sciences as Preparatory Background for studies of Business Management,* Turin Conference on Business Management Education (1956, Turin), *EPA Project* No. 378.

PLANT, A. (1956), *Quel serait le meilleur programme en matière de sciences fondamentales comme préparation à des études d'administration des entreprises?* Conférence de Turin sur la formation des dirigeants des entreprises (1956, Turin), *Projet AEP* nº 378.

SEEAR, B. Nancy (1956), *What Subjects Should be Included in a Full Programme of Business Administration and Management Studies: Personnel Management,* Turin Conference on Business Management Education (1956, Turin), *EPA Project* No. 378.

TABATONI, P. (1956), *What Subjects Should be Included in a Full Programme of Business Administration and Management Studies: Financial Management,* Turin Conference on Business Management Education (1956, Turin), *EPA Project* No. 378.

TERRIER, C. P. (1956), *What Subjects Should be Included in a Full Programme of Business Administration and Management Studies: Financial Management,* Turin Conference on Business Management Education (1956, Turin), *EPA Project* No. 378.

ULF af Trolle (1956), What Subjects Should be Included in a Full Programme of Business Administration and Management Studies: Sales Management, Turin Conference on Business Management Education (1956, Turin), *EPA Project* No. 378.

VLERICK, A. J. (1956), *The Relationship between Management Training Programmes organised inside individual firms and Programmes organised by Universities Training Centres and other outside bodies,* Turin Conference on Business Management Education (1956, Turin), *EPA Project* No. 378.

ZIGNOLI, Vittorio (1956), *What Subjects should be Included in a Full Programme of Business Administration and Management Studies: Production Management,* Turin Conference on Business Management Education (1956, Turin), *EPA Project* No. 378.

Education for Business Leadership (1955, Geneva) (1956), *Report on the International Conference of Directors of Advanced Training Centres, EPA Project* No. 331.

European Productivity Agency (1956), *Productivity in the Wholesale Trade, Technical Assistance Mission* No. 153.

European Productivity Agency (1956), *Statistical Quality Control, Technical Assistance Mission* No. 140.

European Productivity Agency (1956), *Market Research Methods in Europe, Technical Assistance Mission* No. 261.

European Productivity Agency (1957), *Advisory and Consultative Service for Distributive Trades,* No. 1-7, *Technical Assistance Mission* No. 365.

BROMELL, John R. (1957), *Building a Grocery Warehouse, Advisory and Consultative Service for Distributive Trades,* No. 1.

SEEAR, B. Nancy (1956), *Quelles matières convient-il d'inclure dans un programme complet d'études sur l'administration et la gestion des entreprises : direction du personnel,* Conférence de Turin sur la formation des dirigeants des entreprises (1956, Turin), *Projet AEP* n° 378.

TABATONI, P. (1956), *Quelles matières convient-il d'inclure dans un programme complet d'études sur l'administration et la gestion des entreprises: direction financière,* Conférence de Turin sur la formation des dirigeants des entreprises (1956, Turin), *Projet AEP* n° 378.

TERRIER, C.P. (1956), *Quelles matières convient-il d'inclure dans un programme complet d'études sur l'administration et la gestion des entreprises : direction financière,* Conférence de Turin sur la formation des dirigeants des entreprises (1956, Turin), *Projet AEP* n° 378.

ULF af Trolle (1956), *Quelles matières convient-il d'inclure dans un programme complet d'études sur l'administration et la gestion des entreprises: direction commerciale, Conférence de Turin sur la formation des dirigeants des entreprises (1956, Turin), Projet AEP* n° 378.

VLERICK, A. J. (1956), *Quelle peut-être la relation entre les programmes de perfectionnement des cadres organisés dans les firmes et les programmes établis par des organismes extérieurs?* Conférence de Turin sur la formation des dirigeants des entreprises (1956, Turin), *Projet AEP* n° 378.

ZIGNOLI, Vittorio (1956), *Quelles matières convient-il d'inclure dans un programme complet d'études sur l'administration et la gestion des entreprises : Direction de la production,* Conférence de Turin sur la formation des dirigeants des entreprises (1956, Turin), *Projet AEP* n° 378.

La Formation des dirigeants d'entreprises (1955, Genève) (1956), *Rapport de la conférence internationale des directeurs des centres de perfectionnement, Projet AEP* n° 331.

Agence Européenne de Productivité (1956), *Productivité dans le commerce de gros, Mission d'assistance technique* n° 153.

Agence Européenne de Productivité (1956), *Contrôle statistique de la qualité, Mission d'assistance technique* n° 140.

Agence Européenne de Productivité (1956), *Techniques de l'étude des marchés en Europe, Mission d'assistance technique* n° 261.

Agence Européenne de Productivité (1957), *Service d'information et de consultation sur la distribution,* n° 1-7, *Mission d'assistance technique,* n° 365.

BROMELL, John R. (1957), *Construction d'un entrepôt d'épicerie en gros, Service d'information et de consultation sur la distribution,* n° 1.

___. (1957), *Organizing and Operating a Voluntary food Group, Advisory and Consultative Service for Distributive Trade,* No. 2.

___. (1957), *Organisation et fonctionnement d'un groupe volontaire dans le commerce alimentaire, Service d'information et de consultation sur la distribution* n° 2.

___. (1957), *Record Keeping for Delivery Trucks, Advisory and Consultative Service for Distributive Trade* No. 3.

___. (1957), *Contrôle du rendement des camions de livraison, Service d'infomation et de consultation sur la distribution* n° 3.

___. (1957), *Manual Stock Control for Wholesalers, Advisory and Consultative Service for Distributive Trade* No. 4.

___. (1957), *Controle physique des stocks dans le commerce de gros, Service d'information et de consultation sur la distribution,* n° 4.

LARSH, Willard H. (1957), *Materials Handling for Wholesalers, Advisory and Consultative Service for Distributive Trades* No. 5.

LARSH, Willard H. (1957), *Principes élémentaires de manutention à l'usage des grossistes, Service d'information et de consultation sur la distribution,* n° 5.

SWENTOR, August W. (1957), *Modern Layout and Fixtures for Food Stores, Advisory and Consultative Service for Distributive Trades* No. 6.

SWENTOR, August W. (1957), *Modern Layout and Fixtures for Food Stores, Advisory and Consultative Service for Distributive Trades* n° 6. (Disponible seulement en anglais.)

___. (1957), *In Store Merchandising for Food Stores, Advisory and Consultative Service for Distributive Trades* No. 7.

___. (1957), *Présentation et vente des marchandises dans les magasins d'alimentation, Service d'information et de consultation sur la distribution* n° 7.

LEBATAR, Georges G. (1958), *A Voluntary Chain in the Textile Field, Advisory and Consultative Service for Distributive Trades* No. 8.

LEBATAR, Georges G. (1958), *Une chaine volontaire dans les textiles, Service d'information et de consultation sur la distribution* n° 8.

FELLER, Lee (1958), *The Development of Food Distribution in the United States, Advisory and Consultative Service for Distributive Trades* No. 9.

FELLER, Lee (1958), *L'évolution de la distribution des produits alimentaires aux États-Unis, Service d'information et de consultation sur la distribution* n° 9.

CONQUET, A. (1959), *European Colleges for Retail Distribution, Advisory and Consultative Service for Distributive Trades* No. 10.

CONQUET, A. (1959), *Écoles européennes du commerce de détail, Service d'information et de consultation sur la distribution* n° 10.

FRERICHS, G. (1960), *Advisory Services for Wholesalers and Retailers in Germany, Advisory and Consultative Service for Distributive Trades* No. 11.

Agence Européenne de Productivité (1960), *Services consultatifs des commerces de gros et de détail en Allemagne, Service d'information et de consultation sur la distribution* n° 11.

WIRSÄLL, Nils-Erik (1960), *Retailers Buying Co-operatives, Advisory and Consultative Service for Distributive Trades* No. 12.

WIRSÄLL, Nils-Erik (1960), *Les coopératives d'achat de détaillants, Service d'information et de consultation sur la distribution* n° 12.

WICKSTRÖM, Bo (1961), *About Methods to Measure the Effectiveness of Advertising, Advisory and Consultative Service for Distributive Trades* No. 13.

WICKSTRÖM, Bo (1961), *Méthodes utilisées pour mesurer le rendement de la publicité, Service d'information et de consultation sur la distribution* n° 13.

SELIG, L. (1961), *Consumer Credit in the United States, Advisory and Consultative Service for Distributive Trades* No. 13.

SELIG, L. (1961), *Le crédit à la consommation aux États-Unis, Service d'information et de consultation sur la distribution* n° 13.

Dissemination of Management Principles and Techniques (1956, Deauville) (1957), *Report, EPA Project* No. 349.

Diffusion des pincipes et des méthodes de conduite rationnelle des entreprises (1956, Deauville) (1957), *Rapport, Projet AEP* n° 349.

Marketing by Manufacturers (1956, Paris) (1957), *Report.*

La gestion commerciale des entreprises industrielles (1956, Paris) (1957), Rapport.

European Productivity Agency (1957), *Soap, Detergents, Paint, Varnishes: Marketing Techniques in the United States, EPA Project* No. 299.

Agence Européenne de Productivité (1957), *Savons, détergents, peintures, vernis : Techniques de distribution aux États-Unis, Projet AEP* n° 299.

___. (1958), *Company Planning and Production Control: The Story of a Manufacturing Company, EPA Project* No. 173.

___. (1958), *Planning et contrôle de la production dans les entreprises : comment une manufacture a retrouvé la prospérité, Projet AEP* n° 173.

___. (1958), *Technical Information and the Smaller Firm : Facts and Figures on Practices in European and American Industry, EPA Project* No. 296/2.

___. (1958), *Simplification, Standardisation, Specialisation: Case Studies on Variety Reduction, EPA Project* No. 184, 3 vol.

___. (1959), *Budgetary Control: an Effective Tool for the Management of small and medium-sized enterprises, EPA Project* No. 172.

MAGNUS HANNAFORD, R. G. (1959), *Education and Training for Distribution.*

European Productivity Agency (1959), *Improved Methods of Distribution in the Retail Trade for Meat, EPA Project* No. 285/3 Part II.

___. (1959), *Industrial Design in the United States, Technical Assistance Mission* No. 278.

___. (1959), *Organisation of Advisory Services for Handicrafts and Small and Medium Size Firms in Europe, EPA Project* No. 374.

International Conference on Business Management Education (7th, 1960, Paris) (1960), *Report,* by Maurice IDOUX and P. L. SMITH.

IDOUX, Maurice and SMITH, P. L. (1960), *Report,* International Conference on Business Management Education (7th, 1960, Paris).

HENKSMEIER, K. H. (1960), *The Economic Performance of Self Service in Europe, EPA Project* No. 5/33.

European Productivity Agency (1960), *European Guide to General Courses in Business Management.*

European Productivity Agency (1960), *Cost Reduction in Industry: Integrated Approach to the Practical Application of Progressive Management Techniques for the Control and Reduction of Cost.*

MEYNAUD, Jean (1961), *Better Buying through Consumer Information, EPA Project* No. 6/03 G.

KAPFERER, Clodwig (1961), *Sources statistiques des études de marchés : Europe et Amérique du Nord/ Sources of Statistics for Market Research: Europe and North America,* 2 vol.

___. (1961), *Sources statistiques des études de marchés : Europe et Amérique du Nord :* vol. 1 : *appareils de radio/Sources of Statistics for Market Research: Europe and North America:* vol. 1: *radio sets.*

___. (1961), *Sources statistiques des études de marchés : Europe et Amérique du Nord :* vol. 2 : *chaussures/Sources of Statistics for Market Research: Europe and North America:* vol. 2: *footwear.*

___. (1958), *Information technique et les petites et moyennes entreprises : méthodes pratiquées en Europe et aux États-Unis : Quelques chiffres et quelques faits, Projet AEP* n° 296/2.

___. (1958), *Simplification, normalisation, spécialisation : études de cas de réduction de variétés, Projet AEP* n° 184, 3 vol.

___. (1959), *Le budget planifié : instrument efficace pour la bonne gestion des petites et moyennes entreprises, Projet AEP* n° 172.

MAGNUS HANNAFORD, R. G. (1959), Enseignement de la distribution.

Agence Européenne de Productivité (1959), *Amélioration des méthodes de distribution dans le commerce de détail de la viande, Projet AEP* n° 285/3-II.

___. (1959), *Esthétique industrielle aux États-Unis, Mission d'assistance technique* n° 278.

___. (1959), *Organisation des services consultatifs pour l'artisanat et les petites et moyennes entreprises en Europe, Projet AEP* n° 374.

Conférence internationale sur la formation et le perfectionnement en administration des entreprises (7e, 1960, Paris) (1960), *Rapport,* de Maurice IDOUX et de P. L. SMITH.

IDOUX, Maurice et SMITH, P. L. (1960), *Rapport,* Conférence internationale sur la formation et le perfectionnement en administration des entreprises (7e, 1960, Paris).

HENKSMEIER, K. H. (1960), *Le libre service en Europe et son rendement, Projet AEP* n° 5/33.

Agence Européenne de Productivité (1960), *Catalogue Européen des programmes généraux d'enseignement d'administration des entreprises.*

Agence Européenne de Productivité (1960), *Réduction des coûts industriels : Plan coordonné pour l'application des techniques modernes de gestion en vue du contrôle et de la réduction des coûts.*

MEYNAUD, Jean (1961), *Acheter mieux : l'information objective du consommateur, APE Projet* n° 6/03 G.

KAPFERER, Clodwig (1961), *Sources statistiques des études de marchés : Europe et Amérique du Nord/ Sources of Statistics for Market Research: Europe and North America,* 2 vol.

___. (1961), *Sources statistiques des études de marchés : Europe et Amérique du Nord :* vol. 1 : *appareils de radio/Sources of Statistics for Market Research: Europe and North America:* vol. 1: *radio sets.*

___. (1961), *Sources statistiques des études de marchés : Europe et Amérique du Nord :* vol. 2 : *chaussures/Sources of Statistics for Market Research: Europe and North America:* vol. 2: *footwear.*

8.4 Labour and Social Factors

Development of the firm's human capital constituted an essential factor of productivity. Here the EPA's activities focused in particular on vocational training, foremen training, fitting the job to the worker, and effective co-operation between management and representatives of labour in seeking the best methods of production. The Agency encouraged this management-labour co-operation by helping the free trade unions to supplement the information and training of their officials in economic and technical matters ("Trade Union Programme") and by promoting social science research as applied to labour and circulating the results of that research.

These training and documentation activities were supplemented by specific programmes of social science research as applied to labour and studies on the economic and social implications of automation in firms.

Publications:

European Productivity Agency (1955-1958), *Trade Union Information, Technical Assistance Mission* No. 175, 17 Nos.

1956-1958, *Union Studies, Technical Assistance Mission* No. 175, 19 Nos.

VALLSTRAND, Lennart (1956), *Works Councils in Sweden, Union Study* No. 1, *Technical Assistance Mission* No. 175.

___. (1956), *Industrial Democracy in a Swedish Pottery Factory, Union Study* No. 2, *Technical Assistance Mission* No. 175.

CRESPIN, Guy (1956), *Two Case Studies: Belgian Metal Works, Union Study* No. 3, *Technical Assistance Mission* No. 175.

CHAPPELL, F. E. (1956), *Productivity through Joint Consultation, Union Study* No. 4, *Technical Assistance Mission* No. 175.

VERMEULEN, Ad. (1956), *Job Evaluation in the Netherlands, Union Study* No. 5, *Technical Assistance Mission* No. 175.

ETEVENSON, J. (1956), *A French Shoe Factory, Union Study* No. 6, Technical Assistance Mission No. 175.

SCHAEFER, Willfried (1957), *The Unions and Productivity: Practical Experience and Training in Western Germany, Union Study* No. 7, *Technical Assistance Mission* No. 175.

LONGDOZ, J. (1957), *A Belgian electrical apparatus factory, Union Study* No. 8, Technical Assistance Mission No. 175.

PIERRE, J. C. (1957), *Wage Systems in Industry, Union Study* No. 9, *Technical Assistance Mission* No. 175.

8.4 Travail et facteurs sociaux

Le développement des ressources humaines de l'entreprise représentait un facteur essentiel de productivité. A cet égard, les activités de l'AEP ont porté entre autres sur l'amélioration de la formation professionnelle, de celle des contremaîtres, de l'adaptation du travail à l'homme, et de la coopération efficace des chefs d'entreprises et des représentants des travailleurs dans la recherche de meilleures méthodes de production. L'Agence a favorisé cette coopération employeur-travailleur en aidant notamment les organisations syndicales libres à compléter l'information et la formation de leurs cadres en matière économique et technique (« Programme syndical »).

Ces activités de formation et de documentation ont été complétées par des programmes de recherches en sciences humaines appliquées au travail et d'études sur les répercussions économiques et sociales de l'introduction de l'automation dans les entreprises.

Publications :

Agence Européenne de Productivité (1955-1958), *Informations syndicales, Mission d'assistance technique* n° 175, 17 n^os^.

1956-1958, *Documentation syndicale, Mission d'assistance technique* n° 175, 19 n^os^.

VALLSTRAND, Lennart (1956), *Les comités d'entreprise en Suède, Documentation syndicale* n° 1, *Mission d'assistance technique* n° 175.

___. (1956), *Démocratie industrielle dans une usine suédoise, Documentation syndicale* n° 2, *Mission d'assistance technique* n° 175.

CRESPIN, Guy (1956), *Deux histoires de cas de la métallurgie belge envisagées du point de vue syndical, Documentation syndicale* n° 3, *Mission d'assistance technique* n° 175.

CHAPPELL, F. E. (1956), *La consultation paritaire et la productivité, Documentation syndicale* n° 4, *Mission d'assistance technique* n° 175.

VERMEULEN, Ad. (1956), *Évaluation des tâches dans les Pays-Bas, Documentation syndicale,* n° 5, *Mission d'assistance technique* n° 175.

ETEVENSON, J. (1956), *Dans une fabrique française de chaussures, Documentation syndicale* n° 6, *Mission d'assistance technique* n° 175.

SCHAEFER, Willfried (1957), *Syndicats et productivité : formation et application en Allemagne occidentale, Documentation syndicale* n° 7, *Mission d'assistance technique* n° 175.

LONGDOZ, J. (1957), *Dans une entreprise belge d'appareillage électrique, Documentation syndicale* n° 8, *Mission d'assistance technique* n° 175.

PIERRE, J. C. (1957), *Les Modes de rémunération dans l'industrie, Documentation syndicale* n° 9, *Mission d'assistance technique* n° 175.

DOUCY, A. (1957), *Technological Unemployment in Belgium, Union Study* No. 10, *Technical Assistance Mission* No. 175.

THORSRUD, Einar (1958), *The Forty-Hour: Five-Day Week: an Experiment in a Norwegian Garment Factory, Union Study* No. 11, *Technical Assistance Mission* No. 175.

SOUTHWELL, Eric (1957), *Application of Automation in Europe, Union Study* No. 12, *Technical Assistance Mission* No. 175.

PELS, P.S. (1958), *Industrial Relations in the Netherlands, Union Study* No. 13, *Technical Assistance Mission* No. 175.

LUTZ, B. (1958), *Work Study and Collective Agreement in the Metal Industry, Union Study* No. 14, *Technical Assistance Mission* No. 175.

BERTON, J. (1958), *The Unions and Psycho-sociological Techniques,* No. 15, *Technical Assistance Mission* No. 175.

HARLE, R. (1958), *American Trade Unions and Automation, Union Study* No. 16, *Technical Assistance Mission* No. 175.

MOUGIN, G. (1958), *Working Conditions in the European Textile Industry, Union Study* No. 17, *Technical Assistant Mission* No. 175.

MATTHOFER, H. (1958), *Technological Change in the Metallurgy Industry, Union Study* No. 18, *Technical Assistance Mission* No. 175.

NYLEN, Donald A. (1956), *Five Papers on Training in Human Relations: Practice and Theory* by Donald A. Nylen *[et al], Technical Assistance Mission* No. 339.

European Productivity Agency (1956), *Five Papers on Training in Human Relations: Practice and Theory* by Donald A. Nylen *[et al], Technical Assistance Mission* No. 339.

Human Relations in Industry (1955, Florence) (1955), *Papers, EPA Project* No. 312.

Human Relations in Industry (1956, Rome) (1956), *Papers, EPA Project* No. 312.

European Productivity Agency (1956), *Job Analysis: a Tool of Productivity, Technical Assistance Mission* No. 231.

___. (1956), *Inquiry into the Attitudes of Workers in the Steel Industry Towards Technological Changes: Six National Reports, EPA Project* No. 164.

Oil Trade Union Seminar (1955, Hamburg) (1956), *Report, EPA Project* No. 175.

Session d'études syndicales sur les conseils d'entreprise (1956, Bruxelles) (1956), *Report, Projet AEP* No. 175. (available only in French.)

DOUCY, A. (1957), *Le chômage technologique en Belgique, Documentation syndicale* n° 10, *Mission d'assistance technique* n° 175.

THORSRUD, Einar (1958), *Semaine de quarante heures en cinq jours : une expérience dans une manufacture norvégienne d'habillement, Documentation syndicale* n° 11, *Mission d'assistance technique* n° 175.

SOUTHWELL, Eric (1957), *Application de l'automation en Europe, Documentation syndicale* n° 12, *Mission d'assistance technique* n° 175.

PELS, P.S. (1958), *Les relations industrielles aux Pays-Bas, Documentation syndicale* n° 13, *Mission d'assistance technique* n° 175.

LUTZ, B. (1958), *L'étude du travail et les conventions collectives dans la métallurgie, Documentation syndicale* n° 14, *Mission d'assistance technique* n° 175.

BERTON, J. (1958), *Les techniques psychologiques (Point de vue syndical), Documentation syndicale* n° 15, *Mission d'assistance technique* n° 175.

HARLE, R. (1958), *Les syndicats américains et l'automation, Documentation syndicale* n° 16, *Mission d'assistance technique* n° 175.

MOUGIN, G. (1958), *Les conditions de travail dans l'industrie textile européenne, Documentation syndicale* n° 17, *Mission d'assistance technique* n° 175.

MATTHOFER, H. (1958), *L'évolution technologique des industries métallurgiques, Documentation syndicale* n° 16, *Mission d'assistance technique* n° 175.

NYLEN, Donald A. (1956), *Five Papers on Training in Human Relations: Practice and Theory* by Donald A. Nylen *[et al], Technical Assistance Mission* No. 339. (available only in English.)

European Productivity Agency (1956), *Five Papers on Training in Human Relations : Practice and Theory* by Donald A. Nylen *[et al], Technical Assistance Mission* n° 339.

Les relations humaines au cours du travail (1955, Florence) (1955), *Comptes rendus, Projet AEP* n° 312.

Relations humaines dans l'industrie (1956, Rome) (1956), *Comptes rendus, Projet AEP* n° 312.

Agence Européenne de Productivité (1956), *Analyse des tâches : instrument de productivité, Mission d'assistance technique* n° 231.

___. (1956), *Enquête sur les attitudes des travailleurs dans l'industrie de l'acier à l'égard des changements technologiques : Six Rapports nationaux, Projet AEP* n° 164.

Sessions d'étude des syndicats du pétrole (1955, Hambourg) (1956), *Rapport, Projet AEP* n° 175.

Session d'études syndicales sur les conseils d'entreprise (1956, Bruxelles) (1956), *Report, Projet AEP* n° 175.

Sharing out to the Worker the Benefit of Increased Productivity, (1956, The Hague) (1956), *Report* by T. W. CYNOG-JONES and Camillo BENEVENTO, *EPA Project* No. 175.

CYNOG-JONES, T. W. and BENEVENTO, Camillo (1956), *Report,* Sharing out to the Worker the Benefit of Increased Productivity, (1956, The Hague), *EPA Project* No. 175.

COLOMB, Serge and LIENART, Pierre (1957), *About Automation, EPA Project* No. 175.

Trade Union Seminar on Automation (1956, London) (1957), *Final Report, EPA Project* No. 175.

European Productivity Agency (1956), *The Prevention of Occupational Accidents in the United States: role of the Human factor, EPA Project* No. 338.

GRABE, Sven and SILBERER, Paul (1956), *Selection and Training of Foremen in Europe, EPA Project* No. 234.

CLARKE, V. M. (1956), *Training Facilities in the Field of Human Relations: report on France, EPA Project* No. 178.

___. (1956), *Training Facilities in the Field of Human Relations : report on Germany, EPA Project* No. 178.

___. (1956), *Training Facilities in the Field of Human Relations: report on Italy, EPA Project* No. 178.

KING, S. D. M. and CLARKE, V. M. (1956), *Training facilities in the field of human relations: report on the United Kingdom, EPA Project* No. 178.

European Productivity Agency (1956), *Training in Human Relations: an Experience in USA, EPA Project* No. 227.

European Productivity Agency (1956-1957), *Views on Automation, EPA Project* No. 360.

___. (1956), *Views on Automation: Belgium, EPA Project* No. 360.

___. (1956), *Views on Automation: France, EPA Project* No. 360, 4 vol.

___. (1956), *Views on Automation: Germany, EPA Project* No. 360, 2 vol.

___. (1956), *Views on Automation: United Kingdom, EPA Project* No. 360., HMSO, London.

___. (1957), *Views on Automation: Sweden, EPA Project* No. 360.

Conference on Automation (1957, Paris) (1957), *Principal Speeches and Reports of Working Groups, EPA Project* No. 360.

Collective Bargaining and Productivity (1957, Berlin) (1957), *Final Reports.*

International Conference on the Organisation and Administration of Applied Research (3rd, 1956, Vienna) (1957), Scientific Manpower for Applied Research: *Shortage of research workers: how to train and use them, EPA Project* No. 361.

Participation des travailleurs aux avantages découlant d'un accroissement de la productivité (1956, La Haye) (1956), *Rapport* par T. W. CYNOG-JONES et Camillo BENEVENTO, *Projet AEP* nº 175.

CYNOG-JONES, T. W. and BENEVENTO, Camillo (1956), *Rapport,* Participation des travailleurs aux avantages découlant d'un accroissement de la productivité (1956, La Haye), *Projet AEP* nº 175.

COLOMB, Serge et LIENART, Pierre (1957), *A propos de l'automation, Projet AEP* nº 175.

Session d'études syndicales sur l'automation (1956, Londres) (1957), *rapport final, Projet AEP* nº 175.

Agence Européenne de Productivité (1956), *La prévention des accidents du travail aux États-Unis : organisation, rôle de l'élément humain, Projet AEP* nº 338.

GRABE, Sven and SILBERER, Paul (1956), *Sélection et formation des contremaîtres en Europe, Projet AEP* nº 234.

CLARKE, V. M. (1956), *Formation dans le domaine des relations humaines : rapport sur la France, Projet AEP* nº 178.

___. (1956), *Formation dans le domaine des relations humaines : rapport sur l'Allemagne, Projet AEP* nº 178.

___. (1956), *Formation dans le domaine des relations humaines : rapport sur l'Italie, Projet AEP* n° 178.

KING, S. D. M. et CLARKE, V. M. (1956), *Formation dans le domaine des relations humaines : rapport sur le Royaume-Uni, Projet AEP* n° 178.

European Productivity Agency (1956), *Training in Human Relations: an Experience in USA, EPA Project* n° 227. (Disponible seulement en anglais.)

Agence Européenne de productivité (1956-1957), *Vues sur l'automatisme, Projet AEP* nº 360.

___. (1956), *Vues sur l'automatisme : Belgique, Projet AEP* nº 360.

___. (1956), *Vues sur l'automatisme : France, Projet AEP* nº 360, 4 vol.

___. (1956), *Vues sur l'automatisme : Allemagne, Projet AEP* nº 360, 2 vol.

___. (1956), *Vues sur l'automatisme : Royaume-Uni, Projet AEP* nº 360.

___. (1957), *Vues sur l'automatisme : Suède, Projet AEP* nº 360.

Conférence sur l'automatisme (1957, Paris) (1957), *Discours principaux et rapports des groupes de travail, Projet AEP* nº 360.

Négociations collectives et productivité (1957, Berlin) (1957), *Rapports finaux.*

Conférence Internationale sur l'organisation et l'administration de la recherche appliquée (3e, 1956, Vienne) (1957), La recherche appliquée et le problème du personnel scientifique : *pénurie de chercheurs, problèmes de formation et d'utilisation, Projet AEP* nº 361.

National Institute of Industrial Psychology (London) (1957), *The Training of Workers within the Factory: Survey of Industrial In-plant Training Programmes in Seven European Countries, EPA Project* No. 179.

European Productivity Agency (1958), *Fitting the Job to the Worker: Survey of American and European Research into Working Conditions in Industry, EPA Project* No. 335.

International Trade Union Conference (1958, Vienna) (1958), *Trade Union Research and Study Departments: Economic and Technical Problems.*

The Trade Union Seminar on Training Techniques (1958, Poigny-la-forêt, France) (1958), *Final Report,* prepared by Robert MOREAU.

MOREAU, Robert (1958), *Final Report,* The Trade Union Seminar on Training Techniques (1958, Poigny-la-forêt, France).

Fitting the Job to the Worker: International Conference (1959, Zurich) (1960), *General Report,* by Bernard METZ, *EPA Project* No. 6/07 E.

METZ, Bernard (1960), *General Report,* Fitting the Job to the Worker: International Conference (1959, Zurich), *EPA Project* No. 6/07 E.

European Productivity Agency (1958), *Some Aspects of Consultant Engineering in the United States, EPA Project* No. 357.

European Productivity Agency (1959), *Steel Workers and Technical Progress: a Comparative Report on Six National Studies, EPA Project* No. 164.

European Productivity Agency (1960-1961), *Training Possibilities in Europe.*

European Productivity Agency (1960), *Accelerated Vocational Training for Unskilled and Semi-Skilled Manpower, EPA Project* No. 6/08.

European Productivity Agency/Agence Européenne de Productivité (1958), Glossary of Work Study Terms/ Glossaire des termes de l'étude du travail/Wörterbuch des Arbeitsstudiums. (in English, French and German)

European Productivity Agency/Agence Européenne de Productivité (1959), Glossary of Work Study Terms/ Glossaire des termes de l'étude du travail/Wörterbuch des Arbeitsstudiums, 2nd. ed./2e éd. (in English, French and German)

European Productivity Agency/Agence Européenne de Productivité (1960), Glossary of Work Study Terms/ Glossaire des termes de l'étude du travail/Wörterbuch des Arbeitsstudiums, 3rd. ed./3e éd. (in English, French and German)

European Productivity Agency (1960), *Manual on Interviewing for the Use of Instructors in the Employment Services.*

Market Research on a European Scale (1959, Paris) (1960), *[Papers], EPA Project* No. 5/39.

National Institute of Industrial Psychology (Londres) (1957), *La Formation des travailleurs à l'intérieur de l'entreprise : rapport sur l'enquête effectuée dans sept pays européens, Projet AEP* nº 179.

Agence Européenne de Productivité (1959), *Adaptation du travail à l'homme : recherches américaines et européennes sur les conditions de travail dans l'industrie, Projet AEP* nº 335.

Session d'études syndicale internationale (1958, Vienne) (1958), *Les services syndicaux d'études et de recherche : problèmes économiques et techniques.*

Session d'études syndicale internationale sur les techniques de formation (1958, Poigny-la-Forêt, France) (1958), *Rapport final,* établi par Robert MOREAU.

MOREAU, Robert (1958), *Rapport final,* Session d'études syndicale internationale sur les techniques de formation (1958, Poigny-la-Forêt, France).

Adaptation du travail à l'homme : conférence internationale (1959, Zurich) (1960), *Rapport général,* par Bernard METZ, *Projet AEP* nº 6/07 E.

METZ, Bernard (1960), *Rapport général,* Adaptation du travail à l'homme : conférence internationale (1959, Zurich), *Projet AEP* n° 6/07 E.

Agence Européenne de Productivité (1958), *Quelques aspects de la profession d'ingénieur-conseil aux États-Unis, Projet AEP* nº 357.

Agence Européenne de Productivité (1959), *Travailleurs de l'acier et progrès technique : rapport comparatif sur six enquêtes nationales, Projet AEP* nº 164.

Agence Européenne de Productivité (1960-1961), *Possibilités de formation en Europe.*

Agence Européenne de Productivité (1960), *Formation accélèrée de la main-d'œuvre non qualifiée ou semi-qualifiée, Projet AEP* nº 6/08.

European Productivity Agency/Agence Européenne de Productivité (1958), Glossary of Work Study Terms/ Glossaire des termes de l'étude du travail/Wörterbuch des Arbeitsstudiums. (en anglais, français et allemand)

European Productivity Agency/Agence Européenne de Productivité (1959), Glossary of Work Study Terms/ Glossaire des termes de l'étude du travail/Wörterbuch des Arbeitsstudiums, 2nd. ed./2e éd. (en anglais, français et allemand)

European Productivity Agency/Agence Européenne de Productivité (1960), Glossary of Work Study Terms/ Glossaire des termes de l'étude du travail/Wörterbuch des Arbeitsstudiums, 3rd. ed./3e éd. (en anglais, français et allemand)

European Productivity Agency (1960), *Manual on Interviewing for the Use of Instructors in the Employment Services.* (disponible seulement en anglais)

L'étude des marchés européens (1959, Paris) (1960), *[Comptes rendus], Projet AEP* nº 5/39.

European Productivity Agency (1960), *Social Research and Industry in Europe: Problems and Perspectives.*

BERTHON, J. and GHELFI, A. (1961), *About Fitting the Job to the Worker.*

International Trade Union Study Session (1961, Kifissia) (1961), *Areas in Process of Development or Re-Development: Final Report.*

International Trade Union Study Session (1961, Innsbruck) (1961), *Bonus Schemes: Final Report.*

International Trade Union Seminar (1960, Dusseldorf) (1960), *Nuclear Energy Problems: Final Report,* OEEC, Paris.

International Trade Union Seminar (1961, Paris) (1961), *International Trade and Improvement of Labour Conditions: Final Report.*

International Trade Union Seminar (1961, Rattvik, Sweden) (1961), *Productivity Measurement: Final Report.*

European Productivity Agency (1961), *Trade-Union Training in Europe,* 2 vol.

8.5 Applied Research

The OEEC and then the EPA tried to promote the development of applied research and facilitate the use of its findings in industry. The Agency accordingly helped to set up a network of information centres and assisted them by perfecting new methods of information intended mainly for small and medium-sized firms, pointing out the value of Russian scientific and technical literature and taking action to make it more readily available, and showing businessmen how they could use applied research and the benefits to be obtained from encouraging its development.

Publications:

European Productivity Agency (1954), *The Organisation of Applied Research in Europe, the United States and Canada,* 3 vol., *EPA Projects* No. 81, 82, 83.

——. (1955), *Function and Training of the Chemical Engineer, EPA Project* No. 297.

The Organisation of Applied Research in Europe (1954, Nancy) (1955), *Proceedings of the Conference, EPA Project* No. 191.

Technical Information Services in Europe (1st, 1954, London) (1955), *Report, EPA Project* No. 296/1.

Technical Information Services in Europe (2nd, 1955, Frankfurt) (1955), *Report, EPA Project* No. 296/1.

Technical Information Services in Europe (3rd, 1956, Rome) (1958), *Report, EPA Project* No. 296/1.

Agence Européenne de Productivité (1960), *Recherche sociale et l'industrie en Europe : problèmes et perspectives.*

BERTHON, J. et GHELFI, A. (1961), *A propos de l'adaptation du travail à l'homme.*

Session d'études syndicales internationales (1961, Kifissia) (1961), *Régions en voie de développement ou de reconversion : Rapport final.*

Session d'études syndicales internationale (1961, Innsbruck) (1961), *Systèmes de salaires à primes : rapport final.*

Session d'études syndicales internationale (1960, Dusseldorf) (1960), *Problèmes de l'énergie nucléaire : rapport final,* OECE, Paris.

Session d'études syndicales internationale (1961, Paris) (1961), *Commerce international et amélioration des conditions de travail : rapport final.*

Session d'études syndicales internationale (1961, Rattvik, Suède) (1961), *Mesure de la productivité : rapport final.*

Agence Européenne de Productivité (1961), *Formation syndicale en Europe,* 2 vol.

8.5 Recherche appliquée

L'OECE, puis l'AEP, ont favorisé le développement de la recherche appliquée, et facilité son application industrielle. Elle a ainsi encouragé la création et alimenté un réseau de centres d'information, en mettant au point de nouveaux moyens d'information destinés surtout aux entreprises de petite et moyenne dimension, en attirant l'attention sur l'intérêt des publications techniques et scientifiques russes, en cherchant à les rendre plus facilement disponibles, et en démontrant aux industriels l'utilisation qu'ils pouvaient faire de la recherche appliquée et l'intérêt qu'ils auraient à en faciliter le développement.

Publications :

Agence Européenne de Productivité (1954), *L'organisation de la Recherche Appliquée en Europe, aux États-Unis et au Canada,* 3 vol., *Projet AEP* n° 81, 82, 83.

——. (1955), *Rôle et formation de l'ingénieur du génie chimique, Projet AEP* n° 297.

L'organisation de la recherche appliquée en Europe (1954, Nancy) (1955), Documents de la conférence, *Projet AEP* n° 191.

Information technique au service de l'Europe (1re, 1954, Londres) (1955), Rapport, *Projet AEP* n° 296/1.

Information technique au service de l'Europe (2e, 1955, Francfort) (1956), *Rapport, Projet AEP* n° 296/1.

Information technique au service de l'Europe (3e, 1956, Rome) (1958), *Rapport, Projet AEP* n° 296/1.

European Productivity Agency (1955-1956), *EPA Technical Digests,* vol. 1, No. 1 – vol. 2, No. 12. (Replaced by *EPA European Technical Digests.)*

European Productivity Agency (1957-1961), *EPA European Technical Digests,* vol. 2, No. 4 – vol. 9., No. 12, Index 1959, Index 1961. (Replaces *EPA European Technical Digests.)*

DASSEL, E. (1956), *The Importance of Scientific Research for the Teaching of Business Administration.*

Rational Organisation of Industrial Research (1956, Ashridge) (1957), [Report], *EPA Project* No. 352.

European Productivity Agency (1957), *European Co-operation in Research, under the Auspices of the Committee for Applied Research.*

DREYFUS, Gerard A. (1957), *International Guide to European Sources of Technical Information.*

OEEC/OECD (1960-1963), *Russian Technical Literature,* No. 1-4. Index to Issues 1 to 12, 1964.

European Productivity Agency (1960), *Fire Research: Directory, Laboratories and Research Establishments.*

European Productivity Agency (1960), *Technical Services to the Smaller Firm by Basic Suppliers: Case Studies of European and American Industry, EPA Project* No. 296/2.

Administration and Organisation of Research (1st, 1960, Château de Ménars) (1961), [Report of] the First European Regional Seminar.

8.6 Industries, Construction and Public Services

The specialised committees of the OEEC, which were required to monitor developments in the main sectors of industry, concerned themselves with the major technological issues that were liable sooner or later to affect the conditions of production or the structure of the market.

To keep itself informed and to be able to inform European industry, the OEEC called in a great many specialists from as broad a range of fields as possible who, as ''technical assistance missions'', made field trips to the United States or in Europe from which they brought back extremely comprehensive first-hand information on current technology and trends. Other reports are listed in the sections relevant to the committees that commissioned them.

Publications:

OEEC (1953), *Collection and Disposal of Town Refuse Street Cleansing, Technical Assistance Mission* No. 66.

European Productivity Agency (1955-1956), *EPA Technical Digests,* vol. 1, No. 1 – vol. 2, No. 12. (Remplacé par *EPA European Technical Digests)*

European Productivity Agency (1957-1961), *EPA European Technical Digests,* vol. 2, No. 4 – vol. 9, No. 12, Index 1959, Index 1961. (Remplace *EPA European Technical Digests)*

DASSEL, E. (1956), *L'importance de la recherche scientifique pour l'enseignement en matière d'administration des entreprises.*

L'organisation rationnelle de la Recherche Industrielle (1956, Ashridge) (1957), [Rapport]. *Projet AEP* n° 352.

Agence Européenne de Productivité (1957), *Coopération européenne dans le domaine de la recherche, sous le patronnage du Comité de la Recherche Appliquée.*

DREYFUS, Gerard A. (1957), *Guide international des sources européennes d'information technique.*

OECE/OCDE (1960-1963), *Documentation technique russe,* n° 1-4. Index des n° 1 à 17, 1965.

Agence Européenne de Productivité (1960), *Recherche en matière d'incendie : Répertoire, Laboratoires et établissements de recherche.*

Agence Européenne de Productivité (1960), *Services techniques rendus par les fournisseurs aux petites et moyennes entreprises : Études de cas dans les industries américaines et européennes, Projet AEP* n° 296/2.

Administration et organisation de la recherche (1re 1960, Château de Ménars) (1961), [Rapport du] premier colloque régional Européen.

8.6 Secteurs industriels, construction et services publics

Les comités spécialisés de l'OECE, chargés de suivre l'évolution de la conjoncture économique dans les principaux secteurs industriels, se sont intéressés aux grandes questions techniques qui risquaient à plus ou moins longue échéance de modifier de façon importante les conditions de la production ou la structure du marché.

Pour s'informer et informer les industriels européens, l'OECE a eu recours à de très nombreux spécialistes des branches les plus diverses qui, groupés en « mission d'assistance technique », ont accompli, soit aux États-unis, soit en Europe, des voyages d'études qui leur ont permis de recueillir, sur la situation ou les tendances de l'évolution technologique, des renseignements de première main extrêmement complets. D'autres rapports sont énumérés aux sections relatives aux comités qui en ont commandé la rédaction.

Publications :

OECE (1953), *Collecte et évacuation des ordures ménagères, nettoiement des voies publiques, Mission d'assistance technique* n° 66.

——. (1953), *Water Supply and Sewage Disposal, Technical Assistance Mission* No. 46.

OEEC/OECE (1954), *Ideal Foundry in Pictures/Images de la fonderie idéale, Technical Assistance Mission/ Mission d'assistance technique* No. 111.

OEEC (1954), *Increased Thermals Efficiency of Solid Fuel Through Gasification: Technical Progress in the USA and in Europe, Technical Assistance Mission* No. 99.

——. (1954), *Printing and the Graphic Arts in the USA, Technical Assistance Mission* No. 55.

——. (1954), *Recovery of sulphur in all its forms in the textile industry.*

European Congress on Productivity in the Textile Industry (1955, Ostend) (1955), *[Papers]*, 3 vol., *EPA Project* No. 245.

OEEC (1955), *Internal Transports in Iron and Steel Works. Technical Assistance Technique* No. 293.

——. (1955), *Powder Metallurgy, Technical Assistance Mission* No. 141.

——. (1955), *Traffic Engineering and Control in the USA, Technical Assistance Mission* No. 149.

——. (1955), *Zinc and Light Metal Die-Casting, Technical Assistance Mission* No. 155.

——. (1955-1958), *Productivity Measurement Review.*

——. (1956), *The Fibre Building Board Industry in Europe: a study by a specialized working party of the OEEC.*

——. (1956), *Industrial Use of Woodwaste, Technical Assistance Mission* No. 221.

——. (1956), *Long-Distance Gas Transport in the United States, Technical Assistance Mission* No. 118.

——. (1956), *Industrie des pièces détachées et des équipements automobiles aux États-Unis, Mission d'assistance technique No. 131.* (available only in French)

——. (1956), *Magnesium Fabricating and Casting, Technical Assistance Mission* No. 104.

——. (1956), *Titanium, zirconium and some other elements of growing industrial importance, Technical Assistance Mission* No. 247.

VAN den ABEELE, A. M. (1957), *A Method for Analysis and Comparison of Labour Productivity in Cotton Spinning Mills. Special number of the Productivity Measurement Review.*

——. (1957), *Air and Water Pollution: the Position in Europe and in the United States, EPA Project* No. 136 and 145.

——. (1957), *Modern Techniques for the Drying and Conditioning of Timber, Technical Assistance Mission* No. 241.

——. (1953), *Adduction d'eau et traitement des effluents urbains, Mission d'assistance technique* n° 46.

OEEC/OECE (1954), *Ideal Foundry in Pictures/Images de la fonderie idéale, Technical Assistance Mission/ Mission d'assistance technique* n° 111.

OECE (1954), *Valorisation des combustibles solides par la gazéification : évolution de la technique aux USA et en Europe. Mission d'assistance technique* n° 99.

——. (1954), *Arts graphiques aux États-Unis, Mission d'assistance technique* n° 55.

——. (1954), *Récupération du souffre sous toutes ses formes dans l'industie textile.*

Rencontre européenne de productivité dans l'industrie textile (1955, Ostende) (1955), *[Comptes rendus]*, 3 vol., *Projet AEP* n° 245.

OECE (1955), *Les transports intérieurs dans les usines sidérurgiques, Mission d'assistance technique* n° 293.

——. (1955), *Métallurgie des poudres, Mission d'assistance technique* n° 141.

——. (1955), *Organisation de la circulation routière aux États-Unis, Mission d'assistance technique* n° 149.

——. (1955), *Moulage sous pression du zinc et des métaux légers, Mission d'assistance technique* n° 155.

——. (1955-1958), *Revue de la mesure de la productivité.*

——. (1956), *Industrie des panneaux de fibres en Europe : étude préparée par un groupe de travail spécialisé de l'OECE.*

——. (1956), *Utilisation industrielle des déchets de bois, Mission d'assistance technique* n° 221.

——. (1956), *Transport de gaz à longue distance aux États-Unis, Mission d'assistance technique* n° 118.

——. (1956), *Industrie des pièces détachées et des équipements automobiles aux États-Unis, Mission d'assistance technique n° 131.*

——. (1956), *Transformation et moulage du magnesium, Mission d'assistance technique* n° 104.

——. (1956), *Titane, zirconium et autres éléments d'importance croissante pour l'industrie, Mission d'assistance technique* n° 247.

VAN den ABEELE, A. M. (1957), *Une méthode pour l'analyse et la comparaison de la productivité de la main-d'œuvre en filature de coton. Numéro spécial de la Revue de la Mesure de la Productivité.*

——. (1957), *Pollution des eaux et de l'air, la situation en Europe et aux États-Unis, Projet AEP* n° 136 et 145.

——. (1957), *Techniques modernes de séchage et de conditionnement du bois, Mission d'assistance technique* n° 241.

___. (1958), *Prefabricated Building: a Survey of some European Systems, Technical Assistance Mission* No. 226.

1958, *Water Economy in Iron and Steel Works, Technical Assistance Mission* No. 298.

1959, *European Refrigeration Research and its Practical Applications, Technical Assistance Mission* No. 239.

1959, *Production et distribution du béton sur les chantiers : manuel à l'usage des praticiens du bâtiment.* (available only in French)

European Productivity Agency (1960), *Integrated Data Processing and Computers, EPA Project* No. 6/02 B.

European Productivity Agency (1960), *Small Pulp Mills: an Economic Enquiry, EPA Project* No. 419.

European Productivity Agency (1960), *Integrated Data Processing: Working Documents, EPA Project* No. 6/02 B.

European Productivity Agency (1956), *Modular Coordination, EPA Project* No. 174.

European Productivity Agency (1961), *Modular Coordination: Second Report, EPA Project* No. 174.

8.7 Food and Agriculture

The agricultural part of the EPA's programme was drawn up by the Committee of Ministers' Deputies for Agriculture and Food (see Section 7), on the proposal of the Director of Agriculture. Its activities focused on marketing and distribution of fruit and vegetables, livestock products, fish (both fresh and frozen) and selected seed, and on advisory services and training of agricultural advisers in farm management, higher education in agriculture and a food and agricultural technical information service (FATIS).

The Agency helped to raise agricultural efficiency by means of research and circulation of information on the best techniques for modernisation of farm buildings, common methods of testing tractors and knapsack sprayers, control of animal diseases and parasites in stored products, application of nuclear energy to agriculture, non-food use of agricultural produce, and so on.

Publications:

OEEC (1953), *Meetings and Discussions, Technical Assistance Mission* No. 160.

___. (1953), *Pictures Save Words, Technical Assistance Mission* No. 160.

___. (1953), *Use of Aircraft in Agriculture in the USA, Technical Assistance Mission* No. 107.

___. (1958), *Construction préfabriquée en Europe : sélection de procédés et de réalisations, Mission d'assistance technique* n° 226.

1958, *Économie d'eau dans les usines sidérurgiques, Mission d'assistance technique* n° 298.

1959, *Travaux de laboratoires du froid en Europe et leurs applications industrielles, Mission d'assistance technique* n° 239.

1959, *Production et distribution du béton sur les chantiers : manuel à l'usage des praticiens du bâtiment.*

Agence Européenne de Productivité (1960), *Traitement intégré des informations et calculateurs électroniques, Projet AEP* n° 6/02 B.

Agence Européenne de Productivité (1960), *Petites usines de pâtes à papier : enquête économique, Projet AEP* n° 419.

European Productivity Agency (1960), *Integrated Data Processing: Working Documents, EPA Project* n° 6/02 B. (disponible seulement en anglais)

Agence Européenne de Productivité (1956), *Coordination modulaire, Projet AEP* n° 174.

Agence Européenne de Productivité (1961), *Coordination modulaire : deuxième rapport, Projet AEP* n° 174.

8.7 Alimentation et agriculture

La partie agricole du programme de l'AEP fut établie par le Comité des Suppléants des Ministres de l'agriculture et de l'alimentation (voir section 7), sur proposition du Directeur de l'agriculture. Ses activités ont porté sur la commercialisation, la distribution des fruits et légumes, des produits d'élevage, du poisson (frais et congelé) et des semences d'élite; sur la vulgarisation et la formation de conseillers agricoles à la gestion des exploitations; sur l'enseignement supérieur agricole et un service d'information technique sur l'alimentation et l'agriculture (FATIS).

L'Agence a concouru à l'amélioration du rendement des activités agricoles par la recherche et la diffusion des meilleures techniques se rapportant à la modernisation des bâtiments agricoles, aux méthodes communes d'essais pour les tracteurs et pulvérisateurs à dos, à la lutte contre les épizooties et contre les parasites des produits stockés, à l'application de l'énergie nucléaire en agriculture, à l'utilisation non alimentaire des produits agricoles, etc.

Publications :

OECE (1953), *Réunions et discussions, Mission d'assistance technique* n° 160.

___. (1953), *Une image vaut bien des mots, Mission d'assistance technique* n° 160.

___. (1953), *Utilisation de l'aviation dans l'agriculture aux États-Unis, Mission d'assistance technique* n° 107.

——. (1954), *Catalogue of Agricultural Films in European Countries* No. 1, Technical Assistance Mission No. 160.

——. (1954), *Catalogue des films agricoles dans les pays européens* nº 1, Mission d'assistance technique nº 160.

——. (1957), *Catalogue of Agricultural Films* No. 2.

——. (1957), *Catalogue des films agricoles* nº 2.

——. (1954), *Development of the Agricultural Advisory Services in Europe Since 1950.*

——. (1954), *Développement des services consultatifs agricoles en Europe depuis 1950.*

——. (1954), *Manures and fertilizers: Potential Progress in Europe.*

——. (1954), *Fumures minérales et organiques : progrès réalisables en Europe.*

Farm Management (1953, Bonn) (1954), *A Summary of Papers, EPA Project* No. 160.

La Gestion des exploitations agricoles (1953, Bonn) (1954), *Résumé des communications, Projet AEP* nº 160.

OEEC/OECD (1954-1967), *Fatis (Food and Agricultural Technical Information Service) Review.*

OECE/OCDE (1954-1967), *Revue Fatis. (Service d'information technique sur les questions d'alimentation et d'agriculture).*

OEEC (1955), *Agricultural Demonstrations Handbook for Agricultural Advisers, Technical assistance Mission* No. 248.

OECE (1955), *Démonstrations agricoles : Manuel pour les vulgarisateurs agricoles, Mission d'assistance technique* nº 248.

HUBBELING, N. (1955), *Bean Defects, Technical Assistance Mission* No. 160.

HUBBELING, N. (1955), *Maladies et dégats du haricot, Mission d'assistance technique* nº 160.

MULDER, D. (1955), Deficience of Fruit Crops, Technical Assistance Mission No. 160.

MULDER, D. (1955), *Carences des arbres fruitiers, Mission d'assistance technique* nº 160.

OEEC (1955), *Development of seed production and seed trade in european countries, Technical Assistance Mission* No. 214.

OECE (1955), *Développement de la production et du commerce des semences dans les pays européens, Mission d'assistance technique* nº 214.

Farm Planning and Budgeting Services in Farm Management Advisory Work (1954, United Kingdom) (1955), *Report, Technical Assistance Mission* No. 161/1.

Vulgarisation des méthodes et planification du travail et du budget dans la gestion des fermes (1954, Royaume-Uni) (1955), *Rapport, Mission d'assistance technique* nº 161/1.

The Mechanisation of Small Farms (1954, Germany) (1956), *Report, Technical Assistance Mission* No. 161/2.

La mécanisation des petites exploitations (1954, Allemagne) (1956), *Compte rendu, Mission d'assistance technique* nº 161/2.

The Effective Use of Fertilizers Including Lime (1954, Denmark) (1957), *Report, Technical Assistance Mission* No. 161/3.

L'emploi rationnel des engrais et de la chaux (1954, Danemark) (1957), *Compte rendu, Mission d'assistance technique* nº 161/3.

The Effective Use of Modern Pesticides and Herbicides (1954, France) (1955), *Report, Technical Assistance Mission* No. 161/4.

Utilisation rationnelle des pesticides et herbicides modernes (1954, France) (1955), *Compte rendu, Mission d'assistance technique* nº 161/4.

High-quality seed: its production, control and distribution (1954, The Netherlands) (1955), *Report, Technical Assistance Mission* No. 161/5.

La production, le contrôle et la distribution des semences d'élite (1954, Pays-Bas) (1955), *Compte rendu, Mission d'assistance technique* nº 161/5.

Grain Drying Storage and Handling in European Countries (1953, United Kingdom) (1954), *Report, Technical Assistance Mission* No. 161/6.

Les méthodes de séchage, stockage et manutention des céréales en Europe (1953, Royaume-Uni), (1954), *Rapport, Mission d'assistance technique* nº 161/6.

The Production and Marketing of High-quality Milk (1954, Denmark) (1955), *Report, Technical Assistance Mission* No. 161/7.

La production et la vente de lait de haute qualité (1954, Danemark) (1955), *Compte rendu, Mission d'assistance technique* nº 161/7.

The Handling and Marketing of Fruit and Vegetables at Grower-Shippper Level (1954, The Netherlands) (1956), *Report, Technical Assistance Mission* No. 161/8.

La manutention et la commercialisation des fruits et des légumes au stade de la production et de l'expédition (1954, Pays-Bas) (1956), *Compte rendu, Mission d'assistance technique* nº 161/8.

The Production and Marketing of Eggs and Poultry (1954, The Netherlands) (1956), *Report, Technical Assistance Mission* No. 161/9.

La production et la commercialisation des œufs et de la volaille (1954, Pays-Bas) (1956), *Compte rendu, Mission d'assistance technique* nº 161/9.

Improved quality and packing of fresh fish as a means of stimulating consumption (1955, Norway) (1955), *Report, Technical Assistance Mission* No. 161/10.

The Control of Poultry Diseases (1953, France) (1955), *Report, Technical Assistance Mission* No. 161/11.

Grassland Management, Including the Establishment of Pastures and the Conservation of Grass (1954, Germany) (1954), *Report, Technical Assistance Mission* No. 161/12.

The Production and Utilisation of Pasture and Fodder in Mediterranean Regions (1954, Portugal) (1955), *Report, Technical Assistance Mission* No. 161/13.

Cattle Feeding and Management (1954, Belgium) (1956), *Report, Technical Assistance Mission* No. 161/14.

Preparation and Implementation of Special Farm Productivity Campaigns (1954, Germany) (1954), *Report, Technical Assistance Mission* No. 161/15.

Use of Agricultural Press (1954, Sweden) (1955), *Report, Technical Assistance Mission* No. 161/16.

The Use of Radio in Farm Advisory Work and Farmer Education (1954, Italy) (1956), *Report, Technical Assistance Mission* No. 161/17.

Farm Irrigation (1954, Greece) (1955), *Report, Technical Assistance Mission* No. 161/20.

OEEC (1955), *Testing of agricultural seed moving in International Trade, EPA Project* No. 223.

___. (1955), *Advisory Work and the Pen, EPA Project* No. 160.

___. (1955), *Control of Pests and Stored Agricultural Products with Special Reference to Grain, EPA Project* No. 212.

___. (1955), *Frozen fish: Quality and Packing as a Way to Improve Marketing and Consumption, EPA Project* No. 325.

___. (1955), *Marketing of Fruit and Vegetables in Europe, EPA Project* No. 249 C.

___. (1955), *Organisation and Rationalisation of Soil Analysis, EPA Project* No. 156.

___. (1955), *The Agricultural Value of Phosphate Fertilizers which Economise in the Use of Sulphuric Acid, EPA Project* No. 162.

___. (1955), *The Testing of Farms Machinery on a International Basis, EPA Project* No. 251/1.

___. (1955), *The Written Words in Agricultural Advisory Work, EPA Project* No. 323/1.

Comment améliorer l'emballage du poisson frais pour stimuler la consommation? (1955, Norvège) (1955), *Compte rendu, Mission d'assistance technique* n° 161/10.

Le lutte contre les maladies de la volaille (1953, France) (1955), *Compte rendu, Mission d'assistance technique* n° 161/11.

L'exploitation des herbages comprenant la création de pâturages temporaires et la conservation de l'herbe (1954, Allemagne) (1954), *Compte rendu, Mission d'assistance technique* n° 161/12.

La production et l'exploitation des pâturages et des cultures fouragères dans les régions méditerranéennes (1954, Portugal) (1955), *Compte rendu, Mission d'assistance technique* n° 161/13.

L'exploitation et l'alimentation du bétail (1954, Belgique) (1955), *Compte rendu, Mission d'assistance technique* n° 161/14.

La préparation et l'organisation de campagnes consacrées à des programmes de productivité agricole (1954, Allemagne) (1954), *Compte rendu, Mission d'assistance technique* n° 161/15.

Utilisation de la presse agricole (1954, Suède) (1955), *Compte rendu, Mission d'assistance technique* n° 161/16.

Les émissions radiophoniques à l'intention des agriculteurs (1954, Italie) (1956), *Compte rendu, Mission d'assistance technique* n° 161/17.

L'irrigation en agriculture (1954, Grèce) (1955), *Compte rendu, Mission d'assistance technique* n° 161/20.

OECE (1956), *Essais des semences destinées au commerce international, Projet AEP* n° 223.

___. (1955), *La plume au service de la vulgarisation, Projet AEP* n° 160.

___. (1955), *La lutte contre les insectes nuisibles aux denrées emmagasinées et notamment aux céréales, Projet AEP* n° 212.

___. (1955), *Le poisson congelé : qualité et emballage, facteurs du développement du marché et de la consommation, Projet AEP* n° 325.

___. (1955), *Organisations du marché des fruits et légumes en Europe, Projet AEP* n° 249 C.

___. (1955), *Organisation et rationalisation de l'analyse des sols, Projet AEP* n° 156.

___. (1955), *Valeur agricole des engrais phosphatés produits selon des procédés économisant l'acide sulphurique, Projet AEP* n° 162.

___. (1955), *Données internationales sur les essais des machines agricoles, Projet AEP* n° 251/1.

___. (1955), *Le savoir écrire de la vulgarisation agricole, Projet AEP* n° 323/1.

——. (1957), *Breeding Methods for Cattle Pigs and Poultry in the United States Including Inter State Co-operation, Technical Assistance Mission* No. 253.

——. (1957), *Fish Marketing in Western Europe since 1950, EPA Project* No. 325/2.

——. (1957), *Labour Management on the Farm, EPA Project* No. 200.

——. (1957), *Land Consolidation: Cheaper and More Simplified Methods, EPA Project* No. 199.

——. (1957), *Selection, Use and Maintenance of Agricultural Machinery, EPA Project* No. 251/3.

——. (1958), *Advisory Work in Rural Home Economics in Europe, EPA Project* No. 394.

——. (1958), *Agricultural Advisory Services in Europe and North America: 1957, EPA Project* No. 395/A.

——. (1958), *Farm Management in the United States, EPA Project* No. 395/B.

——. (1958), *Application of Atomic Sciences in Agriculture and Food, EPA Project* No. 396.

OEEC/OECE (1958), *Catalogue of the Types and Sizes of Wooden Packaging For Fruit and Vegetables Used in Europe/Catalogue des types dimensionnels d'emballages en bois pour fruits et légumes utilisés en Europe.*

OEEC (1958), *Control of Diseases in Cattle and Sheep at Pasture, EPA Project* No. 204.

——. (1958), *Demonstrations for Improved Seed Multiplication and Trade in Seed 1954-1957, EPA Project* No. 252/4.

1959, *Consumer Education in Food and Agricultural Products with Special Emphasis on Milk and Fish, EPA Project* No. 308.

OEEC/OECD (1959-1964), *Food and Agriculture Documentation.*

OECE (1959), *Cost-Return Relationships in Agriculture, Food and Agriculture Documentation* No. 1, *EPA Project* No. 392.

——. (1959), *Economic Optimum Fertilizer Use, Food and Agriculture Documentation* No. 2, *EPA Project* No. 393.

——. (1959), *Documentation Concerning National Systems of Seed Certification: OEEC Scheme for the Varietal Certification of Herbage Seed Moving in International Trade, Food and Agriculture Documentation* No. 3, *EPA Project* No. 215.

——. (1959), *Consumer education in food and agricultural poducts: with special emphasis on milk and fish, Food and Agriculture Documentation* No. 4, *EPA Project* No. 308.

——. (1957), *Élevage des bovins, des porcins et de la volaille : méthodes d'amélioration génétique appliquées aux États-Unis y compris la coopération entre États, Mission d'assistance technique* n° 253.

——. (1957), *Marché du poisson en Europe occidentale depuis 1950, Projet AEP* n° 325/2.

——. (1957), *Organisation du travail dans l'exploitation agricole, Projet AEP* n° 200.

——. (1957), *Remembrement rural par des méthodes économiques et simplifiées, Projet AEP* n° 199.

——. (1957), *Choix, utilisation et entretien des machines agricoles, Projet AEP* n° 251/3.

——. (1958), *La vulgarisation en matière d'économie domestique rurale, Projet AEP* n° 394.

——. (1958), *Les services de vulgarisation agricole en Europe et en Amérique du Nord : 1957, Projet AEP* n° 395/A.

——. (1958), *La gestion des exploitations agricoles aux États-Unis, Projet AEP* n° 395/B.

——. (1958), *Application des sciences atomiques dans l'agriculture et l'alimentation, Projet AEP* n° 396.

OEEC/OECE (1958), *Catalogue of the Types and Sizes of Wooden Packaging For Fruit and Vegetables Used in Europe/Catalogue des types dimensionnels d'emballages en bois pour fruits et légumes utilisés en Europe.*

OECE (1958), *Lutte contre les maladies des bovins et des ovins au pâturage, Projet AEP* n° 204.

——. (1958), *Démonstration de procédés améliorés pour la multiplication et le commerce des semences 1954-1957, Projet AEP* n° 252/4.

1959, *Éducation du consommateur de produits alimentaires et agricoles, produits laitiers et poissons, Projet AEP* n° 308.

OECE/OCDE (1959-1964), *Documentation alimentation et agriculture.*

OECE (1959), *Rapports charges-Produits en agriculture, Documentation alimentation et agriculture* n° 1, *Projet AEP* n° 392.

——. (1959), *Optimum économique de l'utilisation des engrais, Documentation alimentation et agriculture* n° 2, *Projet AEP* n° 393.

——. (1959), *Documentation relative aux systèmes nationaux de certification des semences : système de l'OECE pour la certification variétale des semences fourragères destinées au commerce international, Documentation alimentation et agriculture* n° 3, *Projet AEP* n° 215.

——. (1959), *Éducation du consommateur de produits alimentaires et agricoles : Produits laitiers et poisson, Documentation alimentation et agriculture* n° 4, *Projet AEP* n° 308.

(1959), *Livestock Diseases and the Organisation of Veterinary Services in Europe, Food and Agriculture Documentation* No. 5, *EPA Project* No. 205.

(1959), *Trial Shipments for European Standardization of Plums, Food and Agriculture Documentation* No. 6, *EPA Project* No. 5/16.

——. (1959), *Marketing of Fruit and Vegetables in Yugoslavia, Food and Agriculture Documentation* No. 7, *EPA Project* No. 372.

——. (1959), *Agricultural Advisory Services in OEEC Countries in the Mediterranean Area, Food and Agriculture Documentation* No. 8, *EPA Project* No. 5/17.

——. (1959), *Farm Records for Farm Management Purposes, Food and Agriculture Documentation* No. 9, *EPA Project* No. 395/2.

——. (1959), *Pre-Packaging for Fruit and Vegetables, Food and Agriculture Documentation* No. 10, *EPA Project* No. 372.

European Productivity Agency/Agence Européenne de Productivité (1959), *List of Agricultural Press and Periodicals in OEEC member countries/Répertoire des quotidiens et périodiques agricoles dans les pays membres de l'OECE, Food and Agricultural Documentation/ Documentation alimentation et agriculture* No. 11, *EPA Project/Projet AEP* No. 5/32.

OEEC (1959), *Slaughterhouse Facilities and Meat Distribution in OEEC Countries, Food and Agriculture Documentation* No. 12, *EPA Project* No. 295.

——. (1959), *Detail Trade for Milk and Milk Products, Food and Agriculture Documentation* No. 13, EPA Project No. 285/3.

——. (1959), *Marketing and Distribution Margins for Livestock and Meat in OEEC Countries, Food and Agriculture Documentation* No. 15, *EPA Project* No. 285.

——. (1959), *Marketing and Distribution Margins for Eggs in OEEC countries, Food and Agriculture Documentation* No. 16, *EPA Project* No. 285.

European Productivity Agency/Agence Européenne de Productivité (1959), Use of Radiations and Radio-Isotopes in Agriculture and Food: *List of research institutes and scientists in OEEC member countries/Utilisation des techniques d'irradiation et des isotopes radioactifs dans la recherche agronomique : répertoire des instituts et des chercheurs dans les pays membres de l'OECE, Food and Agriculture Documentation/Documentation alimentation et agriculture* No. 17, *EPA Project/Projet AEP* No. 396.

——. (1961), *Lexicon of Terminology Used in the Fruit and Vegetables Trade/Répertoire des termes du marché des fruits et légumes, Food and Agriculture Documentation/Documentation alimentation et agriculture* No. 18, *EPA Project/Projet AEP* No. 372/2.

——. (1959), *Lutte contre les maladies du bétail et organisation des services vétérinaires en Europe, Documentation alimentation et agriculture* nº 5, *Projet AEP* nº 205.

——. (1959), *Liaisons commerciales pour la normalisation européennes des prunes, Documentation alimentation et agriculture* nº 6, *Projet AEP* nº 5/16.

——. (1959), *Organisation du marché des fruits et légumes en Yougoslavie, Documentation alimentation et agriculture* nº 7, *Projet AEP* nº 372.

——. (1959), *Services de vulgarisation agricole dans les pays méditerranéens membres de l'OECE, Documentation alimentation et agriculture* nº 8, *Projet AEP* nº 5/17.

——. (1959), *Rôle de la comptabilité dans la gestion des exploitations agricoles, Documentation alimentation et agriculture* nº 9, *Projet AEP* nº 395/2.

——. (1959), *Pré-emballage des fruits et légumes, Documentation alimentation et agriculture* nº 10, *Projet AEP* nº 372.

European Productivity Agency/Agence Européenne de Productivité (1959), *List of Agricultural Press and Periodicals in OEEC member countries/Répertoire des quotidiens et périodiques agricoles dans les pays membres de l'OECE, Food and Agricultural Documentation/ Documentation alimentation et agriculture* nº 11, *EPA Project/Projet AEP* nº 5/32.

OECE (1959), *Abattoirs et la distribution de la viande dans les pays de l'OECE, Documentation alimentation et agriculture* nº 12, *Projet AEP* nº 295.

——. (1959), *Commerce de détail du lait et des produits laitiers, Documentation alimentation et agriculture* nº 13, *Projet AEP* nº 285/3.

——. (1959), *Marges de commercialisation pour le bétail et la viande dans les pays de l'OECE, Documentation alimentation et agriculture* nº 15, *Projet AEP* nº 285.

——. (1959), *Marges de commercialisation pour les œufs dans les pays de l'OECE, Documentation alimentation et agriculture* nº 16, *Projet AEP* nº 285.

European Productivity Agency/Agence Européenne de Productivité (1959), Use of Radiations and Radio-Isotopes in Agriculture and Food: *List of research institutes and scientists in OEEC member countries/Utilisation des techniques d'irradiation et des isotopes radioactifs dans la recherche agronomique : répertoire des instituts et des chercheurs dans les pays membres de l'OECE, Food and Agriculture Documentation/Documentation alimentation et agriculture* nº 17, *EPA Project/Projet AEP* nº 396.

——. (1961), *Lexicon of Terminology Used in the Fruit and Vegetables Trade/Répertoire des termes du marché des fruits et légumes, Food and Agriculture Documentation/Documentation alimentation et agriculture* nº 18, *EPA Project/Projet AEP* nº 372/2.

OEEC (1960), *Training of Young Farmers and Farm Workers, Food and Agriculture Documentation* No. 14, *EPA Project* No. 395/2 and No. 5/17.

——. (1960), *Trial Shipments for the European Standardisation of Table Pears and Citrus Fruit, Food and Agriculture Documentation* No. 19, *EPA Project* No. 372/2.

——. (1959), *OEEC Standard Code and Test Bulletin for Agricultural tractors, Food and Agriculture Documentation* No. 20, *EPA Project* No. 251/4.

——. (1959), *Marketing and Consumption of Frozen Fish in OEEC countries (1959, Verona) (1960), Report, Food and Agriculture Documentation* No. 21, *EPA Project* No. 5/18.

——. (1960), *Consumption of Fruit and Vegetables in OEEC Countries, Food and Agriculture Documentation* No. 22, *EPA Project* No. 372/2.

——. (1960), *Grass, Clover and Lucerne, Food and Agriculture Documentation* No. 23, *EPA Project* No. 209 and 210.

——. (1960), *Marketing and Distribution Margins for Milk and Milk Products in OEEC Countries, Food and Agriculture Documentation* No. 24, *EPA Project* No. 285.

——. (1960), *Standardisation of Wooden Packaging for Fruit and Vegetables, Food and Agriculture Documentation* No. 25, *EPA Project* No. 372/2.

——. (1960), *Contribution of Home Economics Towards Rural Developments Projects, Food and Agriculture Documentation* No. 26, *EPA Project* No. 5/17.

——. (1960), *Agricultural Regions in the European Economic Community, Food and Agriculture Documentation* No. 27.

European Productivity Agency/Agence Européenne de Productivité (1960), *List of Agricultural Press and Periodicals in OEEC Member Countries/Répertoire des quotidiens et périodiques agricoles dans les pays membres de l'OECE, Food and Agriculture Documentation/ Documentation alimentation et agriculture* No. 28, *EPA project/Projet AEP* No. 6/15, rev. ed./éd. révisée.

Marketing of Fruit and Vegetables in Spain and Turkey, Food and Agriculture Documentation No. 29, *EPA Projects* No. 5/16 and No. 6/10.

OEEC (1960), *Higher Education in Agriculture, Food and Agriculture Documentation* No. 30, *EPA Project* No. 6/15.

1961, *Nutritive and Therapeutic Value of Fruit and Vegetables, Food and Agriculture Documentation* No. 31, *EPA Project* No. 7/10-C.

OECE (1960), *Formation des jeunes agriculteurs et des travailleurs agricoles, Documentation alimentation et agriculture* n° 14, *Projet AEP* n° 395/2 et n° 5/17.

——. (1960), *Liaisons commerciales pour la normalisation européenne des poires de table et des agrumes, Documentation alimentation et agriculture* n° 19, *Projet AEP* n° 372/2.

——. (1959), *Code normalisé et bulletin d'essais de l'OECE pour les tracteurs agricoles, Documentation alimentation et agriculture* n° 20, *Projet AEP* n° 251/4.

——. (1959), *Commercialisation et consommation du poisson surgelé dans les pays de l'OECE (1959, Vérone) (1960), Rapport, Documentation alimentation et agriculture* n° 21, *Projet AEP* n° 5/18.

——. (1960), *Consommation des fruits et légumes dans les pays de l'OECE, Documentation alimentation et agriculture* n° 22, *Projet AEP* n° 372/2.

——. (1960), *Essais de comportement des variétés de graminées, de trèfle et de luzerne, Documentation alimentation et agriculture* n° 23, *Projet AEP* n° 209 et 210.

——. (1960), *Marges de commercialisation pour le lait et les produits laitiers dans les pays de l'OECE, Documentation alimentation et agriculture* n° 24. *Projet AEP* n° 285.

——. (1960), *Normalisation des emballages en bois pour fruit et légumes, Documentation alimentation et agriculture* n° 25, *Projet AEP* n° 372/2.

——. (1960), *La contribution apportée par l'économie domestique aux plans agricoles de mise en valeur, Documentation alimentation et agriculture* n° 26, *Projet AEP* n° 5/17.

——. (1960), *Les Grandes régions agricoles dans la communauté économique européenne, Documentation alimentation et agriculture* n° 27.

European Productivity Agency/Agence Européenne de Productivité (1960), *List of Agricultural Press and Periodicals in OEEC Member Countries/Répertoire des quotidiens et périodiques agricoles dans les pays membres de l'OECE, Food and Agriculture Documentation/ Documentation alimentation et agriculture* n° 28, *EPA project/Projet AEP* n° 6/15, rev. ed./éd. révisée.

Organisation du marché des fruits et légumes en Espagne et en Turquie, Documentation alimentation et agriculture n° 29, *Projets AEP* n° 5/16 et n° 6/10.

OECE (1960), *Enseignement supérieur agricole, Documentation alimentation et agriculture* n° 30, *Projet AEP* n° 6/15.

1961, *Valeur alimentaire et thérapeutique des fruits et légumes, Documentation alimentation et agriculture* n° 31, *Projet AEP* n° 7/10-C.

European Productivity Agency/Agence Européenne de Productivité (1961), Meat Cuts in OEEC Member Countries/Les découpes des viandes dans les pays de l'OECE, Food and Agriculture Documentation/Documentation alimentation et agriculture No. 32, *EPA Project/Projet AEP* No. 7/11-IB.

___. (1961), *Catalogue of the Types and Sizes of Wooden Packaging for Fruit and Vegetables Used in Europe: Supplement to the catalogue published in 1958/Catalogue des types dimensionnels d'emballage en bois pour fruits et légumes utilisés en Europe : supplément au catalogue publié en 1958, Food and Agriculture Documentation/Documentation alimentation et agriculture* No. 33, *EPA Project/Projet AEP* No. 5/16.

OEEC (1961), *Farmers Marketing Organisations, Food and Agriculture Documentation* No. 34, *EPA Project* No. 403.

___. (1961), *Agricultural Documentation: the Responsabilities of Libraries and Information Services, Food and Agriculture Documentation* No. 35, *EPA Project* No. 6/15 (FATIS).

___. (1961), *Agricultural Advisory Services in Europe and North America: 1960, Food and Agriculture Documentation* No. 36, *EPA Project* No. 6/14-1.

___. (1961), *Catalogue of Agricultural Films, Food and Agriculture Documentation* No. 37, *EPA Project* No. 8/15 (FATIS).

___. (1961), *Application of Marketing and Consumer Research for Livestock Products in the United States, Food and Agriculture Documentation* No. 40, *EPA Project* No. 5/31-V.

___. (1961), *Agricultural Regions in the OEEC Countries, Food and Agricultural Documentation* No. 41, *EPA Project* No. 417.

___. (1961), *Organisation of the Wholesale Meat Markets in Europe, Food and Agriculture Documentation* No. 42, *EPA Project* No. 5/31-IA.

___. (1961), *Meat Grading in OEEC Member Countries, Food and Agriculture Documentation* No. 43, *EPA Project* No. 5/31-IB.

___. (1961), *Methods of Forecasting Pig Meat Production in OEEC Member Countries, Food and Agriculture Documentation* No. 44, *EPA Project* No. 6/11-IA.

___. (1961), *Programme Planning: a Simple Method of Determining High Profit Production Plans on Individual Farms, Food and Agriculture Documentation* No. 45, *EPA Project* No. 6/14-II.

___. (1961), *Use of Radiations and Radio-Isopes in Food and Agriculture: List of Research Institutes and Researchers in OECD Member Countries, Food and Agriculture Documentation* No. 46, *EPA Project* No. 396. (New and Revised Edition.)

European Productivity Agency/Agence Européenne de Productivité (1961), Meat Cuts in OEEC Member Countries/Les découpes des viandes dans les pays de l'OECE, Food and Agriculture Documentation/Documentation alimentation et agriculture n° 32, *EPA Project/Projet AEP* n° 7/11-IB.

___. (1961), *Catalogue of the Types and Sizes of Wooden Packaging for Fruit and Vegetables Used in Europe: Supplement to the catalogue published in 1958/Catalogue des types dimensionnels d'emballage en bois pour fruits et légumes utilisés en Europe : supplément au catalogue publié en 1958, Food and Agriculture Documentation/Documentation alimentation et agriculture* n° 33, *EPA Project / Projet AEP* n° 5/16.

OECE (1961), *Organisations agricoles de commercialisation, Documentation alimentation et agriculture* n° 34, *Projet AEP* n° 403.

___. (1961), *La documentation agricole : rôle des bibliothèques et des services d'informations, Documentation alimentation et agriculture* n° 35, *Projet AEP* n° 6/15 (FATIS).

___. (1961), *Services de vulgarisation agricole en Europe et en Amérique du Nord : 1960, Documentation alimentation et agriculture* n° 36, *Projet AEP* n° 6/14-1.

___. (1961), *Catalogue des films agricoles, Documentation alimentation et agriculture* n° 37, *Projet AEP* n° 8/15 (FATIS).

___. (1961), *Applications des recherches dans la commercialisation et la consommation des produits de l'élevage aux États-Unis, Documentation alimentation et agriculture* n° 40, *Projet AEP* n° 5/31-V.

___. (1961), *Régions agricoles dans les pays membres de l'OECE, Documentation alimentation et agriculture* n° 41, *Projet AEP* n° 417.

___. (1961), *Organisation des marchés de gros de la viande en Europe, Documentation alimentation et agriculture* n° 42, *Projet AEP* n° 5/31-IA.

___. (1961), *Classification des viandes dans les pays membres de l'OECE, Documentation alimentation et agriculture* n° 43, *Projet AEP* n° 5/31-IB.

___. (1961), *Méthodes de prévision des productions de viande de porc utilisées dans les pays membres de l'OECE, Documentation alimentation et agriculture* n° 44, *Projet AEP* n° 6/11-IA.

___. (1961), *Le « Programme Planning » : Méthode simple de détermination de systèmes de production rentables pour l'exploitation agricole, Documentation alimentation et agriculture* n° 45, *Projet AEP* n° 6/14-II.

___. (1961), *Utilisation des techniques d'irradiation et des isotopes radioactifs dans la recherche agronomique : Répertoire des instituts et des chercheurs dans les Pays Membres, Documentation alimentation et agriculture* n° 46, *Projet AEP* n° 396. (Nouvelle édition révisée.)

___. (1961), *International Standardization of Fruit and Vegetables, Food and Agriculture Documentation* No. 47, *EPA Project* No. 8/10.

___. (1961), *The Development of Agricultural Apprenticeship Schemes, Food and Agriculture Documentation* No. 48, *EPA Project* No. 7/14-III.

___. (1961), *Work Planning Methods in Agriculture and Horticulture, Food and Agriculture Documentation* No. 49, *EPA Project* No. 8/14 *b*.

___. (1961), *Inter disciplinary Cooperation in Technical and Economic Agricultural Research, Food and Agriculture Documentation* No. 50, *EPA Project* No. 8/14 *d*.

___. (1961), *Sanitary Regulations for Fish and Fish Products, Food and Agriculture Documentation* No. 51, *EPA Project* No. 7/12 *c* and 8/12 *c*.

___. (1961), *Agricultural Vocational Training in Europe and North America, Food and Agriculture Documentation* No. 52, *EPA Project* No. 8/16 *b*.

1959, *Development of Farmers' Marketing Co-operatives for Milk, Milk Products and Eggs, Technical Assistance Mission* No. 285.

European Productivity Agency/Agence Européenne de Productivité (1959), *List of Agricultural Press and Periodicals in OEEC member countries/Répertoire des quotidiens et périodiques agricoles dans les pays membres de l'OECE, Food and Agricultural Documentation/ Documentation alimentation et agriculture* No. 11, *EPA Project/Projet AEP* No. 5/32.

___. (1960), *List of Agricultural Press and Periodicals in OEEC Member Countries/Répertoire des quotidiens et périodiques agricoles dans les pays membres de l'OECE, Food and Agriculture Documentation* No. 28/*Documentation alimentation et agriculture* No. 28, *EPA project* No. 6/15/*Projet AEP* No. 6/15, *rev. ed./éd. révisée.*

European Productivity Agency (1959), *Small Family Farm: a European Problem: Methods for Creating Economically Viable Units, Technical Assistance Mission* No. 199/2.

OEEC (1958), *Farm Buildings: Including their Remodelling and Adaptation,* 2 vol., *EPA Project* No. 391.

___. (1958), *Farm Buildings: Including their Remodelling and Adaptation:* vol. 1: *United States, EPA Project* No. 391.

___. (1958), *Farm Buildings: Including their Remodelling and Adaptation:* vol. 2: *Europe, EPA Project* No. 391.

Palletisation of Standard Wooden Containers for Fruit and Vegetables (1960, Lausanne) (1960), *Report, EPA Project* No. 6/10-A.

___. (1960), *Paper and Cardboard Containers for Fruit and Vegetables.*

___. (1961), *Normalisation internationale des fruits et légumes, Documentation alimentation et agriculture* n° 47, *Projet AEP* n° 8/10.

___. (1961), *Le développement des systèmes d'apprentissage agricole, Documentation alimentation et agriculture* n° 48, *Projet AEP* n° 7/14-III.

___. (1961), *Les méthodes d'élaboration des plans de travail pour les exploitations agricoles et horticoles, Documentation alimentation et agriculture* n° 49, *Projet AEP* n° 8/14 *b*.

___. (1961), *Coopération entre les disciplines de recherche technique et économique en agriculture, Documentation alimentation et agriculture* n° 50, *Projet AEP* n° 8/14 *d*.

___. (1961), *Règlements sanitaires pour le poisson et les produits de la pêche, Documentation alimentation et agriculture* n° 51, *Projet AEP* n° 7/12 et 8/12 *c*.

___. (1961), *La formation professionnelle agricole en Europe et en Amérique du Nord, Documentation alimentation et agriculture* n° 52, *Projet AEP* n° 8/16 *b*.

1959, *Développement des coopératives d'agriculteurs pour la commercialisation du lait, des produits laitiers et des œufs, Mission d'assistance technique* n° 285.

European Productivity Agency/Agence Européenne de Productivité (1959), *List of Agricultural Press and Periodicals in OEEC member countries/Répertoire des quotidiens et périodiques agricoles dans les pays membres de l'OECE, Food and Agricultural Documentation/ Documentation alimentation et agriculture* n° 11, *EPA Project/Projet AEP* n° 5/32.

___. (1960), *List of Agricultural Press and Periodicals in OEEC Member Countries/Répertoire des quotidiens et périodiques agricoles dans les pays membres de l'OECE, Food and Agriculture Documentation* n° 28/*Documentation alimentation et agriculture* n° 28, *EPA project* n° 6/15/*Projet AEP* n° 6/15, rev. ed./éd. révisée.

Agence Européenne de Productivité (1959), *La petite exploitation agricole familiale : problème européen : méthodes pour la création d'unités viables, Mission d'assistance technique* n° 199/2.

OECE (1958), *Modernisation des bâtiments de ferme,* 2 vol., *Projet AEP* n° 391.

___. (1958), *Modernisation des bâtiments de ferme:* vol. 1 : *États-Unis, Projet AEP* n° 391.

___. (1958), *Modernisation des bâtiments de ferme :* vol. 2 : *Europe, Projet AEP* n° 391.

Palettisation des emballages en bois normalisés pour fruits et légumes (1960, Lausanne) (1960), *rapport, Projet AEP* n° 6/10-A.

___. (1960), *Emballages en papier et carton pour fruits et légumes.*

___. (1960), *Promotion of Increased Liquid Milk Consumption Through Improved Distribution Methods and Better Quality Control, EPA Project* No. 285/3 – Part III.

___. (1960), *Summary Report on Activities Undertaken by EPA since its Establishment in 1953.*

___. (1961), *Professional Training of Teachers in Vocational Agricultural Schools, EPA Project* No. 6/14-4.

___. (1961), *Hydrological and Biological Conditions in Testing Stations in Europe.*

8.8 Assistance to Underdeveloped Areas

In addition to activities concerned with productivity in the strict sense of the term, the Agency tried to stimulate the economic development of developing areas in Member countries. Italy, Greece and Turkey, for example, were provided with experts who gave the advice needed for the framing of development projects and who were associated with the productivity efforts of those countries. The Agency also encouraged and aided the creation of experimental and demonstration areas.

Publications:

European Productivity Agency (1958), *Uvdal Pilot Community: Norway, EPA Project* No. 323.

OEEC (1960), *Community Development: Some Achievements in the United States and Europe, EPA Project* No. 337.

___. (1960), *Olive Growing in Sardinia.*

___. (1960), *Pilot-area in Sardinia: an International Experiment in Community Development.*

EDELMAN, C. H. (1961), *Soil Survey Activities in Turkey.*

MAYNE, A. (1961), *Designing and Administering: a Regional Economic Development Plan with Specific Reference to Puerto Rico.*

Regional Economic Planning (1960, Bellagio) (1961), *Techniques of Analysis for Less Developed Areas,* OEEC, Paris.

KRIER, H. (1961), *Rural Manpower and Industrial Development: Adaptation and Training: general report.*

9. Office for Scientific and Technical Personnel (OSTP)

The launching of the first Soviet sputnik emphasized the relative shortage of scientists and engineers in the West. In May 1958 the **Special Office for Scientific and Technical Personnel** was set up to direct the campaign undertaken by the Organisation to increase the number of research scientists, technicians and engineers most needed by European industry and to improve the quality of their education and training.

___. (1960), *Encouragement à une consommation accrue de lait grâce à des méthodes rationnelles de distribution et à de meilleurs procédés de contrôle de qualité, Projet AEP* n° 285/3 – Partie III.

___. (1960), *Inventaire des activités de l'AEP depuis sa création en 1953.*

___. (1961), *Formation et perfectionnement des professeurs d'enseignement professionnel agricole, Projet AEP* n° 6/14-4.

___. (1961), *Conditions hydrologiques et biologiques des stations d'essais en Europe.*

8.8 Développement des régions défavorisées

Au-delà des activités relevant de la productivité au sens restreint du terme, l'Agence s'est occupée du développement économique de régions en développement de pays Membres. L'Italie, la Grèce et la Turquie ont bénéficié, par exemple, de conseils d'experts pour l'établissement de projets de développement liés aux efforts de productivité entrepris dans ces pays. Elle a également suscité et facilité la création de zones d'expérimentation et de démonstration.

Publications :

Agence Européenne de Productivité (1958), *Communauté pilote d'Uvdal : Norvège, Projet AEP* n° 323.

OECE (1960), *Action communautaire, quelques exemples de réalisation américaines et européennes, Projet AEP* n° 337.

___. (1960), *Oliviculture en Sardaigne.*

___. (1960), *Zone-pilote en Sardaigne : une expérience internationale de développement communautaire.*

EDELMAN, C. H. (1961). *Étude des sols en Turquie.*

MAYNE, A. (1961), *Établissement et administration d'un plan de développement économique régional : exemple de Porto Rico.*

Planification économique régionale (1960, Bellagio) (1961), *Techniques d'analyse pour les régions moins développées,* OECE, Paris.

KRIER, H. (1961), *Main-d'œuvre rurale et développement industriel : adaptation et formation : rapport général.*

9. Bureau du Personnel Scientifique et Technique (BPST)

Le lancement du premier spoutnik soviétique a fait ressentir le manque relatif de personnel scientifique et technique en occident. En mai 1958, le **Bureau spécial du personnel scientifique et technique,** a été créé pour diriger la campagne entreprise par l'Organisation pour accroître le nombre de chercheurs, techniciens et ingénieurs dont l'industrie européenne avait le plus besoin, et améliorer la qualité de leur instruction et de leur formation.

The activities of the Office were placed under the authority of a **Steering Committee** comprising representatives of all the Member countries of the OEEC and the United States. Set up by Decision of the Council on 19 June 1958 and endowed with the same status as the Governing Body of the EPA, it was responsible for dealing with questions relating to scientific and technical personnel. On 30 May 1961 it was replaced by the **Committee for Scientific and Technical Personnel.**

The Steering Committee adopted the projects for the general sectors of activity covered by the Office for Scientific and Technical Personnel; the Office's programme of work and budget were approved by the Council of the Organisation. The Committee's financial resources were divided into two parts: the ''General Fund'', supplied by contributions from all the Member countries and the United States, was used to finance projects of general interest to the countries participating in the programme; the ''Limited Fund'' financed projects concerning a limited number of countries with common interests by reason of their geographical location, language, or similarity of the basic development problems they had to resolve – these projects were financed as to 50 per cent by the Organisation and 50 per cent by the countries participating in the project concerned.

Publications:

OEEC (1960), *Forecasting Manpower Needs for the Age of Science.*

Investment in Education and Economic Growth (1960, Paris) (1960), *Record of an Informal Meeting.*

OEEC (1960), *Methods and Possibilities of Co-operation in Applied Research.*

___. (1960), *Modern Approach to School Physics.*

___. (1960), *Policy for School Science: Countries with Advanced School System.*

WILGRESS, Dana (1960), *Co-operation in Scientific and Technical Research.*

OECE (1961), *Cinq ans d'assistance technique à l'OECE.* (available only in French)

European Parliamentary and Scientific Conference (1961, London), *[Report],* Council of Europe and OEEC, Strasbourg and Paris.

HALSEY, A.H. (1961), *Ability and Educational Opportunity.*

OEEC (1961), *New Thinking in School Mathematics.*

___. (1961), *School Mathematics in OECE Countries.*

___. (1961), *Supply, Recruitment and Training of Science and Mathematics Teachers.*

Les activités du Bureau furent placées sous l'autorité d'un Comité directeur, composé de représentants de tous les pays Membres de l'OECE, et des États-unis. Créé par décision du Conseil du 19 juin 1958 et doté du même statut que le Comité de direction de l'AEP, il était responsable des questions de personnel scientifique et technique. Le 30 mai 1961, il a été remplacé par le **Comité du personnel scientifique et technique.**

Le Comité directeur adoptait les projets relevant des secteurs généraux d'activité couverts par le programme du Bureau du personnel scientifique et technique. Le programme d'action et le budget du Bureau étaient approuvés par le Conseil de l'Organisation. Les moyens financiers du Comité étaient divisés en deux parties : le «Fonds général», alimenté par des contributions de tous les pays Membres et des États-unis, servait à financer des projets d'intérêt général pour l'ensemble des pays participant au programme ; le «Fonds limité», financait des projets concernant un nombre limité de pays ayant des intérêts communs de par leur situation géographique, leur langue ou une similitude des problèmes fondamentaux de développement qu'ils avaient à résoudre. Ces projets étaient financés à concurrence de 50 % par l'Organisation et pour l'autre moitié par les pays participants au projet considéré.

Publications :

OECE (1960), *Prévoir les cadres de demain.*

Budgets enseignement et expansion économique (1960, Paris) (1960), *Compte-Rendu d'une réunion officieuse,* OECE, Paris.

OEEC (1960), *Methods and Possibilities of Co-operation in Applied Research.* (disponible en anglais)

___. (1960), *Une conception moderne de l'enseignement de la physique.*

___. (1960), *Politique à suivre en matière d'enseignement scientifique : pays disposant d'un système d'enseignement avancé.*

WILGRESS, Dana (1960), *Coopération dans la recherche scientifique et technique.*

OECE (1961), *Cinq ans d'assistance technique à l'OECE.*

Conférence parlementaire et scientifique européenne (1961, Londres), *[Rapport],* Conseil de l'Europe et OECE, Strasbourg and Paris.

HALSEY, A.H. (1961), *Aptitude intellectuelle et éducation.*

OECE (1961), *Mathémathiques Nouvelles.*

___. (1961), *Enseignement des mathématiques dans les pays de l'OECE.*

___. (1961), *Effectifs, recrutement et formation des professeurs de sciences et de mathématiques.*

10. European Nuclear Energy Agency (ENEA)

The Organisation's studies on the energy situation in Europe, and in particular the "Armand Report" (see 6.2.4 above) revealed the importance of establishing co-operation among Member countries in order to develop the production and utilisation of nuclear energy for peaceful purposes. In July 1956 a Steering Committee was instructed to draw up the programme for this co-operation and its proposals led to the creation of the **European Nuclear Energy Agency** by Council Decision of 20 December 1957 (taking effect on 1st February 1958) which established its statute. All the OEEC countries were members of the Agency, Canada and the United States were associated with its work and Euratom participated in it. A co-operation agreement with the International Atomic Energy Agency (IAEA) was concluded on 30 September 1960.

The functions of ENEA, in accordance with its statute as a specialised body of the OEEC, extended to all joint and co-ordinated action decided by the participating governments to facilitate their research and industrial activities in the nuclear energy field.

10.1 Principal activities and organisational structure of the Agency

In the initial phase, which was concerned with R&D, the first and the most original of the Agency's achievements was to create a number of "joint undertakings" in which the countries concerned together financed and carried out R&D projects in various sectors of the nuclear industry. These undertakings, together with education and information activities sponsored by the Agency, played a decisive part in the training of specialists and dissemination of knowledge necessary to the development of this new technology in Europe. To the same end, ENEA also took the initiative of organising exchanges of experience among scientists, notably on reactor physics and constants used in core neutronics.

The other main function of the Agency was to harmonise legislation and regulations concerning nuclear activities in order to help to control the related risks. In this area it drew up basic norms for the protection of workers and the general public from radiation (Recommendation of the Council of 12 June 1959); these were regularly updated and interpreted with a view to their application at national level as experience progressed in this field. At the same time a system of surveillance of ambient radioactivity was established. ENEA also secured the adoption in Europe of an international system of third party liability and insurance for nuclear operators through the Paris Convention of 24 July 1960; this convention and the Agency's work to ensure its application did much to shape the new trends in nuclear

10. Agence Européenne pour l'Énergie Nucléaire (AEEN)

Les études de l'Organisation sur la situation énergétique en Europe et en particulier le « Rapport Armand » (voir ci-dessus 6.2.4) ont mis en lumière l'intérêt d'entreprendre une coopération entre ses pays Membres en vue de promouvoir le développement des utilisations pacifiques et de la production de l'énergie nucléaire. Dès juillet 1956, un Comité de direction a été chargé d'élaborer le programme de cette coopération et ses propositions ont conduit à la création de l'**Agence européenne pour l'énergie nucléaire,** par une décision du Conseil du 20 décembre 1957 (entrée en vigueur le 1er février 1958) qui en établit le Statut. Tous les pays Membres de l'OECE sont devenus membres de l'Agence ; le Canada et les États-Unis s'y sont associés et Euratom y a participé. Un accord de coopération avec l'Agence internationale de l'énergie atomique a été conclu le 30 septembre 1960.

Les compétences de l'AEEN, selon son statut d'organe spécialisé de l'OECE, s'étendaient à l'ensemble des actions communes et coordonnées décidées par les gouvernements participants pour faciliter la mise en œuvre de leurs activités de recherche et d'ordre industriel dans le domaine de l'énergie nucléaire.

10.1 Actions principales et structure de l'Agence

Dans la phase initiale, consacrée aux travaux de recherche et développement, la première et la plus originale des réalisations de l'Agence a été de créer plusieurs « entreprises communes » groupant les pays intéressés, en vue de financer et de mener ensemble de tels travaux dans divers secteurs de l'industrie nucléaire. Ces entreprises combinées aux actions d'enseignement et d'information patronnées par l'Agence ont joué un rôle déterminant dans la formation de spécialistes et la diffusion des connaissances nécessaires au développement de cette technologie nouvelle en Europe. L'AEEN a également pris l'initiative d'organiser des échanges d'expérience entre scientifiques, notamment sur la physique des réacteurs et les constantes neutroniques.

La seconde principale fonction de l'Agence a été d'harmoniser les législations et la règlementation relatives aux activités nucléaires afin de contribuer à la maîtrise des risques liés à ces activités. A ce titre, elle a établi des normes de base pour la protection des travailleurs et de la population contre les radiations (recommandation du Conseil du 12 juin 1959) qui ont régulièrement été mises à jour et interprétées en vue de leur application sur le plan national. De façon parallèle, un système de surveillance de la radioactivité ambiante a été mis en place. L'AEEN a également fait adopter en Europe un régime international de responsabilité civile et d'assurance des exploitants nucléaires par la Convention de Paris du 24 juillet 1960. Cette Convention et les travaux de l'Agence en vue de son application ont largement

law. Finally, a system of security control designed to prevent joint undertakings from being diverted to military purposes was set up by the Convention of 20 December 1957, which also established a European nuclear energy tribunal for the settlement of disputes linked with the application of this control or with other joint action.

As regards the thrust of national policies, the exchanges of views within the Agency among high officials of the participating countries contributed to the co-ordination of research programmes and to the development of prospects in the nuclear industry. Liberalisation of intra-European trade in nuclear equipment and materials was encouraged, in association with Euratom, and within the framework of the more general policy conducted by the OEEC in this connection.

Structure

Under the authority of the Council, the **Steering Committee for Nuclear Energy** was the Agency's governing body and could frame recommendations to the governments of the participating countries; it submitted the Agency's work programmes and budgets to the Council, as well as draft decisions resulting from its activities. The Steering Committee was composed of representatives of the participating governments, representatives of the Euratom Commission and the IAEA taking part in its meetings in an advisory capacity. The Committee was assisted by a secretariat (forming part of the Organisation's secretariat) and by technical commissions, study groups and working parties which it set up in accordance with the needs of the programme. For example, it set up a group of high-level experts to obtain the opinions of leading scientists on projects for co-operation on various types of experimental reactors and prototypes and, later, in other areas of nuclear science. The Statutes devote considerable space to the "restricted agreements" procedure enabling a number of countries to undertake at their own expense specific projects not of interest to all members ("*à la carte*" co-operation).

It also set up *Joint Working Parties* with the *Steering Board for Trade and Study Groups* on:

- *Experimental Reactors*
- *Power Reactors*
- *Joint Undertakings*
- *Nuclear Power Stations*
- *Nuclear Ship Propulsion*
- *Food Irradiation*

Working Parties on:

- *Harmonisation of Legislation*
- *Education*
- *Third Party Liability*
- *Public Health and Safety*

inspiré les tendances nouvelles du droit nucléaire. Enfin, un système de contrôle de sécurité visant à empêcher que les activités des entreprises communes soient détournées à des fins militaires a été mis en place par une Convention du 20 décembre 1957 créant aussi un Tribunal européen de l'énergie nucléaire pour le règlement de litiges qui seraient liés à l'application de ce contrôle ou à d'autres actions communes.

En ce qui concerne l'orientation des politiques nationales, les échanges de vue au sein de l'Agence entre les responsables à haut niveau des pays participants ont contribué, d'une certaine mesure, à la coordination des programmes de recherches et à l'évolution des perspectives de l'industrie nucléaire. La libéralisation des échanges intra-européens d'équipements et de matières nucléaires a été favorisée, en liaison avec Euratom et dans le cadre de la politique plus générale menée par l'OECE.

Structure

Sous l'autorité du Conseil, le **Comité de direction de l'énergie nucléaire** – organe directeur de l'Agence – formulait des recommandations aux gouvernements des pays participants. Il soumettait au Conseil les programmes de travail et budgets de l'Agence ainsi que les projets de décisions résultant de ses activités. Le Comité de direction était composé des représentants des gouvernements participants; les représentants des pays associés d'Euratom et de l'AIEA prenant part aux réunions à titre consultatif. Le Comité de direction était assisté d'un Secrétariat (partie intégrante de celui de l'Organisation), de comités techniques, de syndicats d'études et de groupes de travail qu'il créait en fonction des besoins du programme. Il créa, par exemple, un groupe d'experts à haut niveau pour recueillir l'avis des scientifiques les plus éminents en ce qui concerne les projets de coopération sur divers types de réacteurs expérimentaux ou prototypes et, plus tard, dans d'autres domaines de la science nucléaire. Les Statuts faisaient une large place à la procédure des « accords restreints » permettant à plusieurs pays d'entreprendre à leurs frais des projets particuliers qui n'intéressaient pas la totalité des Membres (coopération « à la carte »).

Il créa aussi des *groupes de travail mixte* avec le *Comité de direction des échanges* ainsi que les *groupes d'études* sur :

- *les réacteurs expérimentaux*
- *les réacteurs de puissance*
- *les entreprises communes*
- *les centrales nucléaires*
- *la propulsion nucléaire des navires*
- *l'irradiation des denrées*

les *groupes de travail* sur :

- *l'harmonisation des législations*
- *l'enseignement*
- *sur la responsabilité civile*
- *la santé publique et la sécurité*

and the

– *Special Group to ensure liaison between the Organisation and the Inter-Governmental Conference in Brussels, and to consider the links to be established between the Institutions to be set up*

Groups of experts, with a membership restricted to the countries concerned, carried out assignments relating to Organisation of the High Temperature Reactor Project, Heavy Water Production and Nuclear Data.

Publications: European Nuclear Energy Agency.

European Nuclear Energy Agency (1956), *Possibilities of Action in the Field of Nuclear Energy.*

___. (1957), *Catalogue of Courses on Nuclear Energy in OEEC Countries: 1957-1958.*

___. (1957), *Experimental Reactors: Proposals for their Co-operative Development in Europe.*

Agence Européenne pour l'énergie nucléaire (1957)/ European Nuclear Energy Agency (1957), *Statuts de l'agence : convention sur le contrôle de sécurité : convention relative à la société Eurochemic/Statute of the Agency: Convention on Security Control: Convention on the Eurochemic Company,* OECE/OEEC, Paris.

The Industrial Challenge of Nuclear Energy (1957, Paris) (1957), *Papers given during the First Information Conference on Nuclear Energy for Management,* OEEC, Paris.

The Industrial Challenge of Nuclear Energy (1957, Amsterdam) (1958), *Research: Uses: Social Problems,* OEEC, Paris.

The Industrial Challenge of Nuclear Energy (1959, Stresa) (1959), *Stresa Conference papers,* 4 parts, OEEC, Paris.

OEEC. Steering Committee for Nuclear Energy (1957), *Experimental Reactors, Proposals for their Co-operative Developments in Europe.*

OEEC. Steering Committee for Nuclear Energy (1958), *The European Nuclear Energy Agency and the Eurochemic Company: First Report,* OEEC, Paris.

Symposium on Health Physics in Nuclear Installations (1959, Riso) (1959)/Symposium sur la physique de santé dans les installations nucléaires (1959, Riso) (1959), *Health Physics in Nuclear Installations/La physique de santé dans les installations nucléaires,* OEEC/OECE, Paris.

OEEC/European Nuclear Energy Agency (1959), *Structure and Functions : First Joint Undertakings,* OEEC, Paris.

Conférence-débat sur les perspectives industrielles de l'énergie nucléaire (1959, Paris) (1959), *[Comptes rendus].* (available only in French)

et un

– *Groupe de travail chargé d'assurer la liaison entre l'Organisation et la Conférence Intergouvernementale de Bruxelles et d'examiner les liens à établir entre les institutions qui seraient créees*

Des groupes d'experts, de composition restreinte aux pays intéressés, ont accompli des tâches relatives à l'organisation du Projet de réacteurs à haute température, à la production d'eau lourde et aux constantes nucléaires.

Publications : Agence Européenne pour l'énergie nucléaire.

Agence Européenne pour l'énergie nucléaire (1956), *Possibilités d'action dans le domaine de l'énergie nucléaire.*

___. (1957), *Catalogue des cours sur l'énergie nucléaire dans les pays de l'OECE : 1957-1958.*

___. (1957), *Propositions concernant la coopération européenne dans le domaine des réacteurs expérimentaux.*

Agence Européenne pour l'énergie nucléaire (1957)/ European Nuclear Energy Agency (1957), *Statuts de l'agence : convention sur le contrôle de sécurité : convention relative à la société Eurochemic/Statute of the Agency: Convention on Security Control: Convention on the Eurochemic Company,* OECE/OEEC, Paris.

L'industrie devant l'énergie nucléaire (1957, Paris) (1957), *Exposés présentés au cours de la première Conférence d'Information Nucléaire pour les dirigeants d'entreprises,* OECE, Paris.

L'industrie devant l'énergie nucléaire (1957, Amsterdam) (1958), *Recherches : applications : problèmes sociaux,* OECE, Paris.

L'industrie devant l'énergie nucléaire (1959, Stresa) (1959), *Papiers de conférence de Stresa,* 4 parties, OECE, Paris.

OECE. Comité de direction de l'énergie nucléaire (1957), *Propositions concernant la Coopération Européenne dans le domaine des réacteurs expérimentaux.*

OECE. Comité de direction de l'énergie nucléaire (1958), *L'agence européenne pour l'énergie nucléaire et la société Eurochemic : premier rapport,* OECE, Paris.

Symposium on Health Physics in Nuclear Installations (1959, Riso) (1959)/Symposium sur la physique de santé dans les installations nucléaires (1959, Riso) (1959), *Health Physics in Nuclear Installations/La physique de santé dans les installations nucléaires,* OEEC/OECE, Paris.

OECE/Agence européenne pour l'énergie nucléaire (1959), *Structure et fonctions : Premières entreprises communes,* OECE, Paris.

Conférence-débat sur les perspectives industrielles de l'énergie nucléaire (1959, Paris) (1959), *[Comptes rendus].*

OEEC/European Nuclear Energy Agency (1960), *Basic Assumptions for Nuclear Power Estimates in Europe.*

——. (1960), *Criticality Control in Chemical and Metallurgical Plant.*

International Trade Union Seminar (1960, Dusseldorf) (1960), *Nuclear Energy Problems: Final Report,* OEEC, Paris.

SMETS, Henri B. (1961), *Non-Linear Analytical Methods in Nuclear Power Reactor Kinetics.* (Paper presented at the European Atomic Energy Society Symposium on "Reactivity Feedback mechanisms and Nuclear Reactor Stability", Zurich, 25th-26th September 1961.)

OEEC/OECE (1959), *Use of Radiations and Radio-Isotopes in Agriculture and Food: List of Research Institutes and Scientists in OEEC Member Countries/Utilisation des techniques d'irradiation et des isotopes radioactifs dans la recherche agronomique : répertoire des instituts et des chercheurs dans les pays membres de l'OECE.*

——. (1961), *Use of Radiations and Radio-Isotopes in Food and Agriculture: List of Research Institutes and Scientists in OECD Member Countries/Utilisation des techniques d'irradiation et des isotopes radioactifs dans la recherche agronomique : répertoire des instituts et des chercheurs dans les pays membres de l'OCDE,* revised edition/nouvelle édition.

10.2 Joint Undertakings

The European Company for the Chemical Processing of Irradiated Fuels (Eurochemic) – Mol, Belgium – was set up under the terms of an International Convention signed on 20 December 1957 (effective from 27 July 1958). The purpose of the company was to construct and operate a plant and a laboratory for the processing of irradiated fuels and to develop technology and specialist training in this field. The company consisted of a General Assembly, which was the plenary body, a *Board of Directors* (16 directors appointed on a personal basis by the General Assembly), a *Study and Research Committee* (5 members personally appointed by the Board of Directors) and a *Managing Director.* The participating countries were: Austria, Belgium, Denmark, France, Germany, Italy, Netherlands, Norway, Portugal, Spain, Sweden, Switzerland and Turkey.

The OEEC's reactor project at Halden (Norway) was formed under an agreement concluded on 11 June 1958 for a programme of research and experiment through joint operation of a heavy water boiling reactor. The project was administered by the *Halden Committee* (a member appointed by each of the participating countries) and the *Halden Technical Group* (one specialist for each country). The participating countries were:

OECE/Agence européenne pour l'énergie nucléaire (1960), *Estimations de production d'énergie nucléaire en Europe : Hypothèses de base.*

——. (1960), *Contrôle de la criticalité dans les installations chimiques et métallurgiques.*

Session d'études syndicales internationale (1960, Dusseldorf) (1960), *Problèmes de l'énergie nucléaire : rapport final,* OECE, Paris.

SMETS, Henri B. (1961), *Non-Linear Analytical Methods in Nuclear Power Reactor Kinetics.* (Disponible seulement en anglais.) (Papier présenté au European Atomic Energy Society Symposium on « Reactivity Feedback mechanisms and Nuclear Reactor Stability », Zurich, 25-26 septembre 1961.)

OEEC/OECE (1959), *Use of Radiations and Radio-Isotopes in Agriculture and Food: List of Research Institutes and Scientists in OEEC Member Countries/Utilisation des techniques d'irradiation et des isotopes radioactifs dans la recherche agronomique : répertoire des instituts et des chercheurs dans les pays membres de l'OECE.*

——. (1961), *Use of Radiations and Radio-Isotopes in Food and Agriculture: List of Research Institutes and Scientists in OECD Member Countries/Utilisation des techniques d'irradiation et des isotopes radioactifs dans la recherche agronomique : répertoire des instituts et des chercheurs dans les pays membres de l'OCDE,* revised edition/nouvelle édition.

10.2 Entreprises communes

La Société Européenne pour le traitement chimique des combustibles irradiés (Eurochemic) – à Mol (Belgique) – a été constituée par une Convention du 20 décembre 1957 (entrée en vigueur le 27 juillet 1958). Elle avait pour objet la construction et l'exploitation d'une usine et d'un laboratoire destinés au traitement des combustibles irradiés, et d'assurer la mise au point de la technique et la formation des spécialistes dans ce domaine. Elle était composée d'une Assemblée générale, organe plénier, d'un *Conseil d'administration* (16 administrateurs nommés à titre individuel par l'Assemblée générale), d'un *Comité scientifique et technique* (5 membres nommés à titre individuel par le Conseil d'administration) et d'un *Directeur général.* Les pays participants étaient : Allemagne, Autriche, Belgique, Danemark, Espagne, France, Italie, Norvège, Pays-Bas, Portugal, Suède, Suisse et Turquie.

Le Projet OECE de réacteur de Halden (Norvège) a été créé par un Accord du 11 juin 1958 pour réaliser un programme de recherches et d'expériences grâce à l'exploitation en commun d'un réacteur à eau lourde bouillante. Il se composait du *Comité Halden* (un membre désigné par pays participant) et du *Groupe technique de Halden* (un spécialiste qualifié par pays). Les pays participant étaient : Autriche, Danemark, Euratom

Austria, Denmark, Euratom (representing Belgium, France, Germany, Italy, Luxembourg and the Netherlands), Norway, Sweden, Switzerland and the United Kingdom; Finland and the United States were associates.

The OEEC High Temperature Gas-Cooled Reactor Project known as "Dragon" (United Kingdom) came into being as the result of an agreement concluded on 23 March 1959. Its purpose was to construct and operate an experimental 10 MW (thermal) power reactor and carry out a joint research programme on the relevant technology. It was administered by a *Board of Management* (each participating country being represented by two or three members) and a *General Purposes Committee* (one specialist for each country). The work of all these joint undertakings was carried out by international teams of research scientists and engineers from the particiating countries. In the case of the Dragon Project those countries were: Austria, Denmark, Euratom (representing Belgium, France, Germany, Italy, Luxembourg and the Netherlands), Norway, Sweden, Switzerland and the United Kingdom.

Publications:

OEEC/OECD (1960-1977), *Dragon: OEEC High Temperature Reactor Project: annual report.*

OEEC (1960), *OEEC Halden Boiling Heavy Water: Second Annual Report.* (First report not published, see the first report of the activities of the ENEA. Third report, see *OECD Halden Boiling Heavy Water Reactor project.)*

Nuclear Graphite (1959, Bournemouth) (1961), *OEEC Dragon Project Symposium.*

11. European Conference of Ministers of Transport (ECMT)

At the beginning of the 1950s it was seen to be necessary to strengthen the executive element in European construction in the field of transport and to ensure that the political will of governments could express itself more directly. The formulation of these considerations in the conclusions of an ad hoc conference held under the aegis of the OEEC on 17 June 1953 (see Section 6.4.1) was followed by the establishment of the European Conference of Ministers of Transport (ECMT).

An intergovernmental organisation set up by a Protocol signed in Brussels on 17 October 1953, the original members of the ECMT were Austria, Belgium, Denmark, France, the Federal Republic of Germany, Greece, Italy, Luxembourg, the Netherlands, Norway, Portugal, Sweden, Switzerland, Turkey and the United Kingdom, together with the authority of the Anglo-American Zone of the Free Territory of Trieste. Ireland and Yugoslavia

(représentant l'Allemagne, la Belgique, la France, l'Italie, le Luxembourg et les Pays-Bas), Norvège, Royaume Uni, Suède et Suisse; les États-Unis et la Finlande y sont associés.

Le Projet OECE du réacteur à haute température refroidi par gaz « Dragon » (Royaume Uni) a été créé par un Accord du 23 mars 1959 et avait pour objet la construction et l'exploitation d'un réacteur expérimental (10 MWt) et l'exécution en commun d'un programme de recherches sur ce type de réacteur. Il se composait d'un *Conseil de direction* (chaque pays participant était représenté par 2 ou 3 membres) et d'un *Comité de gestion* (un spécialiste qualifié par pays Membre). Les travaux de toutes ces entreprises communes étaient confiés à des équipes internationales de chercheurs et d'ingénieurs provenant des pays participants. Ceux-ci étaient pour le projet Dragon : l'Autriche, le Danemark, Euratom (représentant l'Allemagne, la Belgique, la France, l'Italie, le Luxembourg et les Pays-Bas), la Norvège, le Royaume Uni, la Suède et la Suisse.

Publications:

OECE/OCDE (1960-1977), *Dragon : projet OECE de réacteur à haute température : rapport annuel.*

OECE (1960), *Projet OECE de réacteur à eau : deuxième rapport annuel.* (Premier rapport non publié, voir le premier rapport de l'AEEN. Troisième rapport, voir *Projet OCDE de réacteur à eau bouillante de Halden.)*

Nuclear Graphite (1959, Bournemouth) (1961), *OEEC Dragon Project Symposium.* (disponible seulement en anglais)

11. Conférence Européenne des Ministres des Transports (CEMT)

Au début des années 1950, il apparaissait nécessaire de renforcer le caractère exécutif de la construction européenne en matière de transport et de faire en sorte que la volonté politique des gouvernements puisse s'exprimer plus directement. Ces considérations, formulées dans les conclusions déposées à l'issue d'une conférence ad hoc réunie sous l'égide de l'OECE le 17 juin 1953, ont été suivies par la création de la Conférence européenne des Ministres des transports (CEMT).

Organisation intergouvernementale créée par un Protocole signé à Bruxelles le 17 octobre 1953, la CEMT regroupait à l'origine la République fédérale d'Allemagne, l'Autriche, la Belgique, le Danemark, l'Espagne, la France, la Grèce, l'Italie, le Luxembourg, la Norvège, les Pays-Bas, le Portugal, le Royaume-uni, la Suède, la Suisse et la Turquie auxquels s'était jointe l'autorité de la zone anglo-américaine du territoire libre

joined later and in 1954 Canada and the United States were admitted as associate member governments. Since 1961 other countries have become members.

Its aims have remained unchanged and are to:

a) take whatever measures may be necessary to achieve at general or regional level the maximum use and most rational development of European inland transport of international importance;

b) co-ordinate and promote the activities of the international organisations concerned with European inland transport, taking into account the work of supranational authorities in this field.

Activities

During the period of the OEEC's existence the activities of the ECMT were concerned with rail, road, inland waterway and combined means of transport, and general transport policy.

As regards rail transport, the ECMT's first undertaking was to promote the standardisation of rolling material and the use of Diesel locomotives; it set up EUROFIMA, a company with its registered office in Basle, whose purpose was the financing of standardised rolling stock.

With regard to road transport, the ECMT concerned itself in particular with the harmonisation of infrastructures and their international financing, road safety and standardisation of traffic regulations and traffic signs and signals. As of 1956 the ECMT analysed investments in each mode of transport and the services provided and examined national transport policies with a view to promoting their harmonisation.

Structure

The ECMT comprises a **Council of Ministers,** a **Committee of Deputies** and its subsidiary bodies, restricted Groups and a **Secretariat.**

The transport ministers of the Member countries meet twice yearly in the Council of Ministers. Their deliberations are prepared and their conclusions and decisions put into effect by the Committee of Deputies composed of senior transport officials. The Committee may set up subsidiary bodies to assist it, such as the Committee for Co-ordination of Investment.

The Secretariat, housed in the premises of the OEEC and later the OECD, has seen its role evolve over the years. Confined at the outset to tasks of an administrative nature, it has progressively become involved in the preparation of discussions and the drafting of reports.

Publications:

ECMT (1953), *Council of Ministers: Resolutions: I: Final Act, Protocol, Rules of Procedure, Resolutions* (Brussels, 17th October 1957), OEEC, Paris.

de Trieste. L'Irlande et la Yougoslavie s'y sont joints plus tard et, en 1954, les États-Unis et le Canada ont été admis au titre de gouvernements membres associés. Depuis 1961, d'autres pays sont devenus membres.

Ses objectifs sont demeurés inchangés :

a) prendre toutes mesures destinées à réaliser, dans un cadre général ou régional, la meilleure utilisation et le développement le plus rationnel des transports intérieurs européens d'importance internationale ;

b) coordonner et promouvoir les travaux des organisations internationales s'intéressant aux transports intérieurs européens, compte tenu de l'activité des autorités supranationales dans ce domaine.

Activités

Les activités de la CEMT ont porté, au cours de la période OECE, sur les questions de transports ferroviaire, routier, par voie navigable et combiné, et sur la politique générale des transports.

Notons qu'en matière de transport ferroviaire, la CEMT s'est tout d'abord attachée à promouvoir la standardisation du matériel roulant et l'emploi de la traction Diesel et a créé l'EUROFIMA, société qui avait son siège à Bâle et avait pour objet le financement du matériel ferroviaire standardisé.

Dans le domaine de la route, la CEMT s'est notamment préoccupée du problème de l'harmonisation des infrastructures et de leur financement international, de la sécurité et de l'uniformisation des règles de circulation et de signalisation routières. Dès 1956, la CEMT a analysé les investissements réalisés par chaque mode de transport et les prestations fournies ainsi que les politiques nationales des transports en vue de promouvoir, dans ce dernier cas, leur harmonisation.

Structure

La CEMT se compose d'un **Conseil des Ministres,** d'un **Comité des Suppléants** et de ses organes subsidiaires, de Groupes restreints et d'un **Secrétariat.**

Les Ministres des transports des pays Membres se réunissent deux fois par an au sein du Conseil des Ministres. La préparation de leurs délibérations et la mise en œuvre de leurs conclusions et décisions sont assurées par le Comité des Suppléants composé de hauts fonctionnaires. Celui-ci peut, pour l'assister, créer des organes subsidiaires, tel le Comité de coordination des investissements.

Le Secrétariat, installé dans les locaux de l'OECE puis de l'OCDE, a vu son rôle évoluer au fil des ans. Limité à l'origine à assumer des tâches de caractère administratif, il s'est vu progressivement associé à la préparation des discussions et à la rédaction des rapports.

Publications :

CEMT (1953), *Conseil des ministres : résolutions : I : Acte final, Protocole, Règlement intérieur, Résolutions* (Bruxelles, 17 octobre 1957), OECE, Paris.

ECMT/CEMT (1954-1957), *Council of Ministers: Resolutions/ Conseil des Ministres : résolutions,* v.2-v.6, OEEC/OECE, Paris.

ECMT (1957-1961), *Council of Ministers: Resolutions,* v.7-v.11.

ECMT/OECD (1955-), *Report on the Activities of the Conference.*

CEMT/ECMT (1954-1957), *Conseil des Ministres : résolutions/Council of Ministers: Resolutions,* v.2-v.6, OECE/OEEC, Paris.

CEMT (1957-1961), *Conseil des Ministres : résolutions,* v.7-v.11.

CEMT/OCDE (1955-), *Rapport sur l'activité de la Conférence.*

III. PUBLICATIONS ON THE MARSHALL PLAN AND THE OEEC/ PUBLICATIONS SUR LE PLAN MARSHALL ET L'OECE

This chapter aims to provide an overview of monographs and articles on the subjects of the Marshall Plan and the OEEC.

The first part consists of an overview of sources and research instruments, among which are bibliographic tools (1.1), basic collections of printed documents and sources (1.2), memoirs, testimonials and biographies (1.3) and selected monographs and articles dating from the period itself (1.4).

The second part of the chapter compiles publications on the Marshall Plan and the OEEC published *since 1970.*

Ce chapitre est destiné à donner une vue d'ensemble des ouvrages et articles relatifs au Plan Marshall et à l'OECE.

La première partie donne un aperçu des sources et des instruments de recherche, parmi lesquels les outils bibliographiques (1.1), les collections de base des documents imprimés et des sources (1.2), des mémoires, témoignages et biographies (1.3) et une sélection d'ouvrages et d'articles écrits à l'époque (1.4).

La seconde partie de ce chapître regroupe les écrits publiés sur le Plan Marshall et l'OECE *depuis 1970.*

1. Sources and Research Instruments/Sources et instruments de recherche

1.1 Bibliographic Tools/Instruments bibliographiques

BOSSUAT Gérard, CONRAD Yves (1994), *Histoire des constructions européennes au* XXe siècle, Bibliographie thématique commentée des travaux français, Peter Lang, Paris.

BÖTTCHER, Winfried, JANSEN, Jürgen, and WELSCH, Friedrich (1975), *Das britische Parliament und Europa, 1940-1972. Eine Fachbibliographie*, Baden-Baden.

BUCHRUCKER, Petra (1970), *Bibliographie zur Europäisches Integration*, Cologne.

CARSON, Sally (1974), *European Integration and US-European Relations: An Introductory Annotated Bibliography of General Periodical Articles and Pamphlet Material*, New York.

Centre d'Études Européennes, (1985), *Bibliography of historic research studies into European integration 1959-1984*, Brussels.

Centre d'Études Européennes, (1987), *Recherches universitaires sur l'intégration européenne. Enquête réalisée par le Centre d'études européennes, Université Catholique de Louvain à la demande de la Commission des Communautés européennes,* Nr. 13, Brussels.

COLLESTER, Bryan J. (1979), ''The European Communities. A Guide to Information sources'', *International Relations*, Vol. 9, Detroit.

DUMOULIN, Michel, LOTH, Wilfried, BOSSUAT, Gérard, KEOGH, Dermott, VARSORI, Antonio, NIESBERCHEM, Martine, HARRYVAN, Anjo G., JILÉK, Lubor, Actes du Colloque de Louvain-la-Neuve des 11 et 12 septembre 1991, réunis par Michel Dumoulin et Gilbert Trausch. (1992) «Historiographie des constructions européennes», *Lettre d'Information des Historiens de l'Europe Contemporaine*, vol. 7, n° 1-2.

DUMOULIN, Michel (1988), *La construction européenne en Belgique (1945-1957). Aperçu des sources*, CIACO, Louvain-la-Neuve.

KUJATH, Karl (1977), *Bibliographie sur l'intégration européenne/Bibliographie zur europäischen Integration/Bibliography on European Integration*, Institut Für Europäisches Politik, Bonn.

LODGE, Juliet (1983), *The European Community. Bibliographical Excursion*, London.

SEUSING, E. (1983), Bibliographie der EG Zeitschriften, 1952-1980, Kiel.

1.2 Printed Documents and Sources/Documents et sources imprimés

ADENAUER, Konrad, *Briefe, Vol. 1: 1945-1947* (1983) Rudolf MORSEY, Hans-Peter SCHWARZ (editors) Berlin.

___. *Briefe, Vol. 2: 1947-1949* (1984) Rudolf MORSEY, Hans-Peter SCHWARZ (editors) Berlin.

___. *Briefe, Vol. 3: 1949-1951* (1985), Rudolf MORSEY, Hans-Peter SCHWARZ (editors) Berlin.

___. *Briefe, Vol. 4: 1949-1951* (1987), Rudolf MORSEY, Hans-Peter SCHWARZ (editors) Berlin.

___. *Reden 1917-1967. Eine Auswahl* (1975), Hans-Peter SCHWARZ (editor) Stuttgart.

___. *Teegespräche, Vol. 1: 1950-1954* (1984), Hans-Jürgen KÜSTERS (editor) Berlin.

___. *Teegespräche, Vol. 2: 1955-1959* (1986), Hans-Jürgen KÜSTERS (editor) Berlin.

___. *Teegespräche, Vol. 3: 1959-1961* (1988), Hans-Jürgen KÜSTERS (editor) Berlin.

American Assembly of the United States, (1951), *Western Europe. Relationships as Viewed Within the Present World-wide International Enviroment: A Compilation of Research Reports, Documents, and Other Pertinent Information Designed to be Used as a Background for Discussion*, New York.

ARON, Raymond (1990), *Les articles du FIGARO*, vol. 1, *La Guerre Froide* 1947-1955. Paris.

Auswärtiges Amt (editor), (1962), *Dokumente zur Frage der Europäische Einigung*, 3 vol., Bonn.

Auswärtiges Amt, Bundesministerium der Finanzen, Bundesministerium für Wirtschaft, and Bundesministerium für den Marshallplan (editors), *Deutsche Auslandsschulden. Dokumente zu den internationalen Verhandlungen Oktober 1950 bis Juli 1951*, Bonn.

BARING, Arnulf (editor) (1974), *Sehr geehrter Herr Bundeskanzler! Heinrich von Brentano im Briefwechsel mit Konrad Adenauer 1949-1964*, Hamburg.

BLUM, Léon (1958-1963), *L'œuvre de Léon Blum*, vol. 5 : 1. 1945-1947, vol. 5 : 2. 1947-1950, Paris.

BOSSUAT, Gérard (1989), *D'Alger à Rome (1943-1957). Choix de documents*, Brussels.

BRENTANO, Heinrich von (1962), *Deutschland, Europa und die Welt. Reden zur deutschen Außenpolitik*, Bonn.

Bundesarchiv and Institut für Zeitgeschichte (1976-1989), *Akten zur Vorgeschichte der Bundesrepublik Deutschland 1945-1949*. 5 volumes, Munich.

Bundesarchiv (1982-), Die Kabinettsprotokolle der Bundesrepublik, various volumes, Boppard am Rhein.

Bundesministerium für gesamtdeutsche Fragen, *Dokumente zur Deutschlandpolitik, Series 2: 9 May 1945 to 4 May 1955, Series 3: 5 May 1955 to 9 November 1958, Series 4: 10 November 1958 to 30 November 1966*, Frankfurt.

Bundesministerium für den Marshallplan (editor) (1953), *Wiederaufbau im Zeichen des Marshallplanes 1948-1952*, Bonn.

BULLEN, Roger, M.E. PELLY, H.J. YASAMEE, G. BENETT, (editors) (1986), *Documents on British Policy Overseas, various volumes the Schuman Plan, The Council of Europe and Western European Integration Series 2: 1950-1952*, Vol. 1., London.

___. (1986), *Documents on British Policy Overseas. Series 2: 1950-1955*, Vol. 2., London.

___. (1987), *The London Conference, Anglo-American relations and Cold War Strategy*, London.

CHANDLER, Alfred D. and GALAMBOS, Louis (editors) (1970-79), *The Papers of Dwight D. Eisenhower*, 9 volumes, Baltimore.

CLAYTON, Will (1971), *Selected Papers of Will Clayton*, Baltimore.

[Hearings of the] Committee on International Relations (1943-1950), Historical Series, Vol. 3, *U.S. Government Documents*, Washington.

Committee on International Relations (1976), ''Foreign Economic Assistance Programs'', Part II, Extension of the European Recovery Program. *Selected Executive Session Hearings of the Committee on International Relations, 1943-1950, Historical Series*, Vol. 4, Washington.

DE GAULLE, Charles (1984-1985), *Lettres, notes et carnets*, Paris.

___. (1970), *Discours et messages. Avec le renouveau, mai 1958-juillet 1962*, Paris.

ERHARD, Ludwig (1988), *Gedanken aus fünf Jahrzehnten: Reden und Schriften*, Düsseldorf.

ETZOLD, Thomas H. and GADDIS, John Lewis (editors) (1978), *Containment. Documents on American Policy and Strategy, 1945-1950*, New York.

FERRELL, Robert H. (editor) (1980), *Off the Record: The Private Papers of Harry S. Truman*, Boulder, 1980.

___. (1983), *Dear Bess : The Letters from Harry to Bess Truman, 1910-1959*, New York.

Fondation Jean Monnet pour l'Europe, Centre de recherches Européennes (dir.) (1986), *Jean Monnet et Robert Schuman, Correspondance 1947-1953*, Lausanne.

Friedrich Ebert Stiftung (1988), *Kurt Schumacher als deutscher und europäischer Sozialist, Dokumente*, Bonn.

Germany 1947-1949. The Story in Documents (1950), Washington.

HALLSTEIN, Walter (1979), *Europäische Reden*, Thomas OPPERMAN (editor), Stuttgart.

HEUSS, T. (1983), *Lieber Dehler! Briefwechsel mit Thomas Dehler*, F. HENNING (editor) Munich.

KINDLEBERGER, Charles P. (1989), *The German Economy, 1945-1947 : Charles P. Kindleberger's Letters from the Field*, London.

LADEMACHER, Horst, MÜHLHAUSEN, Walter (editors) (1985), *Sicherheit, Kontrole, Souveränität. Das Petersberger Abkommen vom 22 November 1949. Eine Dokumentation*, Melsungen.

LAUDA, R. (1973), "A Survey of Manuscript Collections and Documents Relating to American Foreign Policy and Europe 1945-'50", *Society for Historians of American Foreign Relations Newsletter* .

LIPGENS, Walter (1980), *Sources for the History of European Integration (1945-1955). A Guide to the Archives in the Countries of the Community,* Leyden, London, Boston.

——. (1986), *45 Jahre Ringen um die Europäische Verfassung. Dokumente 1939-1984. Von den Schriften der Widerstandsbewegung bis zum Vertragsentwurf des Europäischen Parlaments*, Bonn.

LIPGENS, Walter and LOTH, Wilfried (1985-1991), *Documents on the History of European Integration, 1939-1950.* 4 volumes, Berlin.

Ministère des Affaires Étrangères, Commission de publications des documents diplomatique (1987), *Documents diplomatique français, 1954 (21 juillet – 31 décembre) et Annexes, 1955 (1er janvier – 30 juin) et Annexes*, Paris.

RUHM VON OPPEN, Beate (editor) (1955), *Documents on Germany under Occupation 1945-1954*, London.

SCHWARZ, Jürgen (editor) (1980), *Der Aufbau Europas. Pläne und Dokumente 1945 bis 1980*, Bonn.

SIEGLER, Heinrich VON (editor) (1961), *Dokumentation der Europäischen Integration (1961), Vol. 1: Mit besonderer Berücksichtigung des Verhältnisses EWG-EFTA. Von der Zürcher Rede Winston Churchills 1946 bis zur Bewerbung Großbritanniens um Mitgliedschaft bei der EWG,* Bonn.

——. (1963), *Dokumentation der Europäischen Integration (1963), Vol. 2: 1961-1963 unter Berücksichtigung der Bestebungen für eine atlantische Partnerschaft*, Bonn.

——. (1968), *Europäische politische Einigung: Dokumente von Vorschlaegen und Stellungnahmen, 1949-1968*, Bonn.

SMITH, Jean Edwards (editor), (1974), *The Papers of General Lucius D. Clay*: Germany 1945-1949, Bloomington: Indiana.

US Department of State (1974-), *Foreign Relations of the United States, various* volumes, Washington.

——. (1983), *The State Department Policy Planning Staff Papers, 1947-1949*, London.

US Senate Committee on Foreign Relations (1973), *Foreign Relief Assistance Act of 1948, Hearings held in Executive Session before the Committee on Foreign Relations, Historical Series, US Senate. 80th Congress, 2nd session 1948*, Washington.

——. (1976), *US Congress, Executive Sessions of the Senate Foreign Relations Committee. Historical Series,* Vol. 2, 81st Congress, 1st and 2nd sessions 1949-1950, Washington.

VANDENBERG, A. (1953), *Private papers of Senator Vandenberg*, London.

VOGEL, Walter, C. WEISZ, W. WOLFRAM, P. WERNER, G. PLUM, H.D. KREIKAMP (editors) (1976-1983), *Akten zur Vorgeschichte der Bundesrepublik Deutschland 1945-1949.* 5 volumes, Munich.

WEISZ, Christoph, and H. WOLLER (editors) (1977), *Wörtliche Berichte und Drucksachen des Wirtschaftsrates des Vereinigten Wirtschaftsgebietes 1947-1949,* 6 Vol., Munich.

1.3 Memoirs, Testimonials and Biographies/Mémoires, témoignages et biographies

ABEN, H. (1967), *Europa onderweg: ooggetuigen brengen verslag uit*, Amsterdam/Brussels.

ACHESON, Dean (1969), *Present at the Creation. My Years in the State Department*, New York.

——. (1960), *Sketches from Men I have Known*, New York.

ADAMS, S. (1961), *First Hand Report: The Story of the Eisenhower Administration*, New York.

ADENAUER, Konrad (1965-1967-1969), *Erinnerungen*, Vol. 1: 1945-1953, Vol. 2: 1953-1956, Vol. 3: 1956-1963, Deutsche Verlags-Anstalt 1965-68, Stuttgart.

ADSTANS, A. (1953), *Alcide de Gasperi nella politica estera italiana, 1944-1953*, Milan.

ALBRECHT, W. (1985), *Kurt Schumacher: Reden, Schriften, Korrespondenzen, 1945-1952*, Berlin, Bonn.

ALEXANDER, E. (1989), *Adenauer und das neue Deutschland: Einführung in das Wesen und Wirken des Staatsmannes*, Recklinghausen.

ALPHAND, Hervé (1977), *L'étonnement d'être, journal 1939-1973*, Paris.

AMBROSE, S. (1983), *Eisenhower: Soldier, General of the Army, President-Elect, 1890-1952*, New York.

___. (1984), *Eisenhower: The President*, New York.

ANDREWS, W. (1959), *Pierre Mendès-France : A Study of Political Ideas in Action*, London.

ARON, Raymond (1983), *Mémoires*, Paris.

ATTLEE, Clement (1954), *As it happened*, London.

___. (1961), *A Prime Minister Remembers: The War and Post-war of the Right Honourable Earl Attlee*, London.

___. (1962), *Twilight of Empire: Memoirs of Prime Minister Clement Attlee*, Barnes.

AUGSTEIN, R. (1964), *Konrad Adenauer*, London.

AURIOL, Vincent (1970), *Mon septennat 1947-1954*, Pierre NORA et Mona OZOUF (dir.), Paris.

___. (1970-78), *Journal du septennat*, 7 vol., Paris.

BACKING, J. (1983), *Winds of History: The German Years of Lucius DuBignon Clay*, New York.

BAKKER, A. and van LENT, M.M.P. (1989), *Pieter Lieftinck 1902-1989. Herinneringen opgetekend door A. Bakker en M.M.P. van Lent*, Utrecht.

BALL, George (1982), *The Past Has Another Pattern: Memoirs*, New York.

BARCLAY, Sir Roderick (1975), *Ernest Bevin and the Foreign Office, 1932-1969*, London.

BARUCH, B. (1958), *My own story*, London.

___. (1960), *The Public Years*, New York.

BEALE, J. (1957), *John Foster Dulles: A Biography*, New York.

BÉRARD, Armand (1976), *Un ambassadeur se souvient.* vol. 1 : *Au temps du danger allemand*, Paris.

___. (1978), *Un ambassadeur se souvient.* vol. 2 : *Washington et Bonn 1945-1955*, Paris.

BEYEN, J. (1968), *Het spel en de knikkers. Een kroniek van 50 jaren*, Rotterdam.

BIDAULT, Georges (1965), *D'une résistance à l'autre*, Paris.

BIRKENHEAD, L. (1961), *The Prof in Two Worlds: The Official Life of Professor F.A. Lindemann, Viscount Cherwell*, London.

BLANKENHORN, Herbert (1980), *Verstandnis und Verständigung. Blätter eines politisches Tagebuchs 1949-1979*, Frankfurt.

BLOCH-LAINÉ, François (1976), *Profession fonctionnaire*, Paris.

BLÜCHER, F. (1953), *Dienst an Deutschland und Europa. Vier Jahre Bundesministerium für den Marshallplan*, Bad Godesberg.

BLUMENWITZ, D. *et. al.* (1976), *Konrad Adenauer und seine Zeit. Politik und Persönlichkeit des ersten Bundeskanzlers. Beiträge von Weg-und Zeitgenossen*, Stuttgart.

BOHLEN, Charles (1973), *Witness to History: 1929-1969*, New York.

BOOTHBY, R. (1962), *My Yesterday, Your Tomorrow*, s.l., 1962.

___. (1987), *Recollections of a Rebel*, London.

BRENDEN, P. (1984), *Winston Churchill: A Brief Life*, London.

BRINKLEY, Douglas (1992), *Dean Acheson: The Cold War Years*, Yale.

BULLOCK, A. (1983), *The Life and Times of Ernest Bevin,* Vol. 3: *Ernest Bevin, Foreign Secretary, 1945-1951*, New York, London.

BURRIDGE, T. (1985), *Clement Attlee: A Political Biography*, London.

BUTLER, R.A. (1971), *The Art of Possible: The Memoirs of Lord Butler*, London.

BUTLER, R.A. (1985), *Years of Recovery 1945-1951*, London.

BYRNES, J (1958), *All in One Lifetime*, New York.

CAIRNCROSS, A. (editor) (1991), *The Robert Hall Diaries, 1947-1953*, London.

CAIRNCROSS, A. (1992), ''From Theory to Policy-Making: Economics as a Profession'', *Banca Nazionale del Lavoro Quarterly Review*, March.

CALLAHAN, R. (1984), *Churchill: Retreat from Empire*, Turnbridge Wells.

CARLTON, A. (1981), *Anthony Eden: A Biography*, London.

CARSTENS, K. (1971), *Politische Führung. Erfahrungen im Dienste der Bundesregierung*, Stuttgart.

CATTI DE GASPERI, M. (1969), *La nostra patria Europea. Il pensiero europeistico di Alcide De Gasperi*, Milan.

CHAPOIS, D. DU (1971), *Paul van Zeeland, au service de la Belgique*, Brussels.

CHAUVEL, Jean (1971), *Commentaire*, vol. 2 : *D'Alger à Berne 1944-1952*, Paris.

CLAY, Lucius (1950), *Decision in Germany*, New York.

COLLOWALD, P., FONTINE, F. (1984), *Interview du Comte Snoy et d'Oppuers. La naissance de l'Europe contemporaine*, Brussels.

COOPER, Duff (1954), *Old men forget: the Autobiography of Duff Cooper*, New York.

COSGRAVE, P. (1981), *R.A. Butler: an English life*, London.

COUDENHOVE-KALERGI, R. (1952), *J'ai choisi l'Europe*, Paris.

COUVE DE MURVILLE, Pierre (1971), *Une politique étrangère, 1958-1969*, Paris.

DAALDER, H. and CRAMER, N. (editors) (1988), *Willem Drees*, Houten.

DALTON, Hugh (1962), *High Tide and After: Memoirs, 1945-1960*, London.

DECONDE, A. (1961), ''George Cattlet Marshall, 1947-1949'' in: N. GREABNER (editor), *An Uncertain Tradition. American Secretaries of State in the Twentieth Century*, New York.

DE GAULLE, Charles (1970), *Mémoires d'espoir*, le renouveau, Paris.

DESCAMPS, Florence (1993), «Une contribution à l'histoire du Plan Marshall : La mémoire des Hauts-Fonctionnaires», in: *Le Plan Marshall et le relèvement économique de l'Europe*. Colloque tenu à Bercy les 21, 22, 23 mars 1991, sous la direction de René GIRAULT et Maurice LEVY-LEBOYER, Comité d'Histoire Économique et Financière de la France, Paris.

DESHORMES, E. (1986), «Camille Gutt – premier Directeur-Général du Fonds Monétaire International 1946-51», *Supplement to Revue de la Banque*, Brussels.

DONOUGHUE, B. and JONES, G. (1973), *Herbert Morrison*, London.

DONOVAN, Robert J. (1977), *Conflict and Crisis: The Presidency of Harry S. Truman, 1945-1948*, Norton, New York.

___. (1982), *Tumultuous Years: the Presidency of Harry S. Truman, 1949-1953*, New York.

DORN, W. (1973), *Inspektionsreisen in der US-Zone. Notizen, Denkschriften und Errinnerungen aus dem Nachlass* (transl. and ed. by L. Niethammer) Stuttgart.

DRUMMOND, R., COBLENTZ, G. (1960), *Duel at the Brink: John Foster Dulles' Command of American Power*, Garden City NY.

DULLES, A. (1963), *The Craft of Intelligence*, New York.

___. (1980), *Chances of a Life-time. A Memoir*, Englewood Cliffs.

DUROSELLE, J. (1977), *Deux types de grands hommes : le général de Gaulle et Jean Monnet*, Geneva.

EDEN, Anthony (1960), *Full Circle: Memoirs 1951-1957*, London.

EDOUARD-ROULET (dir.) (1980), *Max Petitpierre. Seize ans de neutralité active. Aspects de la politique étrangère de la Suisse 1945-61*, Neuchatel.

EISENHOWER, Dwight (1961), *My Years at the White House*, Vol. 1: 1953-1956.

___. (1967), *At Ease: Stories I tell to Friends*, New York.

ERHARD, L. (1978), *Erbe und Auftrag. Aussagen und Zeugnisse*. K. HOHMANN (editor), Düsselcorf.

FAUCCI, R. (1986), *Luigi Einaudi*, Turin.

FAURE, Edgard, (1982), *Mémoires*, Vol. 1 : *Avoir toujours raison, c'est un grand tort*, vol. 2 : *Si tel est mon destin ce soir*, Paris.

FERRAND, C. and SLOOVER, J. (dir.) (1990), *Robert Triffin conseilleur des princes. Témoignage et documents*, Brussels.

FERRELL, Robert H. (1980), *The Autobiography of Harry S. Truman*, New York.

___. (1981), *The Eisenhower Diaries*, New York.

___. (1983), *Harry S. Truman and the Modern American Presidency*, Boston.

FONTAINE, F. (1983), *Plus loin avec Jean Monnet*, Lausanne.

___. (1988), *Jean Monnet : l'inspirateur*, Paris.

FORTE, F. (1982), *Luigi Einaudi : il mercato e il buongoverno*, Turin.

FOSSEDAL, Gregory A. (1993), *Our Finest Hour. Will Clayton, The Marshall Plan and the Triumph of Democracy*, Stanford.

FROHWEIN, A. (1968), *Erinnerungen an seine Tätigkeit im deutschen Wirtschftsrat bei der britischen Kontrollkommission in München*, W. VOGEL (editor), Boppard.

GAITSKELL, Hugh (1983), *The Diary, 1945-1956*, London.

GALBRAITH, John Kenneth (1981), *A Life in Our Times: Memoirs*, Boston.

GARWOOD, E. (1958) *Will Clayton: A Short Biography*, Boston.

GERHARDSEN, Einar (1971), *Samarbeid og strid. Erinderingen 1945-55*, Oslo.

___. (1971), *I medgang og modgang. Erinderinger 1955-65*, Oslo.

GERSON, L. (1986), ''John Foster Dulles'', in: R. FERREL (editor), *The American Secretaries of State and their Diplomacy*, New York.

GOES VAN NATERS, M. VAN DER (1980), *Met en tegen de tijd. Een tocht door de twintigste eeuw*, Amsterdam.

GOOLD-ADAMS, R. (1962), *John Foster Dulles, a Re-appraisal*, New York.

GORDON, Lincoln (1988), ''Recollections of a Marshall Planner'', *Journal of International Affairs* Vol. 41, No. 2, 233-245.

GREABNER, N. (1961), ''Dean Acheson, 1949-1953'' in: N. GREABNER (editor), *An Uncertain Tradition. American Secretaries of State in the Twentieth Century*, New York.

GREWE, Wilhelm G. (1979), *Rückblenden 1976-1951. Aufzeichnungen eines Augenzeugen deutscher Außenpolitik von Adenauer bis Schmidt*, Frankfurt.

GUHIN, M. (1972), *John Foster Dulles: A Statesman and His Time*, New York.

GUINDEY, Guillaume (1977), *The International Monetary Tangle: Myths and Realities*, New York.

HARRIS, K. (1982), *Attlee*, London.

HARTMANN, S. (1971), *Truman and the 80th Congress*, Columbia.

HAUGLAND, J. (1986), *Dagbok fra kongens råd*, Oslo.

___. (1988), *Dagbok fra løvebakken*, Oslo.

HAUSENSTEIN, Wilhelm (1961), *Pariser Erinnerungen. Aus fünf Jahren diplomatischen Dienst 1950-1955*, Munich.

HELMONT, J. VAN (1989), *Jean Monnet comme il était*, Lausanne.

Hessische Sparkasses- und Giroverband, *Frankreich (1990), Deutschland und Europa. Wolfgang Klein in Gespräch mit Pierre Pflimlin und Jhanos Hajdir*, Frankfurt.

HOFFMANN, Johannes (1963), *Das Ziel war Europa. Der Weg der Saar 1945-1955*, Munich.

HOFFMAN, Paul (1951), *Peace Can Be Won*, New York.

HOOPES, T. (1973), *The Devil and John Foster Dulles*, Boston.

HUIZINGH, J. (1961), *Mr. Europe: A Political Biography of Paul-Henri Spaak*, London.

Institut Charles de Gaulle (1992), *De Gaulle en son siècle*, vol. 5 : *l'Europe*, Paris.

JACOBSSON, E. (1979), *A Life for Sound Money: Per Jacobsson, his Biography*, Oxford.

JAHN, H. (1985), *An Adenauers Seite: sein Berater erinnert sich*, Munich, 1985.

JAMES, R.R. (1986), *Anthony Eden, a Biography*, London.

KENNAN, George F. (1967-1972), *Mémoires*, vol. 1 : 1925-1950, vol. 2 : 1950-1967, Boston.

KINDLEBERGER, Charles P. (1987), *Marshall Plan Days*, Boston.

KIRKPATRICK, Ivone (1959), *The Inner Circle*, London.

KOCH, P. (1985), *Konrad Adenauer: eine politische Biographie*, Reinbeck.

LACOUTURE, J. (1984), *Pierre Mendès France*, New York.

LAING, Margaret (1973), *Edward Heath: Prime Minister*, New York.

LAITENBERG, V. (1986), *Ludwig Erhard: der Nationalökonom als Politiker*, Göttingen.

LAPIE, Pierre-Olivier (1971), *De Léon Blum à De Gaulle*, Paris.

LEGOLL, P. (1989), *Konrad Adenauer et l'idée d'unification européenne janvier 1948-mai 1950 : un homme politique « européen » et son environment dans le contexte international*, Bern.

LENNEP, E. VAN (1991), *In de wereldeconomie. Herinneringen van een internationale Nederlander*, Leiden, Antwerpen.

LEVANTROSSER, W. (editor) (1986), *Harry S. Truman, the Man from Independence*, New York.

LILIENTHAL, D. (1964-), *The journals of David E. Lilienthal*, 6 volumes, New York.

LINDEMANN, H. (1987), *Gustav Heinemann. Ein Leben für die Demokratie*, Munich.

LINDSTROM, U. (1969), *I regeringen. Ur min politiska dagbok 1954-1959*, Stockholm.

LINTHORST HOMAN, J. (1974), *Wat zijt ghij voor een vent? Levensherinneringen*, Assen.

LOCHNER, L. (1960), *Herbert Hoover and Germany*, New York.

LUKOMSKI, J. (1965), *Ludwig Erhard. Der Mensch und Politiker*, Düsseldorf.

LUNS, J. (1971), *''Ik herinner mij.'' Vrijmoedige herinneringen van Mr. J.M.A.H. Luns zoals verteld aan Michel van der Plas*, Leiden.

___. (1988), P. HUYSKENS (editor), *Gelooft u mij, het was een genoegen: mijn buitenlandse jaren*, Amsterdam.

LYNG, John (1972), *Brytningsår. Erinderinger 1923-1953*, Oslo.

___. (1973), *Vaktskifte. Erinderinger 1953-1965*, Oslo.

MACMILLAN, Harold (1969), *Tides of Fortune. 1945-1955*, London, Melbourne, Toronto.

___. (1971), *Riding the Storm. 1956-1959*, London, Melbourne, Toronto.

___. (1972), *Pointing the Way. 1959-1961*, London, Melbourne, Toronto.

___. (1973), *At the End of the Day*, London, Melbourne, Toronto.

MARJOLIN, Robert (1986), *Le travail d'une vie, mémoires 1911-1986*, Paris.

___. (1989), *Architect of European Unity: Memoirs 1911-1986*, transl. by William Hall, preface by Raymond Barre, London.

M^al^ JUIN, Alphonse (1960), *Mémoires*, Paris.

MASSIGLI, René (1978), *Une comédie des erreurs : souvenirs et réflexions sur une étape de la construction européenne*, Paris.

MAUDLING, Reginald (1978), *The memoirs of Reginald Maudling*, London.

MCLELLAN, David (1976), *Dean Acheson: The State Department Years*, New York.

MENDES-FRANCE, Pierre (1985), *Œuvres complètes,* vol. 2 : *Une Politique de l'économie, 1943-1954,* vol. 3 : *Gouverner, c'est choisir, 1954-1955,* vol. 4 : *Pour une République moderne, 1955-1962*, Paris.

MILLER, M. (1973), *Plain Speaking; An Oral Biography of Harry S. Truman*, New York.

MILLIS, W. (editor) (1951), *The Forrestal Diaries: The Inner History of the Cold War*, New York.

MONNET, Jean (1966), *Le chancelier Adenauer et la construction de l'Europe*, Lausanne.

___. (1976), *Mémoires*, Paris.

MORAN, Lord (1968), *Winston Churchill: The Struggle for Survival, 1940-1965*, London.

MORRISON, Herbert (1960), *Herbert Morrison: An Autobiography*, London.

MORSEY, R. and REPGEN, K. (editors) (1971-), *Adenauer – Studien* (Various volumes), Mainz.

MOSLEY, Leonard (1982), *Marshall: A Hero for Our Times*, New York.

MÜLLER-ARMACK, A. (1971), *Auf dem Wege nach Europa. Erinnerungen und Ausblicke*, Tübingen.

MULLER FEUGA, Philippe (1993), « Les enseignements tirés des interviews et du Fonds d'archives orales de l'Institut d'Histoire de l'Industrie », in: *Le Plan Marshall et le relèvement économique de l'Europe*. Colloque tenu à Bercy les 21, 22, 23 mars 1991, sous la direction de René GIRAULT et Maurice LEVY-LEBOYER, Comité d'Histoire Économique et Financière de la France, Paris.

MURPHY, R. (1964), *Diplomat among Warriors*, Garden City (NY).

NOVILLE, J. (1954), *Au service de son temps : Paul van Zeeland et la politique étrangère de la Belgique*, Brussels.

OTT, B. (1975), *Georges Bidault, l'indomptable*, Annonay.

OHLIN, B. (1975), *Socialistisk skördetid som kom bort*, Stockholm.
PEARSON, Drew (1972), *Drew Pearson Diaries, 1949-1959*, New York.
PELLING, H. (1984), *Winston Churchill*, London.
PEMBERTON, W. (1989), *Harry S. Truman: Fair Dealer and Cold Warrior*, Boston.
PIKART, E. (1966), *Theodor Heuss und Konrad Adenauer: Die Rolle des Bundespräsidenten in der Kanzlerdemokratie*, Stuttgart, Zürich.
PIMLOTT, B. (editor) (1986), *The Political Diary of Hugh Dalton*, London.
POGUE, F. (1987), *George C. Marshall: Statesman 1945-1959*, New York.
POIDEVIN, Raymond (1986), *Robert Schuman : homme d'État 1886-1963*, Paris.
PRITCHARD, R. (1965), *Will Clayton. A Study of Business Statesmenship in the Formulation of United States Economic Foreign Policy*, PhD. Tufts University.
PRITTIE, T. (1972), *Konrad Adenauer, 1876-1967*, London.
PRUESSEN, R. (1982), *John Foster Dulles, the Road to Power*, New York.
PUCHINGER, G. (1978), *Dr. Jelle Zijlstra: gesprekken en geschriften*, Naarden.
PÜNDER, H. (1968), *Von Preussen nach Europa. Lebenserinnerungen*, Stuttgart.
RAUCHER, A. (1985), *Paul G. Hoffmann: Architect of Foreign Aid*, Lexington.
RHODES JAMES, R. (1987), *Anthony Eden*, New York.
RIEBEN, H. (1971), *Jean Monnet*, Lausanne.
RIOUX, J. (1985), *Pierre Mendès France et le mendésisme : l'expérience gouvernementale (1954-55) et sa postérité*, Paris.
ROLL, E. (1985), *Crowded Hours*, London.
ROSENSTOCK-FRANCK, Louis (1990), *697 Ministres. Souvenirs d'un directeur général des prix 1947-1962*, Paris.
RUTTEN, F. (1989), *De betekenis van Tinbergen en Zijlstra voor de ontwikkeling van de economische wetenschap en het economisch beleid in Nederland na de 2e wereldoorlog*, The Hague.
SAMPSON, A. (1967), *MacMillan: A Study in Ambiguity*, New York.
SCHAPSMEIER, E. and F. (1970), *Prophet in Politics: Henry A. Wallace and the War Years, 1940-1965*, Ames.
SCHWARZ, Hans-Peter (1986), *Adenauer. Der Aufstieg: 1876-1952*, Stuttgart.
___. (1992), *Adenauer. Der Staatsmann: 1952-1967*, Stuttgart.
___. (editor) (1989), *Adenauer und die Hohen Kommissare, 1949-1951*, Munich.
SFORZA, Ciano (1952), *Cinque anni a Palazzo Chigi. La politica estera italiana dal 1947 al 1951*, Rome.
SHUCKBURGH, E. (1986), *Descent to Suez: Diaries, 1951-56*, London.
SMETS, P. (1980), *La pensée européenne et atlantique de Paul-Henri Spaak (1942-1972)*, Brussels.
SMITH, G., ''Dean Acheson'', Vol. 16 of: R. FERREL (editor) (1972), *The American secretaries of state and their diplomacy*, New York.
SNOY et d'OPPUERS, Jean Charles (1973), « La réciproque du Plan Marshall » in: *Chronique de politique étrangère*, vol. 26, nº 6, 681-696.
___. (1982), « Un témoin raconte : du Plan Schuman au traité de Rome » in: *30 jours d'Europe*, nº 285, 23-24.
___. (1989), « Entretiens avec Jean-Claude Ricquier », *Rebâtir l'Europe : mémoires*, Paris, Louvain-la-Neuve, Lausanne.
SPAAK, Paul-Henri (1970-1971), *Combats inachevés,* 2 vols., Paris.
SPEIER, H. (1981), *From the Ashes to Disgrace. A Journal from Germany 1945-1955*, Amherst.
STEEL, R. (1980), *Walter Lippmann and the American Century*, Boston.
STEENHORST, R. and HUIS, F. (1985), *Joseph Luns: biografie*, Amsterdam.
STERNBURG, W. (1990), *Adenauer: eine deutsche Legende*, Frankfurt.
STIKKER, Dirk (1966), *Men of Responsibility. A Memoir*, New York.
STOLER, Mark A. (1989), *Marshall: Soldier and Stateman of the America Century*, Boston.
STRANG, W. (1956), *At Home and Abroad*, London.
STRAUSS, R. (1962), *Men and Decisions*, Garden City (NY).

SULZBERGER, C. (1969) *A Long Row of Candles. Memoirs and Diaries 1934-1954*, Toronto.

——. (1971), *Dans le tourbillon de l'histoire*, Paris.

THOMAS, S. (1989), *Konrad Adenauer und die Entstehung der Bundesrepublik Deutschland*, Berlin.

THORNTON-KEMSLEY, C. (1974), *Through Winds and Tides*, Montrose.

TRAUSCH, G. (1977), *Lambert Schauss. Luxembourg, Belgique, Europe*, Luxembourg.

——. (1978), *Joseph Bech. Un homme dans son siècle. Cinquante années d'histoire luxembourgeoise (1914-1964)*, Luxembourg.

——. (dir.) (1986), *1886-1986. Les racines et l'œuvre d'un grand Européen. Robert Schuman*, Luxembourg.

TRUMAN, Harry (1955-1956), *Memoirs*, Vol. 1: 1945, Vol. 2: 1946-1952, New York.

TRUMAN, M. (1973), *Harry S. Truman*, New York.

URI, Pierre (1991), *Penser pour l'action : un fondateur de l'Europe*, Paris.

VALIANI, L. (1982), *L'Italia di De Gasperi, 1945-1954* (with an eye witness testimony of Giovanni Spadolini), Florence.

VAUBERL, L. (1984), *Zusammenbruch und Wiederaufbau. Ein Tagebuch aus der Wirtschaft 1945-1949*, Munich.

VOGEL, G. (1969), *Diplomat unter Hitler und Adenauer*, Düsseldorf.

WALKER, J. (1976), *Henry A. Wallace and American Foreign Policy*, Westport.

WALLACE, Henry A. (1973), *The Price of Vision. The Diary of Henry A. Wallace 1942-1946*, Boston.

WENZEL, R. (1983), *Konrad Adenauer und die Gestaltung der Wirtschafts- und Sozialordnung im Nachkriegsdeutschland: Ordnungsvorstellungen und politische Praxis*, Flensburg.

WESTERS, F. (1988), *Mr. D.U. Stikker en de na-oorlogse reconstructie van het liberalisme in Nederland: een zakenman in de politieke arena*, Amsterdam.

WEYMAR, P. (1955), *Konrad Adenauer. Die autorisierte Biographie*, Munich.

WHITE, Henry (1978), *In Search of History*, New York.

WIGHTON, C. (1964), *Adenauer: A Critical Biography*, New York.

WILLEQUET, J. (1975), *Paul-Henri Spaak: un homme des combats*, Brussels.

WILLIAMS, F. (1952), *Ernest Bevin: A Portrait of a Great Englishman*, London.

WILLIAMS, P. (1979), *Hugh Gaitskell: A Political Biography*, London.

——. (1983), *The Diary of Hugh Gaitskell, 1945-1956*, London.

WILSON, Harold (1986), *Memoirs: the Making of a Prime Minister, 1916-1964*, London.

ZIJLSTRA, J. (1992), *Per slot van rekening. Memoires*, Leiden, Antwerpen.

1.4 Selected Monographs and Articles from the Period/ Monographies et articles d'époque

ADAM, Henri (1949), *L'organisation européenne de coopération économique*, Paris.

ALBRECHT, Karl (1950), *Zwischenbilanz im Marshallplan*, Munich.

ANDES, W. (1964), *Der Liberalisierungskodex der OECE für den Warenhandel, Inaugural Dissertation*, University of Zürich, Zürich.

BALOGH, T. (1949), *The Marshall Plan in the dollar crisis*, Oxford.

BELOFF, M. (1963), *The United States and the Unity of Europe*, Washington.

BEUGEL, Ernst van der (1966), *From Marshall Plan to Atlantic Partnership, European Integration as a concern of American Foreign Policy*, Amsterdam.

BIDWELL, Percy W., Director (1949), *Germany's contribution to European Economic Life*, Paris.

BOYER, F. and SALLÉ, J.P. (1955) ''The Liberalization of Intra European Trade in the Framework of OEEC'' in: *International Monetary Fund Staff Papers,* Vol. 4, No. 2, 179-216.

BUCHERT, Gerhart (1949), *Der Marshallplan. Ein Weg in die Zunkunft* , Frankfurt.

CAMPS, Myriam (1964), *Britain and the European Community, 1955-1963*, London.

CLAUDE, Henri (1948), *Le plan Marshall*, Paris.

CURZON, G. (1965), *Multilateral Commercial Diplomacy*, London.

DIEBOLD, William Jr., (1952) *Trade and Payments in Western Europe. A study in Economic Cooperation 1947-1951*, New York.

ELKIN, A. (1958) ''The Organization for European Economic Cooperation: its structure and powers'', *European Yearbook*, 96.

FREYMOND, P. (1954), «Les décisions de l'OECE», *Annuaire suisse de droit international*, 65.

GOMBERG, William (1957), ''Labor's Participation in the European Productivity Program: A Study in Frustration'', *Political Science Quarterly* Vol. 74, 240-255.

GROSS, Herbert (1948), *Der Marshallplan, Deutschlands Chance*, Essen-Kettwig.

GUAZZARONI, C. (1958), ''Organizzazione europea di cooperazione economica: Dieci anni di attività'', *Comunità Internazionale* .

HABERLER G. (1948), ''Some Economic Problems of the European Recovery Program'', *American Economic Review*, Vol. 38, No. 4, 495-525.

HARRIS, Seymour (1948), *The European Recovery Program*, Cambridge.

HUET, Pierre (1953), *La commission de recours de l'OECE*, Paris.

___. (1951), *Aspects juridiques de l'Union européenne des paiements*, Paris.

International Cooperation Administration (1957), *European Productivity and Technical Assistance Programs, A Summing Up, 1948-58* , Paris.

JONES, Joseph M. (1955), *The Fifteen Weeks (February 21 – June 5, 1947)*, New York.

de JOUVENEL, Bertrand (1948), *L'Amérique en Europe. Le plan Marshall et la coopération intercontinentale*, Paris.

LUTZ, Friedrich A. (1948), *The Marshall Plan and European economic policy*, Princeton.

MANCEL, Yves (1949), *Le plan marshall. L'Union douanière ou le mariage des nations*, Paris.

MARANTZ, Marcel (1950), *Le Plan Marshall, succès ou faillite ?* Paris.

MARJOLIN, R. (1953), *Europe and the United States in the World Economy*, Durham.

MUZIOL, Roman (1948), *Europaïsche Aussenhandelsverflechtung und Marshallplan*, Frankfurt.

PATTERSON, G. (1966), *Discrimination in International Trade. The Policy Issues 1945-1965*, Princeton.

PERROUX, François (1948), *Le Plan Marshall ou l'Europe nécessaire au monde*, Paris.

PEYRET, Henry (1948), *Le Plan Marshall peut-il sauver l'Europe ?* Paris.

POUGHON, C. (1948), *Le Plan Marshall*, Paris.

PRICE, Harry (1955), *The Marshall Plan and its Meaning*, Ithaca.

SCHMITT, H.A. (1962), *The path to European Union: From Marshall Plan to Common Market*, Baton Rouge.

SCHNEIDER, Wolfgang (1948), *The Marshall Plan and the Dismantling of Industries in Western Germany*, Frankfurt.

SCHULZ, Berthold (1948), *Der Marshallplan. Ein amerikanisch-europäisches Gemeinschaftwerk*, Berlin.

STROHL, Pierre (1959), «L'organisation européenne de coopération économique. I. Les origines de l'OECE et sa place dans l'évolution européenne», *Juris-Classeur de droit international*, vol. 160-A, 1-15.

___. (1959), «L'organisation européenne de coopération économique. II. Structure et fonctionnement de l'OECE», *Juris-Classeur de droit international*, vol. 160-B, 1-26.

___. (1961), «Problèmes juridiques posés par la constitution et le fonctionnement de la Société Eurochemic», *Annuaire français de droit international*, 569-591.

___. (1965), «Les organisations européennes. Introduction. Historique. Bilan et perspectives», *Juris-Classeur de droit international*, vol. 150, 1-32

SVENNILSON, I. (1954), *Growth and Stagnation in the European Economy*, Geneva.

TESSEIDRE, Jean (1948), *Plan Marshall. Naissance et débuts*, Paris.

WAGENFÜHR, Rolf (1948), *Die Marshallplanländer und ihre Stellung in der Weltwirtschaft*, Cologne.

WITTOWSKI, Adolf (1953), *Schrifttum zum Marshallplan und zur Wirtschaftlichen Integration Europas*, Bad Godesberg.

2. Recent publications (after 1970)/Publications récentes (depuis 1970)

By far the largest category of publications on Marshall aid and the OEEC is concerned with the actual preparation, reception and implementation of US foreign aid in Europe. To facilitate access, this category has been divided into four sections, each dealing with different aspects. For the sake of completion, however, those publications dealing with more than one of these topics have been grouped under more than one heading.

The first topic (section 2.1.) provides basic works on the general social, economic, and political context of Marshall Aid and European reconstruction. The second (2.2) seeks to group together general works on the Marshall Plan, whereas the third section (2.3) deals with the various national standpoints on the Marshall Plan by providing a country classification. (For reasons of balance, the Benelux countries and the Scandinavian countries have been grouped together). Finally, the fourth and fifth sections deal with the themes of trade, sectoral cooperation and payments within the OEEC and EPU (2.4) and with the EFTA negotiations (2.5).

La majeure partie des publications sur l'aide du Plan Marshall et l'OECE traitent de la préparation, réception et mise en œuvre de l'aide étrangère américaine en Europe. Afin de faciliter la consultation, cette catégorie a été divisée en quatre sections, chacune d'entre elles traitent d'un aspect différent. Les publications concernant plusieurs rubriques sont mentionnées plusieurs fois.

La première section (2.1) présente les ouvrages de base sur le contexte social, économique et politique du Plan Marshall et de la reconstruction européenne. La seconde (2.2) tente de regrouper les ouvrages généraux sur le Plan Marshall et la troisième (2.3) propose une classification des publications par pays. (Pour conserver un équilibre, les pays du Bénélux et les pays scandinaves ont été regroupés). Enfin, les quatrième et cinquième sections couvrent les thèmes des échanges, de la coopération sectorielle, des paiements au sein de l'OECE et de l'UEP (2.4), et des négociations afférentes à l'AELE (2.5).

2.1 General Context (Basic Works)/ Contexte Général (Ouvrages de base)

ACHESON, A.L.K., J.F. CHANT, M.F.J. PRACHOWNY (editors) (1972), *Bretton Woods revisited*, Toronto.

ARMSTRONG, Philip, Andrew GLYN and John HARRISON (1984), *Capitalism since World War II: The Making and Break Up of the Great Boom*, London.

BARNET, Richard (1983), *The Alliance: America-Europe-Japan, Makers of the Postwar World*, New York.

BECKER, Josef and Franz KNIPPING (1986), *Power in Europe: Great Britain, France, Italy and Germany in a Postwar World, 1945-1950*, Berlin, New York.

BERDING, Helmut (1984), *Wirtschaftliche und politische Integration in Europa im 19 und 20 Jahrhundert*, Göttingen.

BLOCK, Fred (1979), *The Origins of International Economic Disorder. A Study of United States International Monetary Policy from World War II to the Present*, Berkerley.

BOLTHO, Andrea (1982), *The European Economy: Growth and Crisis*, Oxford.

BOSSUAT, Gérard (1992), *L'Europe occidentale à l'heure américaine : le plan Marshall et l'unité européenne, 1945-1952*, Brussels, Paris.

BOSSUAT, Gérard (1994), Les fondateurs de l'Europe, Paris.

BRETT, E.A. (1985), *The World Economy since the War: The politics of uneven development*, New York.

CAIRNCROSS, Alec (1987), "Post-war Planning in Europe, 1945-47", *Okonomi og Politik* Vol. 60, No. 4, 213-223.

De CARMOY, Guy and Jonathan STORY (1986), *Western Europe in World Affairs: Continuity, Change and Challenge*, New York.

CASELLA, A. and B. EICHENGREEN (1993), "Halting Inflation in France and Italy After World War II", in: Michael BORDO and Forrest CAPIE (editors), *Monetary Regimes in Transition*, Cambridge.

DIEBOLD, William, Jr. (1985), *Trade and Payments in Western Europe in Historical Perspective: A Personal View by an Interested Party, European University Insitute Working Papers*, No. 10, European University Institute, Florence.

DI NOLFO, Ennio (1980), "Il Piano Marshall e la guerra fredda", *Colloque sur le Plan Marshall*, Rome.

——. (editor) (1992), *Power in Europe? II Great Britain, France, Italy and the Origins of the EEC 1952-1957*, Berlin, New York.

ELLWOOD, David W. (1992), *Rebuilding Europe: Western Europe, America and Postwar Reconstruction*, London.

FARQUHARSON, John (1991), "'The Essential Division': Britain and the Partition of Germany 1945-9", *German History,* Vol. 9, No. 1, 23-45.

GADDIS, John Lewis (1982), *Strategies of Containment. The United States and the Origins of the Cold War*, New York, 1982.

GERBET, Pierre (1983), *La construction de l'Europe*, Paris.

___. (1987), *La naissance du marché commun, la mémoire du siècle*, Brussels.

GIRAULT René, BOSSUAT Gérard, sous la direction de (1994), Europe brisée, Europe retrouvée, nouvelles réflexions sur l'unité européenne au XXe siècle, Paris.

GRIFFITHS, Richard T. (1990), « A la recherche des débuts de l'intégration européenne », *Revue de synthèse*, vol. 3, 235-252.

___. (1991) ''De economische achtergronden van de Europese integratie 1945-1957'' in W.A.F. CAMPHUIS and C. WILDEBOER SCHUT (editors), *Europese eenwording in historische perspectief*, Zaltbommel.

GROSSER, Alfred (1978), *Les Occidentaux : les pays d'Europe et les États-Unis depuis la guerre*, Paris.

___. (1980), *The Western Alliance: European-American relations since 1945*, London.

HERBST, Ludolf (1986), ''Die Zeitgenössische Integrationstheorie und die Anfänge der Europäischen Einigung 1947-1950'' *Vierteljahrshefte für Zeitgeschichte*, Vol. 34, 161-205.

KATZENSTEIN, Peter J. (1978), *Between Power and Plenty: Foreign Economic Policies of Advanced Industrial States*, Wisconsin.

KINDLEBERGER, Charles P. (1972), *Europe's Postwar Growth*, Harvard.

___. (1984), *A Financial History of Western Europe*, London.

KÜSTERS, Hans Jürgen (1982), *Die Gründung der Europäischen Wirtschaftsgemeinschaft*, Baden-Baden.

LIEBERMAN, Sima (1977), *The Growth of European Mixed Economies, 1945-1970: A Concise Study of the Economic Evolution of Six Countries*, Cambridge (Mass.).

LOTH, Wilfried (1980), *Die Teilung der Welt. Geschichte des Kalten Krieges 1941-1955*, Munich.

___. (1990), *Der Weg nach Europa: Geschichte der Europäischen Integration, 1939-1957*, Göttingen.

MADDISON, Angus (1982), *Phases of Capitalist Development*, Oxford.

MAIER, Charles P. (1978), *The Origins of the Cold War and Contemporary Europe*, New York.

___. (1981), ''The Two Postwar Eras and the Conditions for Stability in Twentieth Century Western Europe'', *American Historical Review*, Vol. 86, 327-367.

MAYNE, Richard (1970), *The Recovery of Europe: From Devastation to Unity*, London.

___. (1986), *Western Europe: A Handbook*, London.

MEERHAEGHE, M.A.G. van (1987), *International Economic Institutions, Fifth Revised Edition*, Dordrecht.

MESER, Robert L. (1982), *The End of an Alliance. James F. Byrnes, Roosevelt, Truman and the Origins of the Cold War*, Chapel Hill.

MILWARD, Alan S. (1984), *The Reconstruction of Western Europe 1945-1951*, London.

___. (1992), *The European Rescue of the Nation State*, London.

MILWARD, Alan S., Frances M.B. LYNCH, Federico ROMERO, Ruggero RANIERI, Vibeke SØRENSEN (1993), *The Frontier of National Sovereignty. History and theory, 1945-1992*, London, New York.

OECD (1978), *From Marshall Plan to Global Interdependence*, Paris.

PATERSON, Thomas J. (1973), *Soviet-American Confrontation: Post-war Reconstruction and the Origins of the Cold War*, Baltimore.

POIDEVIN, Raymond (dir.) (1986), *Histoire des débuts de la Construction européenne (mars 1948-mai 1950). Origins of the European Integration (March 1948-May 1950)*, Actes du Colloque de Strasbourg 28-30 novembre 1984, Brussels, Milan, Paris, Baden-Baden.

POLLARD, Robert A. (1985), *Economic security and the origins of the Cold War, 1945-1950*, New York.

POWASKI, Ronald H. (1991), *Toward an Entangling Alliance. American Isolationism, Internationalism and Europe, 1901-1950*, New York.

PIQUET MARCHALL, Marie-Odile (1985), *Histoire économique de l'Europe des Dix. De la seconde guerre mondiale à aujourd'hui*, Paris.

PIJL, Kees van der (1984), *The Making of an Atlantic Ruling Class*, Amsterdam.

SERRA, Enrico (1987), *Il Rilancio dell'Europa e i Tratti de Roma/La relance européenne et le Traité de Rome, (Actes du Colloque de Rome, 25-28 mars)*, Brussels, Milan, Paris, Baden-Baden.

SILVERMAN, Dan P. (1982), *Reconstructing Europe After the Great War*, Cambridge (Mass.)

SIRACUSA, Joseph M. (1977), *The American Diplomatic Revolution: A Documentary History of the Cold War 1941-1947. Series in American Studies*, New York.

SOLOMON, R. (1982), *The International Monetary System, 1945-1981*, New York.

SMITH R.P. (1980), ''Military Expenditure and Investment in OECD Countries 1954-1973'', *Journal of Comparative Economics*, Vol. 4, No. 1, 19-32.

STIRK Peter M. R, WILLIS, David (1991) (editors), *Shaping postwar Europe: European Unity and Diversity 1945-1957*, New York.

TEW, Brian (1982), *The Evolution of the International Monetary System 1945-1981*, London, Melbourne.

TRAUSCH, Gilbert (Hrsg.), (1993), *Die Europäische Integration vom Schuman-Plan bis zu den Verträgen von Rom. The European Integration from the Schuman-Plan to the Treaties of Rome*. Beiträge des Kolloquiums in Luxemburg, 17-19 mai 1989. Contributions to the Symposium in Luxembourg May 17-19, 1989, Nomos Verlagsgesellschaft, Baden-Baden.

YERGIN, Daniel (1979), *A Shattered Peace: The Origins of the Cold War and the National Security State*, Houghton Mifflin, Boston.

YOUNG, John W. (1984), *Britain, France and the Unity of Europe, 1945-1951*, Leicester.

2.2 General Works on the Marshall Plan/Ouvrages de base sur le Plan Marshall

AGAROSSI, E. (editor) (1983), *Il Piano Marshall e l'Europa*, Rome.

ARKES, Hadley (1972), *Bureaucracy, the Marshall Plan and the National Interest*, Princeton.

BANETH, Jean (1993), «Du Plan Marshall au Plan Brady : la dette des pays en voie de développement à la lumière du Plan Marshall», in: *Le Plan Marshall et le relèvement économique de l'Europe*. Colloque tenu à Bercy les 21, 22, 23 mars 1991, sous la direction de René GIRAULT et Maurice LEVY-LEBOYER, Comité d'Histoire Économique et Financière de la France, Paris.

BAILEY, Thomas A. (1977), *The Marshall Plan Summer. An eyewitness report on Europe and the Russians in 1947*, Stanford.

BOSSUAT, Gérard (1990), «Les grands commencements de l'Europe : Plan Marshall (1947) et aide à l'est européen (1990)», *Vingtième Siècle,* vol. 31, 25-40.

BRÄHLER, R. (1983), *Der Marshallplan: Zur Strategie Weltmarktorientierter Krisenvermeidung*, Cologne.

CAREW, Anthony (1987), *Labour under the Marshall Plan: the Politics of Productivity and the Marketing of Management Science*, Manchester.

CARTAPANIS, André, REIFFERS, Jean-Louis, (1993), «Le Financement Public International à la lumière de l'expérience du Plan Marshall» in: *Le Plan Marshall et le relèvement économique de l'Europe*. Colloque tenu à Bercy les 21, 22, 23 mars 1991, sous la direction de René GIRAULT et Maurice LEVY-LEBOYER, Comité d'Histoire Économique et Financière de la France, Paris.

CERAMI, Charles A. (1989), *A Marshall Plan for the 1990s: An International Roundtable on World Economic Development*, New York.

CHENAUX, Philippe (1990), *Une Europe Vaticane ? Entre le Plan Marshall et les Traités de Rome*, Brussels.

COWEN, Tyler (1986), ''The Great Twentieth-Century Foreign-Aid Hoax'', *Reason,* Vol. 17, No. 11, 37-41.

CRAVERI, Piero (1977), *Sindacato e istituzioni nel dopoguerra*, Bologna.

DANIEL, Ute (1982), *Dollardiplomatie in Europa: Marshall Plan, Kalter Krieg und Aussenwirtschaftspolitik 1945-1952*, Düsseldorf.

DIEBOLD, William Jr. (1988), ''The Marshall plan in Retrospect: a review of recent scholarship'', *Journal of International Affairs*, Vol. 41, No. 2., 421-435.

DONOVAN, Robert J. (1987), *The Second Victory: The Marshall Plan and the Postwar Revival of Europe*, New York.

DORNBUSCH, Rudiger, NOLLING, Wilhelm, LAYARD, Richard (editors), (1993) *Postwar Economic Reconstruction and Lessons for the East Today*, Cambridge (Mass.), London.

DULLES, Allen Welsh (1993), *The Marshall Plan*, Providence.

EICHENGREEN, Barry and UZAN, M. (1992), ''The Marshall Plan: Economic Effects and Implications for Eastern Europe and the Former USSR'', *Economic Policy,* Vol. 14, 13-76.

ELLWOOD, David., ''The Impact of the Marshall Plan'', *History,* Vol. 74, No. 242, 427-436.

ELLWOOD, D. W. (1994), ''The Marshall Plan and the Politics of Growth'', in Richard T. Griffiths (editor), *Explorations in OEEC History*, Paris.

___. (1994), «Le plan Marshall et les aspects politiques de la croissance» in Richard T. Griffiths (dir.), *A la découverte de l'OECE*, Paris.

FAY, Sidney B. (1989), ''The Marshall Plan'', *Current History,* Vol. 88, No. 534, 30-31, 51-52.

FRANKS, Lord (1978), ''Lessons of the Marshall Plan Experience'' in: OECD (editor), *From Marshall Plan to global interdependence*, Paris.

FODOR, G, (1985), ''Perchè nel 1947 l'Europe ebbe bisogno del Piano Marshall?'', Rivista di Storia Economica, Vol. 2, No. 1, 89-123.

GIMBEL, John (1976), *The Origins of the Marshall Plan*, Stanford.

GIRAULT, René, LEVY-LEBOYER, Maurice (dir.), (1993), *Le Plan Marshall et le relèvement économique de l'Europe*, Colloque tenu à Bercy les 21, 22, 23 mars 1991, Comité d'Histoire Économique et Financière de la France, Paris.

HABERL, Othmar, Fritz, NIETHAMMER (1986), *Der Marshall Plan und die Europäische Linke*, Frankfurt.

HOFFMANN, Stanley and Charles S. MAIER (editors) (1984), *The Marshall Plan: A Retrospective*, Cambridge (Mass).

HOGAN, Michael J. (1987) *The Marshall Plan: America, Britain, and the Reconstruction of Western Europe, 1947-1952*, Cambridge.

HOSCHER, Dietmar (1990), ''Anmerkungen zur Diskussion über einen Marshallplan für Osteuropa'', *Europäische Rundschau*, Vol. 18, No. 1, 31-38.

KINDLEBERGER, Charles P. (1987), *Marshall Plan Days*, Boston.

___. (1988), ''The One and Only Marshall Plan'', *National Interest,* Vol. 11., 113-115.

KIRMAN, Alan et Lucrezia REICHLIN (1990), «L'Aide aux pays de l'Est : les leçons du Plan Marshall», *Observations et diagnostics économiques*, n° 34, 281-325.

___. (1991), ''The Marshall Plan'' in J.P. FITOUSSI (dir.), *A l'est en Europe : des économies en transition*, Paris.

KOSTRZEWA, Wojciech, Peter NUNNENKAMP, and Holger SCHMIEDING (1989), ''A Marshall Plan for Middle and Eastern Europe?'', *Kiel Working Papers*, No. 403.

KUKLICK, Bruce (1977), ''The Origins of Marshall Plan'', *Review of American History*, Vol. 5, 292-298.

LACROIX-RIZ, Annie (1993), «Plan Marshall et commerce Est-Ouest : continuités et ruptures», in: *Le Plan Marshall et le relèvement économique de l'Europe.* Colloque tenu à Bercy les 21, 22, 23 mars 1991, sous la direction de René GIRAULT et Maurice LEVY-LEBOYER, Comité d'Histoire Économique et Financière de la France, Paris.

LÉVY-LEBOYER, Maurice (1993), «Conclusion» in: *Le Plan Marshall et le relèvement économique de l'Europe.* Colloque tenu à Bercy les 21, 22, 23 mars 1991, sous la direction de René GIRAULT et Maurice LEVY-LEBOYER, Comité d'Histoire Économique et Financière de la France, Paris.

LOEWENSTEIN, Joseph, TATLOCK, Lynne, (1992) ''The Marshall Plan and the movies: Marlene Dietrich and war incarnations'', *The German Quarterly*, Vol. 65, No. 3/4, 429.

de LONG, J. Bradford, EICHENGREEN, Barry, (1991), ''The Marshall Plan: History's Most Successful Structural Adjustment Program'', in: R. DORNBUSH, R. LAYARD and W. NOLLING (editors), *Postwar Reconstruction 1945-1949: Implications for Eastern Europe*, Cambridge (Mass.), London.

LOTH, W. (1982), ''The West-European Governments and the Impulse given by the Marshall Plan'', in: LIPGENS, W. (editor), *A History of European Integration, Volume 1, 1945-1947. The Formation of the European Unity Movement*, Oxford, 488-506.

MAIER, Charles (1984), ''Supranational Concepts and National Continuity in the Framework of the Marshall Plan'' in: HOFFMANN, Stanley and Charles S. MAIER (editors) (1984), *The Marshall Plan: A Retrospective*, Cambridge (Mass).

MAYNE, Charles S. (1993), ''Premises of the European Recovery Program'', in: *Le Plan Marshall et le relèvement économique de l'Europe.* Colloque tenu à Bercy les 21, 22, 23 mars 1991, sous la direction de René GIRAULT et Maurice LEVY-LEBOYER, Comité d'Histoire Économique et Financière de la France, Paris.

MEE, Charles L. (1984), *The Marshall Plan: the launching of the Pax Americana*, New York.

MILWARD, Alan S. (1984), *The Reconstruction of Western Europe 1945-1951*, London.

___. (1989),''Was the Marshall Plan Necessary?'', *Diplomatic History*, Vol. 13, No. 2, 231-253.

OECD (1978), *From Marshall Plan to global interdependence*, Paris.

POLLARD, R. (1985), ''Economic Security and the Origins of the Cold War: Bretton Woods, the Marshall Plan, and American rearmament'', *Diplomatic History*, Vol. 9, No. 3, 271-289.

——. (1985), *Economic security and the origins of the Cold War*, 1945-1950, New York.

REIFFERS, Jean-Louis, CARTAPANIS, André, (1993), «Le Financement Public International à la lumière de l'expérience du Plan Marshall» in: *Le Plan Marshall et le relèvement économique de l'Europe*. Colloque tenu à Bercy les 21, 22, 23 mars 1991, sous la direction de René GIRAULT et Maurice LEVY-LEBOYER, Comité d'Histoire Économique et Financière de la France, Paris.

ROMERO, Federico (1985), ''Postwar Reconversion Strategies of American and Western European Labor'', *European University Insitute Working Papers*, No. 85/193, September, European University Institute, Florence.

ROMERO, Federico and MERLI BRANDINI, Pietro (1989), *Gli Stati Uniti e il sindicalismo europeo 1944-1951*, Rome.

ROSSI AGA, Elena (ed.), (1983), *Il Piano Marshall e l'Europa*, Rome.

SCHWABE, Klaus (1986), ''Der Marshall-Plan und Europa'', in Raymond POIDEVIN (dir.), *Histoire des débuts de la Construction européenne (mars 1948-mai 1950)*, Actes du Colloque de Strasbourg 28-30 novembre 1984, Brussels, Milan, Paris, Baden-Baden.

WALA, Michael (1986), ''Selling the Marshall Plan at Home: The Committee for the Marshall Plan to Aid European Recovery'', *Diplomatic History*, Vol. 10, No. 3, 247-265.

WEXLER, Imanuel (1983), *The Marshall Plan Revisited: The European Recovery Program in Economic Perspective*, Westport.

WILSON, Theodore A. (1977), ''The Marshall Plan: An Atlantic Venture of 1947-1951 and How It Shaped Our World'', Foreign Policy Association, New York, *Headline Series*, No. 236, June.

WOOD, Robert E. (1986), *From Marshall Plan to Debt Crisis: Foreign Aid and Development Choices in the World Economy*, Berkeley.

2.3 The Marshall Plan from the National Standpoints/Le Plan Marshall: perspectives nationales

2.3.1 Austria/Autriche

ARDELT, Rudolf G. (1975), *Die Westintegration Österreichs nach 1945. Österreichische Zeitschrift für Politikwissensschaft*, Vol. 4, 379-399.

BISCHOF, Günther (1990), ''Der Marshallplan und Österreich'', *Zeitgeschichte* [Austria] Vol. 17, No. 11-12, 463-474.

EGGLESTON, P. (1980), *The Marshall Plan in Austria: a study in American containment of the Soviet Union in the Cold War*, Ph.D University of Alabama.

EINWITSCHLÄGER, ARNO (1986), *Amerikanische Wirtschaftspolitik in Österreich 1945-1959*, Cologne, Vienna.

HUMMEL, N. (editor) (1990), *Österreichs Integration in Europa 1948-1989: von der OEEC zur EG*, Vienna.

MÄHR, Wilfried, (1987), ''Der Marshall-plan in Österreich: wirtschaftspolitischer Nachhilfeunterricht?'' *Zeitgeschichte* [Austria], Vol. 15, No. 3., 91-111.

——. (1989), *Der Marshallplan in Österreich*, Graz.

SENSENIG, Gene R. (1985), ''Gewerkschaftspolitik im Kalten Krieg am Beispiel der Beziehungen der US-Regierung und der US-Gewerkschaften zum ÖGB zwischen 1945 und 1950'', *Zeitgeschichte* Vol. 12, No. 6, 198-216.

SMOLIK, Sabine (1987), ''Die wirtschaftlichen auswirkungen der besatzung in Österreich als didaktisches problem'', *Zeitgeschichte* [Austria], Vol. 14, No. 8, 330-346.

WEBER, Fritz (1987), «Österreichs Wirtschaft in der Rekonstruktionsperiode nach 1945», *Zeitgeschichte* [Austria], Vol. 14, No. 7, 267-298.

——. (1992), ''Die Spuren der NS-Zeit in der österreichischen Wirtschaftsentwicklung'', *Österreichische Zeitschrift für Geschichtswissenschaften,* Vol. 3, No. 2, 135-165.

——. (1994), ''Austria: A Special Case in European Economic Integration'', in Richard T. Griffiths (editor), *Explorations in OEEC History*, Paris.

——. (1994), «L'Autriche : un cas à part dans l'intégration économique européenne?» in Richard T. Griffiths (dir.), *A la découverte de l'OECE*, Paris.

ZIMMERMAN, H. (1983), *Wirtschaftsentwicklung in Österreich 1945-51 am Beispiel der Lohn-und Preisabkommen des Marshallplans*, Ph.D University of Vienna.

2.3.2 The Benelux countries (Belgium, the Netherlands and Luxembourg)/Les pays du Bénélux (Belgique, Pays-Bas et Luxembourg)

BLOEMEN, Erik (1990), ''Hard work! Ideology and Interest in Dutch Economic Policy at Home and Abroad between 1945 and 1951'', *Economic and Social History in the Netherlands*, Vol. 2, 135-148

——. (1993), ''Technical Assistance and Productivity in the Netherlands'' in: *Le Plan Marshall et le relèvement économique de l'Europe*. Colloque tenu à Bercy les 21, 22, 23 mars 1991 sous la direction de René GIRAULT et Maurice LEVY-LEBOYER, Comité d'Histoire Économique et Financière de la France, Paris. Comité d'Histoire Économique et Financière de la France, Paris.

DERCKSEN, W.J. (1986), *Industrialisatiepolitiek rondom de jaren vijftig; een sociologisch-economische beleidsstudie*, Assen, Maastricht.

ENG, P. van der (1987), *De Marshall-hulp. Een perspectief voor Nederland 1947-1953*, Houlen.

——. (1987), ''Marshall Aid as a Catalyst in the Decolonization of Indonesia'', *Journal of Southeast Asian Studies* [Singapore], Vol. 19, No. 2, 335-352.

FEYTER, C.A. de (1981), ''The Selling of an Ideology; The Long Term Expectations of the Marshall Aid and their Impact in the Netherlands'' in: R. KROES (editor), *Image and Impact. American Influences in the Netherlands since 1945*, Amsterdam.

GODTS-PETERS, S. (1987), *La politique européenne du gouvernement belge, septembre 1944-mai 1950*, Ph.D European University Institute, Florence.

GRIFFITHS, Richard T. (1984), ''Economic Reconstruction Policy in the Netherlands and Its International Consequences, May 1945-March 1951'', *European University Institute Working Papers,* No. 76, Florence.

GROSBOIS, Thierry (1993), «Le Bénélux et le Plan Marshall, une union douanière face au roi dollar» in: *Le Plan Marshall et le relèvement économique de l'Europe*. Colloque tenu à Bercy les 21, 22, 23 mars 1991 sous la direction de René GIRAULT et Maurice LEVY-LEBOYER, Comité d'Histoire Économique et Financière de la France, Paris.

HEN, P.E de (1980), *Actieve en re-actieve industiepolitiek in Nederland. De overheid en de ontwikkeling van de Nederlandseindustrie in de jaren zeventig en tussen 1945 en 1950*, Amsterdam.

HOMAN, Gerlof D. (1990), ''The Netherlands, the United States and the Indonesian Question, 1948'' *Journal of Contemporary History*, Vol. 25, No. 1, 123-141.

KLEIN, P.W. (1981), ''Wegen naar economisch herstel 1945-1950'', *Bijdragen en mededelingen betreffende de geschiedenis der Nederlanden*, Deel 96, Aflevering 2, Ministerie van Nationale Opvoeding en Nederlandse Cultuur, 260-276.

KURGAN-VAN HENTENRYK, Ginette (1987), «Le Plan Marshall, un début de la construction européenne? Approche de l'opinion belge», dans Michel Dumoulin, *La Belgique et les débuts de la construction européenne*, CIACO, Louvain-La-Neuve, 77-85.

——. (1993), «La Belgique et le Plan Marshall : les négociations belgo-américaines (juin 1947-juillet 1948)», in: *Le Plan Marshall et le relèvement économique de l'Europe*, Colloque tenu à Bercy les 21, 22, 23 mars 1991 sous la direction de René GIRAULT et Maurice LEVY-LEBOYER, Comité d'Histoire Économique et Financière de la France, Paris.

——. (1993), «La Belgique et le Plan Marshall ou les paradoxes des relations belgo-américaines», *Revue belge de philologie et d'histoire*, vol. 71, n° 2, 290-353.

LANGEVELD, Herman (1986), ''Die Niederländische Gewerkschaftsbewegung und der Marshall-Plan'' in: Othmar HABERL and Fritz NIETHAMMER (editors), *Der Marshall Plan und die Europäische Linke*, Frankfurt am Main.

LIAGRE BÖHL, H. et al. (editors) (1981), *Nederland industrialiseert! Politiek en ideologische strijd rondom het naoorlogse industrialisatiebeleid, 1945-1955*, Nijmegen.

LIAGRE BÖHL, H. (1981), ''Jaren van tucht en ascese. Enige beschouwingen over de stemming in Herrijzend Nederland 1945-1950'', *Bijdragen en Mededelingen Betreffende de Geschiedenis der Nederlanden,* Vol. 96, 300-333.

MEEGENS, Ine (1994), *American Aid to NATO Allies in the 1950s: The Dutch Case*, Ph.D University of Groningen, Groningen.

SCHRAM, Jef (1988), ''Nederland en het Marshallplan. De Nederlandse belangen op de conferentie van Parijs, 1947'', in P. LUYKX and A. MANNING, (editors), *Nederland in de wereld 1870-1950. Opstellen over buitenlandse en koloniale politiek, aangeboden aan dr. N. Boutsma*, Nijmegen.

___. (1993), ''The Netherlands, The Marshall Plan and the European Payments Union (1947-1950)'' in: *Le Plan Marshall et le relèvement économique de l'Europe*, Colloque tenu à Bercy les 21, 22, 23 mars 1991, sous la direction de René GIRAULT et Maurice LEVY-LEBOYER, Comité Pour l'Histoire Économique et Financière de la France, Paris.

WIEBES, Cees and ZEEMAN, Bert (1992), ''United States 'Big Stick' Diplomacy: the Netherlands between Decolonization and Alignment, 1945-1949'', *International History Review*, Vol. 14, No. 1, 45-70.

WIELENGA, Friso (1983), ''De partij van de Arbeid en het Marshall Plan'', *Het vijfde jaarboek voor het democratisch socialisme*, Amsterdam.

WITTE, E., BURGELMAN, J.C. and STOUTHUYSEN, P. (editors) (1989), *Tussen restauratie en vernieuwing. Aspecten van de naoorlogse Belgische politiek (1944-1950)*, Brussels.

2.3.3 France

BANAL, Michel (1993), «Le Plan Marshall et l'électricité», in: *Le Plan Marshall et le relèvement économique de l'Europe*. Colloque tenu à Bercy les 21, 22, 23 mars 1991, sous la direction de René GIRAULT et Maurice LEVY-LEBOYER, Comité d'Histoire Économique et Financière de la France, Paris.

BARJOT, Dominique (1993), «L'industrie Française des Travaux Publics face à la reconstruction : l'impact du Plan Marshall», in: *Le Plan Marshall et le relèvement économique de l'Europe*. Colloque tenu à Bercy les 21, 22, 23 mars 1991, sous la direction de René GIRAULT et Maurice LEVY-LEBOYER, Comité d'Histoire Économique et Financière de la France, Paris.

BOCQUENTIN, Jacques (1991) «État de l'industrie de l'aluminium en 1947», in: *Le Plan Marshall et le relèvement économique de l'Europe*. Colloque tenu à Bercy les 21, 22, 23 mars 1991, sous la direction de René GIRAULT et Maurice LEVY-LEBOYER, Comité d'Histoire Économique et Financière de la France, Paris.

BOSSUAT, Gérard (1983), «Ingérences américaines et dépendance française : la contre-valeur de l'aide Marshall 1948-1951», in *La puissance française en question 1945-1949*, Paris.

___. (1984), «Le poids de l'aide américaine sur la politique économique et financière de la France en 1948», *Relations Internationales*, n° 37, 17-36.

___. (1986), « L'aide américaine à la France après la seconde guerre mondiale», *Vingtième siècle*, n° 9, 17.

___. (1986), *La modernisation de la France sous influence. Premières étapes de l'appel à l'étranger (1944-1949)*, Ph.D University of Paris I, Sorbonne.

___. (1987), «La modernisation de la France (1945-1949), une affaire européenne?» *Le Capitalisme Français*, 307.

___. (1989), «Les Risques et les espoirs du Plan Marshall pour la France», Comité pour l'Histoire Économique et Financière, *Études et Documents*, n° 1989, Paris.

___. (1990), «Paul Ramadier et le Plan Marshall : une rupture en politique étrangère» in: RAMADIER, Paul and BERSTEIN, Serge (dir.), *La République et le socialisme*, Paris.

___. (1993), «La contre-valeur de l'aide américaine à la France et à ses territoires d'outre-mer : la mesure des rapports franco-américains», in: *Le Plan Marshall et le relèvement économique de l'Europe*. Colloque tenu à Bercy les 21, 22, 23 mars 1991, sous la direction de René GIRAULT et Maurice LEVY-LEBOYER, Comité d'Histoire Économique et Financière de la France, Paris.

___. (1992) *La France, l'aide américaine et la construction européenne 1944-1954*, Comité pour l'Histoire économique et financière de la France, Ministère de l'Économie et des Finances, Paris, 2 volumes.

BOUVIER, Jean (1984), «Le Plan Monnet et l'économie française 1947-1952», *European University Institute Working Papers*, No. 83, European University Institute, Florence.

BOUVIER, Jean and BLOCH-LAINÉ, François (1986), *La France restaurée. 1944-1954. Dialogue sur les choix d'une modernisation*, Paris.

BURR, William (1991), ''Marshall Planners and the Politics of Empire: The United States and French Financial Policy, 1948'', *Diplomatic History*, Vol. 15, No. 4, 495-522.

CUTTOLI-UHEL, C. de (1988), «La politique allemande de la France 1945-1948, symbole de son impuissance?» in: GIRAULT, and FRANK, Robert (dir.), *La Puissance française en question, 1945-1949*, Paris.

ESPOSITO, Chiarella (1985), *The Marshall plan in France and in Italy, 1948-1950: counterpart fund negotiations*, University Microfilms International, Ann Arbor, Michigan.

FEIERTAG, Olivier (1993), «Entre la défense du franc et les impératifs de l'economie nationale, les pouvoirs et la politique de Banque de France et de son gouverneur sous la IVe République», in: *Du franc Poincaré à l'écu.* Colloque tenu à Bercy les 3, 4 décembre 1992 sous la direction de Maurice LEVY-LEBOYER, Plessis, Aglietta et de Boissieu Comité d'Histoire Économique et Financière de la France, Paris.

FRANK, Robert, (1983), «Le dilemme français : la modernisation sous influence ou l'indépendance dans la décadence» in: GIRAULT, René and FRANK, Robert (dir.), *La Puissance française en question, 1945-1949*, Paris.

FRIDENSON, Patrick (1993), «L'industrie automobile française et le Plan Marshall» in: *Le Plan Marshall et le relèvement économique de l'Europe.* Colloque tenu à Bercy les 21, 22, 23 mars 1991, sous la direction de René GIRAULT et Maurice LEVY-LEBOYER, Comité d'Histoire Économique et Financière de la France, Paris.

GERBET, Pierre, J. LALOY, J. DUPUY *et al.* (1991), *Le Relèvement 1944-1949*, Paris.

HILL, John S (1992), ''American Efforts to aid French reconstruction between lend-lease and the Marshall Plan'', *The Journal of Modern History*, Vol. 64, No. 3, CHECK

KUISEL, Richard (1985), «Les missions de productivité» in: ROSSI AGA, Elena, (editor), (1983), *Il Piano Marshall e l'Europa*, Rome.

___. (1988), «L'American Way of Life et les mission françaises de productivité», *Vingtième Siècle* vol. 17, n° 1, 21-38.

___. (1993), ''The Marshall Plan in action: Politics, Labor, Industry and the Program of Technical Assistance», in: *Le Plan Marshall et le relèvement économique de l'Europe.* Colloque tenu à Bercy les 21, 22, 23 mars 1991, sous la direction de René GIRAULT et Maurice LEVY-LEBOYER, Comité d'Histoire Économique et Financière de la France, Paris.

LACROIX-RIZ, Annie (1983), *La CGT de la libération à la scission*, Paris.

___. (1986), *Le choix de Marianne : les relations franco-américaines 1944-1948*, Paris.

De LATTRE, André (1993), «Le Plan Marshall et la transition de l'économie française», in: *Le Plan Marshall et le relèvement économique de l'Europe.* Colloque tenu à Bercy les 21, 22, 23 mars 1991, sous la direction de René GIRAULT et Maurice LEVY-LEBOYER, Comité d'Histoire Économique et Financière de la France, Paris.

LOTH, W. (1977), *Sozialismus und Internationalismus. Die französischen Sozialisten und die Nachkriegsordnung Europas 1940-1950*, Stuttgart.

LYNCH, Frances M.B. (1984), *French Reconstruction in a European Context, European University Institute Working Papers,* No. 86/11, European University Institute, Florence.

___. (1986), ''The Impact of Rearmament on French Reconstruction'', *European University Institute Working Paper*, No. 86/253, European University Institute, Florence.

___. (1981), *The Political and Economic Reconstruction of France 1944-1947 in its international context*, Ph.D University of Manchester.

___. (1984), ''Resolving the Paradox of the Monnet Plan: National and International Planning in French Reconstruction'', *Economic History Review*, Vol. 37, No. 2, 229-243.

MARGAIRAZ, Michel (1993), «Les Finances, le Plan Monnet et le Plan Marshall : entre les contraintes, controverses et convergences», in: *Le Plan Marshall et le relèvement économique de l'Europe.* Colloque tenu à Bercy les 21, 22, 23 mars 1991, sous la direction de René GIRAULT et Maurice LEVY-LEBOYER, Comité d'Histoire Économique et Financière de la France, Paris.

MBARAGA, P. (1985), *Le plan Marshall. Louanges et critiques en France 1947-1950*, University of Strasbourg III, Strasbourg.

MIOCHE, Philippe (1984), ''The Origins of the Monnet Plan'', *European University Institute Working Papers*, No. 79/4, European University Institute, Florence.

___. (1987), *Le Plan Monnet : genèse et élaboration, 1941-1947*, Paris.

___. (1993), «Le Plan Marshall et la Sidérurgie française», in: *Le Plan Marshall et le relèvement économique de l'Europe.* Colloque tenu à Bercy les 21, 22, 23 mars 1991, sous la direction de René GIRAULT et Maurice LEVY-LEBOYER, Comité d'Histoire Économique et Financière de la France, Paris.

MORSEL, Henri (1993), «Pechiney et le Plan Marshall» in: *Le Plan Marshall et le relèvement économique de l'Europe.* Colloque tenu à Bercy les 21, 22, 23 mars 1991, sous la direction de René GIRAULT et Maurice LEVY-LEBOYER, Comité d'Histoire Économique et Financière de la France, Paris.

POIDEVIN, Raymond (1985), ''Die Neuorientierung der französischen Deutschlandpolitik 1948-1949'' in: FOSCHEPOTH, J. (editor), *Kalter Krieg und Deutsche Frage*, Göttingen.

——. (1985), ''Der Faktor Europa in der Deutschlandpolitik Robert Schumans (Sommer 1948 bis Frühjahr 1949)'', *Vierteljahrsheft für Zeitgeschichte* 33. Jahrgang, Heft 3, 406-419.

——. (1993), «Plan Marshall et problème allemand : les inquiétudes françaises (1947-1948)» in: *Le Plan Marshall et le relèvement économique de l'Europe.*, Colloque tenu à Bercy les 21, 22, 23 mars 1991, Comité Pour l'Histoire Économique Économique et Financière de la France, Paris.

Du REAU, Elisabeth (1993), «Le gouvernement français, le Quai d'Orsay et la préparation de la Conférence de Paris» in: *Le Plan Marshall et le relèvement économique de l'Europe.* Colloque tenu à Bercy le 21, 22, 23 mars 1991, Comité d'Histoire Économique et Financière de la France, Paris.

RIBEILL, Georges (1993), «La SNCF au temps du Plan Marshall, ou les années noires d'une entreprise publique», in: *Le Plan Marshall et le relèvement économique de l'Europe.* Colloque tenu à Bercy les 21, 22, 23 mars 1991, sous la direction de René GIRAULT et Maurice LEVY-LEBOYER, Comité d'Histoire Économique et Financière de la France, Paris.

ROUSSO, Henri (dir.) (1986), *De Monnet à Massé. Enjeux politiques et objectifs économiques dans le cadre des quatres premiers plans (1946-1951)*, Paris.

SCHARF, Claus, and Hans-Jürgen SCHRÖDER (editors) (1983), *Die Deutschlandpolitik Frankreichs und die französische Zone 1945-1949*, Wiesbaden.

SCHREINER, R. (1985), *Bidault, der MRP und die französische Deutschlandpolitik 1944-1948*, Frankfurt.

SPAGNOLO, Carlo (1993), «L'avis de Jean Monnet sur le contrôle des fonds de contrepartie (1947-1948)», in: *Le Plan Marshall et le relèvement économique de l'Europe.* Colloque tenu à Bercy les 21, 22, 23 mars 1991, sous la direction de René GIRAULT et Maurice LEVY-LEBOYER, Comité d'Histoire Économique et Financière de la France, Paris.

STOFFAES, Christian (1993), «La révolution invisible : une mise en perspective de l'expérience des missions de productivité» in: *Le Plan Marshall et le relèvement économique de l'Europe*, Colloque tenu à Bercy les 21, 22, 23 mars 1991, sous la direction de René GIRAULT et Maurice LEVY-LEBOYER, Comité d'Histoire Économique et Financière de la France, Paris.

SUGIMOTO, Yoshihiko (1986), «Maruseiyu no 1947 nen 11-12 gatsu sutoraiki» [The strikes of November-December 1947 in Marseilles], *Seiyo Shigaku* [Japan], Vol. 143, 36-53.

THUILLIER, Jean-Paul (1993), «Les Charbonnages de France et le Plan Marshall», in: *Le Plan Marshall et le relèvement économique de l'Europe.* Colloque tenu à Bercy les 21, 22, 23 mars 1991, sous la direction de René GIRAULT et Maurice LEVY-LEBOYER, Comité d'Histoire Économique et Financière de la France, Paris.

TREMPÉ, Rolande (1988), «Relations franco-américaines au lendemain de la seconde guerre mondiale» in: Pierre BOUVIER and Olivier KOURCHILD (dir.), *France-USA : Les crises du travail et de la production*, Paris.

WALL, Irvin M. (1989), *L'influence américaine sur la politique française, 1945-1954*, Paris.

——. (1991), *The United States and the Making of Postwar France, 1945-1954*, New York.

——. (1993), ''The American Marshall Plan Mission in France'', in: *Le Plan Marshall et le relèvement économique de l'Europe*, Colloque tenu à Bercy les 21, 22, 23 mars 1991, sous la direction de René GIRAULT et Maurice LEVY-LEBOYER, Comité d'Histoire Économique et Financière de la France, Paris.

WALL, Irwin M. and RAVIART, Philippe-Etienne, transl. (1987), «Les accords Blum-Byrnes : la Modernisation de la France et la Guerre Froide», *Vingtième Siècle*, vol. 13, 45-62.

YOUNG, France W. (1990), *France, the Cold War and the Western Alliance, 1944-1949: French Foreign Policy and Post War Europe*, Leicester, London.

2.3.4 Germany/Allemagne

ABELSHAUSER, Werner, BENZ, Wolfgang, GRAML, Hermann (editors) (1975), ''Wirtschaft in Westdeutschland 1945-1948: Rekonstruktion und Wachstumsbedingungen in der Amerikanischen und Britischen zone'', *Schriftenreihe der Vierteljahreshefte für Zeitgeschichte*, Vol. 30, Stuttgart.

——. (1975), ''Wirtschaft in Westdeutschland 1945-1948'', *Schriftenreihe der Vierteljahrhsefte für Zeitgeschicht*, Vol. 30, 35-42.

——. (1981), ''Wiederaufbau vor dem Marshallplan. Westeuropas Wachstumchancen und die Wirtschaftsordnung in der Zweiten Hälfte der vierziger Jahre'', *Vierteljahrsheft für Zeitgeschichte*, Vol. 29, No. 24, 545-587.

___. (1983), ''Wirtschaft und Besatzungspolitik in der französischen Zone 1945-49'' in: Claus SCHARF and Hans-Jürgen SCHRÖDER (editors), *Die Deutschlandpolitik Frankreichs und die französische Zone 1945-1949*, Wiesbaden.

___. (1984), ''Der Kleine Marshallplan: Handelsintegration durch innereuropäische Wirtschaftshilfe, 1948-1950'', in: Helmut BERDING (editor), *Wirtschaftliche und Politische Integration In Europa im 19. und 20. Jahrhundert*, Göttingen.

___. (1987), ''The economic role of the ERP in German recovery and growth after the war: A macroeconomic perspective'', in: *The Marshall Plan and Germany. West German Development within the Framework of the European Recovery Program*, New York, Oxford.

___. (1989), ''Hilfe und Selbsthilfe: zur Funktion des Marshallplans beim Westdeutschen Wiederaufbau'', *Vierteljahrsheft für Zeitgeschichte*, Vol. 37, No. 1, 85-113.

___. (1991), ''American Aid and West German Economic Recovery: a Macroeconomic Perspective'', in: Charles S. MAIER and Günther BISCHOF (editors), *The Marshall Plan and Germany. West German Development within the Framework of the European Recovery Program*, New York, Oxford.

___. (1993), ''The working of the Marshall Plan in the early phase of the West German construction'' in: *Le plan Marshall et le relèvement économique de l'Europe.* Colloque tenu à Bercy les 21, 22, 23 mars 1991, sous la direction de René GIRAULT et Maurice LEVY-LEBOYER, Comité d'Histoire Économique et Financière de la France, Paris.

ADAMSEN, Heiner R. (1978), ''Faktoren Und Daten der Wirtschaftlichen Deutschland. Entwicklung in der Frühphase der Bundesrepublik 1948-1954'', *Archiv für Socialgeschichte*, Vol. 18, 231.

___. (1981), *Investitionshilfe für die Ruhr: Wiederaufbau, Verbande und soziale Marktwirtschaft, 1948-1952*, Wuppertal.

___. (1984), ''Investitionspolitik in der Bundesrepublik Deutschland 1949-1951'', *European University Institute Working Papers*, No. 82/7, *European University Institute*, Florence.

BACKER, John H. (1971), *Priming the German economy: American Occupational Policies, 1945-1948*, Durham (NC).

BERGHAHN, Volker (1986), *The Americanization of West German Industry 1945-1973*, Lemington Spa.

BORCHARDT, Knut, BUCHHEIM, Christoph (1987), ''Die Wirkung des Marshallplan: hilfe in Schlüsselbranchen der deutschen Wirtschaft'', *Vierteljahrshefte Für Zeitgeschichte*, Vol. 35, 317-347.

___. (1987), ''The Marshall Plan and economic key sectors: A microeconomic perspective'', in Charles S. MAIER and Günther BISCHOF (editors), *Germany and the Marshall Plan. West German Development within the Framework of the European Recovery Program*, New York, Oxford.

BÜHRER, Werner (1988), ''Auftakt in Paris: der Marshallplan und die deutsche Rückkehr auf die Internationale Bühne 1948-1949'', *Vierteljahrshefte Für Zeitgeschichte*, Vol. 36, 529-556.

___. (1990), ''Vom Marshallplan zur EWG'', *Vom Marshall-Plan zum EWG. Die Eingliederung der Bundesrepublik Deutschland in die Westliche Welt 1945-1955*, Munich.

___. (1993), ''Die deutsche Industrie und der Marshallplan (1947-1952)'', in: *Le Plan Marshall et le relèvement économique de l'Europe.* Colloque tenu à Bercy les 21, 22, 23 mars 1991, sous la direction de René GIRAULT et Maurice LEVY-LEBOYER, Comité d'Histoire Économique et Financière de la France, Paris.

von CSERNATONY, Georges (1973), *Le Plan Marshall et le redressement économique de l'Allemagne : Une étape vers l'intégration européenne*, Lausanne.

EISENBERG, Carolyn (1983), ''Working Class Politics and the Cold War: American Intervention in the German Labor Movement, 1945-1949'', *Diplomatic History*, Vol. 7, No. 4, 283-306.

FICHTER, M. (1979), *''Free Trade Unionism'' for Germany: The Planning, Development and Implementation of Trade Union Policy of the US Military Government for Germany 1944-1948*, Ph.D. Free University Berlin, Berlin.

FOSCHEPOTH, J. (editor) (1985), *Kalter Krieg und Deutsche Frage*, Göttingen.

GIMBEL, John (1984), ''Governing the American Zone in Germany'' in: Robert WOLFE (editor), *Americans as Proconsuls. United States Military Government in Germany and Japan, 1944-1952*, Carbondale, Edwardsville.

GROSSER, Alfred (1970), *L'Allemagne de notre temps*, Paris.

___. (1953), *L'Allemagne de l'Occident 1945-1952*, Paris.

HANRIEDER, W.F. (1991), *Deutschland, Europa, Amerika. Die Außenpolitik der Bundesrepublik Deutschland 1949-1989*, Paderborn, Munich, Vienna, Zurich.

HARDACH, Gerd (1987), "The Marshall Plan in Germany, 1948-1952", *The Journal of Economic History*, Vol. 16, No. 1, 433-485.

—. (1993), «Le plan Marshall et l'intégration internationale de l'économie allemande», in: *Le plan Marshall et le relèvement économique de l'Europe*, Colloque tenu à Bercy les 21, 22, 23 mars 1991, sous la direction de René GIRAULT et Maurice LEVY-LEBOYER, Comité d'Histoire Économique et Financière de la France, Paris.

—. (1991) "Transnationale Wirtschaftspolitik: der Marshall Plan in Deutschland 1947-1952" in Dietmar PETZINA (editor), *Ordnungspolitische Weichenstellungen nach dem Zweiten Weltkrieg*, Berlin.

HENNING, Friedrich-Wilhelm (1981), "Wege und Wirkungen des Marshallplans", *Scripta Mercaturae*, No. 15, 91-112.

HERBST, Ludolf, editor (1990), *Vom Marshall-Plan zum EWG. Die Eingliederung der Bundesrepublik Deutschland in die Westliche Welt 1945-1955*, Munich.

—. (1986), *Westdeutschland 1945-1955. Unterwerfung Kontroll, Integration*, Munich.

HERBST, Ludolf (1989), *Option für den Westen, Vom Marshall Plan bis zum deutsch-französischen Vertrag*, Munich.

HILLENBRAND, Martin J. (1983), *Germany in an Era of Transition*, Paris.

KLEMM, Bernd and TRITTEL, Günter J. (1987), "Vor dem 'wirtschaftswunder': durchbruch zum Wachstum oder Lähmungskrise? Eine Auseinandersetzung mit Werner Abelshausers Interpretation der Wirtschaftsentwicklung 1945-1948", *Vierteljahrshefte für Zeitgeschichte,* Vol. 35, No. 4, 571-624.

KNAPP, Manfred (1975) *Die Deutsch-amerikanischen Beziehungen nach 1945*, New York.

—. (1977), "Deutschland und der MarshallPlan: Zum Verhältnis zwischen politischer und ökonomischer Stabilisierung in der Amerikanischen Deutschlandpolitik nach 1945" in: Claus SCHARF and Hans-Jürgen SCHRÖDER (editors) (1977), *Politische und ökonomische Stabilisierung Westdeutschlands: 1945-1949: funf Beiträge zur Deutschland politik der westlichen Allierten*, Wiesbaden.

—. (1978), "Das Deutschlandproblem und die Ursprünge des europäischen Wiederaufbauprogrammes, eine Auseinandersetzung mit John Gimbels Untersuchung 'The Origins of the Marshall Plan'", *Politische Vierteljahresshrift*, No. 9, 48-65.

—. (1981), "Reconstruction and West Integration: the Impact of the Marshall Plan on Germany", *Zeitschrift für die gesammte Staatswissenschaft,* Vol. 17, 415-433.

—. (1984), "Die Anfänge westdeutscher Außenwitschafts- und Außenpolitik im bizonalen Vereinigten Wirtschaftsgebiet (1947-1949)" in: Manfred KNAPP (editor), *Von der Bizonengründung zur ökonomisch-politischen Westintegration*, Frankfurt.

LINK, Werner (1978), *Deutsche und amerikanische Gewerkschaften und Geschäftsleute 1945-1975*, Düsseldorf.

—. (1980), "Der Marshallplan und Deutschland", *AusPolitik und Zeitgeschichte*, No. B50/80, 3-18.

—. (1991), "Nongovernmental German American Linkages" in: Charles S. MAIER and Günther BISCHOF (editors), *Germany and the Marshall Plan. West German Development within the Framework of the European Recovery Program*, New York, Oxford.

MAYER, Herbert C. (1969), *German Recovery and the Marshall Plan*, Bonn, Brussels.

MORGAN, Roger (1974), Royal Institute of International Affairs and Harvard Center for International Affairs, *The United States and West Germany, 1945-1973: A study in alliance policy*, London.

OTT, E. (1980), "Die Bedeutung des Marshall-Plans für die Nachkriegsentwicklung in Westdeutschland", *Aus Politik und Zeitgeschichte*, No. B4/80, 19-37.

—. (1990), "Die Bedeutung des Marshall-Planes für die Nachkriegsenwicklung Deutschlands" in: Hans-Jürgen SCHRÖDER (editor), *Marshallplan und Westdeutscher Wiederaufstieg. Positionen, Kontroversen*, Stuttgart.

SCHARF, Claus, and SCHRÖDER, Hans-Jürgen (editors) (1977), *Politische und ökonomische Stabilisierung Westdeutschlands: 1945-1949: funf Beiträge zur Deutschland politik der westlichen Allierten,* Wiesbaden.

—. (1983), *Die Deutschlandpolitik Frankreichs und die französische Zone 1945-1949*, Wiesbaden.

SCHRÖDER, Hans-Jürgen (1987), "Marshall Plan, Amerikanische Deutschlandpolitik und Europäische integration 1947-1950", *Aus Politik und Zeitgeschichte*, Vol. 18/87, No. 2, 3-17.

SCHRÖDER, Hans-Jürgen (editor) (1990), *Marshallplan und westdeutscher Wiederaufstieg. Positionen, Kontroversen*, Stuttgart.

SCHWABE, Klaus (1991), "German Policy responses to the Marshall Plan" in: Charles S. MAIER and Günther BISCHOF (editors), *Germany and the Marshall Plan. West German Development within the Framework of the European Recovery Program*, New York, Oxford.

SCHWARTZ, Thomas (1991), ''European Integration and the 'Special Relationship': Implementing the Marshall Plan in the Federal Republic of Germany, 1948-1951'', in: Charles S. MAIER and Günther BISCHOF (editors), *Germany and the Marshall Plan. West German Development within the Framework of the European Recovery Program*, New York, Oxford.

TURNER, Ian D. (editor) (1989), *Reconstruction in Postwar Germany. British Occupation Policy and the Western Zones, 1945-1955*, Oxford, New York, Munich.

WINKLER, H.A. (editor), *Politische Weichenstellungen im Nachkriegsdeutschland 1945-1953*, Göttingen.

WURM Clemens (1995), *Western Europe and Germany, the beginnings of European Integration 1945-1960*, Oxford.

2.3.5 Greece/Grèce

AMEN, M.M. (1978), *American Foreign Policy in Greece: 1944-1949*, Frankfurt.

FRERIS, A. (1986), *The Greek Economy in the Twentieth Century*, London, Sydney.

IATRIDES, J.O. (editor) (1981), *Greece in the 1940s. A Nation in Crisis*, Hannover, N.H.

STATHAKIS, George (1990), ''Appproaches to the Early Postwar Greek Economy: A Survey'', *Journal of Modern Hellenism,* No.7.

___. (1991), ''Finance and Industrial Reconstruction: The Case of the Marshall Plan in Greece'' in: Association Interdiscipline Franco-hellenique 1992 (dir.), *L'entreprise en Grèce et en Europe, XIXe-XXe siècles*, Athens.

___. (1993), *The Civil War Economy, 1944-1953: The Truman Doctrine and the Marshall Plan in Greece*, Athens.

___. (1993), ''The Marshall Plan in Greece'' in: *Le Plan Marshall et le relèvement économique de la France*. Colloque tenu à Bercy les 21, 22, 23 mars 1991, sous la direction de René GIRAULT et Maurice LEVY-LEBOYER, Comité d'Histoire Économique et Financière de la France, Paris.

THOMAKADIS, S. (1989), ''The Truman Doctrine: Was there a Development Agenda?'', *Journal of Modern Hellenism,* No. 6.

WITTNER, Lawrence S. (1982), *American Intervention in Greece, 1943-1949*, New York.

2.3.6 Ireland/Irlande

GIRVIN, Brian (1989), *Between Two Worlds: Politics and Economy in Independent Ireland*, Dublin.

___. (1994), ''Ireland and the Marshall Plan: A Cargo Cult in the North Atlantic?'', in Richard T. Griffiths (editor), *Explorations in OEEC History*, Paris.

___. (1994), « L'Irlande et le plan Marshall : un culte du cargo dans l'Atlantique nord ? » in Richard T. Griffiths (dir.), *A la découverte de l'OECE*, Paris.

KEOGH, Dermot (1990), *Ireland and Europe 1919-1989: A Diplomatic and Political History*, Cork.

LEE, J.J. (1989), *Ireland 1912-1985*, Cambridge.

MAHER, D.J. (1984), *The tortuous Path. The Course of Ireland's Entry into the EEC, 1948-1973*, Dublin.

MCCARTHY, John F. (editor) (1990), *Planning Ireland's Future: the Legacy of T.K. Whitaker*, Dublin.

MJOSTET, Lars (1992), *The Irish Economy in a Comparative Institutional Perspective*, Dublin.

O'GRADY, Joseph Patrick (1988), ''J.W. Fulbright and the Fulbright Program in Ireland'', *Arkansas Historical Quarterly,* Vol. 47, No. 1, 47-69.

RAYMOND, Raymond J. (1985), ''The Marshall Plan and Ireland, 1947-1952'', in P.J. DRUDY (editor), *The Irish in America: Emigration, Assimilation and Impact*, Cambridge.

___. (1985), ''The Marshall Plan and Ireland, 1947-52'', *Irish Studies* 4, 295-328.

WHELAN, Bernadette (1989), ''The European Recovery Program (the Marshall Plan) and Ireland: Summary and Assessment'' *Eire-Ireland,* Vol. 24, No. 3, 78-84.

2.3.7 Italy/Italie

BAGNATO, Bruna (1993), « Le Plan Marshall et l'Union douanière Franco-italienne (juillet 1947-mars 1948) » in: *Le Plan Marshall et le relèvement économique de la France*. Colloque tenu à Bercy les 21, 22, 23 mars 1991, sous la direction de René GIRAULT et Maurice LEVY-LEBOYER, Comité d'Histoire Économique et Financière de la France, Paris.

BARUCCI, Piero (1978), *Ricostruzione, pianificazione, Mezzogiorno. La politica economica in Italia, 1943-1955*, Bologna.

D'ATTORE, Pier Paolo (1985), ''Anche noi possiamo essere prosperi: Aiuti ERP e politiche della produttività negli anni cinquanta'', *Quaderni Storici*, Vol. 58, 55-93.

——. (1985), ''ERP aid and the Problems of Productivity in Italy during the 1950s'', *European University Institute Working Paper*, No. 85/199, European University Institute, Florence.

——. (1985), ''Il piano Marshall: politica, economia, relazioni internazionali nella ricostruzione italiana'', *Passato e Presente*, No. 7, 31-63.

——. (1986), ''Riconstruzione e anni depressi: il piano Marshall in Sicilia'', *Italia Contemporanea*, Vol. 164, 5-35.

——. (1988), ''Il piano Marshall: politica, economia, relazioni internazionali nella ricostruzione italiana'' in: di NOLFO, Ennio, RAINERO, R. and VIGEZZI, B. (editors), *L'Italia e la politica di potenza in Europa, 1945-1950*, Milan.

DE CECCO, M. (1972), ''Italian economic policy during the reconstruction'', in S.J. WOOLF, (editor), *The Rebirth of Italy 1943-1950*, London.

DI NOLFO, Ennio (1986), *Le paure e le speranze degli italiani 1943-1953*, Milan.

——. (1993) , *«L'Italie et le Plan Marshall. Aux origines de la participation italienne»* in: *Le Plan Marshall et le relèvement économique de l'Europe.* Colloque tenu à Bercy les 21, 22, 23 mars 1991, sous la direction de René GIRAULT et Maurice LEVY-LEBOYER, Comité d'Histoire Économique et Financière de la France, Paris.

DI NOLFO, Ennio, RAINERO, R. and VIGEZZI, B. (ed.) (1988), *L'Italia e la politica di potenza in Europa, 1945-1950*, Milan.

ELLWOOD, David (1983), ''Il Piano Marshall e il processo di modernizzazione in Italia'' in: ROSSI AGA, Elena (ed.) (1983), *Il Piano Marshall e l'Europa*, Roma, 149-161.

——. (1985), ''La propaganda del Piano Marshall in Italia'', *Passato e Presente,* No. 9, 153-171.

FAENZA, R., FINI, M. (1976), *Gli Americani in Italia*, Milan.

FOA, Vittorio (1974), ''La ricostruzione capitalistica nel secondo dopoguerra'', *Il secondo dopoguerra in Italia*, Torino.

HARPER, John L. (1986), *America and the reconstruction of Italy, 1945-1948*, New York.

——. (1986), *L'America e la reconstruzione dell'Italia, 1945-1948,* Bologna.

MILLER, James E. (1986), *The United States and Italy 1940-1950. The Politics and Diplomacy of Stabilization*, Chapel Hill, London.

QUARTARARO, Rosaria (1984), ''L'Italia e il Piano Marshall (1947-1952)'', *Storia contemporanea,* Vol. 15, No. 4, 647-722.

——. (1986), *Italia e Stati Uniti Gli anni difficili (1945-1952),* Roma.

RANIERI, Ruggero (1985), ''Europeismo e politica europea: osservazioni sulla presenza italiana in Europa occidentale dal 1947 al 1951'', *Storia delle Relazioni Internazionali,* No. 1, 161-181.

——. (1993), ''The Marshall Plan and the reconstruction of the Italian steel industry (1948-1954)'', in: *Le Plan Marshall et le relèvement économique de l'Europe.* Colloque tenu à Bercy les 21, 22, 23 mars 1991, sous la direction de René GIRAULT et Maurice LEVY-LEBOYER, Comité d'Histoire Économique et Financière de la France, Paris.

ROMERO, Federico (1987), *Guerra fredda e stabilizzazione sociale: politiche americane sulla questione sindacale nella recostruzione postbellica dell'Europa e dell'Italia, 1944-1953*, Rome.

——. (1988), ''Oltre il piano Marshall: gli USA e la modernizzazione del sindacalismo italiano (1950-1955)'', *Italia Contemporanea*, No.170, 71-96.

——. (1988), ''Gli Stati Uniti e la ricostruzione postbellica dell'Europa: il ruolo dei sindacati americani'', *Storia delle Relazioni Internazionali*, Vol. 4, No. 2, 367-394.

——. (1989), *Guerra fredda e stabilità sociale: gli Stati Uniti e il sindacalismo europeo 1944-1951. Il caso italiano*, Rome.

——. (1991), *Emigrazione e integrazione europea 1945-1974*, Rome.

SAVONA, P. (1983), ''La stabilizzazione monetaria in Italia e il Piano Marshall'' in: AGAROSSI, E. (ed.), *Il Piano Marshall e l'Europa*, Rome.

SEBESTA, L. (1988), ''I programmi di aiuto militare nella politica americana per l'Europa: l'esperienza italiana 1948-1952'', *Italia Contemporanea*, No. 173, 43-64.

VARSORI, Antonio (1986), ''Italian diplomacy and contrasting perceptions of American policy after World War II (1947-1950)'', *Storia Nordamericana*, Vol. 3, No. 2, 73-91.

___. (1993), ''Italy and European integration from the Marshall plan to the Pleven Plan'' in: *Le Plan Marshall et le relèvement économique de l'Europe*. Colloque tenu à Bercy les 21, 22, 23 mars 1991, sous la direction de René GIRAULT et Maurice LEVY-LEBOYER, Comité d'Histoire Économique et Financière de la France, Paris.

VECCHIO, Giorgio, ''Movimenti Pacifisti ed Antiamericano in Italia (1948-1953)'', *European University Institute Working Papers*, No. 249, November, EUI, Florence.

WOOLF, Stuart J. (ed.) (1974), *Italia 1943-1950. La ricostruzione*, Bari.

ZAMAGNI, Vera (1986), ''Betting on the Future. The Reconstruction of Italian Industry, 1946-1952'' in: BECKER, Josef and Franz KNIPPING (editors), *Power in Europe: Great Britain, France, Italy and Germany in a Postwar World, 1945-1950*, Berlin, New York.

___. (1988), ''Una somessa sul futuro; l'industria italiana nella ricostruzione (1946-1952)'' in: di NOLFO, Ennio, RAINERO, R. and VIGEZZI, B. (ed.) (1988), *L'Italia e la politica di potenza in Europa, 1945-1950*, Milan.

2.3.8 Portugal

FUNDACO, A. (1976), ''Caluste Gulbenkian and the German Marshall Funds of the United States'' in: *Conferencia Internacionale sobre Economica Portogesa.*

2.3.9 Scandinavian Countries (Denmark, Finland, Norway and Sweden)/ Pays Scandinaves (Danemark, Finlande, Norvège et Suède)

AASTAD S.A. (1974), *Marshallhljelpens organisering gjennom OEEC – konsekvenser for Norge. Hovedoppgave i historie*, Oslo.

ANDERSEN, Poul Nyboe (1987), ''Marshall-planens betydningen for dansk okonomi'' [The impact of the Marshall Plan on the Danish economy], *Okonomi og Politik,* Vol. 60, No. 4, 278-288.

BROFOSS, E. (1977), ''The Marshall Plan and Norway's Hesitation'', *Scandinavian Journal of History*, Vol. 2, No. 3, 241-242.

EMBLEM, T. (1977), *Arbeiderpartiet og Norges tilslutning til Marshallplanen. Hovedoppgave i historie*, Oslo.

ERIKSEN, Knut (1977), ''Norge i det vestlige samarbeid'' in: Trond BERGH (editor), *Vekst og velstand. Norsk politisk historie 1945-1965*, Oslo, Bergen, Tromsø.

GELTING, Jorgen H. (1987), ''Danske genopbygningsproblemer 1945-1947'' [Danish reconstruction problems, 1945-47], *Okonomi og Politik,* Vol. 60, No. 4, 234-239.

JENSEN, Leon Dalgas (1987), ''Nogle tal om Marshallplanen og hjaelpen til Danmark'' [Some figures on the Marshall Plan and aid to Denmark], *Okonomi og Politik,* Vol. 60, No. 4, 210-212.

___. (1987), ''Marshallplanen og Danmark: en litteraturliste'' [The Marshall Plan and Denmark: a bibliography], *Okonomi og Politik,* Vol. 60, No. 4, 297-304.

___. (1991), ''Denmark and the Marshall Plan, 1947-48: the Decision to Participate'', *Scandinavian Journal of History,* Vol. 14, No. 1, 57-83.

___. (1991), ''Mod en langsigtet erhvervspolitik'' [Toward a long-term industrial policy], *Okonomi og Politik,* Vol. 60, No. 4, 255-262.

___. (1993), *Politisk kamp om Danmarks Importpolitik 1945-1948*, Ph.D University of Copenhagen, Copenhagen.

LACROIX-RIZ, Annie (1991), *L'economie suédoise entre l'Est et Ouest 1944-1949 : neutralité et embargo, de la guerre au Pacte Atlantique*, Paris.

LUNDESTAD, Geir (1980), *America, Scandinavia and the Cold War*, Oslo.

MÜLLER, Otto (1987), ''De handels- og valutapolitiske sporgsmål, som Marshall-planen rejser for Danmark'' [The effects of the Marshall Plan on Danish trade and monetary policies], *Okonomi og Politik,* Vol. 60, No. 4, 266-276.

PAAVONEN, Tapani (1989), ''Neutrality, Protectionism and the International Community: Finnish Foreign Economic Policy in the Period of Reconstruction of the International Economy, 1945-1950'', *Scandinavian Economic History Review,* Vol. 37, No. 1. 23-40.

PEDERSEN, K.R. (1988), *The United States and Norwegian Reconstruction 1945-1953, PhD. University of Rochester*, New York.

PHARO, Helge (1976), ''Bridge-building and Reconstruction: Norway faces the Marshall Plan'', *Scandinavian Journal of History,* Vol. 1, No. 1, 128-130.

___. (1984), ''Domestic and International Implications of Norwegian Reconstruction'', *European University Institute Working Papers*, No. 83/81, European University Institute, Florence.

___. (1988), ''Marshallplanen sett fra amerikansk side. Norge i komparativt perspektiv'' [The Marshall Plan seen from the American side: Norway in a comparative perspective], *Historisk Tidsskrift,* Vol. 68, No. 2, 184-209.

___. (1989), ''Gjenreisning og utenrikspolitikk'' in: T. BERGH and Helge PHARO (editors), *Historiker og Veileder*, Oslo.

___. (1993), ''The Marshall Plan and the Modernization of the Norwegian Economy'', in *Le Plan Marshall et le relèvement économique de l'Europe*, Colloque tenu à Bercy les 21, 22, 23 mars 1991, sous la direction de René GIRAULT et Maurice LEVY-LEBOYER, Comité d'Histoire Économique et Financière de la France, Paris.

___. (1993), ''Denmark, the Marshall Plan and European Integration, 1945-1963'', *The International History Review,* Vol. 1, 23-45.

___. (1994), ''Norway, the United States and the Marshall Plan, 1947-52'', in Richard T. Griffiths (editor), *Explorations in OEEC History*, Paris.

___. (1994), «La Norvège, les États-Unis et le plan Marshall 1947-1952'' in Richard T. Griffiths (dir.), *A la découverte de l'OECE*, Paris.

SCHMIDT, Erik Ib. (1987), ''De okonomiske og politiske overvejelser ved beslutningen om deltagelse i Marshallplanen'' [The economic and political considerations concerning the decision to participate in the Marshall Plan], *Okonomi og Politik,* Vol. 60, No. 4, 242-251.

SØRENSEN, Vibeke (1987), *Social Democratic Government in Denmark under the Marshall Plan, 1947-1950*, Ph.D. European University Institute, Florence.

___. (1993), ''The Politics of Closed Markets: Denmark, the Marshall Plan and European Integration 1945-1963'', *International History Review,* Vol. 15, No. 1, 23-45.

STEIRO, Jens R. (1973), *Om opprettelsen av Norsk produktivitetsinstitutt*, Oslo.

2.3.10 Switzerland/Suisse

FLEURY, Antoine (1993), «Le patronat suisse et l'Europe : du Plan Marshall aux Traités de Rome» in: Michel DUMOULIN *et. al.* (dir.), *L'Europe du patronat. De la Guerre froide aux années 1960*, Louvain-La-Neuve.

___. (1993), «Le Plan Marshall et l'économie suisse» in: *Le Plan Marshall et le relèvement économique de l'Europe*. Colloque tenu à Bercy les 21, 22, 23 mars 1991, sous la direction de René GIRAULT et Maurice LEVY-LEBOYER, Comité d'Histoire Économique et Financière de la France, Paris.

KEEL, Guido Alberto (1980), *Le grand patronat suisse face à l'integration européenne*, Bern.

WEHNER, Gerd (1992), ''Die Schweiz und der Marshallplan'', *Vierteljahrschrift für Sozial- und Wirtschaftsgeschichte,* Vol. 79, No. 3, 341-356.

2.3.11 Turkey/Turquie

THOBIE, Jacques (1987), «France et Turquie, les relations entre un ancien et un nouveau pays industriels depuis 1945» in: *Actes du colloque d'Istanbul*, 2-4 décembre 1985, Istanbul, Paris.

THOBIE, Jacques and BACQUÉ-GRAMMONT (1987), «L'accession de la Turquie à la civilisation industrielle» in: *Actes du colloque d'Istanbul*, 2-4 décembre 1985, Instanbul, Paris.

THOBIE, Jacques (1993), «La Turquie et le Plan Marshall vus de France» in: *Le Plan Marshall et le relèvement économique de l'Europe*, Colloque tenu à Bercy, les 21, 22, 23 mars 1991, sous la direction de René GIRAULT et Maurice LEVY-LEBOYER, Comité d'Histoire Économique et Financière de la France, Paris.

2.3.12 United Kingdom/Royaume Uni

ANSTEY, Caroline (1986), ''Foreign Office Publicity, American aid and European unity: mobilising public opinion 1947-1949» in: Josef BECKER and Franz KNIPPING (editors), *Power in Europe? Great Britain, France, Italy and Germany in the Post-War World, 1945-1950*, Berlin, New York.

BECKER, Joseph and KNIPPING Franz (editors), (1986) *Power in Europe? Great Britain, France, Italy and Germany in the Post-War World, 1945-1950*, Berlin, New York.

BOYLE, Peter G. (1987), ''Britain, America and the Transition from Economic to Military Assistance, 1948-51'', *Journal of Contemporary History,* Vol. 22, No. 3, 521-538.

BRIVATI, Brian and JONES, Harriet (1993), *From Reconstruction to Integration: Britain and Europe since 1945*, London.

CAIRNCROSS, Alec (1985), *Years of recovery: British Economic Policy 1945-1951*, London, New York.

CAREW, Anthony (1991), ''The Anglo-American Council on Productivity (1948-52): the Ideological Roots of the Post-War Debate on Productivity in Britain'', *Journal of Contemporary History,* Vol. 26, No. 1, 49-69.

CLARKE, Richard W. (1982) Alec CAIRNCROSS (editor), *Anglo-American Economic Collaboration in War and Peace 1942-1949*, Oxford.

CROMWELL, William C. (1987), ''The Marshall Plan, Britain and the Cold War'', *Review of International Studies,* Vol. 8, No. 4, 233-249.

HOGAN, Michael J. (1987) *The Marshall Plan: America, Britain and the Reconstruction of Western Europe 1947-1952*, New York.

NEWTON, Scott (1984), ''The Sterling Crisis of 1947 and the British Response to the Marshall Plan'', *Economic History Review,* Vol. 37, No. 3, 391-408.

PELLING, Henry (1988), *Britain and the Marshall Plan*, London.

TOMLINSON, J. (1990), ''The failure of the Anglo-American Council on Productivity'', *Business History,* Vol. 33, No. 1, 82-92.

YOUNG, John (1984), *Britain, France and the Unity of Europe 1945-1951*, Leicester.

2.3.13 The United States/Les États-Unis

ANSTEY, Caroline (1986), ''Foreign Office Publicity, American aid and European unity: mobilising public opinion 1947-1949'' in: Josef BECKER and Franz KNIPPING (editors), *Power in Europe? Great Britain, France, Italy and Germany in the Post-War World, 1945-1950*, Berlin, New York.

BACKER, John H. (1978), *The decision to divide Germany: American Foreign policy in transition*, Durham (NC).

BERNSTEIN, Barton J. (1970), *Politics and Policies of the Truman Administration*, Chicago.

BOLTANSKI, L. (1981), ''America, America... Le plan Marshall et l'importation du management'', *Actes de la Recherche en Sciences Sociales*, May, 19-41.

BOYLE, Peter G. (1987), ''Britain, America and the Transition from Economic to Military Assistance, 1948-51'', *Journal of Contemporary History,* Vol. 22, No. 3, 521-538.

BRYAN, Ferald J. (1991), ''George C. Marshall at Harvard: a study of the Origins and Construction of the Marshall Plan Speech'', *Presidential Studies Quarterly*, Summer 1991, Vol. 21, No. 3, 489-507.

BURR, W. (1990), *The Truman Administration and European Reconstruction, 1947-1950: Corporate internationalism and foreign aid*, Gostone Surrey (UMI).

CHOTARD, Jean-René (1991), *La politique américaine en Europe : 1944/1948, étude des archives officielles US*, Paris.

CLARKE, Richard W. et Alec CAIRNCROSS (1982), *Anglo-American Economic Collaboration in War and Peace 1942-1949*, Oxford.

CROMWELL, William C. (1979), ''The Marshall Non-Plan, Congress and the Soviet Union'', *Western Political Quarterly*, Vol. 32, No. 4, 422-443.

FOSSEDAL, Gregory A. (1993), *Our finest hour: Will Clayton, the Marshall Plan and the triumph of democracy*, Stanford.

GADDIS, John Lewis (1985), ''The United States and the Question of a Sphere of Influence in Europe, 1945-1949'', in: Olav RISTE (editor), *Western Security: The Formative Years. European and Atlantic Defence, 1947-1953*, New York.

___. (1987), ''The United States and the Question of a Sphere of Influence in Europe, 1945-1949'', in: GADDIS, John Lewis (editor), *The Long Peace: Inquiries into the History of the Cold War*, New York.

GARRETT, Crister S. (1990), ''Faith in the name of America's self interest: an analysis of the Marshall Plan and its historiography'', *UCLA Historical Journal,* Vol. 10.

GATZKE, Hans W., and Edwin O. REISCHAUER (1980), ''Germany and the United States: A Special Relationship,'' in: *The American Foreign Policy Library*, Cambridge (Mass.)

HAMBY, Alonzo L. (1973), *Beyond the New Deal: Harry S. Truman and American Liberalism*, New York.

HARPER, John L. (1986), *America and the reconstruction of Italy, 1945-1948*, New York.

HELLER, Francis H. (1981), *Economics and the Truman Administration*, Lawrence.

HOGAN, Michael J. (1982), ''The search for a 'Creative Peace': The United States, European Unity and the Origins of the Marshall Plan'', *Diplomatic History,* Vol. 6, 267-285.

___. (1992), ''Paths to Plenty: Marshall Planners and the debate over European Integration 1947-1948'', *Pacific Historical Review,* Vol. 53, No. 3, 337-366.

___. (1985), ''American Marshall Planners and the Search for a European Neocapitalism'', *American Historical Review*, Vol. 90, No. 1, 44-72.

___. (1987) *The Marshall Plan: America, Britain and the Reconstruction of Western Europe 1947-1952*, New York.

JACKSON, Scott (1979), ''Prologue to the Marshall Plan: The Origins of the American Commitment for a European Recovery Program'', *Journal of American History,* Vol. 65, No. 4, 1043-1068.

KENNETH, Joseph V. (1988), ''A Reexamination of Professional and Popular Thought on Assistance for Foreign Economic Development: 1949-1952'', *Journal of Development Areas,* Vol. 20, No. 3, 297-326.

KINDLEBERGER, Charles P. (1987), ''The Marshall Plan seen from the United States, 1947 and 1987'', *Okonomi og Politik,* Vol. 60, No. 4, 224-230.

KOLKO, Gabriel and Joyce (1972), *The Limits of Power: The World and United States Foreign Policy, 1945-1954*, New York.

LACROIX-RIZ, Annie (1987), «Crédits américains et coopération européenne (1949-1954)», in: FRIDENSON, Patrick and STRAUSS, André (dir.), *Le capitalisme français XIXe-XXe : blocages et dynamismes d'une croissance*, Paris.

LUNDESTAD, Geir (1980), *America, Scandinavia and the Cold War*, Oslo.

MAIER, Charles S. (1977), ''The Politics of Productivity: Foundations of American International Economic Policy after World War II'', *International Organization,* Vol. 31, No. 4, 607-633.

___. (1981), *''You People in Europe'': Regional Concepts and National Roles within the Marshall Plan.*

___. (1987), *In Search of Stability; Explorations in Historical Political Economy*, Cambridge.

___. (1990), ''American Visions and British Interests: Hogan's Marshall Plan'', *Reviews in American History,* Vol. 18, No. 1, 102-111.

MANDERSON-JONES, R.B. (1972), *The Special Relationship: Anglo-American Relations and Western European Unity, 1947-1956*, London.

MELANDRI, Pierre (1979), *L'Alliance atlantique*, Paris.

___. (1980), *Les États-Unis face à l'unification de l'Europe 1945-1954*, A. Pedone, Paris.

___. (1980), «L'apprentissage du leadership occidental, les États-Unis et le monde 1941-1949», *Relations Internationales*, No. 22, 175-192.

___. (1986), «Le rôle de l'unification européenne dans la politique extérieure des États-Unis 1948-1950», in Raymond POIDEVIN (dir.), *Histoire des débuts de la construction européenne (mars 1948-mai 1950).* Actes du Colloque de Strasbourg 28-30 novembre 1984, Brussels, Milan, Paris, Baden-Baden.

___. (1993), «L'intégration contre la désintégration : les États-Unis, le Plan Marshall et l'unification de l'Europe (1947-1950)» in: *Le Plan Marshall et le relèvement économique de l'Europe.* Colloque tenu à Bercy les 21, 22, 23 mars 1991, sous la direction de René GIRAULT et Maurice LEVY-LEBOYER, Comité d'Histoire Économique et Financière de la France, Paris.

MILWARD, Alan S. (1993), ''The Marshall Plan and Europe's Foreign Trade'', in: *Le Plan Marshall et le relèvement économique de l'Europe.* Colloque tenu à Bercy les 21, 22, 23 mars 1991, sous la direction de René GIRAULT et Maurice LEVY-LEBOYER, Comité d'Histoire Économique et Financière de la France, Paris.

PASTOR, R. (1980), *Congress and the Politics of the US Foreign Economic Policy*, 1929-1976, Berkerly.

RAPPAPORT, A. (1981), ''The United States and European Integration: The First Phase'' in *Diplomatic History,* Vol. 5, No. 2, 121-150.

ROMERO, Federico (1987), ''United States Policy for Post-war European Reconstruction: The Role of American Trade Unions'', *European University Institute Working Papers*, No. 87, European University Institute, Florence.

___. (1987), *Guerra fredda e stabilizzazione sociale:politiche americane sulla questione sindacale nella recostruzione postbellica dell'Europa e dell'Italia, 1944-1953*, Rome.

ROMERO, Federico and MERLI BRANDINI, Pietro (1989), *Gli Stati Uniti e il sindicalismo europeo 1944-1951*, Rome.

SCHRÖDER, Hans Jürgen (1986) ''Die amerikanische Deutschlandpolitik und das Problem der Westeuropäischen Kooperation 1947/1948-1950'', in Raymond POIDEVIN (dir.), *Histoire des débuts de la construction européenne (mars 1948-mai 1950)*, Actes du Colloque de Strasbourg 28-30 novembre 1984, Brussels, Milan, Paris, Baden-Baden.

___. (1987), ''Marshall Plan, Amerikanische Deutschlandpolitik und Europäische integration 1947-1950'', *Aus Politik und Zeitgeschichte*, Vol. 18/87, No. 2, 3-17.

SENSENIG, Gene R. (1985), ''Gewerkschaftspolitik im Kalten Krieg am Beispiel der Beziehungen der US-Regierung und der US-Gewerkschaften zum ÖGB zwischen 1945 und 1950'', *Zeitgeschichte,* Vol. 12, No. 6, 198-216.

WALA, Michael (1985), ''Selling War and Peace: the Non-Partisan Committee for Peace, the Committee to Defend America and the Committee for the Marshall Plan'', *Amerikastudien,* Vol. 30, No. 1, 91-105.

___. (1986), ''Selling the Marshall Plan at home: the Committee for the Marshall Plan to Aid European Recovery'', *Diplomatic History,* Vol. 10, No. 3, 247-265.

WALL, Irvin M. (1989), *L'influence américaine sur la politique française, 1945-1954*, Paris.

WEILER, Peter (1981), ''The United States, International Labor and the Cold War: The Breakup of the World Federation of Trade Unions'', *Diplomatic History*, Vol. 5, No. 1, 1-22.

WINAND, Pascaline (1990), Presidents, *Advisers and the Uniting of Europe. American Policy toward European Integration 1939-1963, Ph.D Free University Brussels.*

___. (1993) Eisenhower, Kennedy, and the United States of Europe, London.

WITTNER, Lawrence S. (1982), *American Intervention in Greece, 1943-1949*, New York.

2.3.14 Other Countries/Autres pays

ANDERSON, Sheldon (1991), *''Poland and the Marshall Plan, 1947-1949'',* Diplomatic History, Vol. 15, No. 4, 473-494.

___. (1992), ''A Dollar to Poland is a Dollar to Russia: United States Economic Diplomacy toward Poland, 1945-1950'', *East European Quarterly,* Vol. 26, No. 1, 77-108.

ARSENIEVA, Marina (1974), *Histoire de la politique extérieure de l'URSS, 1945-1970*, Moscow.

BARNOVSKY, Michal (1985), ''Die politische Krise in der Slowakei im Herbst 1947'', *Studia Historica Slovaca,* Vol. 14, 220-256.

BERNAT I PONS, Alí (1990), ''La historia 'imaginada': bienvenido Mr. Marshall'', [''Imagined'' history: Welcome Mr. Marshall], *Historia y Vida* [Spain], Vol. 23, No. 265, 96-102.

BLACK, Cyril, ''The View from Bulgaria de Cyril Black'' in: *Witnesses of the Origins of the Cold War,* Washington, 1982.

CROMWELL, William C. (1979), ''The Marshall Non-Plan, Congress and the Soviet Union'', *Western Political Quarterly,* Vol. 32, No. 4, 422-443.

GARSON, R.A. (1986), ''American Foreign Policy and the Limits of Power: Eastern Europe 1946-50'', *Journal of Contemporary History*, Vol. 21, No. 3, 347-366.

GOLDSMITH-ZAIMOV, Martin (1993), «Le refus bulgare de participer au Plan Marshall: une décision imposée ou l'établissement d'un régime politique», in: *Le Plan Marshall et le relèvement économique de l'Europe*, Colloque tenu à Bercy les 21, 22, 23 mars 1991, sous la direction de René GIRAULT et Maurice LEVY-LEBOYER, Comité d'Histoire Économique et Financière de la France, Paris.

HARA, Akira (1993) ''American aid and the reconstruction of the Japanese economy'' in: *Le Plan Marshall et le relèvement économique de l'Europe*, Colloque tenu à Bercy les 21, 22, 23 mars 1991, sous la direction de René GIRAULT et Maurice LEVY-LEBOYER, Comité d'Histoire Économique et Financière de la France, Paris.

JIRANOVA, Dagmar and KUCERA, Jaroslav (1985), ''Die Tschechoslowakischen Nachkriegspläne zur Herstellung einer Friedensordnung in Europa durch Partner der Antihitlerkoalition'', *Bulletin des Arbeitskreises ''Zweiter Weltkrieg''* [East Germany], (1-4), 205-217.

KAPLAN, Karel and PRIBIK, Petr (1985), ''Die Tschechoslowakei und der Marshall-Plan'', *Bohemia* [West Germany], Vol. 26, No. 2, 347-371.

KAPLAN, Karel (editor) (1991), ''Stalin, Czechoslovakia, and the Marshall Plan: New Documentation from Czechoslovak Archives'', *Bohemia,* Vol. 32, No. 1, 133-144.

KOPECKY, Peter, I. (1985), ''Revolucno-demokraticka vlada v rumunsku a jej program obnovy narodného hospodarstva v r. 1945-1947 [The first revolutionary democratic government in Romania and its program for the revival of the national economy, 1945-47]'', *Slovansky Prehled* [Czechoslovakia], Vol. 71, No. 5, 353-364.

——. (1987), ''Mezinarodné postavenie rumunska poprotifasistickom povstaniu'' [The international situation of Romania after the antifascist uprising], *Slovansky Prehled,* Vol. 73, No. 1, 27-35.

LUNDESTAD, Geir (1986), ''Der Marshall-Plan und Osteuropa'' in: Othmar HABERL, Lutz NIETHAMMER, *Der Marshall Plan und die Europäische Linke*, Frankfurt.

NARINSKI, Mikhail (1993), «Le Plan Marshall et l'URSS» in: *Le Plan Marshall et le relèvement économique de l'Europe*, Paris.

PETRUF, Pavel (1985), ''K niektorym otazkam ceskoslovensko-sovietskej sohospodarskej spoluprace v rokoch 1945-1948'' [Some questions in Czechoslovak-Soviet economic cooperation, 1945-48]. *Slovanské Stúdie* [Czechoslovakia], Vol. 25, No. 2, 69-77.

PIKE, David Wingeate (1991), «Franco et l'admission aux Nations Unies», *Guerres Mondiales et Conflits Contemporains*, Vol. 41, No. 162, 105-114.

SCHREURS, R. (1994), ''A Marshall Plan for Africa? The Overseas Territories Committee and the Origins of European Cooperation in Africa'', in Richard T. Griffiths (editor), *Explorations in OEEC History*, Paris.

——. (1994), «Un plan Marshall pour l'Afrique? Le comité des territoires d'outre-mer et les origines de la coopération européenne en Afrique» in Richard T. Griffiths (dir.), *A la découverte de l'OECE*, Paris.

TEICHOVA, Alice (1993), ''For and against the Marshall Plan in Czechoslovakia'' in: *Le Plan Marshall et le relèvement économique de l'Europe*, Colloque tenu à Bercy les 21, 22, 23 mars 1991, sous la direction de René GIRAULT et Maurice LEVY-LEBOYER, Comité d'Histoire Économique et Financière de la France, Paris.

TÉTÉ-ADJALOGO, Têtêvi G. (1989), *La question du Plan Marshall et l'Afrique*, Paris.

ZEDEK, Vesely (1985), *Ceskoslovensko a Marshalluv prispevekproblematice mezinarodnich souvislosti revolucniho procesu u Ceskoslovensku v letech 1945-1948*, Karlov.

2.4 Organisation for European Economic Co-operation (OEEC)/ Organisation européenne de Coopération Économique (OECE)

2.4.1 Trade liberalisation/Libération des échanges

ABELSHAUSER, Werner (1984), ''Der Kleine Marshallplan: Handelsintegration durch innereuropäische Wirtschaftshilfe, 1948-1950'', in: Helmut BERDING (editor), *Wirtschaftliche und Politische Integration In Europa im 19. und 20. Jahrhundert*, Göttingen.

AMBROSIUS G. (1984), ''Europäische Integration und wirtschaftliche Entwicklun der Bundesrepublik Deutschland in den fünfziger Jahren'' in: Helmut BERDING (editor), *Wirtschafliche und politische Integration in Europa im 19. und 20. Jahrhundert*, Göttingen.

ASBEEK BRUSSE, W. (1989), ''The Stikker Plan'' in GRIFFITHS, Richard T. (editor) *The Netherlands and the Integration of Europe, 1945-1957*, Amsterdam.

——. (1991), *West European Tariff Plans, 1947-1957. From Study Group to Common Market*, PhD. European University Institute, Florence.

——. (1992), ''De tariefpolitiek van de Benelux-landen. 1948-1955'' in BLOEMEN, E.S.A. (editor) *Het Benelux-effect. België, Nederland en Luxemburg en de Europese integratie, 1945-1957*, Amsterdam.

——. (1993), ''The failure of European Tariff plans in GATT (1951-1954)'' in Gilbert Trausch (Hrsg.) *Die Europäische Integration vom Schuman-Plan bis zu den Verträgen von Rom. European Integration from the Schuman-Plan to the Treaties of Rome.* Beiträge des Kolloquiums in Luxemburg, 17.-19. Mai 1989. Contributions to the Symposium in Luxembourg May 17-19, 1989, Nomos Verlagsgesellschaft, Baden-Baden.

___. (1994), ''The OEEC and the Liberalisation of European Trade'', in Richard T. Griffiths (editor), *Explorations in OEEC History*, Paris.

___. (1994), «Libéralisation des échanges intra-européens» in Richard T. Griffiths (dir.), *A la découverte de l'OECE*, Paris.

BAGNATO, Bruna (1993), «Le Plan Marshall et l'Union douanière franco-italienne (juillet 1947-mars 1948)» in: *Le Plan Marshall et le relèvement économique de l'Europe.* Colloque tenu à Bercy les 21, 22, 23 mars 1991, sous la direction de René GIRAULT et Maurice LEVY-LEBOYER, Comité d'Histoire Économique et Financière de la France, Paris.

BARBEZAT, Daniel (1994), ''The Marshall Plan and the Origin of the OEEC'', in Richard T. Griffiths (editor), *Explorations in OEEC History*, Paris.

___. (1994), «Le plan Marshall et les origines de l'OECE» in Richard T. Griffiths (dir.), *A la découverte de l'OECE*, Paris.

BAUER, Gérard-F. (1982), «L'adhésion de la Suisse à l'Organisation Européenne de Coopération Économique : ses conditions principales», *Relations Internationales,* vol. 30, 209-219.

BÉVANT, Didier (1993), «De l'opération de décembre 1958 au 'Discours sur le crédit' (décembre 1961) de J. Rueff», in: *Du franc Poincaré à l'écu.* Colloque tenu à Bercy les 3, 4 décembre 1992 sous la direction de Maurice LEVY-LEBOYER, Plessis, Aglietta et de Boissieu, Comité d'Histoire Économique et Financière de la France, Paris.

BOCCIA, C.P. (1992), *L'amministrazione Eisenhower e l'integrazione economica dell'Europa occidentale, 1953-1961*, Ph.D. University of Genoa, Genoa.

BOSSUAT, Gérard (1988), SCHWABE, Klaus (dir.) «La politique française de libération des échanges en Europe et le plan Schuman (1950-1951)», Colloque d'Aachen, Mai 1986, *Die Anfänge des Schuman-Plan*, Contributions to the Colloquium in Aachen, May 28-30 1986, Nomos Verlagsgesellschaft, Baden-Baden.

___. (1993), «La vraie nature de la politique européenne de la France (1950-1957)» in Gilbert Trausch (Hrsg.) *Die Europäische Integration vom Schuman-Plan bis zu den Verträgen von Rom. European Integration from the Schuman-Plan to the Treaties of Rome.* Beiträge des Kolloquiums in Luxemburg, 17-19 mai 1989. Contributions to the Symposium in Luxembourg May 17-19, 1989, Nomos Verlagsgesellschaft, Baden-Baden.

BUCHHEIM, Christoph (1990), *Die Wiedereingliederung Westdeutschlands in die Weltwirtschaft 1945-1958*, Oldenbourg Verlag, München.

BÜHRER, Werner (1990), ''Erzwungene oder freiwillige Liberalisierung? Die USA, die OEEC und die westdeutsche Aussenhandelspolitik 1949-1952'', in Herbst, Ludolf, Werner Bührer, Sowade Hanno, *Vom Marshallplan zur EWG. Die Eingliederung der Bundesrepublik Deutschland in die westliche Welt*, Oldenboug Verlag, München.

___. (1993), ''Die deutsche Industrie und der Marshallplan (1947-1952)'', in *Le Plan Marshall et le relèvement économique de l'Europe*, Colloque tenu à Bercy les 21, 22, 23 mars 1991, sous la direction de René GIRAULT et Maurice LEVY-LEBOYER, Comité d'Histoire Économique et Financière de la France, Paris.

CAVALCANTI, Maria Luisa (1984), *La politica commerciale italiana 1945-1952: uomini e fatti*, Naples.

CLERX, J. (1986), *Nederland en de liberalisatie van het Europese handels- en betalingsverkeer*, Groningen.

D'ATTORE, Pier Paolo (1986), *L'Italia e il piano Marshall: L'adhesione all'OECE e la partecipazione nazionale all'integrazione economica europea*, Bologna, Doctoral Dissertation.

FAURI, F. (1994), ''Free but Protected? Italy and the Liberalisation of Foreign Trade in the 1950s'', in Richard T. Griffiths (editor), *Explorations in OEEC History*, Paris.

___. (1994), «Libre mais protégée? L'Italie et la libéralisation des échanges dans les années 50» in Richard T. Griffiths (dir.), *A la découverte de l'OECE*, Paris.

FERREIRA, Margarida Ponte (1992), ''Norge og den europeiske okonomiske integrasjonen: fra den andre verdenskrig til eos'' [Norway and European economic integration: from World War II to the EEA], *Internasjonal Politik,* Vol. 50, No. 3, 313-321.

FLEURY, Antoine (1986), «La situation particulière de la Suisse au sein de l'Organisation européenne de cooperation économique (OECE)» in: Raymond POIDEVIN (dir.), *Histoire des débuts de la Construction européenne (mars 1948-mai 1950). Origins of European Integration (March 1948–May 1950),* Actes du Colloque de Strasbourg 28-30 novembre 1984, Brussels, Milan, Paris, Baden-Baden.

___. (1990), «La Suisse et le retour au multilatéralisme dans les échanges internationaux après 1945» in: P. BAIROCH and M. KÖRNER (dir.), *La Suisse dans l'économie mondiale*, Zurich.

——. (1993), «La position des autorités suisses face à la crise économique et financière de la France, 1956-58», in: *Du franc Poincaré à l'écu.* Colloque tenu à Bercy les 3, 4 décembre 1992 sous la direction de Maurice LEVY-LEBOYER, Plessis, Aglietta et de Boissieu, Comité d'Histoire Économique et Financière de la France, Paris.

FORTHOMME, P.A. (1981), «Les travaux de l'OECE», *Studia Diplomatica,* Vol. 34, 199-200.

FRANK, Robert (1988), «France-Grande-Bretagne : la mésentente commerciale 1945-1958», *Relations Internationales,* Vol. 55, 303-321.

GERBET, Pierre (1971), «Le rôle des représentants permanents dans la transformation de l'OECE en OCDE», Carnegie Foundation for International Peace, *Les missions permanentes auprès des organisations internationales,* Brussels.

GIOVAGNOLI, A. (1984), ''L'Italia nel'OECE e le prospettive della politica estera degapseriana'' in: *De Gasperi e l'età del centrismo (1947-1953),* Rome.

GRIFFITHS, Richard T. (1987), ''De eerste fase van de Westeuropese eenwording'' in: T. van der KROGT *et al.* (editors), *Big is Beautiful? Schaalproblemen in overheid en samenleving,* The Hague.

——. (1988), ''The Abortive Dutch Assault on European Tariffs, 1950-52'' in M. WINTLE (editor), *Modern Dutch Studies. Essays in Honour of Peter King,* London.

GRIFFITHS, Richard T. (1994), '''An Act of Creative Leadership': The end of OEEC Europe and the birth of the OECD'', in Richard T. Griffiths (editor), *Explorations in OEEC History,* Paris.

——. (1994), «'Une initiative créatrice'. La fin de l'OECE et la naissance de l'OCDE» in Richard T. Griffiths (dir.), *A la découverte de l'OECE,* Paris.

GRIFFITHS, Richard T. and ASBEEK BRUSSE, Wendy (1989), ''The Dutch Cabinet and the Rome Treaties'' in: E. SERRA (ed.), *Il rilancio dell'Europa e i Trattati di Roma,* Brussels, Milan, Paris, Baden-Baden.

GRIFFITHS, Richard T. and ASBEEK BRUSSE, Wendy (1994), ''Exploring the OEEC's Past: the Potentials and the Sources'', in Richard T. Griffiths (editor), *Explorations in OEEC History,* Paris.

——. (1994), «A la découverte de l'OECE : le potentiel et les sources» in Richard T. Griffiths (dir.), *A la découverte de l'OECE,* Paris.

GRIFFITHS, R.T. and LYNCH, Frances M.F.B. (1985) «L'échec de la 'petite Europe' : les négociations Fritalux-Finebel 1949-1950», *Revue Historique,* vol. 274, n° 1, 159-193.

——. (1988), «L'échec de la 'Petite Europe'? Le Conseil Tripartite, 1944-1948», in: *Guerres mondiales et conflits contemporains,* vol. 38, n° 152, 39-62.

GRIFFITHS, Richard T. and MILWARD, Alan (1986), ''The Beyen Plan and the Europen Political Community'' in: *Noi si mura. Selected Working Papers of the European University Institute,* Florence.

GROSBOIS Thierry, (1991), *Le Bénélux, laboratoire de l'Europe? Témoignage et réflexions du Comte Jean-Charles SNOY et d'OPPUERS,* Louvain-La-Neuve.

——. (1993), «Le Bénélux et le Plan Marshall, une union douanière face au roi dollar» in: *Le Plan Marshall et le relèvement économique de l'Europe.* Colloque tenu à Bercy les 21, 22, 23 mars 1991 sous la direction de René GIRAULT et Maurice LEVY-LEBOYER, Comité d'Histoire Économique et Financière de la France, Paris.

GUILLEN, Pierre (1984), «L'echec du project d'union douanière franco-italienne 1947-1951» in: G. GILIBERT (ed.), *Regioni e comunità montane delle Alpi Occidentali,* Milan.

——. (1986), «Le project d'union économique entre la France, l'Italie et le Benelux» in: Raymond POIDEVIN (dir.), *Histoire des débuts de la Construction européenne (mars 1948-mai 1950),* Actes du Colloque de Strasbourg 28-30 novembre 1984, Brussels, Milan, Paris, Baden-Baden.

HARDACH, Gerd (1993), «Le plan Marshall et l'intégration internationale de l'économie allemande», in: *Le plan Marshall et le relèvement économique de l'Europe,* Colloque tenu à Bercy les 21, 22, 23 mars 1991, sous la direction de René GIRAULT et Maurice LEVY-LEBOYER, Comité d'Histoire Économique et Financière de la France, Paris.

HOMMEL, K. (1993), ''Spanien: Von der OEEC zur Europäischen Wirtschaftsgemeinschaft. Zum Wirken der 'Comision Interministerial para el Estudio de las Comunidades Economica y Atomica Europeas' 1957-1961'', *Zeitschrift für Geschichtswissenschaft,* Vol. 41, No. 9, 792-797.

HUMMEL, N. (editor) (1990), *Österreichs Integration in Europa 1948-1989: von der OEEC zur EG,* Vienna.

ILGEN, T. (1985), *Autonomy and Interdependence: US-Western European Monetary and Trade Relations, 1950-1984,* New York, Ottawa.

JENSEN, Leon Dalgas (1993), *Politisk kamp om Danmarks Importpolitik 1945-1948*, Ph.D University of Copenhagen, Copenhagen.

JERCHOW, Friedrich (1979), ''Außenhandel im Widerstreit. Die Bundesrepublik auf dem Wege in das GATT 1949-1951'' in: H.A. WINKLER (editor), *Politische Weichenstellungen im Nachkriegsdeutschland 1945-1953*, Göttingen.

KAUFMAN, Burton I. (1982), *Trade and Aid: Eisenhower's Foreign Economic Policy 1953-1961*, The Johns Hopkins University Press, Baltimore.

KURGAN-VAN HENTENRYK, Ginette (1987), «La Belgique et le relèvement économique de l'Allemagne 1945-1948», *Relations Internationales*, n° 51, 343-363.

KÜSTERS, H.J. (1984), ''Zollunion oder Freihandelszone? Zur Kontroverse über die Handelspolitik Westeuropas in den fünfziger Jahren'' in: Helmut BERDING (editor), *Wirtschaftliche und politische Integration in Europa im 19. und 20. Jahrhundert*, Göttingen.

LACROIX-RIZ, Annie (1991), *L'économie suédoise entre l'Est et l'Ouest 1944-1949 : neutralité et embargo, de la guerre au Pacte Atlantique*, Paris.

LACROIX-RIZ, Annie (1993), «Plan Marshall et commerce Est-Ouest : continuités et ruptures (cas français et perspective comparative) 1945-1952» in: *Le Plan Marshall et le relèvement économique de l'Europe*, Colloque tenu à Bercy les 21, 22, 23 mars 1991, sous la direction de René GIRAULT et Maurice LEVY-LEBOYER, Comité d'Histoire Économique et Financière de la France, Paris.

LANGE, E. and PHARO, H.Ø. (1994), ''Norwegian Trade Patterns and Domestic Policies in the Twentieth Century'', *Scandinavian Journal of History*.

LAPPENKÜPER, U. (1991), '''Ich bin wirklich ein gute Europäer'. Ludwig Erhards Europapolitik 1949-1966'', *Francia*, Vol. 18. No. 3, 85-122.

LAURENT, Pierre-Henri (1987), ''America's Ally, Britain's Opponent: Belgium and the OEEC/EPU debates, 1947-50'', *Millennium: Journal of International Studies*, Vol. 16, No. 3, 453-466.

LAURSEN, J. (1994), ''Integration at Crosscurrents. The OEEC and the European Coal and Steel Community, 1952-56'', in Richard T. Griffiths (editor), *Explorations in OEEC History*, Paris.

___. (1994), «Les méandres de l'intégration : L'OECE et la Communauté européenne du charbon et de l'acier, 1952-1956» in Richard T. Griffiths (dir.), *A la découverte de l'OECE*, Paris.

LOUIS, J.V. (1975), «Le fonds de soutien financier de l'OCDE», *Studia Diplomatica*, vol. 27, n° 4.

MALMBORG, M. (1994), «From Bridge Building to West European Economic Integration: Sweden in the OEEC», in Richard T. Griffiths (editor), *Explorations in OEEC History*, Paris.

MALMBORG, M. (1994), «La Suède dans l'OECE : De la stratégie tous azimuts à l'intégration dans l'Europe de l'Ouest» in Richard T. Griffiths (dir.), *A la découverte de l'OECE*, Paris.

MAYRZEDT, H. (1979), *Multilaterale Wirtschaftsdiplomatie zwischen westliche Industriestaaten als Instrument zur Stärkung der multilateralen und liberalen Handelspolitik*, Bern.

MARX, Roland (1988), «Le problème du Commonwealth dans les choix européens de la Grande-Bretagne de 1948 à 1975», *Relations Internationales,* vol. 55, 361-376.

MILWARD, Alan S. (1981), *''OEEC and the Origins of the Customs Union''* in: Wilfried LOTH (editor), *The Origins of European Unity*, Oxford.

___. (1982), ''The Committee of European Economic Cooperation (CEEC) and the Advent of the Customs Union'' in: W. LIPGENS (editor), *A History of European Integration,* Vol. 1, 1945-1947, Oxford.

___. (1984), *The reconstruction of Western Europe 1945-1951*, London.

___. (1992), *The European Rescue of the Nation State*, London.

___. (1993), ''The Marshall Plan and Europe's Foreign Trade'', in: *Le Plan Marshall et le relèvement économique de l'Europe*. Colloque tenu à Bercy les 21, 22, 23 mars 1991, sous la direction de René GIRAULT et Maurice LEVY-LEBOYER, Comité d'Histoire Économique et Financière de la France, Paris.

___. (1993), «La livre sterling, le franc et le deutschemark, 1950-55», in: *Du franc Poincaré à l'écu*. Colloque tenu à Bercy les 3, 4 décembre 1992 sous la direction de Maurice LEVY-LEBOYER, Plessis, Aglietta et de Boissieu, Comité d'Histoire Économique et Financière de la France, Paris.

MINX, E.P.W. (1980), *Von der Liberalisierung bis zur Wettbewerbspolitik. Internationale Wirtschaftspolitik zwischen Industrieländern nach dem Zweiten Weltkrieg*, Berlin, New York.

MUIRHEAD, B.W. (1992), ''Britain, Canada, and the Collective Approach to Freer Trade and Payments, 1952-57'', *Journal of Imperial and Commonwealth History*, Vol. 20, No. 1, 108-126.

POHL, Hans (1993), ''Die westdeustche Währungsreform von 1948 und ihre wirtschaftlichen Folgen'', in *Le Plan Marshall et le relèvement économique de la France*, Paris.

SCHMIEDING, H. (1987), ''How to Fill a 'Dollar Gap'?: Observations on the Liberalisation of West Germany's External Trade and Payments, 1947-1958'', *Working Paper No. 291*, Institut für Weltwirtschaft, Kiel.

SCHWERDTEL, Gunther (1992), *The Swiss Participation in the European Payments Union 1950-1958*, Bern.

SERRA, Enrico (1988), ''L'union doganale italo-francese e la conferenza e la conferenza di Santa Margherita 1947-1951'' in: Enrico SERRA and J.B. DUROSELLE (editors), *Italia e Francia 1946-1954*, Milan.

SØRENSEN, Vibeke (1986), ''Danish Economy Policy and the European Cooperation on Trade and Currencies, (1948-1950)'', *European University Institute Working Papers*, No. 251, December, EUI, Florence.

___. (1993), ''The Politics of Closed Markets: Denmark, the Marshall Plan and European Integration 1945-1963'', *International History Review*, Vol. 15, No. 1, 23.

___. (1994), ''Denmark and the OEEC'', in Richard T. Griffiths (editor), *Explorations in OEEC History*, Paris.

___. (1994), «Le Danemark et l'OECE» in Richard T. Griffiths (dir.), *A la découverte de l'OECE*, Paris.

ZAMAGNI, Vera (1990), ''L'apertura internazionale dell'economia italiana 1945-1957'', *Communicazione preparata per l'incontro di studio*, Castiglione Fiorentino.

2.4.2 European Payments Union (EPU)/Union Européenne des Paiements (UEP)

AGLIETTA, Michel (1985), *«De l'Union Européenne des Paiements à l'ECU : une investigation dans les arcanes de la coopération monétaire»,* Cahiers du CERNEA n° 8, University of Paris X, Nanterre.

AGLIETTA, Michel, de BOISSIEU, Christian, (1993), «Pour une organisation des paiements entre les pays de l'Est» in: *Le Plan Marshall et le relèvement économique de l'Europe.* Colloque tenu à Bercy les 21, 22, 23 mars 1991, sous la direction de René GIRAULT et Maurice LEVY-LEBOYER, Comité d'Histoire Économique et Financière de la France, Paris.

BLOEMEN, E.S.A. (1992), ''Harde franken, zachte guldens en de oprichting van de Europese Betalingsunie (1950)'' in: E.S.A. BLOEMEN (editor), *Het Benelux-effect. België, Nederland en Luxemburg en de Europese integratie, 1945-1957*, Amsterdam.

___. (1994), ''A Creditor's Dreams and Nightmares: Benelux and the Foundation of the Europeans Payments Union'', in Richard T. Griffiths (editor), *Explorations in OEEC History*, Paris.

___. (1994), «Rêves et cauchemars d'un créancier : Le Bénélux et la fondation de l'Union européenne de paiements» in Richard T. Griffiths (dir.), *A la découverte de l'OECE*, Paris.

BOCCIA, C. P. (1994), ''The United States, Convertibility, and the Reform of the European Payments Union in 1954: A View on the Debate in the Eisenhower Administration'', in Richard T. Griffiths (editor), *Explorations in OEEC History*, Paris.

___. (1994), «Les États-Unis, la convertibilité et la réforme de l'union européenne des paiements en 1954 : le débat au sein de l'Administration Eisenhower» in Richard T. Griffiths (dir.), *A la découverte de l'OECE*, Paris.

BOEL, B. (1994), ''The European Productivity Agency, 1953-1961'', in Richard T. Griffiths (editor), *Explorations in OEEC History*, Paris.

___. (1994), «L'Agence Européenne de Productivité, 1953-1961» in Richard T. Griffiths (dir.), *A la découverte de l'OECE*, Paris.

BOFINGER, P. (1990), ''A Multilateral Payments Union for Eastern Europe?'', *CEPR Discussion Papers,* No. 458.

CAIRNCROSS, A., EICHENGREEN, B. (1983), *Sterling in Decline: the Devaluations of 1931, 1949 and 1967*, Oxford.

CHÉLINI, Michel-Pierre (1993), «Inflation, dévaluations et politique monétaire en France, 1944-52», in: *Du franc Poincaré à l'écu.* Colloque tenu à Bercy les 3, 4 décembre 1992 sous la direction de Maurice LEVY-LEBOYER, PLESSIS, AGLIETTA et de BOISSIEU Comité d'Histoire Économique et Financière de la France, Paris.

CLERX, J. (1986), *Nederland en de liberalisatie van het Europese handels- en betalingsverkeer*, Groningen.

DICKHAUS, Monica (1993), «L'ouverture internationale de l'économie allemande et la convertibilité du mark allemand, 1949-1958», in: *Du franc Poincaré à l'écu.* Colloque tenu à Bercy les 3, 4 décembre 1992 sous la direction de Maurice LEVY-LEBOYER, PLESSIS, AGLIETTA et de BOISSIEU Comité d'Histoire Économique et Financière de la France, Paris.

___. (1994), ''It is only the provisional that lasts': The European Payments Union'', in Richard T. Griffiths (editor), *Explorations in OEEC History*, Paris.

___. (1994), « 'Il n'y a que le provisoire qui dure' : L'Union européenne des paiements » in Richard T. Griffiths (dir.), *A la découverte de l'OECE*, Paris.

EICHENGREEN, Barry (1993), ''A Payments Mechanism for the Former Soviet Union: is the EPU a Relevant Precedent?'', *CEPR Discussion Paper,* No. 824, London.

___. (1993), *Reconstructing Europe's Trade and Payments. The European Payments Union*, Manchester.

FLEURY, Antoine (1986), « La situation particulière de la Suisse au sein de l'Organisation européenne de coopération économique (OECE) » in: Raymond POIDEVIN (dir.), *Histoire des débuts de la Construction européenne (mars 1948-mai 1950). Origins of the European Integration (March 1948-May 1950), Actes du Colloque de Strasbourg 28-30 novembre 1984. Brussels, Milan, Paris, Baden-Baden.*

___. (1993), « Le Plan Marshall et l'économie suisse » in: *Le Plan Marshall et le relèvement économique de l'Europe.* Colloque tenu à Bercy les 21, 22, 23 mars 1991, sous la direction de René GIRAULT et Maurice LEVY-LEBOYER, Comité d'Histoire Économique et Financière de la France, Paris.

___. (1990), « La Suisse et le retour au multilatéralisme dans les échanges internationaux après 1945 », in Paul BAIROCH (dir.), *La Suisse dans l'économie mondiale*, Zürich.

GODTS-PETERS, S. (1987), « Le rôle des belges dans l'élaboration d'un système de paiements en Europe, de 1947 à l'Union européenne de paiments », in: DUMOULIN, M. (dir.) *La Belgique et les débuts de la construction européenne de la guerre aux traités de Rome*, Louvain-la-Neuve.

GROSBOIS, Thierry (1993), « Le Bénélux et le Plan Marshall, une union douanière face au roi dollar » in: *Le Plan Marshall et le relèvement économique de l'Europe*. Colloque tenu à Bercy les 21, 22, 23 mars 1991 sous la direction de René GIRAULT et Maurice LEVY-LEBOYER, Comité d'Histoire Économique et Financière de la France, Paris.

___. (1993), « Les relations monétaires bilatérales franco-belges de la Guerre à l'Union européenne des paiements », in: *Du franc Poincaré à l'écu.* Colloque tenu à Bercy les 3, 4 décembre 1992 sous la direction de Maurice LEVY-LEBOYER, PLESSIS, AGLIETTA et de BOISSIEU Comité d'Histoire Économique et Financière de la France, Paris.

HENTSCHEL, Volker (1989), ''Die Europäische Zahlungsunion und die deutschen Devisenkrisen 1950/51'', *Viertel-jahrshefte für Zeitgeschichte*, Vol. 37, No. 4, 715-758.

ILGEN, T. (1985), *Autonomy and interdependence : US-Western European Monetary and Trade relations, 1950-1984*, New York, Ottawa.

JANSSENS, V. (1981), « La Coopération et l'Integration Monétaires Européennes (1945-1975) », *Studia Diplomatica.* Vol. XXXIV, Nos. 1-4, 345-366.

KAPLAN, Jacob and Günther SCHLEIMINGER (1989), *The European Payments Union-Financial Diplomacy in the 1950s*, Oxford.

LAURENT, Pierre-Henri (1987), America's Ally, Britain's Opponent: Belgium and the OEEC/EPU debates, 1947-50, *Millennium: Journal of International Studies*, Vol. 16, No. 3, 453-466.

LIEFTINCK, P. (1973), *The Post-War Financial Rehabilitation of the Netherlands*, The Hague.

LYNCH, Frances M.B (1990), « La France, la Grande-Bretagne et le problème du dollar, 1945-1950. Une profonde mésentente », *Matériaux pour l'histoire de notre temps*, n° 18, 12-19.

___. (1993), « France and the European Payments Union » in: *Le Plan Marshall et le relèvement économique de l'Europe.* Colloque tenu à Bercy les 21, 22, 23 mars 1991, sous la direction de René GIRAULT et Maurice LEVY-LEBOYER, Comité d'Histoire Économique et Financière de la France, Paris.

MARGAIRAZ, Michel (1991), *L'État, les finances et l'économie en France (1932-1952).* Histoire d'une conversion, vol. 2, Paris.

MARSEILLE J. (1984), *Empire colonial et capitalisme français, histoire d'une divorce*, Paris.

MILWARD, Alan S. (1984), *The Reconstruction of Western Europe 1945-1951*, London.

___. (1987), ''Belgium and Western European interdependence in the 1950s: some unexplained problems'', in Michel Dumoulin, *La Belgique et les débuts de la construction européenne : de la guerre au Traité de Rome*, Louvain-la-Neuve.

___. (1989), ''Motives for Currency Convertibility. The Pound and the Deutschmark, 1950-55'' in: C.L. HOLTFRE-R I C H
(editor), *Interaction in the World Economy. Perspectives from Economic History*, Hemel Hempstead.

___. (1992), *The European rescue of the nation state*, London.

NEWTON, Scott (1984), ''The Sterling Crisis of 1947 and the British Response to the Marshall Plan'', *Economic History Review* Vol. 37, No. 3, 391-408.

NEWTON, Scott (1985), *''The 1949 Sterling Crisis and British Policy towards European Integration'', Review of International Studies Vol. 11, No. 3, 169-182.*

___. (1985), ''Britain, The Sterling Area and European Integration, 1949-1950'', *Journal of Imperial and Commonwealth History* Vol. 13, No. 3, 163-182.

PITMAN, Paul (1993), «Le retour à la convertibilité monétaire en Europe occidentale et le redressement financier français», in: *Du franc Poincaré à l'écu*. Colloque tenu à Bercy les 3, 4 décembre 1992 sous la direction de Maurice LEVY-LEBOYER, PLESSIS, AGLIETTA et de BOISSIEU Comité d'Histoire Économique et Financière de la France, Paris.

___. (1994), ''The French Crisis and the Dissolution of the European Payments Union, 1956-1958'', in Richard T. Griffiths (editor), *Explorations in OEEC History*, Paris.

___. (1994), «La crise française et la dissolution européenne des paiements, 1956-1958» in Richard T. Griffiths (dir.), *A la découverte de l'OECE*, Paris.

SAVONA, P. (1983), ''La stabilizzazione monetaria in Italia e il Piano Marshall'' in: AGAROSSI, E. (ed.), *Il Piano Marshall e l'Europa*, Rome.

SCHLEIMINGER, Günther (1979), *Europäische Zahlungsunion.* Handwörterbuch der Wirtschaftswissenschaft, Stuttgart, New York.

SCHRAM, Jef (1993), ''The Netherlands, The Marshall Plan and the European Payments Union (1947-1950)'' in: *Le Plan Marshall et le relèvement économique de l'Europe*, Colloque tenu à Bercy les 21, 22, 23 mars 1991, sous la direction de René GIRAULT et Maurice LEVY-LEBOYER, Comité Pour l'Histoire Économique et Financière de la France, Paris.

SCHWERDTEL, Gunter (1993) *The Swiss Participation in the EPU*, Berne.

TRIFFIN, Robert (1989), «L'histoire de l'unification monétaire européenne : de l'UEP à nos jours», *Revue d'Économie Financière*, vol. 8–9, mars-juin, 13-18.

SØRENSEN, Vibeke (1986), ''Danish Economy Policy and the European Cooperation on Trade and Currencies, (1948-1950)'', *European University Institute Working Papers*, No. 251, European University Institute, Florence.

WALLICH, H., WILSON, J. (1981), ''Economic Orientations in Postwar Germany: Critical Choices on the Road to Convertibility'', *Zeitschrift für die gesammte Staatswissenschaft,* Vol. 137, No. 3, 390-406.

2.4.3 Sectorial cooperation within the OEEC/Coopération sectorielle au sein de l'OECE

BRABERS, Jan (1993), ''The failure of European transport integration (1945-1955)'' in Gilbert Trausch (Hrsg.) *Die Europäische Integration vom Schuman-Plan bis zu den Verträgen von Rom. The European Integration from the Schuman-Plan to the Treaties of Rome*. Beiträge des Kolloquiums in Luxemburg, 17.-19. Mai 1989. Contributions to the Symposium in Luxembourg May 17-19, 1989, Nomos Verlagsgesellschaft, Baden-Baden.

BUSEKIST, Otto VON (1982), *«Eurochemic : échec ou exemple ?»*, Consensus revue belge d'information sur l'énergie, n° 1, 1-15.

GRIFFITHS, Richard T. and MILWARD, Alan S. (1986), The European Agricultural Community, 1948-1954, *European University Institute Working Papers*, No. 86/254, European University Institute, Florence.

GUILLEN, Pierre, (1987) «La France et les négociation du Traité d'Euratom» in: *Relations Internationales,* No. 51, 391-412.

HELMERICH, J.E. (1986), *Gathering Rare Ores. The Diplomacy of Urnanium Acquisition 1943-1954*, Princeton.

KAPSTEIN, E.B. (1990), *The Insecure Alliance: Energy Crisis and Western Politics since 1944*, New York.

KLUGE, Ulrich (1989), ''Du Pool noir au Pool vert : Wirtschafts-und Sozialprobleme des 'Marchés Communs Agricoles de l'Europe' 1949-1957 aus deutscher Sicht'' in: E. SERRA (ed.), *Il rilancio dell'Europa e i Trattati di Roma*, Brussels, Milan, Paris, Baden-Baden.

___. (1990), ''Wege europäischer Agrarintegration 1950-1957'', HERBST, Ludolf, Werner BÜHRER, SOWADE Hanno, *Vom Marshallplanzur EWG. Die Eingliederung der Bundesrepublik Deutschland in diewestliche Welt*, Munich.

NOEL, Gilbert (1979), «Les tentatives de Communauté agricole européenne, 1947-1955», Revue d'Histoire Moderne et Contemporaine. Octobre-Décembre, 579-611.

STROHL, Pierre (1981), *«La coopération internationale dans le domaine de l'énergie nucléaire, Europe et pays de l'OCDE»*, L'Europe dans les relations internationales. Unité et Diversité, Actes du Colloque de Nancy tenu les 21-22-23 mai 1981, Paris.

VERMEULEN, W. (1989), *Europees landbouwbeleid in de maak. Mansholts eerste plannen, 1945-1954*, Groningen.

WEILEMANN, Peter (1983), *Die Anfänge der europäischen Atomgemeinschaft: zur Gründungsgeschichte von Euratom 1955-1957*, Baden-Baden.

2.5 European Free Trade Area/Zone européenne de libre-échange

ANGELL, V. (1971), ''Det europeisk fellesskap og 'Rest-EFTA' '', *Internasjonal Politikk.*

BJØRKLUND, T. (1982), *Mot strømmen. Kampen mot EF 1961-1972*, Oslo.

BURGESS, S. and EDWARDS, G. (1988), ''The Six Plus One: British Policy-Making and the Question of European Economic Integration, 1955'' in: *International Affairs* Vol. 63, No. 3, 393-413.

CORBET, H. and D. ROBERTSON (1970), *Europe's Free Trade Area Experiment: EFTA and Economic Integration*, Oxford, New York.

CURZON, Victoria (1974), *The Essentials of Economic Integration: Lessons from the EFTA Experience*, London.

Du BOIS, Pierre (1987), *EFTA from yesterday to tomorrow*, Geneva.

ERIKSEN, Knut (1977), ''Norge i det vestlige samarbeid'' in: Trond BERGH (editor), *Vekst og velstand. Norsk politisk historie 1945-1965*, Oslo, Bergen, Tromsø.

FERREIRA, Margarida Ponte (1992), ''Norge og den europeiske okonomiske integrasjonen: fra den andre verdenskrig til eos'' [Norway and European economic integration: from World War II to the EEA], *Internasjonal Politik,* Vol. 50, No. 3, 313-321.

FLEURY, Antoine (1987), *«La Suisse et le projet de Grande Zone Européenne de Libre-Échange et la création des Communautés Européennes»*, in: E. SERRA (ed.), *Il Rilancio dell'Europa e i Tratti de Roma/La relance européenne et le Traité de Rome, (Actes du Colloque de Rome, (25-28 mars)*, Brussels, Milan, Paris, Baden-Baden.

___. (1993), «La neutralité suisse à l'épreuve de l'Union européenne» in: J. NEVAKIVI (editor), *Neutrality and History. Proceedings of the Conference on the History of Neutrality organized in Helsinki 9-12 September 1992*, Helsinki.

FUKUDA, H. (1970), *First decade of EFTA's Realisation*, in H. COBET, D. ROBERTS (1970), *Europe's Free Trade Experiment*, Oxford, New York.

GRIFFITHS, Richard T. (1991), ''The changing concept of Europe'', *EFTA Bulletin*, Vol. 32, No. 1, 2-5.

___. (1991), ''British attitudes towards European Integration'', *EFTA Bulletin*, Vol. 32, No. 2, 17-22.

___. (1991), ''The Failure of the Wider European Free Trade Area'', *EFTA Bulletin*, Vol. 32, No. 3/4, 15-20.

___. (1992), ''The Importance of Fish for the Creation of EFTA'', *EFTA Bulletin*, Vol. 33, No. 1, 34-40.

HANSEN, S.O. (1990), *Det norske EFTA-sporet i 1950 åre. Hovedoppgave i historie*, Oslo.

KLEPPE, P. (1990), *Norges vei til Europa*, Oslo.

LANDQUIST, Ake (1992), ''Focus on the Creation of EFTA History Conference in Oslo'', *EFTA Bulletin*, Vol. 33, No. 2, 13-16.

MILWARD, Alan S. (1989), ''Patterns of Western European Trade in the 1950s and the Motivation towards a Customs Union'', *European University Institute of Europe 141/89,* European University Institute, Florence.

PHARO, Helge (1989), *The Creation of EFTA*, European University Institute, Florence.

___. (1993), ''Denmark, the Marshall Plan and European Integration, 1945-1963'', *The International History Review,* Vol. 1, 23-45.

RØHNE, N.A. (1989), *De første skritt inn i Europa. Norsk Europa-politikk fra 1950*, Oslo.

SAETER, M. (1989), *Europa i forandring. EF – EFTA og all-Europa*, Oslo.

IV. CHRONOLOGY

1947

01/01 **George C. Marshall** appointed US Secretary of State in succession to James Byrnes.

12/03 ''Containment'' speech by **Harry Truman.** Aid to Greece and Turkey.

05/06 Speech by US Secretary of State **George C. Marshall** at Harvard University. Offer of aid to Europe.

17/06 France and the United Kingdom accept **Marshall Aid.**

27/06-02/07 **Franco-Anglo-Soviet Conference** in Paris. Soviet rupture.

12/07-22/09 Conference on European Economic Co-operation convened in Paris by France and Great Britain to prepare the report to the US Government on economic aid.

22/09 The report puts the European deficit at 22 billion for the four years to come.

17/12 The Interim Aid Act for assistance to certain European countries comes into force.

1948

02/01 The US Congress passes the Economic Co-operation Act releasing $5 million in economic aid to Europe for the first of the four years covered by the European Recovery Programme (ERP). Paul G. Hoffmann appointed Administrator of the Economic Co-operation Administration (ECA).

16/04 Signing of the **Convention for European Economic Co-operation** by the Foreign Ministers of sixteen European countries and the Commanders in Chief of the Anglo-American and French zones of occupation in Germany, bringing the **Organisation for European Economic Co-operation (OEEC)** into being. Council elections for 1948-1949. **Robert Marjolin** is appointed to the post of Secretary-General. It is decided that the Organisation's headquarters shall be in Paris. **Paul Henri Spaak** is appointed Chairman of the Council.

17/04 Establishment of the **Methods Committee** and the **Budget Commission.**

11/05 Establishment of the following **Committees**:

- Balance of Payments
- Intra-European Trade and Payments
- Coal
- Electricity
- Oil
- Iron and Steel
- Food and Agriculture (Sub-Committee on Agricultural Machinery)
- Raw Materials
- Inland Transport
- Maritime Transport

22/05 Establishment of the following **Committees**:

- Textiles
- Chemical Products
- Timber
- Pulp and Paper
- Non-Ferrous Metals
- Hides and Skins

05/06 The **Machinery Committee** is set up.

11/06 Establishment of the Working Party to study problems relating to **Trade.**

28/06 Bilateral Franco-American agreement on **Marshall Aid.**

16/07 Approval of the basic principles for the establishment of the 1948-1949 **Annual Programme**; the principle of division of American aid by the OEEC is adopted.

Establishment of a Restricted Group on preliminary repartition of ERP aid.

20/07 Establishment of the Restricted Working Group on Intra-European **Trade and Payments.**

24/07 Adoption of the general principles of the **Intra-European Payments Scheme**.

25/07 Meeting of the ministers of member countries with Paul G. Hoffman of the Economic Co-operation Administration.

05/08 Establishment of the Committee to Study the Final Scale of **Contributions.**

20/09 Establishment of the **Supervisory** Sub-Committee (supervision of the system of payments and clearing between European countries).

04/10 Establishment of the Working Party on **Overseas Territories.**

14/10 The Anglo-American Zone of the Free Territory of **Trieste** accedes to the Convention.

16/10 Meeting of ministers of Member countries. The 1948-1949 Annual Programme is handed to W. Averell Harriman, United States Special Representative in Europe.

The **Agreement for Intra-European Payments and Compensation** is signed.

Establishment of the **Committee of Ministers** to study possible changes to be made in the structure of the Organisation.

31/12 The Council adopts the Report on the 1949-50 Annual Programme and the Interim Report on the European Recovery Programme.

Approval of the Interim Report on the European Recovery Programme 1948-1949 to 1952-1953 (1st Annual Report of the OEEC).

1949

01/01 At the invitation of the ECA, Baron Snoy (Chairman of the Council), Sir Edmund Hall-Patch (Chairman of the Executive Committee), Robert Marjolin (Secretary-General) and a group of experts leave for Washington to provide additional information on the 1949-50 Annual Programme and the **Interim Report.**

17/02 Establishment of a **Consultative Group of Ministers** to assist the Chairman of the Council in reviewing the most important issues facing the Organisation.

14/03 Establishment of a Working Party on Systems of Observation and Review.

26/03 On the basis of the Consultative Group's proposals, implementation of the 1949-1950 Programme, including intensification of the OEEC's activities in regard to **agriculture** and the development of tourism in Europe.

28/03 The **Overseas Territories Committee** is set up.

10/05 Establishment of the Working Party to consider Member countries' reports on internal **financial stability.**

04/06 The Consultative Group of Ministers frames **trade liberalisation** proposals, which are transmitted to Member country governments for consideration.

09/06 The following **Sub-Committees** are set up:

- Food and Agriculture, amending the Council Declaration of 12 April 1949
- Import and Export Programmes
- Agricultural Production Plans and Programmes
- Agricultural Machinery
- Fertilisers, Insecticides and Fungicides
- Working Party on Food Consumption Levels
- Fisheries.

02/07 On the Consultative Group of Ministers's proposal, the Council adopts the principles of the **Payments and Compensation Agreement for 1949-50.**

	Member countries are requested to take the necessary steps to phase out their quantitative import restrictions so as to achieve as high as possible a degree of trade **liberalisation** in Europe by 1951.
13/08	It is decided that Member countries will specify, by 1st October 1949 at the latest, those products from other Member countries in respect of which they have decided, or are ready to decide, unilaterally or by negotiation, to abolish **import restrictions** or automatic issue of import licences.
31/08	Approval of the recommendations made by the Chairman of the Council and the Secretary-General on the **distribution of US aid** and on drawing rights for 1949-50.
07/09	Signing of the **Agreement for Intra-European Payments and Compensations** for 1949-50.
29/09	On the Consultative Group of Ministers's proposal, the Council adopts new co-operation measures. The Council decides to submit a second report to the ECA on 15 January 1950 and approves a new method of **fixed allocation** of US aid for the last two years of the ERP.
30/09	Establishment of Restricted Special Committees to examine cases covered by Articles 33 and 34 of the **Payments and Compensation Agreement** between European countries for 1949-50.
31/10	Delegates of the Federal Republic of Germany take their seat in the Council for the first time.
02/11	The Council takes its first decision on liberalisation of intra-European trade, which is to bear on 50 per cent by 15 December 1949.
01/12	Establishment of the International Technical Association concerned with **Artificial Textiles.**
09/12	Establishment of the European **Trade Fair** Board.

1950

20/01	The Council approves measures to increase productivity in Europe.
	Working parties are set up to deal with questions relating to **productivity** and co-operation in scientific research and technical development.
31/01	The Council entrusts Dirk U. Stikker, Netherlands Minister of Foreign Affairs, with a mission as political **conciliator** of the Organisation.
	New decision of the Council concerning **trade liberalisation.**
22/02	Approval of the terms of the reply sent to the Secretary General of the Council of Europe concerning the proposals contained in the economic Recommendations adopted by the Consultative Assembly of the **Council of Europe.**
	Decision to establish official relations with the **Council of European Industrial Federations.**
	The Sub-Committee for **Food and Agriculture** is set up.
09/03	Establishment of a working party to consider Member countries' reports on internal **financial stability.**
04/04	End of the activity of the **Consultative Group** of Ministers.
25/04	Establishment of the Organisation's Committee for consultations with the **Council of Europe.**
03/05	Adoption of the first decision on liberalisation of invisible transactions.
19/05	Establishment of the Joint Working Party of the **Overseas Territories** Committee.
02/06	**Canada** and the **United States** are invited to participate unofficially in the work of the OEEC to review problems of common interest.
06/07-07/07	Approval of the provisions for the establishment of a **European Payments Union**; within fifteen days of signing an agreement establishing a European Payments Union, Member countries shall derestrict at least 60 per cent of their imports on private account from other Members.
07/08-20/08	Participation of Member countries in the first **International Trade Fair** in Chicago.
18/08	The **Code of Liberalisation** is adopted; Member countries pledge to phase out among themselves quantitative restrictions on merchandise imports. Decision to set up the European Payments Union. Appointment of the Managing Board of the European Payments Union.
04/09	Approval of a report on international **investment.**
19/09	The seventeen Member countries of the OEEC sign the Agreement establishing the **European Payments Union** (EPU).
21/09	Establishment of the **Co-ordinating Group for Trade Liberalisation.**
04/10	Member countries **derestrict** among themselves 60 per cent of their imports on private account.

07/10 The Council examines a memorandum by the Secretary-General concerning urgent economic problems and establishes a list of measures to be taken as a result of the changes which have occurred in the economic situation since the outbreak of the **Korean War.**

20/10 The Executive Committee instructs the Vertical Committees of the Organisation immediately to undertake a study on the scarcity of **raw materials.**

27/10 The Council adopts a new decision concerning the **liberalisation of trade.** Member countries undertake to derestrict 75 per cent of their imports on private account from other Member countries, taken as a whole, by 1 February 1951.

30/10 Establishment of a committee to consider the problems posed by relations between the **Council of Europe** and the Organisation.

02/12 Consideration of the Report by the Economic Committee on scarcity of raw materials. Recommendation to increase the output of and reduce the demand for **scarce raw materials.** Adoption of international cooperation measures and recommendations concerning **skilled labour** shortages in Europe.

06/12 At the invitation of the ECA, an OEEC delegation led by Sir Edmund Hall-Patch, Chairman of the Executive Committee, leaves for Washington to discuss all matters affecting possibilities of supply of **raw materials.**

13/12 The EPU opens a special line of credit to Germany.
The following bodies are set up:

- Food and Agriculture Committee on coarse grain production in the Overseas Territories
- Joint Working Party of the Overseas Territories Committee
- Textiles Committee on cotton production in the Overseas Territories

1951

21/02 Germany suspends liberalisation of intra-European trade.

09/03-10/03 The Council accepts the invitation by the Governments of the United States, Great Britain and France to participate in the Central Group of the **International Raw Materials Conference.**

25/04 The Council approves the first report on European Economic Co-operation for transmission to the **Council of Europe.**

20/07 The OEEC organises a European campaign for increased **agricultural production.** The Council adopts the **Code of Liberalisation** of Trade and Invisible Transactions.

29/07 The representatives of the governments of OEEC Member countries, at a meeting of the Council, declare that their general policy aim is to increase **overall production** in Western Europe by 25 per cent over the next five years.

10/10 The President of the United States approves the **Mutual Security Act** replacing the ECA and bringing the Marshall Plan to an end.

08/11 The United Kingdom reduces from 90 to 61 per cent the degree of liberalisation of its trade with other European countries.

21/11 The Report on internal **financial stability** and inflation control is adopted and transmitted to the Council of Europe.

13/12 A European network of **Technical Information Centres** is set up on the initiative of the OEEC Committee for Scientific and Technical Matters.

1952

11/01 Establishment of a ''Ministerial **Coal Production** Group'' comprising the ministers in charge of coal production of France, Germany and the United Kingdom and headed by Dirk U. Stikker, Chairman of the Council, with instructions to frame proposals for increased coal production so as to enable Member countries to avoid recourse to exceptional imports in 1954.

01/03 France suspends liberalisation of intra-European trade.

11/03 The United Kingdom reduces from 61 to 46 per cent the degree of liberalisation of its trade with other European countries.

21/03 The **Ministerial Coal Production Group** produces its first report, with recommendations to the governments of European coal-producing countries to **increase coal output.**

28/03-29/03 The Council decides to introduce annual reviews of the domestic economic and financial situation of Member countries.

29/03 The Steering Board for Trade is set up.

30/06 Adoption of formal decisions concerning renewal of the **EPU** after 30 June 1952 for a period of one year, entry into force of a new scale for gold payments by debtors in respect of deficits incurred within the limits of their quotas, settlement of the position of certain extreme creditors and establishment of a guarantee fund.

18/07 Report on the domestic **financial situation** of OEEC Member and Associated countries, drawn up by a group of independent experts and examined by a Temporary Ministerial Committee set up by Decision of 29 March.

21/08 First liaison established between the OEEC and the **European Coal and Steel Community** (ECSC). An observer from the High Authority attends the meeting of the Supply and Distribution Sub-Committee of the Organisation's Coal Committee.

03/09-12/09 Attilio Cattani, Chairman of the Executive Committee, and Robert Marjolin, Secretary-General, attend the seventh meeting of the Board of Governors of the **International Bank for Reconstruction and Development** (IBRD) and the **International Monetary Fund** (IMF) in Mexico City. The Secretary-General reports on recent developments in the economic situation in Europe.

21/09-26/09 A workshop on **agricultural information and advisory services,** organised by the OEEC and the Ministry of Agriculture and Fisheries of England and Wales, is held at Wye College, Kent (UK).

15/10 The Council approves the procedure for liaison between the Organisation and the High Authority of the **European Coal and Steel Community** (ECSC) until the establishment of the Common Market. The High Authority will send an observer to meetings of the Coal and Iron and Steel Committees and will appoint a permanent liaison officer to the Organisation's secretariat.

20/10-21/10 First meeting of the Council under the chairmanship of Anthony Eden; exchange of views on the broad lines of the organisation's **Annual Report** on the economic situation and prospects of Member countries, the United States and Canada. Approval of the Report by the Temporary Ministerial Committee on internal financial stability of Member and Associated countries.

27/11 Conference on the dollar export drive, attended by representatives of the organisations in Member countries responsible for directing and coordinating this drive.

09/12 Adoption of recommendations for strengthening Member countries' co-operation on **trade liberalisation.**

13/12 4th Annual Report of the Organisation.

1953

07/02 The Council settles some practical problems arising out of the establishment of the **common coal and steel market,** with particular reference to the provisions of the OEEC Code of Liberalisation of Trade.

18/03 An OEEC conference on European **inland transport,** attended by representatives of the sixteen Member countries of the OEEC, the United States, Spain and Yugoslavia, is held at the Château de la Muette.

24/03 The Council creates, within the OEEC, the **European Productivity Agency** (EPA); this decision is to take effect on 1 May 1953.

30/03 The Council approves the import and export of **electric power** between eight Member countries of the OEEC whose power systems are already interconnected. This exchange of electric power will prevent a spill of hydro-energy and ensure continuity of supply.

10/04 An OEEC mission led by Sir Hugh Ellis-Rees, Chairman of the Council of the Organisation, visits Washington, at the invitation of the United States Government, for talks with the US Administration concerning the **economic situation** in Europe and the recommendations of the OEEC's 4th Report adopted by the Council in December 1952. The mission also discusses with the US authorities the problems connected with the establishment of an enlarged trade and payments system.

15/06 The Council of the OEEC takes a decision on the financing of the **European Productivity Agency** (EPA), and approves an arrangement between the US Mutual Security Administration and the OEEC regarding food and agricultural productivity.

17/06 The **European Inland Transport** Conference, after holding three sessions at the Château de la Muette, reaches the conclusion that a ''European Conference of Ministers of Transport'' must be set up.

19/06 Approval of the arrangements to renew the **EPU** for one year from 30 June 1953, the only changes for the period 1953-54 being an extension of quota overruns and an increase in interest rates on credits made available through the EPU.

24/07 A Recommendation for the establishment of a **European Conference of Ministers of Transport** is adopted.

17/10 The Transport Ministers of seventeen European countries meet in Brussels at the invitation of the Belgian Government and, pursuant to the OEEC Council's recommendation of 24 July, approve and sign the Statute of the **European Conference of Ministers of Transport**.

29/10 The United Kingdom raises to 75 per cent the degree of liberalisation of its trade with other European countries.

30/10 Resolution of the OEEC Ministerial Council reaffirming its ultimate objective of completely eliminating quantitative import restrictions among Member countries. The Council instructs the Managing Board of the EPU to produce a report by 31 March 1954 on possible problems in the event of reestablishment of **convertibility** of one or more Member countries' currencies. The Board is mandated to prepare a report by 1 March on the conditions in which the EPU would remain in force until 30 June 1955. Adoption of a Resolution concerning relaxation of quantitative restrictions on imports from the dollar area.

1954

21/01 The OEEC publishes the first year's programme of the **European Productivity Agency** (EPA).

29/01 The Council lays down the procedures for its association with the **European Conference of Ministers of Transport** (ECMT), set up in 1953.

12/02 Conference of experts of OEEC countries and the United States to consider administrative and legislative obstacles to American private investment in Europe.

17/02 The Organisation's Oil Committee undertakes a study on crude **oil and natural gas prospection and exploitation in Member countries.**

29/03 Adoption of new measures to liberalise **invisible transactions,** designed in particular to facilitate travel and study trips to OEEC countries as well as transactions and transfers relating to promotional operations.

07/04 Approval of the recommendations of the Report by the Economic Committee on the causes of the disequilibrium within the EPU leading to the extreme creditor position of Germany.

05/05-05/06 The Council meeting at ministerial level:

- lays down the broad lines of the renewal of the EPU for one year after 30 June 1954;
- sets up a Ministerial Study Group on Convertibility to study the practical problems of restoring **convertibility** to the currencies of a certain number of Member countries;
- adopts a resolution concerning the implementation of its October 1952 Resolution on the extension of **liberalisation** of trade in Europe;
- adopts a resolution on the reinforcement of the **Code of Liberalisation of Trade** in order to prevent excessive recourse to the derogation clauses in the Code, reduce their period of utilisation and alleviate the possible consequences of such derogations;
- adopts a resolution to request the Steering Board for Trade to submit proposals for enabling Member countries to abolish artificial **export** aids;
- instructs the Joint Trade and Intra-European Payments Committee to submit concrete proposals for action which the Organisation might take in co-operation with the United States and Canada to ease **quantitative restrictions** on imports from the dollar area.

14/05 The OEEC publishes its comments on the **Strasbourg Plan.**

30/06 Adoption of formal provisions for a one-year renewal of the EPU after 30 June 1954, with arrangements between certain creditor and debtor countries for the repayment of debt balances. These arrangements provide for new lending and borrowing facilities. The machinery of the Union is modified.

15/07-16/07 First meeting in London of the Ministerial Study Group on **Convertibility.**

09/09 Resignation of **Robert Marjolin, Secretary-General** of the Organisation; he leaves the OEEC early in 1955.

02/12 Publication of the Report on the Timber Industry in Europe, the first in a series on the situation in the different economic sectors.

22/12 The Council recommends that Member countries ease their quantitative restrictions on merchandise import trade and invisible transactions with the dollar area.

1955

13/01-14/01 The Council:

- adopts a Decision concerning the extension and stabilisation of **trade liberalisation;** Member countries are to derestrict, as from 1 July 1955, 10 per cent of their imports which are not already liberalised, and, as from 1 October 1955, 90 per cent of their total imports on private account and 75 per cent of their imports on private account in each of the three categories specified in the Code of Liberalisation;
- establishes a **Ministerial Committee for Agriculture and Food.** The OEEC takes over the tasks of the ''Green Pool'';
- Spain, a member of the Pool, is enabled to participate fully in the Organisation's work connected with agriculture and food.

15/02 Appointment of **Roger Grégoire** as Director of the European Productivity Agency; he succeeds Karl P. Harten.

25/02 The Yugoslav Government is invited to be represented by an observer at meetings of the Council, the Technical Committees and the latter's sub-committees.

04/03 Declaration of intention by Member countries on the goals of **trade liberalisation.**

01/04 **René Sergent** takes up his duties as Secretary-General of the OEEC.

01/05 France raises to 75 per cent the degree of liberalisation of its trade with other European countries.

09/06-10/06 The Council:

- takes a Decision concerning the renewal of the EPU, the establishment of a **European Fund** and the trade policy rules to be followed by Member countries in the event of a return to convertibility;
- appoints a Working Party of the Council to explore the possibilities of economic cooperation within the Organisation as regards the peaceful uses of **nuclear power.**

Creation of a Commission for Energy under the chairmanship of Sir Harold Hartley.

29/06 Adoption of further measures to liberalise **invisible transactions** and transfers; decision to set up a Committee for Invisible Transactions.

01/08 EPU settlements to be made as to 25 per cent in credits and 75 per cent in gold.

05/08 Representatives of Member countries sign the **European Monetary Agreement** establishing a European Fund and a multilateral system to facilitate payments between Member countries.

1956

20/01 The Council decides that the **Benelux** countries will in future be treated as a single entity for the purposes of the Code of Trade Liberalisation. This is the first time that Belgium, the Netherlands and Luxembourg are considered as a single country in an international organisation.

27/01 The **Gas Committee** is set up to study problems connected with the production, transportation, distribution and utilisation of gas in Member countries.

28/02-29/02 12 Member countries sign an international agreement establishing their first joint undertaking, the European Company for the Chemical Processing of Irradiated Fuels – EUROCHEMIC.

Establishment of a Special Committee of the Council to deal with matters relating to the utilisation of nuclear energy for peaceful purposes.

The Council adopts a Resolution giving directives for the **future work of the Organisation. It directs, in particular:**

- **that studies on the longer-term** problems of economic expansion in Europe should be pressed forward;
- that investigations should be made in the economic sectors giving cause for concern: **agriculture, textiles** and **energy**;
- **that 90 per cent** liberalisation of intra-European trade should be consolidated at 30 September 1956, and that the Organisation should concentrate on other trade barriers such as high tariffs, restrictive state trading and artificial aids to exports, as well as on quantitative restrictions;
- that the Organisation should carry forward the study of the problem of reducing bilateralism and discrimination in trade and payments with third countries.

16/03 The **Fiscal Committee** is set up.

22/06 The Council decides to prolong the existence of the **European Productivity Agency** (EPA) until June 1960.

17/07-19/07 Establishment of a Steering Committee for **Nuclear Energy** composed of representatives of interested Member countries, the governments of the United States and Canada to be associated with its work.

19/07 First meeting of the Special Group set up by the Council to study the problems of the **European textile industry.** A special working party is set up to investigate the possibility of creating a free trade area in Europe.

24/09 First meeting of the Special Working Party set up to study the possible forms and methods of multilateral association between the **Customs Union** envisaged by the six member countries of the Brussels Intergovernmental Committee and the other OEEC countries.

14/11 The Anglo-Icelandic **fisheries** dispute is settled on the basis of OEEC proposals. The Council requests the Executive Committee to consider the general repercussions in Member countries of the current difficulties in obtaining **supplies of fuels** and other commodities, and instructs it to coordinate, for this purpose, the work of the Technical Committees for Coal, Gas and Maritime Transport, the Economic Committee, the Joint Trade and Intra-European Payments Committe and the Managing Board of the European Payments Union.

26/11 Establishment of the **Energy** Advisory Commission and the Energy Committee as recommended by the Commission for Energy's report: ''Europe's Growing Needs of Energy. How can they be met?''.

30/11 Establishment of the **OEEC Petroleum Emergency Group** to advise the Oil Committee about the available supplies of oil for Europe and to help that committee to implement its recommendations.

14/12 The Council takes steps to reduce current pressure on **freight** rates; measures to the same end are taken by the United States Government.

1957

17/01 The **Oil** Committee distributes the first 200 000 tonnes of oil products being held as a reserve for distribution by the OEEC to countries experiencing particular difficulties.

13/02 Negotiations to determine the ways and means of establishing a **European Free Trade Area** associating the Common Market of the Six and the other OEEC countries.

12/03 Three working parties are set up to study the problems posed by the establishment of a European free trade area.

21/03 The Steering Committee for Nuclear Energy creates a Group of Experts to draw up common **health standards** for European countries.

25/03 In Rome the Six sign the treaties establishing the European Economic Community and EURATOM.

05/06 Ceremonies to mark the **tenth anniversary** of the speech made by US Secretary of State George C. Marshall at Harvard University on 5 June 1947.

18/06 France suspends its liberalisation of intra-European trade.

17/10 The Council declares its intention to secure the establishment of a **European Free Trade Area** and sets up an Intergovernmental Committee at ministerial level.

18/10 The Intergovernmental Committee holds a first procedural meeting under the chairmanship of **Reginald Maudling,** Her Majesty's Paymaster General.

20/12 Adoption of the statute of the **European Nuclear Energy Agency** (ENEA), which will be established within the framework of the OEEC as from 1 February 1958; signature of the Convention on Security Control ensuring the exclusively peaceful character of the Agency's objectives. Twelve Member countries of the Organisation sign the International Agreement to set up a first joint undertaking, the European Company for the Chemical Processing of Irradiated Fuels (EUROCHEMIC).

1958

10/01 Signing of the agreement associating **Spain** with the work of the OEEC.

30/01 France receives special loans from the EPU-IMF and from the US Government.

01/02 The ENEA comes into being.

01/02-03/02 Belgium, the Netherlands and Luxembourg sign the Treaty of the Benelux Economic Union.

14/05 A Special Office of **Scientific and Technical Personnel** is set up.

28/07-29/07 The Council, after considering a report from the Working Party set up on 18 July 1956 to examine the current economic situation in Member countries, recommends that Member countries should pursue policies encouraging sustainable economic growth.

15/12 The work of the Intergovernmental Committee for the establishment of a **European Free Trade Area** is suspended.

27/12 The **European Monetary Agreement** comes into force.

1959

30/01 **Spain** participates in the OEEC's first joint nuclear project.

23/03 Signing of the agreement on the high-temperature reactor project of the European Nuclear Energy Agency (**DRAGON project).**

25/05-26/05 First meeting of the **Economic Policy Committee.**

12/06 OEEC countries adopt measures for protection against **radiation.**

01/07 The obligation as to 90 per cent **liberalisation** of **trade among OEEC countries is extended until 30 June 1960.**

07/07 On the Fiscal Committee's proposal, measures against double taxation are adopted.

20/07 **Spain** becomes the 18th Member country of the OEEC.

29/07 Yugoslavia joins the Ministerial Committee for Agriculture and Food.

10/08 The Convention on Security Control in the nuclear field comes into force.

04/12 The Code of Liberalisation of **Capital Movements** is adopted.

21/12 The multilateral settlement system set up under the **European Monetary Agreement** is prolonged for an indefinite period.

1960

07/07 Work begins on the construction of the EUROCHEMIC plant at Mol (Belgium).

28/07 **Thorkil Kristensen** is appointed **Secretary-General of the OEEC** with effect from 1 September and Secretary-General designate of the Organisation for Economic Co-operation and Development (OECD). He is to chair the meetings of the **OECD** Preparatory Committee.

29/07 Signing of the Convention on Third-Party Liability in the field of **nuclear energy.**

03/08 Prolongation of the OEEC **HALDEN** reactor project. First session of the **nuclear safety** tribunal set up by the OEEC.

30/09 Agreement on collaboration between ENEA and the **International Atomic Energy Agency** (IAEA).

05/10 The **HALDEN** heavy-water boiling reactor becomes operational.

14/12 Signing of the Convention on the Organisation for Economic Co-operation and Development (OECD), which takes effect on 30 September 1961 and replaces the Convention for European Economic Co-operation.

IV. REPÈRES CHRONOLOGIQUES

1947

01/01	**George C. Marshall** est nommé Secrétaire d'État américain à la place de James Byrnes.
12/03	Discours du « containment » de **Harry Truman**. Aide à la Grèce et à la Turquie. Discours de **George C. Marshall** Secrétaire d'État américain à Harvard. Offre d'aide à l'Europe.
17/06	La France et la Grande-Bretagne acceptent l'**Aide Marshall**.
27/06-02/07	**Conférence franco-anglo-soviétique** à Paris. Rupture soviétique.
12/07-22/09	**Conférence de Coopération Économique Européenne** à Paris pour préparer le rapport au Gouvernement des États-Unis sur l'aide économique à l'invitation de la France et de la Grande-Bretagne.
22/09	Le Rapport européen évalue à 22 milliards le déficit des 4 années à venir.
17/12	Entrée en vigueur de la Loi d'aide intérimaire au profit de certains pays européens.

1948

02/01	Le Congrès des États-Unis adopte la Loi de coopération économique accordant une aide économique de 5 millions de dollars à l'Europe pour la première des 4 années prévues pour le Programme de relèvement européen (ERP). Paul G. Hoffman est nommé Administrateur de l'Administration de Coopération Économique (ECA).
16/04	Signature de la **Convention de Coopération Économique Européenne** par les Ministres de seize pays européens et les Commandants en Chef des zones d'occupation anglo-américaine et française en Allemagne, Acte de naissance de l'Organisation Européenne de Coopération Économique (OECE). Élections au sein du Conseil pour l'année 1948-1949 et nomination de **Robert Marjolin** au poste de Secrétaire Général. Le siège de l'Organisation est fixé à Paris. **Paul-Henri Spaak** est Président du Conseil.
17/04	Création du Comité des **Méthodes** et de la Commission du **Budget**.
11/05	Création des **Comités** suivants : – Balance des Paiements – Échanges et Paiements Intra-européens – Charbon – Électricité – Pétrole – Sidérurgie – Alimentation et Agriculture (Sous-Comité du Machinisme Agricole) – Matières Premières – Transports Intérieurs – Transports Maritimes
22/05	Création des Comités suivants : – Textiles – Produits Chimiques – Bois – Pâtes et Papier – Métaux non ferreux – Cuirs et Peaux
05/06	Création du Comité de l'Équipement.

11/06 Création du Groupe de Travail chargé d'étudier les problèmes relatifs aux **échanges**.

28/06 Accord bilatéral franco-américain sur l'**Aide Marshall**.

16/07 Approbation des principes fondamentaux pour l'établissement du **Programme annuel** 1948-1949; le principe de la division de l'aide américaine est adopté par l'OECE.

Création du Groupe Restreint chargé de proposer une répartition préliminaire de l'aide ERP.

20/07 Création du Groupe de Travail Restreint des **Échanges et Paiements** Intra-européens.

24/07 Adoption des principes généraux du Plan de **paiements** intra-européens.

25/07 Réunion des Ministres des pays participants avec Paul G. Hoffmann, de l'**Administration de Coopération Économique** (ECA).

05/08 Création du Comité d'Étude du Barème définitif des **Contributions**.

20/09 Création du Sous-Comité de **Surveillance** (contrôle du système des paiements et de compensations entre les pays européens).

04/10 Création du Groupe de Travail des **Territoires d'Outre-Mer**.

14/10 Adhésion à la Convention de la zone anglo-américaine du Territoire libre de **Triestre**.

16/10 Réunion des Ministres de pays participants. Le Programme annuel 1948-1949 est remis à **W. Averell Harriman,** Représentant spécial des États-Unis en Europe.

Signature de l'**Accord de Paiements et de Compensation** entre les pays européens.

Création du Comité des Ministres pour l'Étude des Modifications éventuelles à apporter à la structure de l'Organisation.

31/12 Adoption par le Conseil du Rapport sur le Programme annuel 1949-1950 et du Rapport Intérimaire sur le Programme de Relèvement Européen.

Approbation du Rapport Intérimaire sur le Programme de Relèvement Européen 1948-1949 à 1952-1953. (1er rapport annuel de l'OECE)

1949

01/01 Visite à Washington, sur l'invitation de l'ECA, du **Baron Snoy** (Président du Conseil), de **Sir Edmund Hall Patch** (Président du Comité Exécutif), de **Robert Marjolin** (Secrétaire Général) et d'un groupe d'experts pour apporter des renseignements complémentaires sur le Programme annuel 1949-1950 et le **Rapport intérimaire**.

17/02 Création d'un **Groupe Consultatif** des Ministres pour assister le Président du Conseil dans l'examen des questions les plus importantes se posant à l'Organisation.

14/03 Création d'un Groupe de Travail pour l'Étude des Mécanismes de **Surveillance et de Contrôle**.

26/03 Sur la base des propositions faites par le Groupe Consultatif, mise en application du Programme 1949-1950 comprenant l'intensification des activités de l'OECE, en matière agricole et de développement du tourisme en Europe.

28/03 Création du Comité des **Territoires d'Outre-Mer**.

10/05 Création du Groupe de Travail chargé d'examiner les rapports des pays Membres sur la **stabilité financière** intérieure.

04/06 Élaboration par le Groupe Consultatif des propositions concernant la **libération des échanges** qui sont transmises pour examen aux gouvernements des pays Membres.

09/06 Création des **Sous-Comités** suivants :

- Alimentation et agriculture, portant amendement à la Déclaration du Conseil du 12 avril 1949
- Programmes d'importation et d'exportation
- Programmes des plans de production agricole
- Machinisme agricole
- Engrais et des produits insecticides et fongicides
- Groupe de travail des niveaux de l'alimentaire
- Pêche

02/07 Adoption par le Conseil, sur la proposition du Groupe Consultatif, des principes de l'**Accord de Paiement et de Compensation** pour l'année 1949-1950.

Invitation aux pays Membres à prendre les mesures nécessaires pour l'élimination progressive et réciproque des restrictions quantitatives à l'importation en vue d'arriver en 1951 à une **libération** aussi complète que possible des échanges en Europe.

13/08 Décision en vertu de laquelle les pays Membres indiqueront, au plus tard le 1er octobre 1949, les produits en provenance des autres pays Membres pour lesquels ils ont décidé, ou sont prêts à décider, soit unilatéralement ou par voie de négociation, la suppression des **restrictions d'importation** ou de délivrance automatique des licences d'importation.

31/08 Approbation des recommandations faites par le Président du Conseil et le Secrétaire Général sur la **répartition de l'aide** américaine et sur les droits de tirage pour l'année 1949-1950.

07/09 Signature de l'**Accord de Paiements et de Compensation** entre les pays européens pour l'année 1949-1950.

29/09 Le Conseil adopte sur proposition du Groupe Consultatif, de nouvelles mesures de coopération. Décision du Conseil de soumettre à l'ECA, le 15 janvier 1950, un second rapport et approbation d'une nouvelle méthode de **répartition forfaitaire** de l'aide américaine pour les deux dernières années de l'ERP.

30/09 Création de Comités Spéciaux Restreints chargés d'examiner les cas prévus aux Articles 33 et 34 de l'**Accord de Paiements et de Compensation** entre les pays européens pour 1949-1950.

31/10 Les délégués de la République Fédérale d'**Allemagne** siègent pour la première fois au Conseil.

02/11 Le Conseil adopte sa première décision sur la libéralisation des échanges intra-européens ; celle-ci devra porter sur 50% des échanges avant le 15 décembre 1949.

01/12 Création de l'Association Technique de **Textiles Artificiels**.

09/12 Création du Bureau Européen des **Foires Commerciales**.

1950

20/01 Le Conseil approuve des mesures destinées à intensifier la productivité en **Europe**.

Création de Groupes de Travail chargés des questions de **productivité** et de coopération dans la recherche scientifique et le développement technique.

31/01 Le Conseil confie à Dirk U. Stikker, Ministre des Affaires Étrangères des Pays-Bas, une mission de **conciliateur** politique de l'**Organisation**.

Nouvelle décision du Conseil relative à la **libéralisation des échanges.**

22/02 Approbation des termes de la réponse adressée au Secrétaire Général du Conseil de l'Europe concernant les propositions contenues dans les Recommandations adoptées par l'Assemblée Consultative du **Conseil de l'Europe** en matière économique. Décision d'établir des relations officielles avec le Conseil des **Fédérations Industrielles** de l'Europe.

Création du Sous-Comité de l'**Alimentation et de l'Agriculture**.

09/03 Création du Groupe de Travail chargé d'examiner les rapports des pays Membres sur la **stabilité financière** intérieure.

04/04 Fin de l'activité du **Groupe Consultatif**.

25/04 Création de la Commission de l'Organisation chargée des consultations avec le **Conseil de l'Europe.**

03/05 Adoption de la première décision sur la libération des transactions invisibles.

19/05 Création du Groupe de Travail Mixte du Comité des Territoires d'**Outre-Mer**.

02/06 Invitation du **Canada** et des **États-Unis** à s'associer officieusement aux travaux de l'OECE sur l'examen des problèmes d'intérêt commun.

06/07-07/07 Approbation des dispositions relatives à la création de l'**Union Européenne de Paiements** ; dans un délai de quinze jours après la signature d'un accord créant une Union Européenne des Paiements, les pays Membres devront libérer 60 % au moins de leurs importations dans le secteur privé en provenance des autres pays Membres.

07/08-20/08 Participation des pays Membres à la première **Foire Internationale** de Chicago.

18/08 Adoption du **Code de la Libération** ; les pays Membres s'engagent à abolir progressivement entre eux les restrictions quantitatives à l'importation des marchandises. Décision portant création de l'Union Européenne des paiements. Désignation du Comité de Direction de l'Union Européenne de Paiements.

04/09 Approbation d'un rapport sur les **investissements** internationaux.

19/09 Signature par les dix-huit pays Membres de l'OECE de l'Accord créant l'**Union Européenne de Paiements**.

21/09 Création du Groupe de Coordination et de **Libération des Échanges**.

04/10 **Libération** par les pays Membres entre eux de 60 % de leurs importations privées.

07/10 Examen du memorandum du Secrétaire Général relatif aux problèmes économiques urgents et création d'une liste de mesures à prendre à la suite des modifications intervenues dans la conjoncture économique depuis la **Guerre de Corée.**

20/10 Le Comité Exécutif charge les Comités Verticaux d'entreprendre immédiatement une étude sur les pénuries de **matières premières**.

27/10 Nouvelle décision sur la **libéralisation des échanges**. Les pays Membres s'engagent à libérer, pour le 1er février 1951, 75 % de leurs importations privées en provenance des autres pays Membres pris dans leur ensemble.

30/10 Création de la Commission chargée d'examiner les problèmes posés par les relations entre le **Conseil de l'Europe** et l'Organisation.

02/12 Examen du Rapport du Comité Économique sur la raréfaction des matières premières. Recommandation d'accroissement de la production et de la réduction de la demande de **matières premières rares**. Adoption de mesures de coopération internationale, de recommandations concernant les pénuries de main-d'œuvre qualifiée en Europe.

06/12 Visite à Washington d'une délégation de l'OECE, conduite par Sir Edmund Hall Patch, Président du Comité Exécutif, sur l'invitation de l'ECA, pour discuter des facteurs affectant les possibilités d'approvisionnement en **matières premières**.

13/12 L'UEP ouvre un crédit spécial à l'Allemagne.

- Comité de l'Alimentation et de l'Agriculture sur la production de céréales secondaires dans les territoires d'Outre-Mer
- Groupe de Travail Mixte du Comité des Territoires d'Outre-Mer
- Comité des Textiles sur la production du coton dans les territoires d'Outre-Mer

1951

21/02 L'Allemagne suspend la libération des échanges intra-européens.

09/03-10/03 Acceptation de l'invitation des Gouvernements des États-Unis, de Grande Bretagne et de France, de participer au Groupe Central de la **Conférence Internationale des Matières Premières**.

25/04 Approbation du premier rapport sur la Coopération Économique Européenne destiné au **Conseil de l'Europe**.

20/07 L'OECE organise une campagne européenne en faveur d'un accroissement de la **production agricole**. Le Conseil adopte le Code de la Libération des échanges et des transactions invisibles.

29/07 Déclaration par les représentants des Gouvernements de pays Membres de l'OECE, réunis en Conseil, de leur objectif général : accroître de 25 % dans les cinq prochaines années la **production globale** de l'Europe Occidentale.

10/10 Approbation par le Président des États-Unis de la **Loi de Sécurité Mutuelle** (« Mutual security act ») qui remplace l'ECA et consacre la fin du Plan Marshall.

08/11 Le Royaume-Uni ramène de 90 à 61 le pourcentage de libération des échanges avec les autres Européens.

21/11 Adoption du Rapport sur la **stabilité financière** intérieure et la lutte contre l'inflation, transmission au Conseil de l'Europe.

13/12 Création d'un réseau européen de centres d'**information technique** sur l'initiative du Comité des Questions Scientifiques et Techniques.

1952

11/01 Création d'un « Groupe Ministériel de la **Production Charbonnière** » comprenant les Ministres responsables de la production charbonnière de l'Allemagne, de la France, du Royaume-Uni, présidé par Dirk U. Stikker, Président du Conseil, et chargé de faire des propositions visant à l'accroissement de la production de charbon, pour permettre aux Pays Membres d'éviter en 1954 des importations exceptionnelles.

01/03 La France suspend la libération des échanges intra-européens.

11/03 Le Royaume-Uni ramène de 61 à 46 le pourcentage de libération de ses échanges avec les autres pays européens.

21/03 **Le Groupe Ministériel de la Production Charbonnière** élabore son premier rapport, avec recommandations aux Gouvernements des pays européens producteurs de charbon, pour accroître la **production**.

28/03-29/03 Le Conseil décide un examen annuel de la situation économique et financière intérieure des pays Membres.

29/03 Création du Comité de Direction des Échanges.

30/06 Adoption des décisions formelles permettant le renouvellement de l'**UEP** après le 30 juin 1952 pour une période d'un an, concernant l'entrée en vigueur d'un nouveau barème applicable aux versements d'or par les débiteurs pour les déficits encourus dans les limites de leur quota, le règlement de la position de certains créditeurs extrêmes et la constitution d'un fonds de garanties.

18/07 Rapport sur la **situation financière** intérieure des pays Membres de l'OECE et des pays Associés, établi par un Groupe d'experts indépendants, et examiné par un Comité Ministériel Temporaire, créé en application de la Décision du 29 mars.

21/08 Première liaison établie entre l'OECE et la **Communauté Européenne du Charbon et de l'Acier** (CECA). Un observateur de la Haute Autorité assiste à la réunion du Sous-Comité des Approvisionnements et de la Distribution du Comité du Charbon de l'Organisation.

3/09-12/09 Attilio Cattani, Président du Comité Exécutif, et Robert Marjolin, Secrétaire Général, assistent à Mexico à la septième Réunion du Conseil des Gouverneurs de la **Banque Internationale pour la Reconstitution et le Développement** (BIRD) et du **Fonds Monétaire International** (FMI). Le Secrétaire Général expose les récents développements de la situation économique en Europe.

21/09-26/09 Une session d'étude sur les moyens d'information et de **vulgarisation agricoles**, organisée par l'OECE et le Ministère de l'Agriculture et de la Pêche d'Angleterre et du Pays de Galles se tient à Wye College (Kent).

15/10 Approbation des modalités de la liaison entre l'Organisation et la Haute Autorité de la **Communauté Européenne du Charbon et de l'Acier** (CECA), jusqu'à l'établissement du marché commun. La Haute Autorité enverra un observateur aux Comités du Charbon et de la Sidérurgie et désignera un Agent de liaison permanent auprès du secrétariat de l'Organisation.

20/10-21/10 Première réunion du Conseil sous la présidence de Anthony Eden; échange de vues sur les grandes lignes du **Rapport Annuel** de l'Organisation sur la situation et les perspectives économiques des pays Membres, des États-Unis et du Canada. Approbation du Rapport du Comité Ministériel Temporaire sur la **stabilité financière** intérieure des pays Membres et des pays Associés.

27/11 Conférence sur l'effort d'exportation vers la zone dollar; participation des représentants des organismes chargés, dans les pays Membres, d'orienter et de coordonner cet effort.

09/12 Adoption de recommandations pour renforcer la coopération des pays membres en matière de **libération des échanges**.

13/12 4e Rapport annuel de l'Organisation.

1953

07/02 Le Conseil examine les problèmes posés par l'établissement du **Marché Commun** du charbon et de l'acier au regard des dispositions du Code de la Libération des Échanges de l'OECE.

18/03 Une conférence OECE sur les **transports intérieurs** européens à laquelle participent les représentants des seize pays membres de l'OECE, des États-Unis, de l'Espagne et de la Yougoslavie, se réunit au Château de la Muette.

24/03 Création dans le cadre de l'OECE, d'une **Agence Européenne de Productivité** (AEP), à dater du 1er mai 1953.

30/03 Approbation concernant l'exportation d'**énergie électrique** entre huit pays Membres de l'OECE dont les réseaux sont interconnectés. Ces échanges d'énergie permettront d'éviter soit des pertes d'énergie hydraulique, soit des coupures de courant.

10/04 Une mission de l'OECE dirigée par Sir Hugh Ellis-Rees, Président du Conseil de l'Organisation, procède à Washington, sur l'invitation du Gouvernement des États-Unis, à des entretiens avec l'Administration américaine consacrés à l'étude de la **situation économique** de l'Europe et à l'examen des recommandations du quatrième Rapport de l'OECE adopté par le Conseil en décembre 1952. La mission examine également avec les Autorités américaines les problèmes relatifs à l'établissement d'un système plus vaste d'échanges et de paiements.

15/06 Le Conseil de l'OECE prend une décision concernant le financement de l'**Agence Européenne de Productivité** (AEP), approuve un arrangement entre l'Administration américaine de sécurité mutuelle et l'OECE en ce qui concerne la productivité alimentaire et agricole.

17/06 La Conférence sur les **transports intérieurs européens** conclut, à l'issue des trois sessions tenues au Château de la Muette depuis cette date, à la nécessité d'organiser en Europe une «Conférence Européenne des Ministres des Transports».

19/06 Approbation des dispositions portant sur le renouvellement de l'**UEP** pour un an à partir du 30 juin 1953 avec pour seules modifications en 1953-1954 un rallongement des excédents des quotas et un accroissement des taux d'intérêts des crédits accordés dans le cadre de l'UEP.

24/07 Adoption d'une Recommandation relative à l'établissement d'une **Conférence Européenne des Ministres des Transports.**

17/10 Réunion à Bruxelles des Ministres des Transports de dix-sept pays européens sur l'invitation du Gouvernement belge; adoption, sur la base d'une recommandation du Conseil de l'OECE du 24 juillet, du Statut de «**Conférence Européenne des Ministres des Transports**».

29/10 Le Royaume-Uni porte de nouveau à 75 % la libération des échanges avec les autres pays européens.

30/10 Résolution du Conseil Ministériel de l'OECE réaffirmant son objectif de s'acheminer vers l'élimination complète des restrictions quantitatives à l'importation entre les pays Membres. Il charge le Comité de Direction de l'UEP de faire un rapport pour le 31 mars 1954 sur les problèmes éventuels au rétablissement de la **convertibilité** d'une ou de plusieurs monnaies des Pays Membres. Mandat est donné au Comité de Direction de préparer pour le 1er mars un rapport sur les conditions dans lesquelles l'UEP resterait en vigueur jusqu'au 30 juin 1955. Adoption d'une Résolution concernant l'assouplissement des restrictions quantitatives aux importations en provenance de la zone dollar.

1954

21/01 L'OECE publie le premier programme annuel de l'**Agence Européenne de Productivité** (AEP).

29/01 Le Conseil arrête les modalités de sa collaboration avec la **Conférence Européenne des Ministres des Transports** (CEMT), créée en octobre 1953.

12/02 Conférence d'experts des pays Membres de l'OECE et des États-Unis pour examiner les obstacles d'ordre administratif et législatif aux **investissements** privés américains en Europe.

17/02 Le Comité du Pétrole de l'Organisation entreprend une étude sur la recherche et l'exploitation du **pétrole** brut et du gaz naturel dans les Pays Membres.

29/03 Adoption de nouvelles mesures de libération des **transactions invisibles** qui ont notamment pour but de faciliter les voyages et séjours pour des études dans les pays de l'OECE et les transactions et transferts relatifs aux opérations de publicité.

07/04 Approbation des recommandations du Rapport du Comité Économique sur les causes du déséquilibre au sein de l'**UEP** conduisant à la position de créditeur extrême de l'Allemagne.

05/05-05/06 Le Conseil réuni au rang des Ministres :

- fixe les lignes générales du renouvellement pour un an de l'**UEP** après le 30 juin 1954;
- crée un Groupe d'Étude Ministériel chargé d'étudier les problèmes pratiques du rétablissement de la **convertibilité** par un certain nombre de pays Membres;
- adopte une résolution concernant la mise en œuvre de sa résolution d'octobre 1952 sur l'extension de la **libération** des échanges en Europe;
- adopte une résolution sur le renforcement du **Code de la Libération** des Échanges pour prévenir un recours excessif aux clauses dérogatoires du Code, réduire leur période d'utilisation et atténuer la gravité des conséquences possibles de ces dérogations;
- adopte une résolution invitant le Comité de Direction des Échanges à lui soumettre des propositions permettant aux pays Membres d'abolir les mesures artificielles d'**aide aux exportateurs**;
- charge le Comité Mixte des Échanges et des Paiements Intra-européens de soumettre des propositions concrètes pour l'action éventuelle de l'Organisation, en coopération avec les États-Unis et le Canada, pour assouplir les **restrictions quantitatives** aux importations en provenance de la zone dollar.

14/05 L'OECE publie ses commentaires sur le **Plan de Strasbourg.**

30/06 Adoption des dispositions formelles pour renouvellement d'un an de l'UEP après le 30 juin 1954 avec arrangements entre certains pays créditeurs et débiteurs. Ces arrangements ont pu permettre l'octroi de nouvelles facilités de crédit et d'emprunt. Modifications apportées au mécanisme de l'Union.

15/07-16/07 Première réunion à Londres du Groupe d'Étude Ministériel sur la **Convertibilité**.

09/09 Démission de **Robert Marjolin, Secrétaire Général** de l'Organisation; il quitte l'Organisation début 1955.

02/12 Publication d'un Rapport sur l'Industrie du Bois en Europe, le premier d'une série consacrée à la situation des différents secteurs économiques.

22/12 Le Conseil recommande aux pays Membres d'assouplir les restrictions quantitatives aux importations de marchandises et aux transactions invisibles avec la zone dollar.

1955

13/01-14/01 Le Conseil :

- adopte une décision relative à l'extension et à la stabilisation de la **libération des échanges**; les pays Membres devront libérer, à dater du 1er juillet 1955, 10 % de l'ensemble de leurs importations privés et 75 % dans chacun des trois secteurs définis au Code de la Libération;
- créé un **Comité Ministériel de l'Agriculture et de** l'Alimentation. L'OECE a repris les tâches du «Pool Vert»;
- l'Espagne, membre du «Pool Vert», devient membre de plein droit pour les travaux sur l'agriculture et l'alimentation.

15/02 Nomination de **Roger Grégoire** comme Directeur de l'Agence Européenne de Productivité; il remplace Karl P. Harten.

25/02 Le Gouvernement Yougoslave est invité à se faire représenter par un Observateur aux séances du Conseil, Comités Techniques et Sous-Comités qui en dépendent.

04/03 Déclaration d'intention des pays Membres sur les objectifs de la **libération des échanges.**

O1/04 **René Sergent** prend ses fonctions de Secrétaire Général de l'OECE.

01/05 La France porte à nouveau à 75 % la libération de ses échanges avec les autres pays européens.

09/06-10/06 Le Conseil :

- décide le renouvellement de l'UEP, l'établissement d'un **Fonds Européen** et les règles de politique commerciale applicables aux pays Membres à l'occasion d'un retour éventuel de **convertibilité**;
- charge un Groupe de Travail du Conseil d'explorer les possibilités d'une coopération économique et financière au sein de l'Organisation pour l'utilisation pacifique de l'**énergie nucléaire.**

Création d'une Commission de l'Énergie sous la Présidence de Sir Harold Hartley.

29/06 Adoption de nouvelles mesures de libération des **transactions invisibles** et des transferts; décision de créer un Comité des Transactions Invisibles.

01/08 Les règlements de l'UEP s'effectuent à raison de 25 % en crédits et 75 % en or.

05/08 Signature par les représentants des pays Membres de l'**Accord Monétaire Européen** qui établit un Fonds Européen et un système multilatéral pour faciliter les règlements entre les pays Membres.

1956

20/01 Décision qui, pour la première fois, considère les pays du **Bénélux** comme une unité et cela au regard des dispositions du Code de la Libération des Échanges. C'est la première fois que la Belgique, les Pays-Bas et le Luxembourg sont considérés comme une unité dans une organisation internationale.

27/01 Création d'un Comité du **Gaz** qui étudiera les problèmes de production, transport, distribution et l'utilisation du gaz des pays Membres.

28/02-29/02 12 pays Membres ont signé un Accord international instituant la 1ere entreprise commune, la Société Européenne pour le Traitement Chimique des Combustibles Irradiés : EUROCHEMIC ; Création d'un Comité Spécial du Conseil nucléaire pour l'utilisation de l'énergie à des fins pacifiques.

Le Conseil adopte une Résolution donnant des directives sur les travaux futurs de l'Organisation, en demandant en particulier :

- l'intensification de l'étude des problèmes à **long terme** créés par l'expansion économique en Europe ;
- des enquêtes dans les secteurs économiques préoccupants : **agriculture, textiles** et **énergie** ;
- la consolidation au 30 septembre 1956 de 90% de la libéralisation des échanges intra-européens ;
- que l'Organisation œuvre sur les barrières au commerce telles les tarifs élevés, le commerce d'États restrictifs et l'aide artificielle aux exportations ainsi que sur les restrictions quantitatives ;
- l'étude de la réduction du bilatérisme et des discriminations à l'égard des pays tiers en matière d'échange et de paiements.

16/03 Création du Comité **Fiscal**.

22/06 Prorogation de la durée de l'**Agence Européenne de Productivité** (AEP) jusqu'en juin 1960.

17/07-19/07 Création d'un Comité de Direction de l'**Énergie Nucléaire** composé des représentants de tous les pays Membres intéressés et aux travaux duquel seront associés les Gouvernements des États-Unis et du Canada.

19/07 Première réunion du Groupe Spécial créé par le Conseil pour étudier les problèmes de l'**industrie textile**. Un Groupe de Travail Spécial est chargé d'examiner la possibilité de créer une zone libre d'échange en Europe.

24/09 Première réunion du Groupe de Travail Spécial chargé d'examiner les formes et méthodes possibles d'associations multilatérales entre l'**Union Douanière** envisagée par les six pays Membres du Comité Inter-gouvernemental de Bruxelles et les autres pays de l'OECE.

26/09 Création d'une Commission Consultative de l'**Énergie** et d'un Comité de l'Énergie.

14/11 Le différend anglo-islandais en matière de **pêche** est réglé sur la base des propositions de l'OECE. Le Conseil invite le Comité Exécutif à examiner les répercussions générales sur les pays Membres des difficultés actuelles d'**approvisionnement en combustibles** et autres produits, et le charge de coordonner les travaux des Comités Techniques du Charbon, du Pétrole, des Transports Maritimes, Économiques, Mixtes des Échanges et Paiements Intra-européens et de la Direction de l'UEP.

26/11 L'Europe face à ses besoins croissants en énergie. Rapport de la Commission de l'Énergie amenant à la création de la Commission Consultative de l'Énergie et du Comité de l'Énergie.

30/11 Création d'un **Groupe Industriel Spécial pour le Pétrole** (OPEG) chargé de conseiller le Comité du Pétrole sur les disponibilités en pétrole de l'Europe et de l'aider à appliquer ses recommandations.

14/12 Mesures prises pour réduire la hausse des taux de **fret** ; dispositions également prises à cet effet par le Gouvernement des États-Unis.

1957

17/01 Le Comité du **Pétrole** procède à la répartition de la première tranche de 200 000 tonnes de produits pétroliers pour constituer une réserve à distribuer par l'OECE aux pays ayant des difficultés particulières.

13/02 Négociations pour déterminer les modalités éventuelles de l'établissement d'une **Zone de libre-échange** en Europe associant le Marché Commun des six et les autres pays Membres de l'OECE.

12/03 Création de trois Groupes de Travail sur les problèmes posés par l'établissement d'une zone européenne de libre-échange.

21/03 Le Comité de Direction de l'Énergie Nucléaire constitue un Groupe d'experts chargés d'élaborer les **normes sanitaires** communes aux pays européens.

25/03 Les six signent à Rome les Traités établissant la Communauté Économique Européenne et EURATOM.

05/06 Célébration du dixième **anniversaire** du discours prononcé le 5 juin 1947 par le Secrétaire d'État Américain, George C. Marshall, à l'Université de Harvard.

13/06 Le Conseil se déclare déterminé à assurer l'établissement d'une zone européenne de **libre-échange** et crée un Comité Ministériel Inter-gouvernemental, au niveau Ministériel.

18/06 La France suspend la libération des échanges intra-européens.

18/10 Première réunion du Comité Inter-gouvernemental de Procédure sous la Présidence de **Reginald Maudling,** Her Majesty's Paymaster-General.

20/12 Adoption des Statuts de l'**Agence Européenne pour l'Énergie Nucléaire** qui sera créée dans le cadre de l'OECE le 1er février 1958 ; signature d'une Convention sur le Contrôle de Sécurité pour respecter le caractère exclusivement pacifique des objectifs de l'Agence. Signature des douze pays Membres de l'Organisation de l'Accord international créant une première entreprise commune, la Société Européenne pour le Traitement Chimique des Combustibles Irradiés (EUROCHEMIC).

1958

10/01 Signature de l'Accord associant l'**Espagne** aux travaux de l'OECE.

30/01 La France reçoit des prêts spéciaux de l'UEP-FMI et du Gouvernement américain.

01/02 Création de l'Agence Européenne pour l'Énergie Nucléaire (AEEN).

01/02-03/02 La Belgique, les Pays-Bas, le Luxembourg signent le Traité d'Union Économique du Bénélux.

14/05 Création d'un Bureau Spécial du **Personnel Scientifique et Technique.**

28/07-29/07 Le Conseil, après étude du rapport du Groupe de travail créé le 18 juillet 1956 pour examiner la situation économique courante des pays Membres, recommande à ces derniers d'adopter des politiques favorisant une saine expansion économique.

15/12 Suspension des travaux du Comité Inter-gouvernemental pour la Création d'une Zone de **libre-échange.**

27/12 L'**Accord Monétaire Européen** entre en application.

1959

30/01 L'**Espagne** participe au premier projet nucléaire commun de l'OECE.

23/03 Signature de l'Accord sur le projet de réacteur à haute température de l'Agence Européenne pour l'Énergie Nucléaire **(Projet DRAGON).**

25/05-26/05 Première réunion du Comité de **Politique Économique.**

12/06 Les pays de l'OECE adoptent des mesures de protection contre les **radiations**.

01/07 Prolongation jusqu'au 30 juin 1960 des obligations de **libération** à 90 % des échanges entre les pays Membres de l'OECE.

07/07 Adoption sur proposition du Comité **Fiscal** de Mesures pour lutter contre la double imposition.

20/07 L'**Espagne** devient le 18e pays Membre de l'OECE.

29/07 La **Yougoslavie** entre au Comité Ministériel de l'Agriculture et de l'Alimentation.

10/08 Entrée en vigueur de la Convention sur le Contrôle de Sécurité dans le domaine nucléaire.

04/12 Adoption du Code de la Libération des **Mouvements de Capitaux.**

21/12 Prorogation pour une durée indéfinie du Système multilatéral de règlement institué par l'Accord Monétaire Européen.

1960

07/07 Inauguration à Mol (Belgique) de l'ouverture des travaux de construction de l'Usine de traitement des combustibles nucléaires (EUROCHEMIC).

28/07 Nomination de **Thorkil Kristensen comme Secrétaire Général de l'OECE** à partir du 1er septembre et Secrétaire Général désigné de l'Organisation de Coopération et de Développement Économiques (OCDE). Il assurera la présidence des réunions du Comité Préparatoire de l'**OCDE.**

29/07 Signature de la Convention sur la Responsabilité Civile dans le domaine de l'**énergie nucléaire**.

03/08 Prolongation du Projet OECE de réacteur de **HALDEN.** Première séance du Tribunal de **sécurité nucléaire** créé par l'OECE.

30/09 Accord de collaboration entre l'AEEN et l'**Agence** Internationale de l'Énergie Atomique (AIEA).

05/10 Le réacteur à eau lourde bouillante de **HALDEN** entre en ébullition.

14/12 Signature de la Convention relative à l'Organisation de Coopération et de Développement Économiques (OCDE) qui entre en vigueur le 30 septembre 1961 et se substitue à la Convention de Coopération Économique Européenne.

STRUCTURE DE L'ORGANISATION EUROPÉENNE DE COOPÉRATION ÉCONOMIQUE

STRUCTURE OF THE ORGANISATION FOR EUROPEAN ECONOMIC CO-OPERATION

1948-1958

STRUCTURE DE L'ORGANISATION EUROPÉENNE DE COOPÉRATION ÉCONOMIQUE – 1948
STRUCTURE OF THE ORGANISATION FOR EUROPEAN ECONOMIC CO-OPERATION – 1948

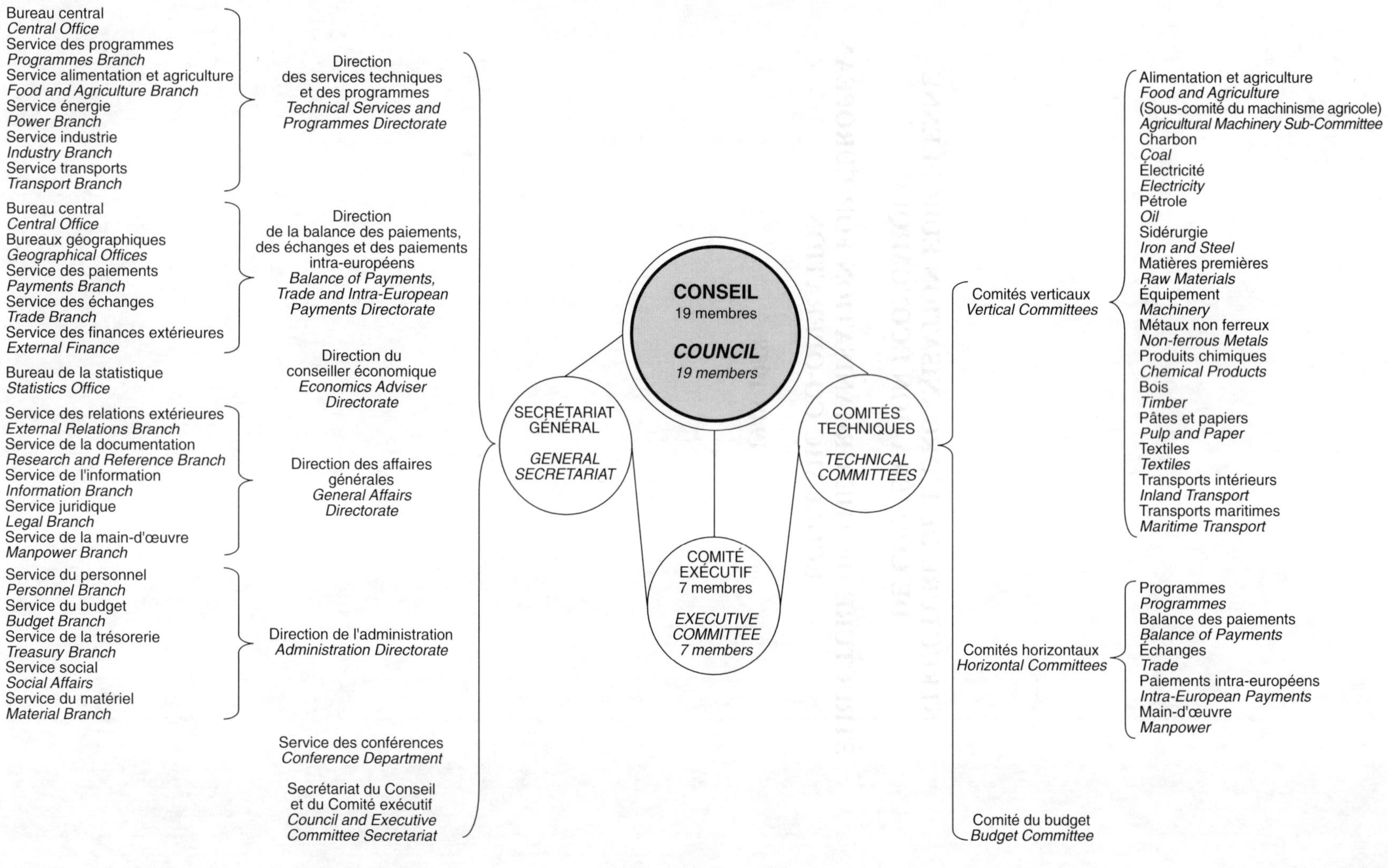

Source : OCDE/OECD.

STRUCTURE DE L'ORGANISATION EUROPÉENNE DE COOPÉRATION ÉCONOMIQUE – 1958
STRUCTURE OF THE ORGANISATION FOR EUROPEAN ECONOMIC CO-OPERATION – 1958

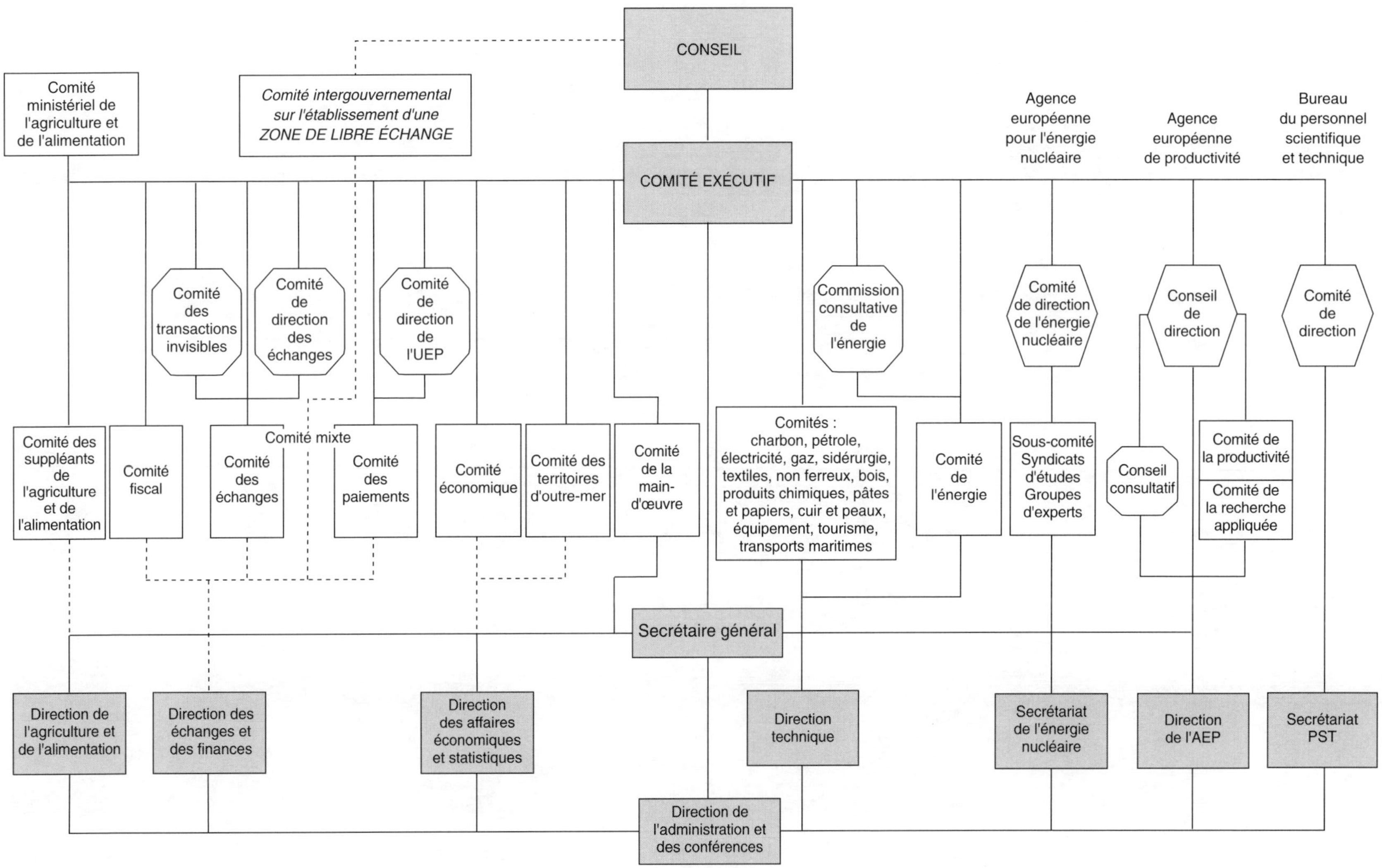

Source : OCDE/OECD.

MAIN SALES OUTLETS OF OECD PUBLICATIONS
PRINCIPAUX POINTS DE VENTE DES PUBLICATIONS DE L'OCDE

ARGENTINA – ARGENTINE
Carlos Hirsch S.R.L.
Galería Güemes, Florida 165, 4° Piso
1333 Buenos Aires Tel. (1) 331.1787 y 331.2391
Telefax: (1) 331.1787

AUSTRALIA – AUSTRALIE
D.A. Information Services
648 Whitehorse Road, P.O.B 163
Mitcham, Victoria 3132 Tel. (03) 9210.7777
Telefax: (03) 9210.7788

AUSTRIA – AUTRICHE
Gerold & Co.
Graben 31
Wien I Tel. (0222) 533.50.14
Telefax: (0222) 512.47.31.29

BELGIUM – BELGIQUE
Jean De Lannoy
Avenue du Roi 202 Koningslaan
B-1060 Bruxelles Tel. (02) 538.51.69/538.08.41
Telefax: (02) 538.08.41

CANADA
Renouf Publishing Company Ltd.
1294 Algoma Road
Ottawa, ON K1B 3W8 Tel. (613) 741.4333
Telefax: (613) 741.5439

Stores:
61 Sparks Street
Ottawa, ON K1P 5R1 Tel. (613) 238.8985
12 Adelaide Street West
Toronto, ON M5H 1L6 Tel. (416) 363.3171
Telefax: (416)363.59.63

Les Éditions La Liberté Inc.
3020 Chemin Sainte-Foy
Sainte-Foy, PQ G1X 3V6 Tel. (418) 658.3763
Telefax: (418) 658.3763

Federal Publications Inc.
165 University Avenue, Suite 701
Toronto, ON M5H 3B8 Tel. (416) 860.1611
Telefax: (416) 860.1608

Les Publications Fédérales
1185 Université
Montréal, QC H3B 3A7 Tel. (514) 954.1633
Telefax: (514) 954.1635

CHINA – CHINE
China National Publications Import
Export Corporation (CNPIEC)
16 Gongti E. Road, Chaoyang District
P.O. Box 88 or 50
Beijing 100704 PR Tel. (01) 506.6688
Telefax: (01) 506.3101

CHINESE TAIPEI – TAIPEI CHINOIS
Good Faith Worldwide Int'l. Co. Ltd.
9th Floor, No. 118, Sec. 2
Chung Hsiao E. Road
Taipei Tel. (02) 391.7396/391.7397
Telefax: (02) 394.9176

CZECH REPUBLIC – RÉPUBLIQUE TCHÈQUE
Artia Pegas Press Ltd.
Narodni Trida 25
POB 825
111 21 Praha 1 Tel. (2) 242 246 04
Telefax: (2) 242 278 72

DENMARK – DANEMARK
Munksgaard Book and Subscription Service
35, Nørre Søgade, P.O. Box 2148
DK-1016 København K Tel. (33) 12.85.70
Telefax: (33) 12.93.87

EGYPT – ÉGYPTE
Middle East Observer
41 Sherif Street
Cairo Tel. 392.6919
Telefax: 360-6804

FINLAND – FINLANDE
Akateeminen Kirjakauppa
Keskuskatu 1, P.O. Box 128
00100 Helsinki

Subscription Services/Agence d'abonnements :
P.O. Box 23
00371 Helsinki Tel. (358 0) 121 4416
Telefax: (358 0) 121.4450

FRANCE
OECD/OCDE
Mail Orders/Commandes par correspondance :
2, rue André-Pascal
75775 Paris Cedex 16 Tel. (33-1) 45.24.82.00
Telefax: (33-1) 49.10.42.76
Telex: 640048 OCDE

Internet: Compte.PUBSINQ @ oecd.org

Orders via Minitel, France only/
Commandes par Minitel, France exclusivement :
36 15 OCDE

OECD Bookshop/Librairie de l'OCDE :
33, rue Octave-Feuillet
75016 Paris Tel. (33-1) 45.24.81.81
(33-1) 45.24.81.67

Dawson
B.P. 40
91121 Palaiseau Cedex Tel. 69.10.47.00
Telefax : 64.54.83.26

Documentation Française
29, quai Voltaire
75007 Paris Tel. 40.15.70.00

Economica
49, rue Héricart
75015 Paris Tel. 45.78.12.92
Telefax : 40.58.15.70

Gibert Jeune (Droit-Économie)
6, place Saint-Michel
75006 Paris Tel. 43.25.91.19

Librairie du Commerce International
10, avenue d'Iéna
75016 Paris Tel. 40.73.34.60

Librairie Dunod
Université Paris-Dauphine
Place du Maréchal-de-Lattre-de-Tassigny
75016 Paris Tel. 44.05.40.13

Librairie Lavoisier
11, rue Lavoisier
75008 Paris Tel. 42.65.39.95

Librairie des Sciences Politiques
30, rue Saint-Guillaume
75007 Paris Tel. 45.48.36.02

P.U.F.
49, boulevard Saint-Michel
75005 Paris Tel. 43.25.83.40

Librairie de l'Université
12*a*, rue Nazareth
13100 Aix-en-Provence Tel. (16) 42.26.18.08

Documentation Française
165, rue Garibaldi
69003 Lyon Tel. (16) 78.63.32.23

Librairie Decitre
29, place Bellecour
69002 Lyon Tel. (16) 72.40.54.54

Librairie Sauramps
Le Triangle
34967 Montpellier Cedex 2 Tel. (16) 67.58.85.15
Tekefax: (16) 67.58.27.36

A la Sorbonne Actual
23, rue de l'Hôtel-des-Postes
06000 Nice Tel. (16) 93.13.77.75
Telefax: (16) 93.80.75.69

GERMANY – ALLEMAGNE
OECD Publications and Information Centre
August-Bebel-Allee 6
D-53175 Bonn Tel. (0228) 959.120
Telefax: (0228) 959.12.17

GREECE – GRÈCE
Librairie Kauffmann
Mavrokordatou 9
106 78 Athens Tel. (01) 32.55.321
Telefax: (01) 32.30.320

HONG-KONG
Swindon Book Co. Ltd.
Astoria Bldg. 3F
34 Ashley Road, Tsimshatsui
Kowloon, Hong Kong Tel. 2376.2062
Telefax: 2376.0685

HUNGARY – HONGRIE
Euro Info Service
Margitsziget, Európa Ház
1138 Budapest Tel. (1) 111.62.16
Telefax: (1) 111.60.61

ICELAND – ISLANDE
Mál Mog Menning
Laugavegi 18, Pósthólf 392
121 Reykjavik Tel. (1) 552.4240
Telefax: (1) 562.3523

INDIA – INDE
Oxford Book and Stationery Co.
Scindia House
New Delhi 110001 Tel. (11) 331.5896/5308
Telefax: (11) 332.5993

17 Park Street
Calcutta 700016 Tel. 240832

INDONESIA – INDONÉSIE
Pdii-Lipi
P.O. Box 4298
Jakarta 12042 Tel. (21) 573.34.67
Telefax: (21) 573.34.67

IRELAND – IRLANDE
Government Supplies Agency
Publications Section
4/5 Harcourt Road
Dublin 2 Tel. 661.31.11
Telefax: 475.27.60

ISRAEL – ISRAËL
Praedicta
5 Shatner Street
P.O. Box 34030
Jerusalem 91430 Tel. (2) 52.84.90/1/2
Telefax: (2) 52.84.93

R.O.Y. International
P.O. Box 13056
Tel Aviv 61130 Tel. (3) 546 1423
Telefax: (3) 546 1442

Palestinian Authority/Middle East:
INDEX Information Services
P.O.B. 19502
Jerusalem Tel. (2) 27.12.19
Telefax: (2) 27.16.34

ITALY – ITALIE
Libreria Commissionaria Sansoni
Via Duca di Calabria 1/1
50125 Firenze Tel. (055) 64.54.15
Telefax: (055) 64.12.57

Via Bartolini 29
20155 Milano Tel. (02) 36.50.83

Editrice e Libreria Herder
Piazza Montecitorio 120
00186 Roma Tel. 679.46.28
Telefax: 678.47.51

Libreria Hoepli
Via Hoepli 5
20121 Milano Tel. (02) 86.54.46
Telefax: (02) 805.28.86

Libreria Scientifica
Dott. Lucio de Biasio 'Aeiou'
Via Coronelli, 6
20146 Milano Tel. (02) 48.95.45.52
Telefax: (02) 48.95.45.48

JAPAN – JAPON
OECD Publications and Information Centre
Landic Akasaka Building
2-3-4 Akasaka, Minato-ku
Tokyo 107 Tel. (81.3) 3586.2016
Telefax: (81.3) 3584.7929

KOREA – CORÉE
Kyobo Book Centre Co. Ltd.
P.O. Box 1658, Kwang Hwa Moon
Seoul Tel. 730.78.91
Telefax: 735.00.30

MALAYSIA – MALAISIE
University of Malaya Bookshop
University of Malaya
P.O. Box 1127, Jalan Pantai Baru
59700 Kuala Lumpur
Malaysia Tel. 756.5000/756.5425
Telefax: 756.3246

MEXICO – MEXIQUE
OECD Publications and Information Centre
Edificio INFOTEC
Av. San Fernando no. 37
Col. Toriello Guerra
Tlalpan C.P. 14050
Mexico D.F.
Tel. (525) 606 00 11 Extension 100
Fax : (525) 606 13 07

Revistas y Periodicos Internacionales S.A. de C.V.
Florencia 57 - 1004
Mexico, D.F. 06600 Tel. 207.81.00
Telefax: 208.39.79

NETHERLANDS – PAYS-BAS
SDU Uitgeverij Plantijnstraat
Externe Fondsen
Postbus 20014
2500 EA's-Gravenhage Tel. (070) 37.89.880
Voor bestellingen: Telefax: (070) 34.75.778

NEW ZEALAND – NOUVELLE-ZÉLANDE
GPLegislation Services
P.O. Box 12418
Thorndon, Wellington Tel. (04) 496.5655
Telefax: (04) 496.5698

NORWAY – NORVÈGE
NIC INFO A/S
Bertrand Narvesens vei 2
P.O. Box 6512 Etterstad
0606 Oslo 6 Tel. (022) 57.33.00
Telefax: (022) 68.19.01

PAKISTAN
Mirza Book Agency
65 Shahrah Quaid-E-Azam
Lahore 54000 Tel. (42) 353.601
Telefax: (42) 231.730

PHILIPPINE – PHILIPPINES
International Booksource Center Inc.
Rm 179/920 Cityland 10 Condo Tower 2
HV dela Costa Ext cor Valero St.
Makati Metro Manila Tel. (632) 817 9676
Telefax : (632) 817 1741

POLAND – POLOGNE
Ars Polona
00-950 Warszawa
Krakowskie Przedmieácie 7 Tel. (22) 264760
Telefax : (22) 268673

PORTUGAL
Livraria Portugal
Rua do Carmo 70-74
Apart. 2681
1200 Lisboa Tel. (01) 347.49.82/5
Telefax: (01) 347.02.64

SINGAPORE – SINGAPOUR
Gower Asia Pacific Pte Ltd.
Golden Wheel Building
41, Kallang Pudding Road, No. 04-03
Singapore 1334 Tel. 741.5166
Telefax: 742.9356

SPAIN – ESPAGNE
Mundi-Prensa Libros S.A.
Castelló 37, Apartado 1223
Madrid 28001 Tel. (91) 431.33.99
Telefax: (91) 575.39.98

Mundi-Prensa Barcelona
Consell de Cent No. 391
08009 – Barcelona Tel. (93) 488.34.92
Telefax: (93) 487.76.59

Llibreria de la Generalitat
Palau Moja
Rambla dels Estudis, 118
08002 – Barcelona
(Subscripcions) Tel. (93) 318.80.12
(Publicacions) Tel. (93) 302.67.23
Telefax: (93) 412.18.54

SRI LANKA
Centre for Policy Research
c/o Colombo Agencies Ltd.
No. 300-304, Galle Road
Colombo 3 Tel. (1) 574240, 573551-2
Telefax: (1) 575394, 510711

SWEDEN – SUÈDE
CE Fritzes AB
S–106 47 Stockholm Tel. (08) 690.90.90
Telefax: (08) 20.50.21

Subscription Agency/Agence d'abonnements :
Wennergren-Williams Info AB
P.O. Box 1305
171 25 Solna Tel. (08) 705.97.50
Telefax: (08) 27.00.71

SWITZERLAND – SUISSE
Maditec S.A. (Books and Periodicals - Livres et périodiques)
Chemin des Palettes 4
Case postale 266
1020 Renens VD 1 Tel. (021) 635.08.65
Telefax: (021) 635.07.80

Librairie Payot S.A.
4, place Pépinet
CP 3212
1002 Lausanne Tel. (021) 320.25.11
Telefax: (021) 320.25.14

Librairie Unilivres
6, rue de Candolle
1205 Genève Tel. (022) 320.26.23
Telefax: (022) 329.73.18

Subscription Agency/Agence d'abonnements :
Dynapresse Marketing S.A.
38 avenue Vibert
1227 Carouge Tel. (022) 308.07.89
Telefax: (022) 308.07.99

See also – Voir aussi :
OECD Publications and Information Centre
August-Bebel-Allee 6
D-53175 Bonn (Germany) Tel. (0228) 959.120
Telefax: (0228) 959.12.17

THAILAND – THAÏLANDE
Suksit Siam Co. Ltd.
113, 115 Fuang Nakhon Rd.
Opp. Wat Rajbopith
Bangkok 10200 Tel. (662) 225.9531/2
Telefax: (662) 222.5188

TUNISIA – TUNISIE
Grande Librairie Spécialisée
Fendri Ali
Avenue Haffouz Imm El-Intilaka
Bloc B 1 Sfax 3000 Tel. (216-4) 296 855
Telefax: (216-4) 298.270

TURKEY – TURQUIE
Kültür Yayinlari Is-Türk Ltd. Sti.
Atatürk Bulvari No. 191/Kat 13
Kavaklidere/Ankara
Tel. (312) 428.11.40 Ext. 2458
Telefax: (312) 417 24 90

Dolmabahce Cad. No. 29
Besiktas/Istanbul Tel. (212) 260 7188

UNITED KINGDOM – ROYAUME-UNI
HMSO
Gen. enquiries Tel. (171) 873 8242
Postal orders only:
P.O. Box 276, London SW8 5DT
Personal Callers HMSO Bookshop
49 High Holborn, London WC1V 6HB
Telefax: (171) 873 8416
Branches at: Belfast, Birmingham, Bristol, Edinburgh, Manchester

UNITED STATES – ÉTATS-UNIS
OECD Publications and Information Center
2001 L Street N.W., Suite 650
Washington, D.C. 20036-4922 Tel. (202) 785.6323
Telefax: (202) 785.0350

Subscriptions to OECD periodicals may also be placed through main subscription agencies.

Les abonnements aux publications périodiques de l'OCDE peuvent être souscrits auprès des principales agences d'abonnement.

Orders and inquiries from countries where Distributors have not yet been appointed should be sent to: OECD Publications Service, 2, rue André-Pascal, 75775 Paris Cedex 16, France.

Les commandes provenant de pays où l'OCDE n'a pas encore désigné de distributeur peuvent être adressées à : OCDE, Service des Publications, 2, rue André-Pascal, 75775 Paris Cedex 16, France.

1-1996

OECD PUBLICATIONS, 2, rue André-Pascal, 75775 PARIS CEDEX 16
PRINTED IN FRANCE
(03 96 02 3) ISBN 92-64-04362-4 – No. 47598 1996